The New Warriors

The New Warriors
Native American Leaders
since 1900

EDITED BY R. DAVID EDMUNDS

University of Nebraska Press
Lincoln & London

✳

© 2001 by the University of Nebraska Press
All rights reserved
Manufactured in the United States of America

(∞)

Library of Congress Cataloging-in-Publication Data
The New Warriors : Native American leaders since 1900 /
edited by R. David Edmunds.
p.   cm.
Includes bibliographical references and index.
ISBN 0-8032-1820-6 (cloth: alk. paper)
1. Indian civic leaders—United States—Biography. 2. Indian activists—
United States—Biography. 3. Indians of North America—
Politics and government. 4. Indians of North America—
Government relations.
I. Edmunds, R. David (Russell David), 1939–
E89 .N48 2001
305.897'073'0922—dc21
[B]   2001027146

PHOTO CREDITS

page 16 Charles Curtis, 1924. Courtesy, Kansas State Historical Society, Topeka KS.
page 34 Gertrude Bonnin (Zitkala Ša), 1920. Courtesy, Marquette University Archives.
page 54 Robert Yellowtail, 1934. Courtesy, Hardin Photo Service, Hardin MT.
page 78 Vine V. Deloria Sr., *right*, ca. 1980. Courtesy, Philip J. Deloria.
page 96 D'Arcy McNickle, ca. 1970. Courtesy, The Newberry Library, Chicago. Peter Weil, Photographer.
page 122 LaDonna Harris, 1997. Courtesy, LaDonna Harris.
page 146 Russell Means, 1998. Courtesy, *Well Nations Magazine*.
page 170 Howard Tommie, ca. 1980. Courtesy, Howard Tommie.
page 194 Phillip Martin, 1999. Courtesy, Phillip Martin.
page 210 Wilma Mankiller, 1999. Courtesy, Sammy Still, Cherokee Nation.
page 238 Ada Deer, 2000. Courtesy, Ada Deer.
page 262 Ben Nighthorse Campbell, 2000. Courtesy, Ben Nighthorse Campbell.
page 280 Janine Pease Pretty-on-Top, 1999. Courtesy, Kyle Brehm, Billings MT.
page 298 Walter Echo-Hawk, 1999. Courtesy, Native American Rights Fund.

For LeeAnne,
a special daughter from across the sea.
Ready smile, black eyes flashing.
Give 'em hell, Wiggleb . . .

CONTENTS

✳

Introduction
Twentieth-Century Warriors   1
by R. David Edmunds

The New Warriors

Introduction

Twentieth-Century Warriors

R. DAVID EDMUNDS

During the twentieth century Native American leadership evolved to reflect the particular challenges that faced Native American people during those years. From a dwindling population confined on rural enclaves, controlled by federal agents, and characterized by their isolation from mainstream American life, Native Americans have emerged as a growing member of America's modern multiethnic community. The Indian urban residency rate now exceeds 50 percent, and Indian people have assumed a growing sovereignty over their own communities and their lives. Many of these changes were facilitated by Native American leaders who responded to a series of challenges and seized opportunities to improve the quality of their people's lives. The patterns of their leadership vary in time and circumstance, and some have been more successful than others. The contours of their ascendancy offer insights into the evolving status and influence of Indian people during their times and reflect the changing nature of Native American leadership over the past one hundred years.

To understand this evolution it is first necessary to examine its antecedents. In 1900 the Native American population had reached its nadir (237,196), and most non-Indians were convinced that Indian people were on the brink of extinction. Images of "vanishing redmen" permeated newspapers, magazines, and dime novels, while James Earle Frazer's popular sculpture "The End of the Trail," which featured a defeated Plains warrior slumped forward over a downcast horse, seemed to epitomize what was believed to be the Native Americans' fate. The U.S. government had moved the vast majority of Native Americans onto reservations, and opportunities for meaningful armed resistance were gone. In 1887 Congress had passed the General Allotment Act (Dawes Act), which stipulated that at the president's discretion most Indian reservations could be "allotted" or divided into small one-hundred-sixty-acre farms. The act essentially forced acculturation upon tribal people and aimed eventually to assimilate them into American society. That the majority of Native Americans might reject such acculturation and wish to retain a separate ethnic identity was unfathomable to non-Indians. Still, most Indian people were determined to defend their remaining land-bases, protect their tribal communities, and forge a viable, if uncertain, place within a new American society characterized by considerable chauvinism, an optimistic appraisal of the future, and a growing reliance upon an industrial economy.

Throughout the nineteenth century a growing number of tribal communities had come to terms with both the federal government and the onrush of non-Indians who surrounded them. Some tribal peoples, such as the Five Southern Tribes in Oklahoma, had achieved at least a limited sovereignty, since they controlled certain facets of their political and economic lives. Other tribes, ensconced on reservations, were dependent upon the federal government for their economic well-being and were more subject to the whims of their local Indian agents. Those tribal people whose lives were most closely circumscribed by federal policies still maintained a modicum of control over their personal lives, but within the reservation communities most Native Americans needed the permission of federal officials if they wished to lease or sell their allotments, or even leave the physical confines of those reservations that remained extant.

Within this milieu of dependency, federal officials, missionaries, and other agents of acculturation labored to transform the remaining Indian communities. Missionaries, reformers, and other "progressives" were convinced that the key to transforming Native American ways lay within the realm of education. If Indian children could be processed through a school system that championed the ideas and values of a middle-class American society, then they would absorb the ethos of their teachers and emerge as useful citizens of the United States. Moreover, they could then serve as models for their less acculturated kinsmen and accelerate the rate of change within the tribal communities.

Not surprisingly, many of these initial graduates were Native Americans of mixed Indian-white lineage. Mixed-blood children often were products of families in which at least one parent already had some formal education; these families were more willing to enroll their children in the mission or government schools. In addition, because such families often were more familiar with the academic or vocational skills needed for success outside the reservation environment, they realized that a formal education could be utilized to either lead or defend the surviving Indian communities. It is not surprising, therefore, that many of the leaders featured in this volume are individuals of mixed ancestry and that many are relatively well-educated, by both Native American and non-Indian standards.

The missionaries and reformers who championed Native American education at the beginning of the twentieth century would most certainly be surprised at the results of their efforts. As the following essays illustrate, most Native American leaders have utilized their formal "white" education for Indian purposes. Although they have attended and/or graduated from non-Indian educational institutions, they have taken the Crow chief Plenty Coups's maxim to heart: "Education is your most powerful weapon. With education you are the white man's equal, without it you are his victim." Indeed it seems doubtful that few white educators or reformers would ever have envisioned Native American leaders such as Ada Deer, Walter Echo-Hawk, Phillip Martin, or Janine Pease Pretty-on-Top using their formal training to establish new institutions and policies to protect and strengthen the tribal communities and their resources from further infringement by the non-Indian world. Instead most white reformers envisioned that well-educated and relatively acculturated Native Americans would quickly blend into the white "mainstream," willingly relinquishing their Indian identity in return for the acceptance of their white peers. In one reformer's words, the Indian of the twentieth century would "gladly lay aside his picturesque blanket and moccasin, and, clad in the panoply of American citizenship, seek his chances of fortune or loss in the stern battle of life with the Aryan races."[1]

The reformers' prognostications were mistaken. Many Native American people have joined the mainstream of American life, but almost all have proudly retained their Indian identity. Indeed, the evolution of such identity continues to be one of the most complex and controversial aspects of Native American existence. In the twentieth century Indian identity has manifested itself on several levels and has assumed different parameters for different people, at different places, and at different times. Within the reservation communities at the beginning of the century, Indian identity was equated with tribal identity, which in turn was well delineated through traditional systems of clan and family ties. If an individual was a member of a Comanche family, the Comanches considered that person to be one of their own. He or she was part of the Comanche community, was envisioned as "Comanche," and therefore was also identified as an "Indian." In other words, if the tribal community said you were a member of the tribe, you *were* a member of the tribe (and also considered Indian). Tribal membership and Indian identity were defined by kinship and tribal consensus.

During the twentieth century, federal enrollment procedures incorporated into the Dawes Act have markedly altered these tribal definitions. Following the passage of the Dawes Act, federal agents entered the tribal communities and attempted to "enroll" or list all members of the tribe. Initially, this procedure was designed to discover how many tribe members were extant and to ascertain their eligibility to receive allotments. Enrollment agents usually listed each individual's "blood quantum," or percentage of biological Native American ancestry. Therefore, individual enrollees were listed as "full-blood," "half-blood," "one quarter," "one-eighth," and so on. In many cases the blood-quantum assessments were incorrect, but they became part of the "official roll" of the tribe.

The enrollment criteria reflected the American fixation on defining "race" only in biological terms and completely ignored an individual's adherence to, or rejection of, traditional tribal values. Ironically, in the twentieth century most tribal governments embraced the blood-quantum rationale and used biological descent as the primary criteria for tribal membership. Most tribes now demand that all members be direct descendants of those individuals first enrolled on the allotment lists or other federal census reports taken in the late nineteenth century. Although the percentage of tribal ancestry necessary for modern tribal membership varies from tribe to tribe, the most widely utilized standard stipulates that the minimal biological ancestry be one-quarter or one-eighth, and that at least one parent should be enrolled in the tribe.

This reliance upon biological descent offers some advantages, since it requires that tribal members produce legal documents (such as birth certificates), which prove that they are entitled to tribal membership; however, it also raises serious questions regarding the parameters of modern tribal (and Native American) identity. Throughout the twentieth century Native Americans have increasingly intermarried with non-Indians, producing a growing population of "mixed-bloods" or people of Indian and non-Indian descent. Moreover, as some of these mixed-bloods or their descendants also marry non-Indians, their children and grandchildren's tribal blood-quantum declines. Thus, regardless of their residency within, and acceptance by, an established tribal community, they are no longer eligible for tribal enrollment. Ironically, in some cases, these individuals of limited blood-quantum may adhere to traditional tribal values much more closely than enrolled tribe members of a higher blood-quantum who no longer reside within the tribal community or participate in its activities.

Since the federal government provides certain limited services (the Indian Health Service, and so on) only to members of recognized tribes, en-

rollment has been critical to one's identity as an "official" Indian. Moreover, within the past decade, as some tribal economic enterprises have
prospered, tribal governments have carefully guarded the boundaries of
tribal membership in order to protect tribal assets from being depleted by
individuals who are eager to jump on the "buckskin bandwagon" for a
share of gaming profits or other largesse but who have little claim to tribal
membership. Nevertheless, many individuals of tribal descent who have
no aspirations of using government services or of sharing tribal assets
continue to personally identify themselves as members of specific tribes
and as Native Americans, regardless of their lack of official enrollment. In
addition, other tribal people, such as the Lumbees of North Carolina or
the Mashpees of Cape Cod (Massachusetts) are members of tribes recognized by a state government but not the federal government.

This entanglement of federal, state, tribal, and personal claims and
identities is further complicated by the question of an individual's participation within a tribal community and adherence to a particular way of
life. Obviously a federally enrolled member of a reservation community
who has resided on the reservation all of his or her life and who is an active participant in that community's activities, is certainly a bona fide
member of the tribe and an Indian. But as the twentieth century progressed, a diminishing percentage of Native Americans were able to meet
such standards. During the last two decades of the century, almost half of
the Native American population lived in large metropolitan regions, often
far removed from the tribal communities on reservations or old homelands. Many of these individuals still proudly identify themselves as tribal
members, and they periodically return to the reservation communities to
renew old family and ceremonial obligations, but they have spent or will
spend decades apart from these communities. Moreover, although many
urban Native American parents have taken special pains to regularly take
their children back to the reservation, many of them will grow up in urban environments far removed from reservation life. Consequently, if adherence to a particular ceremonialism or value system is critical to tribal
identity, what does the future hold for Native Americans separated from
the wellsprings of such traditions?

To combat this seeming inevitability, some urban-dwelling Native
American people have joined together to form urban Indian communities
particularly adapted to city life. These urban Indians still retain their tribal
ties, but they often face issues different from the ones that confront their
relatives back on the reservations. They have banded together in urban intertribal organizations designed to address the particular problems of life

in the city. It is from these urban Native American communities that activist organizations such as the American Indian Movement (AIM) originated.

Maintaining one's identity and ties with a tribal community sometimes has been difficult for Native American leaders in the twentieth century. Obviously, leaders such as Robert Yellowtail, Howard Tommie, and Phillip Martin, who have focused their efforts on improving the lives of people within their reservations, have retained close ties to their communities and are identified primarily as tribal leaders. They are considered to be Crow, Seminole, or Mississippi Choctaw leaders: individuals closely associated with their respective tribes. By contrast, other individuals featured in this volume (such as D'Arcy McNickle, Gertrude Bonnin, and Ben Nighthorse Campbell) are leaders whose efforts have been waged on the national level. Unlike the tribal leaders whose achievements are initiated at the grassroots level and then transcend their local reservations to provide benefits or examples to other tribal communities, the national leaders have initiated much of their efforts at the national level, and the results of their actions are then applied to the local reservation communities. Both types of leaders have made significant contributions to Native American people, but since national leaders wage their battles in Washington or other venues far removed from the reservation communities, they have found it difficult to maintain close ties to their tribes. In contrast to Yellowtail, Tommie, or Martin, national leaders are usually identified (at least by non-Indians) first as "Native American" or "Indian," and second by their tribal affiliation.

Regardless of their primary identification, almost all the individuals discussed in this volume have fought to maintain and expand the sovereignty of the tribes. Tribal sovereignty, which is the ability of a tribal community to control its own political, social, economic, and religious life, has increased during the twentieth century. Prior to the 1930s few Indian agents, reformers, or Native Americans would have envisioned tribal councils essentially governing and policing reservation lands, negotiating their own contracts with outside businesses or agencies, maintaining their own legal staffs, and administering the broad spectrum of economic programs and policies that recently have developed within the communities. Moreover, Native American control over indigenous (and adopted) religious ceremonies has also increased, as have tribal claims and hegemony over the sites of graves and over skeletal remains, sacred objects, and other culturally significant items. Tribal governments now administer many of the services once provided by the Bureau of Indian Affairs (BIA), or sponsor tribal school systems and colleges whose curricula are designed to meet the specific needs of the tribal communities. Although improvements still need to be made, life expectancy and per capita income within many of the communities has significantly increased.

Some of this "progress" may have come at a price. Traditional, clan-based tribal councils whose decisions were made only after lengthy debate and a general consensus have been replaced by federally designed, democratically elected councils or tribal business committees whose decisions have spurred the resentment of more traditional tribespeople and have aggravated tribal politics. Economic development has been uneven, and the material wealth it has engendered sometimes has upset the harmony of tribal life. Native American leaders have been hard-pressed to provide the economic resources and training necessary to allow their people to compete in a twentieth-century world while protecting those things that enable them to retain their unique Indian way of life. Moreover, both Indian people and tribal governments still have an ongoing, continued relationship with the federal government. Very few Native Americans wish to see that relationship terminated. Thus tribal leaders have been forced to walk a very fine line between negotiating with the government to ensure that federal services are continued, and becoming a part of the very bureaucracy with which they are negotiating. And finally, during the last third of the twentieth century, as the rural reservation communities have become less isolated, they have been inundated by a cultural invasion creating changes that will unquestionably alter the parameters and quality of Native American life. Bombarded by radio, television, video games, and the Web, young Native Americans now are exposed to a spectrum of educational and entertainment offerings undreamed of by their grandparents. Channeling this new technology and the changes it will bring for the general benefit of their people may emerge as one of the greatest challenges for Native American leaders in the years to come.

The chapters in this volume generally address Native American leaders who have focused upon political or economic issues. Although Vine V. Deloria Sr. and Janine Pease Pretty-on-Top have been recognized for their contributions in the areas of religion and education, their efforts also have markedly influenced the political and economic climate in their tribes. Obviously, there are other Native American leaders worthy of inclusion in this volume. Since this volume concentrates on politics and economics, it does not include Native Americans who have excelled in literature, the arts, or athletics. Moreover, there are many individuals within the local communities who are highly esteemed by their friends and families and who have spent their lives as religious leaders, counselors, or resource people whose knowledge of tribal traditions is treasured by all who know them. These people, often known only to members of their immediate community, are also worthy of our respect. They are the elders to whom people turn with their daily problems, and they often form the warp in the fabric of local communities. Many are unsung heroes, but others recently have been featured in the University of Nebraska Press's *American Indian Lives* series. Their lives also teach us much about Indian leadership.

Of all the Native Americans featured in the volume, Charles Curtis probably would have given the late-nineteenth-century reformers the most satisfaction. As William Unrau illustrates, Curtis seemed to epitomize the ideal acculturation model at the beginning of the twentieth century. Of mixed Kaw-white lineage, Curtis was a product of frontier Kansas, received some formal education, and was first reared by a strict Protestant grandmother determined to wean him from both his tribal past and his Catholic faith. When Curtis was six years old he lived for two years with his dead mother's relatives on the Kaw reservation before returning to Topeka. He briefly rejoined the reservation community when he was fourteen, but left when the Kaw tribe was removed to Oklahoma. In Topeka, Curtis first entered business and then politics, where he capitalized on his tribal heritage and his image as a "self-made man" and "progressive Indian." Elected first to Congress, then to the Senate, he sponsored the nefarious "Curtis Act," which eventually allotted the lands of the Five Southern Tribes, abolished their tribal governments, decimated tribal sovereignty, and opened their former reservations to white exploitation.

Curtis's biography has been included in this volume because it provides an interesting case study in Native American identity. Although he was an enrolled member of the Kaw tribe, Curtis's identification with the white power structure and his subscription to its value system raise serious questions about his identity. As William Unrau points out, Charles Curtis was Kaw by birth, but whether he was either Kaw or Native American in spirit after 1890 remains open to question.

If Gertrude Bonnin had problems with her Indian identity, they were of a different sort. Also of mixed ancestry, Bonnin was born on the Yankton Reservation in South Dakota, spent six years in a boarding school, and enrolled in Earlham College in Indiana. Following college, she taught at Carlisle Indian School, published a series of essays, and moved to Boston where she met and was temporarily engaged to Carlos Montezuma, a Yavapai physician and Indian activist. When Bonnin refused to relocate with Montezuma to Chicago, the engagement was broken.

In contrast to Charles Curtis, Bonnin championed her Yankton and Native American identity, preferred to be known by her Yankton name, Zitkala-Ša, and even denied that her father was a non-Indian. Although she spent most of her life away from the Yankton Reservation, Bonnin identified so strongly with the Dakota people that she defined "being Indian" in Sioux terms. Deborah Welch indicates that Bonnin's chauvinism debilitated the pan-Indian causes that she espoused, but Bonnin provides an interesting case study of the contradictions found among many Native American activists during the first quarter of the twentieth century. Moreover, she exemplifies a pattern of Native American leadership that has flowered in the second half of the twentieth century: dedicated and highly motivated Indian women who have risen to positions of prominence within their tribes and as members of a larger, pan-Indian community.

Questions of tribal or Native American identity were never an issue for Robert Yellowtail. Unlike Curtis and Bonnin, Yellowtail spent almost all of his life on the Crow Reservation in Montana. Although he was educated within the boarding school system, Yellowtail used his training and his skill as an orator to emerge as a leading tribal spokesman, and then served as the BIA's superintendent of the Crow Reservation. As historians Tim Bernardis and Frederick Hoxie indicate, Yellowtail's career provides a good example of how intelligent and adaptive tribal leaders have been able to work within the system, using positions of authority vested by the federal government to increase tribal sovereignty and protect their reservation and its resources from exploitation. Tribal leaders who become part of the federal bureaucracy are often objects of suspicion by members of their community, but Yellowtail was able to balance the opposing interests of the government and the Crows, and by remaining within the system he attempted to protect his people from its abuses.

Philip Deloria's essay indicates that his grandfather utilized traditional patterns of Sioux culture to serve his people in South Dakota. As most Sioux people are aware, holy men or influential religious figures have always exercised considerable power within Sioux society. Although non-Indians usually have portrayed Crazy Horse and Sitting Bull primarily as war chiefs or political leaders, during their lifetime their kinsmen respected them more as holy men, possessors of powerful medicine that they used for the good of the people. Indeed, they did exercise considerable political influence, but the basis of that power was their spirituality.

Vine V. Deloria Sr. also combined religious and political power to assist the Sioux people. Ordained as a deacon in the Episcopal Church, he spent most of his adult life using his position of religious leadership to strengthen and stabilize Native American communities in South Dakota. An energetic advocate of the social gospel, Deloria established a series of religious or social organizations that added cohesion to the reservation communities and resembled the ceremonial societies that were part of Dakota culture during the prereservation era. Moreover, his utilization of consensual decision making appealed to the Dakota people, although it sometimes engendered criticism from his superiors in the church. He labored to build bridges between the Indian and white worlds, but his (unsuccessful) efforts to champion a distinct cadre of Indian clergy reflect his commitment to the retention of a separate and distinct "Indian" identity. Deloria spent his adult life as an Episcopal priest, but he remained an Indian.

D'Arcy McNickle's identity seems to be more complicated. The consummate Native American intellectual, McNickle was born on the Flathead Reservation in Montana, but was not raised within a tribal community. As a young man he studied in England and in Paris before settling in New York, where he worked part-time jobs while writing *The Surrounded,* an autobiographical novel about a young mixed-blood man who flees a reservation in Montana only to return and become enmeshed in the tragedies of reservation life.

Essayist Dorothy Parker argues that McNickle's efforts to compose, refine, and publish his work markedly strengthened his Native American identity and was instrumental is his decision to seek employment with the BIA in Washington. Yet McNickle became suspicious of BIA paternalism, left the BIA, and spent the rest of his life sponsoring or directing other organizations that fostered education and leadership among younger Native Americans. Well known among American intellectuals, McNickle's ties to his own reservation, and other reservations, were tenuous. His efforts fostered the growth of pan-Indian causes and influenced federal Indian policy, but he seems to have been more comfortable associating with other Native American intellectuals than with reservation communities. His identity may have been more "Indian" than tribal.

LaDonna Harris also has spent much of her life attempting to influence federal Indian policy. Utilizing her access to prominent political figures, Harris has worked as an "insider" attempting to focus the government's attention on the needs of Native Americans people. As historian Gary Anderson illustrates, Harris was heavily influenced by her close association with leading Democratic politicians during the Kennedy and Johnson administrations, and she has worked hard to guarantee that Indian people have access to the state and federal programs and services to which they are entitled.

Harris's public career offers some similarities but also some stark contrasts to that of Charles Curtis. Both are of mixed-lineage and were born in or near reservation communities. Both achieved considerable influence within the power structure in Washington. Yet unlike Curtis, Harris retained her roots in her state and tribal communities and used her influence specifically to meet the needs of tribal people. She remains a highly successful, sophisticated Native American woman, but regardless of her years in Washington, she remains an Indian.

Russell Means's leadership also flowered in the late 1960s and 1970s, but it followed a different path. Although he was born on the Pine Ridge Indian Reservation in South Dakota, Means grew up in California, is a product of an urban Indian environment, and exemplifies many of the Native American activists who emerged during the turbulent 1960s and 1970s. A graduate of "the school of hard knocks," the charismatic Means rose through the ranks of AIM and played a leading role in AIM's confrontations with government officials during this period. Raymond Wilson demonstrates that Means's leadership was based on a "Red Power" or national identity, rather than within his tribal affiliation. Although AIM's leadership has fragmented, and confrontational Indian activism has declined, Wilson argues persuasively that Means and AIM played a major role in raising the political consciousness of younger Native Americans and in focusing the public's attention upon many of the issues facing Indian people. Wilson also demonstrates that Means's career has remained controversial and that he has engendered considerable criticism from other Native American leaders, particularly because of his participation in films and television productions. Despite the criticism, he remains one of the most widely recognized Native American leaders, and his career continues.

Like Russell Means, Wilma Mankiller was born in an Indian community on the fringe of the Great Plains, and her family also moved to California. Mankiller also came of age in an urban California environment, became an activist during the 1960s, and assisted in the occupation of Alcatraz. But in 1977 she returned to Oklahoma where she applied her grassroots activism within the Cherokee Nation, entered tribal politics, and eventually emerged as the elected chief of the tribe.

Historian Brad Agnew argues that Mankiller's leadership initially focused on a broad spectrum of social problems, particularly housing, health care, and other social services. Her labors in improving such conditions among the Oklahoma Cherokees brought her considerable media coverage, which she then used to champion Native American causes on both the state and national levels. Mankiller's identity and political power remain based within the Cherokee Nation, but her career illustrates how successful tribal leaders can transcend tribal boundaries to emerge as national leaders. Agnew also indicates that Mankiller's administration has not been without controversy, and her critics have charged that she has been more successful in promoting social services than economic development. But her forceful leadership has provided a viable model for other Native American women and she has proven that strong, effective leadership transcends gender lines. Moreover, her promotions of Cherokee tribal controls over gaming and taxation have strengthened the Cherokee Nation's political sovereignty, sometimes at the expense of other Cherokee bands. Mankiller has emerged as the most widely recognized female Indian leader of the last quarter of the twentieth century.

Howard Tommie also has been successful in strengthening tribal government and expanding tribal sovereignty. Born and raised on the Seminole reservation in Florida, Tommie gained valuable experience directing the Seminole's Neighborhood Youth Corps and in 1971 was elected chairman of the Seminole tribal council. Harry Kersey perceptively argues that the passage of the Indian Self-Determination Act in 1975 enabled Tommie to shrewdly bypass the BIA and use tribal agencies to administer federal funds made available through the War on Poverty. Consequently the Seminole tribal government markedly expanded its role, and Tommie's administration established the Human Resources Division, which oversaw many of the social, educational, and medical programs previously managed by the BIA.

Tommie pushed the envelope of tribal sovereignty even further. Since tribal lands are not subject to state taxation, Tommie's administration championed Seminole "smoke shops," which sold "tax-free" cigarettes at lower prices than those of non-Indian merchants, and established "high-stakes" bingo halls that attracted large numbers of non-Indians to the reservation. Of course such entrepreneurship engendered criticism, both from within the Seminole community and from state and local politicians in Florida, and Tommie's gains in personal income amid this general economic growth has raised some eyebrows, but most Seminoles have prospered during his administration. Though his efforts have focused almost entirely upon the Seminoles, his success has paved the way for similar economic enterprises among many other tribes.

Like Tommie, Phillip Martin also is a tribal leader, but as historians Benton and Christine Schulz White illustrate, he has taken Native American entrepreneurship even further. Born and raised amidst the poverty of the Mississippi Choctaw Reservation, Martin enlisted in the U.S. Air

Force. He then returned to Mississippi, entered tribal politics, and in 1959 was elected chairman of the Choctaw Tribal Council. Martin believed that the Choctaws' future initially lay in the development of reservation-based industry, not in smoke shops or gaming. Following Martin's leadership, the Choctaws established a tribal "enterprise zone" and lured outside industries to the reservation with offers of low taxes, inexpensive labor, and legal benefits. Martin was even willing to adopt non-Indian labor practices to ensure these industries' prosperity, and after an initial period of languor, the venture became very successful. Under Martin's leadership, the Choctaw industrial complex expanded and now employs considerable numbers of non-Indians in addition to Choctaws.

Martin has been criticized for emphasizing economic development over social services and for encouraging his kinsmen to join an industrial economy, since participation in these activities stands in marked contrast to the slower, more traditional Choctaw way of life. Yet funds generated by the economic growth enable tribal schools and a tribal television station to offer courses in Choctaw language and culture. Moreover, as the authors point out, Native American cultures, like all cultures, continually evolve. They are not fixed in stone.

Since Ada Deer's leadership is so multifaceted, it's much more difficult to characterize. Of mixed-lineage, she is well educated, and has worked as a social worker, college professor, and tribal administrator, and has been a candidate for Congress. She was born in, and retains strong ties to a reservation community, but has spent most of her adult life in an urban setting. Yet as Clara Sue Kidwell indicates, Deer has functioned effectively as an "outsider" and an "insider" in both tribal and federal environments and has provided leadership at both the tribal and national levels. As a Menominee activist she led the fight for Menominee restoration. Later, as chair of the Restoration Committee, she mediated the disputes among the BIA, the state of Wisconsin, and the Menominee Warrior Society. As a member of the American Indian Policy Review Commission she championed tribal sovereignty, and as the first female assistant secretary of Indian Affairs she continued to use her position as a member of the Clinton administration to support important amendments to both the American Indian Religious Freedom Act, and the Indian Self-Determination and Educational Assistance Act. Deer remains a viable member of the Menominee community, and her national stature has enabled her to serve as a role model for young Indian women across the United States. More than any other Native American leader of the twentieth century, she has bridged the gap between reservation and "mainstream" life.

Ben Nighthorse Campbell's ties to a reservation community are more tenuous. Born in 1933 near Sacramento, California, Campbell has always been proud of his Native American ancestry, but had no opportunity to visit the Northern Cheyenne reservation as a child. Campbell's Native American identity strengthened as he matured, and he was officially enrolled into the Northern Cheyenne tribe in 1980. He remains the sole Indian voice in the United States Senate. Donald Fixico points out that Campbell's support of Native American causes has been tempered by his transcendence of solely Indian issues; Campbell also has championed legislation supporting small business and the environment. Still, Campbell generally has supported the expansion of tribal economic and political sovereignty, although he has been reluctant to endorse gaming as an economic panacea for Native American communities. Campbell remains a complex figure—a Native American leader with significant influence on Capitol Hill, but a leader who continues to chart his own course. He refuses to adhere to any political or ideological line within either the greater Indian community or the halls of Congress.

Janine Pease Pretty-on-Top also was born and raised away from her tribal reservation, but she was able to maintain her ties to the Crow community. Unlike the other leaders in this volume, Pretty-on-Top's primary contribution has been in the field of education, and she epitomizes the best of those Native American educators who have spearheaded the growth and development of tribal colleges. As Douglas Nelson and Jeremy Johnston illustrate, Little Big Horn College, under Pretty-on-Top's guidance, has emerged as a leading institution among tribal colleges. It provides its students with skills both to meet the needs of local markets and to attend other institutions of higher education. The college also has become a repository of tribal traditions, a place where Crow scholars can enrich their sense of tribal culture and identity. Pretty-on-Top's role in building this institution has attracted the admiration of the Crow community and has placed her in the foremost ranks of Native American educators across the United States. Similar to Wilma Mankiller and Ada Deer, she functions as both a leading figure within her tribe and as a Native American woman of considerable national prominence.

In the nineteenth century many tribes had warrior societies dedicated to protecting their people and their homelands. Today such societies still function, but their warriors are armed with briefcases rather than trade muskets. As John Wunder points out, Walter Echo-Hawk is one of those legal warriors, and his society is the Native American Rights Fund (NARF).

Although Echo-Hawk was born in the Indian Health Service hospital near Pawnee, Oklahoma, and retains his ties to the Pawnee people, he is a Native American leader whose prominence rests upon his leadership at the national level. Obviously, the demands of the profession have forced Echo-Hawk and other NARF attorneys to reside in urban areas, often far removed from the reservation communities, but their involvement in issues that affect these communities both enables and forces them to remain attuned to the political, economic, and social climates of the reservations. Moreover, in the final decades of the twentieth century, Echo-Hawk and other legal warriors emerged as the foremost defenders of Native American rights. Armed with legal expertise, they are protecting and expanding Native American sovereignty in the courtroom and in the halls of Congress. Sometimes these contests have been protracted, and Echo-Hawk and his colleagues have not always been successful, but they have counted many coups. The struggle continues.

In conclusion, the Native American leaders featured in this volume persisted in their efforts to help their people adjust to the changes of the twentieth century. Like Indian people throughout the United States, some of these leaders have been forced to forge a personal identity amidst pressures and conditions much different from those faced by their predecessors. Yet many of the old challenges endure. Like tribal leaders in the past, most of these twentieth-century warriors developed and employed a series of strategies to strengthen and defend tribal sovereignty, retain Native American identity, and protect Native American rights. Some retained close ties to their tribes and focused their efforts on the reservation communities; others fought their battles at the state or national level. Many are of mixed lineage; some are well educated. And finally, like the tribes in which they are enrolled, the individuals discussed in these essays have differing opinions about what "being Indian" entails, but they all were, or are, proud to be Indian.

NOTE

1. *Little Big Horn College Catalog, 1997–1999* (Crow Agency MT: Little Big Horn College, 1997), iii; Phillip Garrett, "Indian Citizenship," *Proceedings of the Fourth Annual Lake Mohonk Conference,* quoted in *Americanizing the American Indians: Writings by the "Friends of the Indian," 1880–1890,* edited by Francis Paul Prucha (Cambridge: Harvard University Press, 1973), 65.

Charles Curtis

Kaw

BY WILLIAM E. UNRAU

Few Indians who rose to national prominence were born in a more unsettled political and social environment than Charles Curtis, a mixed-blood member of the Kaw (or Kansa) tribe.[1] Born on 25 January 1860, in Eugene (North Topeka), Kansas Territory, to Ellen Pappan Curtis, a quarter-blood Kaw and Oren A. Curtis, a non-Indian, Curtis was raised in a setting where outbursts of violence over slavery and the political future of what is now Kansas prompted eastern journalists and politicians to call the territory "Bleeding Kansas." That tension, followed by a striking growth in the Kansas economy during and after the Civil War and a burgeoning of the Kansas Republican Party in the wake of statehood (29 January 1861), would have a dramatic influence on the development of Charles Curtis's social, political, and economic values.

Since the mid-1830s, the area west of Missouri had been a focal point of the government's policy of tribal concentration, and after the passage of the Kansas-Nebraska Act in 1854, Kansas emerged as a region of brazen exploitation where white farmers, land speculators, railroad corporations, town promoters, and myriad squatters of diverse political persuasions contested for control of the region in defiance of federal law.[2] Such lawlessness also loomed in the education and acculturation of the young mixed-blood, whose family had been leading members of the Kaw tribe from its earliest recorded contacts with white Americans.[3]

Centuries before, when Europeans first arrived in the Western Hemisphere, Curtis's Kaw forebears resided in the lower Ohio Valley and were part of a Hopewellian group ethnologists have termed the Dhegihan-Siouans. Also included in this group were relatives of the modern Omaha, Osage, Ponca, and Quapaw tribes. Sometime prior to 1673—the year Pére Jacques Marquette recorded the Dhegian-Siouan presence west of the Mississippi River—the Quapaws moved down the Mississippi while the other tribes journeyed to the mouth of the Missouri and then up that river where further divisions took place between present St. Louis and Kansas City. The Omahas and the Poncas established their villages in southeastern Nebraska; the Osages traveled up the Osage River to modern Vernon County, Missouri.

The Kaws took the middle road to the mouth of the Kansas River (near the present site of Kansas City) and then west up the Kansas Valley until the Pawnees turned them back at the mouth of the Blue River. By the time the United States had purchased the area from France in 1803, Curtis's distant relatives claimed roughly the northern three-fifths of future Kansas as their domain, a claim that was officially recognized by the United States in the Kansa (Kaw) Treaty of 1825.

That same treaty reduced the Kaw domain from twenty million acres to an area less than half that amount west of the future site of North Topeka. The treaty also included an article that granted 640-acre sections in fee simple to each of the twenty-three half-bloods of the Kaw tribe—one of whom was Curtis's maternal grandmother, Julie Gonville Pappan. The government justified the provision on grounds that the owners of these half-blood tracts would abandon gardening and hunting in favor of commercial agriculture and thus serve as models for their less acculturated kinsmen. This proved not to be the case. In fact the agreement was divisive in the extreme. Most of the half-bloods were minors who in 1825 did not reside on the tribal reservation west of North Topeka. In fact these fertile and well-timbered tracts along the Kansas River became the objects of intense speculation by white land-jobbers and provided the future vice president with good reason to question supposed harmonious relations between Indians and non-Indians in Indian Country.

Curtis was aware that his own family reflected a blending of ethnic, tribal, and religious diversity common to the American frontier. Curtis's great-great-grandfather, White Plume (Nompawarah), whom he later described as "one of the ablest and most progressive Indians of his day,"[4] was one of the leading chiefs who signed the Kansa Treaty. In about 1800 White Plume married a daughter of Pawhuska, the celebrated Osage chief, and their union produced several children. One of White Plume's daughters, Wyhesse (Waisjasi), married Louis Gonville, a French-Canadian fur trader from St. Louis; their marriage was confirmed in a Catholic ceremony in late 1817 or early 1818. Julie, a daughter born to this union, married Louis Pappan, a fur trader from St. Louis who with his brother Joseph (who married Julie's sister Josette) established a ferry service on the Kansas River at the site of future Topeka. There, in 1840, Charles Curtis's mother was born in a log cabin situated on "Kaw Mile Three," the allotment that the Treaty of 1825 granted her sister Josette.

Whether by her own decision or that of her parents, young Ellen was sent to a Catholic convent in St. Louis. But as she approached legal maturity her interest in the 640-acre tract granted to her mother in 1825 prompted her to return to Kansas Territory, where in 1859 she married Oren A. Curtis, an emigrant from Eugene, Indiana, who had secured employment in her father's ferry business at North Topeka.

On 25 January 1860, the future vice president of the United States was born in a crude cabin on his grandmother's allotment. The young Curtis received Catholic baptism at St. Mary's Immaculate Conception Church on the nearby Potawatomi reservation. During the next three years Ellen raised Curtis and taught him English and French, since she had received training in the latter while in the convent in St. Louis. Evidence suggests that Curtis's parents intended to raise their son at their home near modern Topeka, well removed from the traditional culture of his blood relatives on the Kaw reservation some sixty miles to the west.

But in 1863 Charles's mother died, and his father faced the unexpected task of raising the young boy alone. Moreover, shortly following his wife's death, Oren Curtis obtained an appointment in the Union Army in Kansas, and his duties as an officer required that he be absent from his home. Oren Curtis placed Charles with his parents, William and Permelia Hubbard Curtis, who had followed their son from Indiana to Kansas. William Hubbard soon became involved in attempts to promote the development of a town on the Pappan family's allotment, while his wife—a stern homemaker who believed that "being Methodist and a Republican [were] essential for anyone expected to go to heaven"—saw to it that young Charles was diverted from "pagan Indian culture and the Catholic heresy" of his deceased mother in favor of Methodist doctrine and Republican Party ideals so fashionable in Kansas during and after the Civil War.[5]

Three years later, in 1866, Charley (as he was now called) was sent to live with his maternal grandmother on the Kaw reservation, near Council Grove. Talk of a Kaw removal treaty and final settlement of land claims in Kansas offered the possibility of financial disbursements to individual tribal members living on the reservation. It is possible that Julie Pappan was determined to have her grandson share in the bounty if in fact a treaty was negotiated. There is the possibility also that Julie was opposed to the rigid social and religious values of Permelia Curtis and wanted Charley to learn more about his Indian heritage. In any case, the young mixed-blood's environment at Council Grove was more relaxed and certainly in dire contrast to the stern will and rigid Methodism of his white grand-mother in Topeka.

Life for young boys on the Kaw reservation was a mixture of leisure activities such as fishing, foot-racing, and horseback riding, coupled with more serious endeavors such as hunting with bow and arrow or with a lance, and preparing for the vision-quest that would signify advancement from adolescence to manhood. Charley adjusted well to reservation life and quickly displayed unusual skill in horseback riding—a skill that he soon put to practical purpose in the burgeoning horse-racing business of frontier Kansas. By all accounts, Charley enjoyed his life with his maternal grandmother but his residency on the Kaw reservation was cut short by old tribal quarrels that originated long before Charlie had been born.

For more than half a century relations between the Kaws and the Southern Cheyennes and Arapahos had deteriorated, mainly over the dwindling bison supply on the high plains of western Kansas. In the winter of 1866 the Cheyennes stole forty-two horses from a Kaw hunting party on the upper Arkansas, and following a murder of a Kaw herder at a buffalo camp near Fort Zarah a year later, the Kaws attacked a Cheyenne encampment, killing fourteen and losing only one of their own. The death of sixty starving Kaw warriors in bitterly cold weather during the retreat back to Council Grove severely depleted the Kaw's military strength and led to a near panic in the Kaw villages, particularly when it was rumored that the Cheyennes were planning a counterattack on the reservation at Council Grove. The "attack" came on 3 June 1868, when approximately one hundred Southern Cheyennes fired a few scattered shots at the Kaw Agency Headquarters. No one was killed or injured; the entire affair lasted less than four hours. The Cheyennes gained some booty from outlying white farms but had to pay for it out of annuities granted them in the Medicine Lodge Treaty of 1867.

Like other young boys on the reservation, Charley was unaware of the events leading up to the attack. For him the minor attack was a harrowing experience; in later years he never wearied of relating the trying circumstances under which he returned to the home of his paternal grandparents in Topeka. There were many variations to his story,[6] but the high points were that because he could speak good English, because he was an expert runner, and because his people were besieged on their reservation (no horses were available for the journey to Topeka), the chief of the Kaws entrusted him with the responsibility of seeking help from the white man some sixty miles to the east. But the facts are that, under orders from Kaw Indian agent E. S. Stover and tribal leaders, Charley made the journey to

Topeka accompanied by Little Chief Joe Jim (Kyhegashinga), who served as the government interpreter for the Kaws and who was a trusted friend of Charley's Indian grandmother.

Charley never returned to the Kaw reservation and, so far as is known, had few contacts with Indians until elected to Congress in 1892. Once again he took up residence with his white grandparents—this time in the hamlet of Eugene (soon to be renamed North Topeka), located on a parcel of Kaw half-blood land William Curtis had only recently purchased from Julie Pappan. The town site was on the proposed route of the Union Pacific, Eastern Division Railroad, directly across the Kansas River from Topeka proper, where William Curtis also built a hotel, saloon, livery stable, and racetrack. The track became a popular attraction, especially for young Charley, who with not a little experience riding Indian ponies on the Council Grove reservation soon became an expert jockey. In fact, by the early 1870s he was winning more than his share of races at county fairs in Kansas, Texas, and the Indian Territory, and seemed content to live out his life near his paternal grandparents in Topeka.

In 1872 the Kaws relinquished their 250,000-acre reservation near Council Grove in exchange for a 100,000-acre tract in Indian Territory, just south of the Kansas border. In the following year most of the Kaws from the Council Grove reservation moved to their new lands, which were located at the confluence of Beaver Creek and the Arkansas River. Charley's name remained on the tribal roll, and in 1874 members of the Kaw tribe contacted him, asking him to also move to the new reservation. Charley refused. During the previous fall (1873) he had enrolled at Topeka High School. Moreover, he continued to ride in horse races at county fairs on weekends, and he enjoyed both the races and the prize money that he won.

Yet other factors also kept him in Kansas. In 1873 his grandfather, William Curtis, died suddenly and Charley was forced to help support his grandmother. To augment her income he sold apples and peanuts at the North Topeka railroad station, and worked as a hack driver and bookkeeper in the evening and on weekends during the winter. During the summer of 1874 he returned to the racetrack, mainly in eastern Kansas, Council Grove, and Wichita. Then came what Curtis termed a pivotal event in his life, one that by his own admission loomed large in his development as an American and an Indian.

In the fall of 1874, accompanied by several other tribal members, Louis and Julie Pappan journeyed to Topeka to visit their grandson as well as other friends and relatives residing on the nearby Potawatomi reservation. Disheartened by his labors as a depot vender, hack driver, and book-keeper, Charlie remembered his carefree days among the Kaws on the old Council Grove reservation and listened longingly to descriptions of life on the new lands in Indian Territory. In addition, Curtis later recalled that "the men folks of the tribe induced me to go to their reservation," reminding him that "under an old treaty provision the government was issuing free rations to all members of the tribe."[7]

Envisioning a life free from some of the responsibilities that now seemed to overwhelm him, the fourteen-year-old Curtis packed his few belonging in a flour sack, saddled his brown mare, and without even stopping to consult with his grandmother he left home and rode to Six Mile Creek, south of Topeka, where the Kaws were camped while visiting their relatives. But there his other grandmother intervened. As in most tribal societies, grandmothers are respected and revered for their wisdom. Julie Pappan called Charley to her wagon and asked him why he wanted to rejoin the tribe. When Charley recounted that the Kaw men who were part of the visiting party had admonished him for remaining in Topeka, his grandmother: "told me what I might expect on the Indian Reservation and that I would likely become like most of the men on it; that I would have no schooling, would put in my time riding racehorses or ponies, and become a reservation man with no future, and that if I ever expected to make anything out of myself I should return to Topeka and start school again." Curtis continues, "I took her advice. . . . No man or boy ever received better advice. It was the turning point in my life."[8]

Consequently, although Curtis temporarily remained on the Kaw tribal roll, as he moved from adolescence to adulthood he moved more permanently into the white world. He remained with his widowed grandmother, whose dedication to Republican conservatism had a profound impact on the young man. Permelia insisted that Charley complete his public school education, encouraged him to seek additional part-time jobs, and made sure that he understood that the Republican Party had won the Civil War, that the anti-black and anti-Indian sentiments of the Democrats were proof of that party's demagogy, and that the Methodist Church was the bastion of everything decent in Kansas and the nation.

Following high school Curtis read law with A. H. Case, a prominent Topeka attorney, and in 1881—the year that the Kansas prohibition amendment went into effect—he was admitted to the Kansas Bar. He also became active in state and local politics and gave notice of his ambition for public office and his commitment to the Republican Party. William Allen White concluded that the Kaw mixed-blood was a regular Republican "by inheritance," and quite an attractive politician at that: "He was handsome, slight, with the jockey's litheness, with affectionate, black, caressing eyes that were hard to forget; with a fine olive skin, and a haymow of black hair and a curling mustache. Add to that a gentle, ingratiating voice, an easy flow of innocuous conversation unimpeded by pestiferous ideas, and you have a creature God-sent into politics."[9] Thus in 1884 he was elected Shawnee County Attorney, one of the youngest men to hold such an office in the Jayhawk State. In the meantime, from Julie Pappan he inherited a parcel of land in North Topeka that was exempt from the Kansas prohibition law because of federal trustee regulations dating back to the Kansa Treaty of 1825. He sold several large lots to a distillery and a brewer who then produced the very commodities needed by bootleggers to contend with the Kansas prohibition law. But to the surprise of most Republicans and certainly all "resubmissionist" Democrats, within a few weeks after taking office Curtis closed the door of virtually every illicit bar in Shawnee County even though he personally did not favor prohibition.

The consequence was dramatic. Here was a person of humble origins who could support a law contrary to his personal beliefs, and more important, a dedicated politician who had demonstrated that personal sacrifice and individual performance were not beyond the grasp of an Indian whose ancestors had been dispossessed by the very society the Topeka mixed-blood now was taking by political storm.

Not surprisingly, then, "Our Charley" Curtis became the darling of the Republican Party, and given what William Allen White insisted were his emotional but simplistic political tactics that included a "bloody shirt" speech on the Civil War accompanied by a plea to "vote the way you shot"; a mindless, indeed incomprehensible appeal for higher tariffs; "and a very carefully poised straddle on the currency question," which Curtis "knew little about and cared absolutely nothing for,"[10] he was easily elected to Congress in 1892. During the next four decades, accompanied by what his detractors called his inherent talent to manipulate the political system from behind the scenes, his rise to the most distinguished position in the U.S. Senate and then to the second highest office in the land was short of phenomenal.[11]

Curtis's initial election to Congress was a testament to his hand-shaking energy and skill in getting to know his constituents at a personal, human, level. He carried a book with the names, occupations, and personal relations of virtually every family in every township in the Kansas Fourth District, and his dramatic victory over the Populist candidate John G. Otis in the same year that Kansas supported Populist James B. Weaver for the presidency, attracted national attention. Some attributed his success to the fact that he was French, Indian, and American at a time when census data indicated that the Native American population was rapidly nearing its nadir or, in more literary terms, when the "Vanishing American" epithet appeared to be reaching demographic fulfillment.

Still others viewed Curtis's political success in terms of his tribal ancestry and the prowess they felt was a characteristic of Native Americans. Following his dramatic 1892 victory, the Kaw mixed-blood easily won consecutive terms to the House until the Kansas legislature elevated him to the Senate in 1907. While his success obviously was the result of his ability to campaign effectively and to respond to his constituents' concerns—farm issues, veterans pensions, monetary matters, and the concerns of railroad corporations and the petroleum industry in the Jayhawk state—one commentator nevertheless concluded: "Although slightly less than one-quarter Indian, Curtis might from his features and swarthy skin, be taken for a full-blood. 'The Indian' he has been called, sometimes in hate, sometimes in admiration, throughout his political career. 'Beat the Indian' was the battle cry in many a hard-fought campaign. But it was not enough to beat the Indian who has just reached a dominating place in Kansas politics. Curtis has the wily persistence and dogged determination in a fight that marks him a true son of his Kaw ancestors."[12] The Washington press corps quickly appropriated this stereotype. "He has all the wisdom of his aboriginal ancestors," wrote one member.[13] "The pure possession of his ancestral qualities—the Indian tendencies toward taciturnity and general powers of self-repression and control—have something to do with the career of Curtis," suggested another.[14]

Finally a national magazine editor ferreted out the essential quality that made Curtis so attractive to non-Indian America. Even with his coal-black hair, copper complexion, and Fenimore Cooper–like demeanor, it was argued, the mixed-blood senator refused to conduct himself in the manner of the more traditional "braves who came on from the West every year to see their Great Father in Washington and to spend money which their kind and devoted Indian Commissioner gave them."[15] In short, for most Americans, Senator Charles Curtis was a *progressive* Indian, a self-made man whose success seemed to vindicate the Horatio Alger optimism of his age. Moreover, Curtis's political accomplishments seemed to prove that federal efforts to assimilate Indian people could be successful. Indian policies formulated in the 1880s were working. Charles Curtis was proof of their success and, in 1924, when Curtis eventually succeeded Henry Cabot Lodge as majority leader of the Senate, private citizens and government leaders alike (including Indian commissioner Charles H. Burke) characterized Senator Curtis as loyal, hardworking, frugal, and self-reliant—a self-made man who epitomized what Indian people could do if they seized the initiative.[16]

Curtis's image of himself seemed less certain. Although he had opted to remain in Topeka with his maternal grandmother in 1874, he still envisioned himself as an Indian. In 1878 Kaw Indian agent Laban J. Miles arbitrarily dropped his name from the tribal roll since he was not living on the reservation. Curtis did not immediately contest Miles's action, but in 1887, shortly after the passage of the Dawes Severalty Act, Curtis wrote to the Office of Indian Affairs and requested re-enrollment. In response, the matter was sent back to Miles. In the spring of 1889 Miles summarily reinstated Curtis and his sister Elizabeth on the Kaw tribal roll. In retrospect, Curtis may have been motivated by opportunities to receive an allotment if and when the Kaw reservation lands were divided, but Curtis argued that his decision to live with his grandmother in Topeka did not negate his tribal status. According to Curtis, he was a blood descendant of Chief White Plume, he had inherited part of his Indian grandmother's "half-breed" allotment, he had lived on the Kaw reservation and had received annuities prior to 1874, and therefore, legally, he was a Kaw Indian.[17]

Yet Curtis envisioned himself as an Indian far removed from the more traditional ways of his kinsmen in Indian Territory, or on other reservation communities in the West. Educated in the white man's world, Curtis evidently subscribed wholeheartedly to the accepted canons of federal Indian policy at the turn of the century and sincerely believed that the dissolution of the reservation communities and the assimilation of Native American peoples into mainstream American society were viable goals. In retrospect, his subscription to such policies may seem shortsighted, but like many other Americans of his era, Curtis believed that the federal policies he championed were conceived on the Indians' behalf. In 1900, after pushing through Congress legislation that provided for the further allotment of tribal lands in Indian Territory, Curtis wrote to Secretary of the Interior Ethan Allen Hitchcock and proudly proclaimed, "I have done more to secure legislation for the [Indian] Territory than all others put together since the 54th Congress [of 1896]."[18]

The legislation to which Curtis referred was entitled "An act for the protection of the people of the Indian Territory, and for other purposes," but it was more commonly known as the "Curtis Act." With Curtis's strong support it passed Congress in June 1898.[19] Without question the most important piece of Indian legislation between the General Allotment (Dawes) Act of 1887 and the Indian Reorganization (Wheeler-Howard) Act of 1934, the Curtis Act forced the allotment of the Five Southern Tribes and several smaller tribes in Indian Territory and elsewhere that previously had been excluded from the provisions of the Dawes legislation. The act was strongly opposed by most tribal leaders but Curtis maneuvered the bill through congressional committees and when it reached the floor of the House of Representatives, the House passed the bill with less than three minutes of consideration. A newspaper reporter from the Cherokee Nation who watched the proceedings from the gallery noted that the bill's passage was such a foregone conclusion that when it reached the floor "an air of indolence prevailed."[20] One congressman commented that any resistance to Curtis in this matter was "absolutely useless." In Indian Territory, the editor of the *Muskogee Phoenix*, the most prominent newspaper in the Creek Nation, agreed: "He [Curtis] is now not only the most powerful man in the House of Representatives in matters concerning this Indian country, but his influence is equally great with members of the Senate."[21]

The Curtis Act had a profound impact upon tribal people in Indian Territory. Under Curtis's deftly fashioned law, the Five Southern Tribes eventually fell under the allotment hammer, as did the smaller tribes that had been spared ten years earlier. No less important, the act abolished tribal laws and courts, provided a comprehensive code for the legalization of town sites in Indian Territory, maintained the authority of federal inspectors and inspections districts in Indian Country, and gave the Interior Department discretionary authority over oil, gas, and other mineral leases on Indian lands; in effect, it established the political foundation for Oklahoma statehood nine years later. If reformers or boosters of Oklahoma statehood wanted a law designed to encourage the dissolution of tribal government and the forced assimilation of tribal people into mainstream America, they got it. Moreover, to their great delight, the act had been pushed through Congress by "the Indian," Charles Curtis. As both the reformers and Curtis later would perceive, the act proved generally disastrous for many Indian people.

Four years later, in 1902, Curtis, who then presided over the House Committee on Indian Affairs, pushed the Kaw Allotment Act through Congress.[22] Each member of the tribe, including Curtis and his two children, received an allotment of approximately six hundred acres of former reservation land. To Curtis it must have seemed that a golden age for the Kaw people soon would arrive. They too could follow his path down the road to progress and prosperity.[23]

While Curtis was drafting legislation, he also was climbing the political ladder in Washington. Early in his career he had caught the attention of House Speaker Thomas B. "Czar" Reed who called the young congressman from Kansas "the Indian." On one occasion Curtis happened to stumble into a meeting of the Gold Standard Committee in Reed's conference room. Reed asked him to sit in on the proceedings, which at that point had reached a deadlock. Reed turned to Curtis, who by no means was a currency expert, and asked him what he would do. Without wavering, "the Indian" suggested appointing a select committee that had little or no experience in monetary matters. After laughter among the assembled Solons subsided, Reed queried further. "Just what do you mean by that?" he asked. "I mean just this," replied Curtis as he sized up the assemblage, "if you put these specialists on that committee, each with a bill of his own in mind, you won't get anywhere. . . . You had better let the thing out to fellows who may not know so much about currency but who will bring in a bill." A few days later such a committee was appointed. To include Curtis, the Speaker increased the traditional membership from ten to eleven, and it was this committee that framed what became the Gold Standard Act of 1900.[24]

His success with this event and with other legislation, buttressed by Reed's support, led to Curtis's membership on the powerful House Committee on Ways and Means. His other committee assignments suggest a personal preference for roles dealing with Indian people and Indian affairs. He sat on the Committee on Territories, which at the turn of the century played a major role in the statehood movements in Oklahoma, Arizona, and New Mexico—states with large Indian populations. He served on Public Lands and Expenditures in the Interior Department (the latter had significant control over fiscal matters in the Office of Indian Affairs) and, most important of all, as chairman (1900–1906) of the House Committee on Indian Affairs.

In 1907 Curtis was appointed to the U.S. Senate, and although he occasionally encountered prejudicial remarks (his enemies called him the "whispering Indian"), he rose through the ranks of the upper house to a position of leadership. During the decade following his appointment he authored no major Native American legislation but served faithfully on Senate committees, and was elected and re-elected by the people of Kansas on four occasions between 1908 and 1926.

Most political analysts have concluded that the zenith of Curtis's public career came in the half decade between his selection as Senate majority leader in 1924 and his inauguration as vice president under Herbert Hoover in 1929. It is true that during this period virtually every piece of Republican legislation in one way or another bore the stamp of Curtis. According to one study his bills and amendments saved the federal government eighty three million dollars between 1924 and 1929. He was an indefatigable spokesman for prohibition, women's rights, veterans' pensions, and child labor laws. He was intractable in support of President Coolidge's conservative agenda in general and, as senior statesman from a powerful farm state, played a critical role in sustaining Coolidge's veto on the McNary-Haugen Farm Relief Bill in 1927.

Yet by the mid-1920s Curtis must have realized that the allotment and assimilationist policies he had championed at the turn of the century had proven unsuccessful. While some tribespeople had accepted and developed their allotments into successful farms, many others had lost their lands to opportunistic whites who readily purchased the properties when the Indians became impoverished. Valuable Native American mineral resources had been depleted, while the proceeds from oil and mining leases often ended in the hands of white, court-appointed "guardians" who pocketed the majority of the profits while returning only a pittance to their Indian wards. Meanwhile, tribal governments among the Five Southern Tribes were decimated, and Cherokees, Choctaws, Creeks, and others now found the cadence of their daily lives more closely controlled by non-Indians.

The Kaws, Curtis's own tribe, provide a microcosm of the debacle. By 1923, twenty years after its lands were allotted, the tribe was in shambles. Aware that his policies had failed, Curtis wrote to an Office of Indian Affairs official in Oklahoma: "I, like you, am exceedingly sorry the Kaws sold so much land so quickly. I tried to keep them from selling. I even agreed with [Kaw chief] Washungah that I would let my [allotment] titles remain as they were during the twenty-five year period, so as to set an example."[25] And so he did, but to no avail. Both the Dawes and the Curtis acts stipulated that the allotted lands would be placed in trust for twenty-five years—until Indian people supposedly became experienced enough to prevent their property from being swindled away from them. Yet after 1908, Indian agents, in conjunction with officials in Washington, could declare individual Indians "competent," enabling these "more sophisticated" individuals to sell their lands prior to the end of the twenty-five-year trust period. Between 1903 and 1923 Indian agents among the Kaws arbitrarily declared the majority of the tribe to be "competent" (whether they understood the responsibilities of Anglo-American land tenure or not), and most sold their land outright or had it mortgaged to the degree that foreclosure was virtually inevitable. Even those "incompetent" Kaws who still retained their allotments in trust were so far in debt that at the end of their twenty-five-year trust period most would have to give up their property in order to liquidate their indebtedness. The dream of a self-sufficient Kaw people settled happily on their individual allotments was an empty one. By the mid-1920s the Kaw tribe had disintegrated and poverty was rampant on what formerly had been the Kaw reservation.

Thus in 1924, as Curtis held the position of Senate majority leader and even entertained the possibility of running for the presidency, it was obvious that his efforts to mold Indian people in his own mixed-blood image had not succeeded. His legislative handiwork had accelerated allotment, but it had not ushered in a new golden age for Indian people. Back in 1910 his good friend Indian commissioner Francis E. Leupp had written: "With his Indian blood he [Curtis] inherits keenness of observation, stoicism under suffering, love of freedom, a contempt of the petty things which lay so heavy a burden on our convention-bound civilization; with his white blood the competitive instinct, individual initiative; resourcefulness in the face of novel obstacles, and a constitution hardened to the drafts made upon its strength by the artificialities of modern life."[26] At the time these words had been written they were pleasing to Curtis, but by the mid-1920s the mixed-blood man from Kansas had become disillusioned about providing any future guidance in the realm of Indian policy. Policies he long championed had failed. He seemed to retreat into other arenas.

In 1928, Curtis made a bid for the Republican nomination for the presidency. He enjoyed strong support in Kansas and significant support among delegates from New England, New York, Pennsylvania, Oklahoma, and some states in the upper Midwest, but his campaign budget was limited. Moreover, his campaign remained so unimaginative that some political analysts believed that he came to the convention in Kansas City more interested in the vice presidency than in contending for the presidential nomination. If such was the case, he succeeded. Most of his public statements focused on his long and dedicated service to the Republican Party, and few delegates were surprised when Curtis readily accepted the invitation to become Hoover's running mate after the latter amassed enough delegates to win the primary nomination. The Kaw from Kansas garnered a decisive 1,052 votes—250 more than Hoover received for the presidency—on the first vice presidential ballot. It was as if most delegates knew well that, while Charley may not have been bona fide presidential timber, he absolutely deserved the second office for his long service and loyalty to the GOP.

In keeping with the norm of the times, Curtis's contribution to public affairs while in office as vice president was minimal. Hoover invited him to attend cabinet meetings but because relations between the two men were never very close or cordial, Curtis exhibited more interest in wielding the gavel in the Senate, adding a kind of aloof dignity to the second highest office in the land. He decorated his office with Native American artifacts and memorabilia, and attended seemingly endless receptions and dinner parties while the nation plunged deeper into the economic morass culminating in the great stock market crash of 1929. Yet if Curtis was moved by the plight of the many Americans who were suffering the effects of the economic plunge, he did not voice his sympathies. When asked about the rising clamor for relief and reform that arose over the stock market crash and the subsequent business failures, he replied that "it is not pleasing to note the wave that is sweeping over the country which disregards law and order and the Constitution, and substitutes man's desire, and weakens opinion of law."[27]

During the 1928 campaign Curtis insisted that he supported legislation to improve the status of American Indians, but unlike Hoover, who at least publicly supported the reforms proposed by a Brookings Institute study compiled by Lewis Merriam, Curtis issued no public statement regarding the poverty and shocking conditions on most Indian reservations. And again, in the campaign in 1932 that pitted Hoover and Curtis against Franklin D. Roosevelt and John N. Garner, he failed to adequately address the important issues facing Indian people. On the very eve of Indian commissioner John Collier's call for dramatic changes in American Indian policy, it was clear that Curtis's leadership in such matters lay in the past.

The victory of the Roosevelt-Garner ticket in November 1932 ended the political career of Charles Curtis. He retained a nominal association with a law firm in Topeka and made occasional trips back to Kansas and Oklahoma. There was even talk that he might try to regain his old seat in the Senate. But his main interest was his law office in Washington, which became well known as a rendezvous for Republican regulars to discuss the future of the GOP. On 8 February 1936, he was found dead of a heart attack in the Washington home of his half-sister, Dolly Gann.[28] Thousands paid their last respects to Curtis in the Gann house, after which his body was taken to Topeka for a memorial service in the rotunda of the state capitol. Only a bow and arrows, gifts from Chief Deerfoot of the Apaches, adorned his coffin. A Wichita newspaper printed a large photograph of Curtis beside a photograph of Kaw chief Washungah, who died in 1908, with the caption: "Who can say but that they are together in the happy hunting grounds." Final interment was in a North Topeka cemetery not far from the small cabin where Curtis was born three quarters of a century earlier.[29]

NOTES

1. Prior to 1850 the Kaw tribe was known as the Kansa (or Konza) tribe. The change to Kaw was the consequence of reports filed by field agents of the U.S. Bureau of Indian Affairs.

2. For the details of this activity, see Paul Wallace Gates, *Fifty Million Acres: Conflict over Kansas Land Policy, 1854–1890* (Ithaca: Cornell University Press, 1954).

3. For a general study of Curtis and his roles in Indian and non-Indian society, see William E. Unrau, *Mixed-Bloods and Tribal Dissolution: Charles Curtis and the Quest for Indian Identity* (Lawrence: University Press of Kansas, 1989).

4. Charles Curtis, "Autobiography," article 1, 1–5. A typed copy of the manuscript is in the possession of Tom Dennison, Ponca City, Oklahoma. Dennison, whose permission to quote from the "Autobiography" is hereby acknowledged, obtained the typed copy from William P. Colvin, Charles Curtis's nephew.

5. Dolly Gann, *Dolly Gann's Book* (Garden City NY: Doubleday, Doran and Company, Inc., 1933), 1. Dolly Gann was Charles Curtis's half-sister.

6. The most romanticized versions are in Don C. Seitz, *From Kaw Teepee to Capitol: The Story of Charles Curtis, Indian, Who Has Risen to High Estate* (New York: Frederick A. Stokes, 1928), 121–25, and *New York Times*, 14 April 1929. For a summary and analysis of the several versions see Unrau, *Mixed-Bloods and Tribal Dissolution*, 72–75.

7. Curtis, "Autobiography," article 5, 7.

8. Curtis, "Autobiography," article 5, 8.

9. William Allen White, *Calvin Coolidge: The Man Who Is President* (New York: Macmillan, 1925), 178.

10. William Allen White, *The Autobiography of William Allen White* (New York: Macmillan, 1946), 106.

11. The best summary of Curtis's political career after 1892 is in Marvin Ewy, "Charles Curtis of Kansas: Vice President of the United States, 1929–1933," *Emporia State Research Studies* 10 (December 1961): 1–58.

12. Sheffield Cowdrick, "From Saddle to Senate, the Remarkable Career of Charles Curtis, Indian," *The World Today*, March 1907, 313–14.

13. *National Tribune* (Washington DC), 27 July 1920.

14. *Inquirer* (Washington DC), 7 December 1924.

15. "Lo, the Poor Senator," *Saturday Evening Post*, 9 February 1907, 14.

16. As a freshman congressman, Curtis received 1400 letters during one twenty-four-hour period. With the help of his family, a variety of form letters, and several secretaries, he answered most of them within the day. See Ewy, "Charles Curtis of Kansas," 23.

17. Unrau, *Mixed-Bloods and Tribal Dissolution,* 130–35.

18. "Curtis to Hitchcock," n.d., 1900, Ethan Allen Hitchcock Papers, RG 200, National Archives.

19. *U.S. Statutes at Large* 30: 495–519.

20. *Vinita Indian Chieftain* (Vinita, Indian Territory), 21 April 1908.

21. *Muskogee Phoenix* (Muskogee, Indian Territory), 26 March 1900.

22. *U.S. Statutes at Large* 32: 686–90.

23. For an assessment of Curtis's role in the allotment of the Kaw tribe, see William E. Unrau, "Charles Curtis: The Politics of Allotment," in *Indian Lives: Essays on Nineteenth and Twentieth Century Native American Leaders,* edited by L. G. Moses and Raymond Wilson (Albuquerque: University of New Mexico Press, 1985), 113–37.

24. Unrau, *Mixed-Bloods and Tribal Dissolution,* 115.

25. Curtis to J. W. Clendening, 22 January 1923, Kaw Indian Agency Collection, Western History Collections, University of Oklahoma Library, Norman, Oklahoma.

26. Francis E. Leupp, *The Indian and His Problem* (New York: Charles Scribner and Sons, 1910), 344.

27. *New York Times,* 5 July 1930.

28. Curtis's wife Anna (Baird) Curtis, a native of Topeka, died 29 June 1924. Excluding his stay in a ten-room suite in the Mayflower Hotel during the vice presidential years, Curtis resided with his half-sister, Permelia ("Dolly") Gann after his wife's death. Gann served as Curtis's official hostess during the vice presidential years.

29. *Wichita Eagle,* 9 February 1936.

Gertrude Simmons Bonnin
(Zitkala-Ša)

Dakota

BY DEBORAH WELCH

Gertrude Simmons Bonnin (Zitkala-Ša) stands almost alone as an American Indian woman who sought a national leadership role in shaping U.S.-Indian policy during the early years of the twentieth century. She first rose to fame while a young woman at the turn of the century, publishing numerous short stories that celebrated an unstintingly proud, if highly romanticized, view of Indian history. From 1912 to 1913, she co-wrote with William Hanson the opera *Sun Dance,* first performed in Salt Lake City. Later, as a leader in the political pan-Indian movements of the 1910s, 1920s, and 1930s, the Society of American Indians, and the National Council of American Indians, Zitkala-Ša demanded her right to be heard in all arenas—from the halls of Congress to tribal council meetings held on reservations throughout the country. In this crucial period of Native American history, at the height of U.S. allotment and assimilation policies, Zitkala-Ša grappled with the central issues of her day, drawing new attention to questions of an American Indian identity and Native American rights to land and water. Sometimes in alliance, but more often in sharp disagreement with other Indian and Anglo reformers, and plagued by personal difficulties of poverty and illness, Zitkala-Ša battled on. Her life provides a blueprint of the challenges and issues that would face Indian leadership throughout the twentieth century.

Born in 1876 on the Yankton Sioux Reservation in southeastern South Dakota, young Zitkala-Ša spent the first eight years of her childhood solely in the company of her mother, Ellen Simmons, a woman embittered by family loss and the grinding poverty of reservation life at the end of the nineteenth century. Ellen Simmons hated all white men and later her daughter would remember how her mother sought to teach her children to feel the same way. Following the death of her Yankton Sioux husband, which left her with small children to raise, Zitkala-Ša's mother took a white man, Simmons, for her second husband and gave birth to two children: Dawee (or David) and Gertrude (Zitkala-Ša). But Simmons, an often drunk and violent man, beat the children, so husband and wife parted. Ellen Simmons effectively expunged him from her children's memories. Throughout her life, Zitkala-Ša never acknowledged her biological father, seeking instead to present herself always as a full Sioux. She crafted for herself an identity of "a warrior's daughter," the title of one of her later short stories. This fierce pride in her Sioux identity—a pride that would shape her entire life—led her to use her Dakota name, Zitkala-Ša, as a young author.

Zitkala-Ša's childhood, which she later described in her book, *American Indian Stories,* was short-lived.[1] For many years, Quaker missionaries visited the Yankton Reservation and gathered children to be educated in the East, away from the reservation and the "barbarism" of their parents. In these boarding schools, Indian children were compelled to speak English, to adopt Anglo modes of dress along with Anglo values of individualism and property ownership, and most important, to become Christians and learn a trade.

The Quakers had taken Zitkala-Ša's older brother David to White's Manual Labor Institute in Wabash, Indiana, for three years of education. Zitkala-Ša's turn came in 1884 when she was only eight years old. Lured by the missionaries' promises of bright red apples and wonderful Eastern lands, Zitkala-Ša begged her mother to let her go. Ellen Simmons, like Indian parents throughout the West, had to make a heartrending decision. She hated whites and had heard stories of the harsh conditions and high mortality rates in the boarding schools. But the rapid changes she had seen in her own lifetime, including the steady encroachment of white populations around her, meant that if her daughter were to have a future, she must learn how to live with whites. So Ellen Simmons relented, and young Zitkala-Ša was put on the wagon alongside the other Yankton children to be taken away.

Unlike Charles Eastman and other Indian writers who have somewhat charitably described their painful boarding school experiences in their memoirs, Zitkala-Ša was less forgiving. She later vividly recalled the humiliation and mistreatment she underwent as a result of her Anglo teachers' total scorn for Indian cultures. While recognizing that her teachers were well-meaning, she nonetheless spiritedly refused to be inculcated with their "superstitious ideas" or broken by their hard hearts.[2] Zitkala-Ša was a good student, discovering a keen appreciation for literature and music, but she hated those first years at White's. After three years she left and returned to her mother's house. She spent the next four years, from age eleven to fifteen, trying to reconcile her longing for Anglo education with the trauma she had undergone in defying her mother and placing herself in the hands of ethnocentric Anglo missionaries. Her exposure to the Anglo world of books and writing awakened in her a desire to learn more, but she felt unable to defy her mother and return to school. She spent four years trying to fit back into a reservation society where she no longer seemed to belong. "During this time I seemed to hang in the heart of chaos, beyond the touch or voice of human aid. My brother, being almost ten years my senior, did not quite understand my feelings. My mother had never gone inside a schoolhouse, and so she was not capable of comforting a daughter who could read and write. Even nature seemed to have no place for me. I was neither a wee girl nor a tall one; neither a wild Indian nor a tame one. This deplorable situation was the effect of my brief course in the East and the unsatisfactory 'teenth' in a girls' years."[3] In 1892 Zitkala-Ša returned to White's, receiving her diploma in 1895. At nineteen, she again disobeyed her mother's demands that she return home and went on to Earlham College in Richmond, Indiana.

Zitkala-Ša's years at Earlham were among the happiest in her life. In a collegiate atmosphere, her talents and keen mind blossomed as she discovered her gifts for writing, oratory, and music. She became an accomplished pianist and violinist and won several oratorical contests. In her public speeches, Zitkala-Ša urged her listeners to accept the Indian as a fellow man, to afford him equal opportunities, and to live the Christian message of brotherhood. This youthful zeal was common among other Indian reformers also coming of age in this era of American progressivism marked by the belief that past injustices could be redressed if only the American public were made aware of them. But Zitkala-Ša encountered bigotry as well. Even as she accepted an award at the state oratorical contest in 1896, some students from an opposing college dropped from a balcony a white banner on which was drawn a caricature of an Indian girl with the word "squaw" crudely lettered beneath. No one forced the students to remove the banner and it was left hanging throughout the ceremony.[4]

Nonetheless, Zitkala-Ša persevered. While still at Earlham, she began to experience stomach problems and an overwhelming sense of weariness, which would eventually compel her to withdraw from college before she could receive her degree. This early pattern of illness would remain with her throughout her life. Though weak and frequently in low spirits, Zitkala-Ša still could not return home. To do so would have been to admit failure, and Zitkala-Ša's pride would not permit it. Instead she turned her attention to writing as an outlet for the ever-present guilt she felt at having "abandoned" her mother and thus her culture, as well as for her desire for more education and the opportunity to seek recognition of her talents in the East. She began contacting literary societies in Boston and Washington DC that were anxious to help her publish her short stories and provide opportunities for her to speak and to perform as a musician. Moreover, she found a teaching job at Carlisle, the most famous Indian school of her day. Although she did not particularly relish her teaching responsibilities, the classroom provided Zitkala-Ša with a small salary necessary to remain in the East.

During the spring of her first year at Carlisle, a Washington literary club invited her to give a recitation and violin concert at a meeting that President McKinley would be attending. This event provided Zitkala-Ša one of her first opportunities to act as a spokesperson for her race, a purpose she adopted to assuage the guilt she felt at remaining away from Yankton. Before the president himself, she demonstrated the heights an Indian could reach when given the opportunity. In January 1900 her first article, "Impressions of an Indian Childhood," appeared in the *Atlantic Monthly*. The February and March issues of the magazine published two additional stories, "The School Days of an Indian Girl" and "An Indian Teacher among Indians," respectively.

The response to this new author proved overwhelming. In April of 1900, *Harper's Bazaar* included a brief overview of her work in the column "Persons Who Interest Us." These and other accolades abounded for the young author, encouraging her further work and attracting scholarships that would make possible her further study.

In late 1900 Zitkala-Ša left Carlisle and went to Boston where she enrolled in the New England Conservatory of Music. She traveled to France where she played at the Paris Exposition. Moreover, Boston literary society welcomed her and provided the incentive to publish more stories.

Zitkala-Ša loved her time in Boston, the intellectual company, and the happy life full of good friends and long lazy picnics. Perhaps she enjoyed her time all the more because she knew it would be cut short. News from Yankton troubled her. During a brief visit the year before, she witnessed firsthand the rapid inroads being made onto both Yankton lands and culture by the surrounding Anglo populations. Yet she was well aware of the difficulties she would face in returning to the reservation. In 1901 she published two more stories, "The Trial Path" and "The Soft-Hearted Sioux," as well as a book, *Old Indian Legends*, all of which provide palpable evidence of the doubts she felt. The stories dealt with the dilemma faced by Indian peoples educated in the East who attempt to return to the reservation, bringing their adopted Anglo culture with them, and facing great sadness and often tragedy in their efforts to live in two worlds.

Nonetheless, Zitkala-Ša decided to go back. It was not a decision without cost. While in Boston, she had become engaged to another Indian activist, the Yavapai physician Carlos Montezuma. Montezuma practiced in Chicago, where he wanted his future wife to join him. Zitkala-Ša's compulsion to return to the Yankton reservation and Montezuma's equally stubborn insistence that she would only waste her talents at Yankton, meant that the two eventually had to part. Montezuma, educated in Anglo boarding schools, was then a firm believer in assimilation and making equal opportunities available to all Indian peoples. He was a lifelong critic of the Indian Bureau, which he maintained imprisoned Indians in reservations of poverty.[5] Zitkala-Ša continually reiterated her belief that there was an equally valuable education to be found in the traditional ways that would soon be lost if young Indians were not encouraged to embrace their identities as Indians. The engagement was broken and a rift formed between these two friends that would last for several years.

Zitkala-Ša's long and often haranguing letters to Montezuma revealed her intention to maintain her hard-won identity as an independent, capable, and wholly Sioux woman. She was not prepared to relinquish her accomplishments to become a wife or allow her identity to become lost in that of her husband's, as she well knew would happen in American society of 1901. Zitkala-Ša's fierce pride in her Sioux heritage governed her choice of a mate. Shortly after her final breakup with Montezuma, in June 1902, Zitkala-Ša married a Sioux man, eight years her junior, named Raymond T. Bonnin. He was not an educated man, but he was an ambitious one. Following their marriage, he began to read law. Seven months after their marriage, a son, Raymond O. Bonnin, was born to the couple. However, there was no work for Bonnin on the Yankton reservation, and in 1903 he was forced to relocate his young family to Utah, where he had been offered a position as government clerk on the Uintah reservation.

Settling in at Whiterocks, Zitkala-Ša undertook to make a home for her husband and new son. Domesticity had never interested her, however, and she did not remain home long. Despite repeated requests for an agency teaching position, no offer was forthcoming from the Indian Bureau. Zitkala-Ša's bitterness toward Anglo administrators and policy makers deepened.[6] However, she soon found ways to become involved with the school and the Ute community. Discovering that a shipment of brass instruments had been delivered to the school years before, though promised funds for a music teacher had never materialized, Zitkala-Ša began teaching music. By the fall of 1904, she had formed a band from among the Ute school children and begun offering concerts for their parents.

Next she organized a basket-weaving class among the Ute women. These baskets would be sold to help alleviate, however slightly, the desperate poverty she saw about her. Moreover, bringing these women into her home for classes gave Zitkala-Ša the opportunity to share information about new medicines, hygiene, and education for the children. Her desire to help was sincere, but her feelings of Sioux superiority can be found in her descriptions of the Utes, a people she described as "victims" of their "ignorance, superstition, and degradation."[7]

Most of all, however, she was lonely. The Uintah Agency appeared to be in every sense a desert. The writing through which she had once successfully pursued her goal of acting as a spokesperson for her race was abandoned. One of the rationales she had given Montezuma for her decision to return to the reservation was that she would use the opportunity to gather more materials for her stories. Yet those stories never materialized after she went to Utah. While at Carlisle, and especially in Boston, the young Zitkala-Ša had enjoyed a network of literary friends who supported her efforts to write about the Indian past. Publishing her stories had helped to alleviate the guilt she had felt at defying her mother and staying in the East. With this motivation, she had been amazingly prolific. In Utah, however, there was no network of friends and fellow writers. Her mother died in 1905, and with the fulfillment of her self-imposed obligation to live among her own race, the incentive to write and speak was gone. For ten years Zitkala-Ša's voice disappeared only to be resurrected in 1913 by the emergence of a new political stage for her talents in the creation of the Society of American Indians.

The idea of a pan-Indian organization, a reform society whose leadership and full membership would be open only to Indian peoples, had long been discussed among groups such as the Indian Rights Association (IRA) and the Friends of the Indian. The beginning of the twentieth century saw the coming of age of a large number of young Indian people like Zitkala-Ša, who were the products of a nineteenth-century U.S. policy of acculturation through education. The dream of an Indian-only organization materialized in 1911 when sociologist Fayette McKenzie organized the first meeting of the Society of American Indians (SAI) in Columbus, Ohio. McKenzie drew together some of the most capable young Indian leaders of this generation, including Sherman Coolidge, Arapahoe minister; Henry Roe Cloud, Winnebago educator; Arthur C. Parker, Seneca anthropologist; Charles Eastman, Sioux physician; and others. Though a vastly diverse group of people in some respects, they all possessed highly educated backgrounds, success in their fields, and a keen awareness of a responsibility to share the benefits enjoyed in their own lives with the rest of their race. They hoped to organize the Indian voice for self-determination within the parameters of the Progressive Era, which stressed hard work, moral uprightness, and above all, assimilation into the Anglo-American dream.

The progressive mood of the country in the early twentieth century influenced the formation of the SAI. More directly, these young Indian leaders were an unforeseen outgrowth of the nation's policy of Indian education and acculturation. To varying degrees, the men and women who formed the SAI had internalized the lessons of their teachers. They recognized the benefits of such things as education and health care offered by Anglo society and saw themselves as the bearers of these blessings to their race. They had not forgotten injustice, for tangible and immediate evidence of America's inhumanity to its Indian peoples could be observed on every reservation. But they saw themselves as realists concerned not with the past but with the present, and the role their organization could play in bringing the benefits of Anglo society to other Indian peoples.

One of the Society's principal purposes was to hold annual conferences where Indian peoples from throughout the country could express their views. In addition, Society members recognized the importance of publicizing their findings, both for Indian peoples and Anglo society, through the publication of the *Quarterly Journal*, later renamed the *American Indian Magazine*. The Society mailed hundreds of letters to Indian people throughout the country in an effort to secure membership and badly needed contributions. Shortly after the Society's founding, Zitkala-Ša began a collaboration with composer William Hansen that resulted in their creation of the opera "Sun Dance," which was first performed in 1913 in Salt Lake City and received rave reviews. In that same year, she once again contacted Montezuma explaining that like Rip Van Winkle, she had been asleep for the last decade but was now awake.[8] Possibly through Montezuma's intercession, Zitkala-Ša joined the SAI's advisory board in 1914 and immediately began to publish in the *Quarterly Journal* stories about her work in establishing sewing and other classes among the Utes. Such community work was in keeping with SAI goals to bring the benefits of Anglo civilization to the Indian. But in her articles to the *Quarterly Journal*, one can discern the old Zitkala-Ša reemerging from the pen of Mrs. Raymond

Bonnin. Here, once again, is the young Sioux girl taking on the mantle of being the "warrior's daughter" and its incumbent responsibilities for the care of the fathers and mothers. These articles reveal her profound commitment to the past and to the uniqueness of Indian cultures.

No less than other SAI members, Zitkala-Ša knew too well the need for the knowledge and technology of Anglo-American civilization to be extended to reservation peoples. At the same time, she, more than many Society members, continued to nurture a keen appreciation for and identity with Indian civilizations. Zitkala-Ša felt deeply the assault on Indian cultures made by advocates of acculturation. Publishing in the *Quarterly Journal,* Zitkala-Ša once again relived the pain of her early schoolgirl days and the cruel ethnocentrism of Anglo teachers she had witnessed at Carlisle as well as on the Yankton and Uintah reservations. She criticized the Anglo-Christian society, which offered platitudes of brotherhood while robbing Indian peoples of land and culture. Her youthful idealism gone, Zitkala-Ša was now ready to fight for the Indian right to survive as Indian.

By 1915 Zitkala-Ša had assumed an active role in all of the Society's annual meetings, and in 1916 was elected national secretary, which meant relocating her family to SAI headquarters in Washington DC. Her husband willingly joined her to pursue his own career working as an attorney for reform of national Indian policy. Shortly after their arrival, he was also commissioned by the army as second lieutenant in preparation for U.S. entry into World War I.

From the outset, the Society of American Indians had been governed by Indian men. A few women, in particular Nora McFarland from Carlisle and Laura Cornelius Kellogg, participated actively in the early days of the Society. McFarland is notable as the only one of the SAI's founders who appeared in Indian dress in a group photograph of the organizers taken in 1911. Other women worked long and hard in primarily clerical roles to maintain communication, do the paperwork for membership drives, and solicit contributions. Certainly women typed the *Quarterly Journal* but, until Zitkala-Ša, they contributed to it infrequently. Not until 1916 did a woman join the journal's editorial board. Nor could the voices of women members be heard much in the early annual conferences. When they were heard, it was through their writings on issues of education or childrearing—traditional Anglo women's concerns.

Men vastly outnumbered women in the Society. Of the 219 active members on the Society's rolls by 1912, only 66 were women, most of them single young teachers at reservation schools. While their relative youth and small numbers may have contributed to the subordinate role women played in SAI leadership, gender appears to have been a more important factor. Drawing its female membership from the small group of highly educated and acculturated young Indian women in the 1910s, the SAI acquired women who were assimilated into the subordinate gender role assigned by Anglo societal mores. However, these women's commitment to the SAI's success in effecting national policy change appears to be far more of a determining factor in their willingness to accept background roles. The SAI had been founded as the voice of Indian America to Anglo America. In the second decade of the twentieth century, only the Indian male voice would be heard and seriously considered. Even Marie Baldwin, a trained attorney and suffragist, kept her feminist interests apart from the Society, serving only as treasurer and occasionally writing articles for the *Quarterly Journal* emphasizing women's proper roles as helpmates.[9] She and other SAI women remained voluntarily in the background, bolstering the confidence and supporting the achievements of Indian men.

Zitkala-Ša stood alone as a female member of the SAI who sought both power and leadership within the organization. By the end of 1916, Zitkala-Ša served as the only woman on the executive council. Moreover, she was not prepared to limit herself to what the Anglo world saw as traditional female concerns. While she had written about education and health care as an entree to the Society, after being elected secretary, she never again contributed articles on community-center work. Rather she sought to turn the Society's attention to what she viewed as more important questions, contributing essays to the *Quarterly Journal* on the importance of water rights and land ownership, resources under continual assault by whites and crucial to the survival of Indian peoples as distinct communities. "For the sake of our children's children, we must hold onto a few acres. . . ."[10]

Zitkala-Ša's actions raised questions within the organization, both about her choice of subjects and her role as a woman in addressing these issues. In response, she began contributing articles to the *Quarterly Journal* dealing for the first time with the historic roles played by famous Indian women leaders. She wrote of Pocahontas, whom she called "the first emissary of democratic ideas to cast-ridden Europe," and of "Chipeta, Widow of Chief Ouray."[11] These women had nurtured and supported their men, but had also provided leadership to their people when the need arose. So, too, Zitkala-Ša saw the need for new leadership within the Society of American Indians and took action to achieve it.

By 1918 she had maneuvered both Chippewa Marie Baldwin, treasurer, and Seneca Arthur C. Parker, editor of the *Quarterly Journal,* out of their positions, and assumed both jobs herself. She supported the election of Charles Eastman, a fellow Sioux, to the office of SAI president. But her triumph in bringing the SAI under Sioux leadership was short-lived. The tensions that would eventually tear the organization apart were already well-established; Zitkala-Ša was powerless to control them, and her forceful personality rendered her ill-suited to mediate them.

Factionalism had been present in the SAI from its inception. Questions over the role of the Indian Bureau, the increasing use of peyote on reservations, and, most centrally, the role of the SAI itself, divided the membership. Carlos Montezuma led the fight for immediate abolition of the Indian Bureau. He strongly believed that its reservation system served only to keep Indian peoples imprisoned in poverty. Questions consequently arose about the loyalty of SAI members, such as Marie Baldwin, who worked for the bureau. Others took a more gradualist view; they sincerely believed that as Indian peoples became increasingly able to assume a self-sufficient role in American society, the need for the bureau would diminish. Zitkala-Ša tried to mediate between the two groups even as she presented a third and vital view: that reservations were necessary to the maintenance of Indian homelands and served as centers of Indian cultures where all Indians, even those like herself who lived in cities, could return to reinforce their identities as Indians.

The issue of peyote was equally destructive to the Society. Zitkala-Ša continually hearkened back to a romantic view of the Indian past in her stories; because of this, members who advocated peyote, like Thomas Sloan, anticipated Zitkala-Ša's support for the Native American Church and its ceremonial peyote use. However, the defense of peyote as a religious right, as part of the cultural heritage of Indian peoples, deeply angered Zitkala-Ša. Throughout her life, she had continually promoted the ongoing viability of Indian societies. But Zitkala-Ša had defended those cultures as she defined her identity—within the narrow parameters of Sioux tradition. In speaking of Indian cultures, Zitkala-Ša invariably meant Sioux society as it had existed in the late 1870s and early 1880s, during the years of her girlhood. Those happy, if faint and highly picturesque memories celebrated in her stories, colored her outlook of what constituted Indian traditional distinctiveness. She was not prepared to include any evolution in culture, such as the Native American Church, to that definition of "Indianness." To that end, she joined those members of the Society who opposed peyote and offered her services to Arizona Congressman Carl M. Hayden, who introduced yet another bill to outlaw its use in 1917.

Zitkala-Ša's determination to thwart the supporters of peyote would cost her dearly. As an erudite and polished Indian speaker, she provided the authentic star quality Hayden sought in his repertoire of witnesses. To that end, Zitkala-Ša appeared before the Senate Subcommittee on Indian Affairs in native dress wearing her hair in two long traditional braids. A photograph of her appeared in the *Washington Times* announcing her forthcoming testimony.

In arranging for this publicity, the bill's supporters emphasized the importance of her testimony. They had, however, overextended themselves. In attempting to impress upon the reading public Zitkala-Ša's qualifications, the article presented a number of falsehoods, including one that proclaimed Zitkala-Ša was a relative of Sitting Bull.

Two days after the article appeared, ethnologist James Mooney took the stand before the Senate subcommittee and charged that Zitkala-Ša had no right to speak on the peyote issue. Unlike himself, Zitkala-Ša had never participated in or even attended a peyote meeting. He refuted all of her charges of indecent sexual excesses, which she asserted resulted from peyote use. Most devastatingly, he displayed the *Washington Times* article and photograph charging that while Zitkala-Ša claimed to be a Sioux woman, the traditional costume she wore was not Sioux at all, but from a southern tribe and that her belt was a Navajo man's belt. Finally, Mooney pointed out, that in her complete ignorance, Mrs. Bonnin carried a peyote man's fan in the photo.

A severely shaken Zitkala-Ša appeared before the subcommittee on the following day providing all the testimony she could muster regarding peyote's ill effects, which she had witnessed while in Utah. Moreover, she darkly warned that Anglo young people would soon also fall prey to peyote's "drug users" if Congress did not act. But her humiliation had been complete. On a national stage, Mooney's charges had portrayed her as someone not only ignorant of peyote, but of the very Sioux culture so central to her own constructed identity.

The trials Zitkala-Ša faced in the U.S. Senate were mirrored by growing factionalism within the SAI. As editor of the *Quarterly Journal*, newly renamed the *American Indian Magazine*, Zitkala-Ša continued to pursue her own agenda of celebrating Indian, especially Sioux, heritage. At the end of 1917 she published a special issue of the magazine devoted to the Sioux. But this celebration of individual tribal identity served only to further rend the Society. Too late, Zitkala-Ša sought to bridge the tribal divisions that her own actions had fostered through a celebration of Indian patriotism in the wake of America's entry into World War I. In her articles, Zitkala-Ša proudly proclaimed that five thousand Indian men, including her husband, were saving their country in the armed forces. Moreover, she pointed out, Indian civilians were also making contributions, especially those farmers whose crops were sorely needed both at home and by the Allied forces abroad. As always, she emphasized the contributions of Indian women who were knitting sweaters and socks for the soldiers. Finally, she announced that Indian peoples had subscribed to roughly ten million dollars in Liberty Bonds. The SAI's annual conference of 1917 was canceled as a sacrifice made for the war effort.

A conference was held during the following year in the heart of Sioux country in Pierre, South Dakota, but fewer than thirty members attended. Zitkala-Ša publicly blamed poor attendance on the war, but in fact the pro-peyote faction boycotted the meeting. Others stayed away in part because of a growing disappointment over the inability of the SAI to influence U.S. government policy. Zitkala-Ša and Society president Charles Eastman were pushing Congress hard for passage of Indian citizenship legislation. To create public awareness of this issue, Zitkala-Ša went so far as to petition President Woodrow Wilson to include Indian representatives at the peace conference in Versailles. Preoccupied with his self-proclaimed role of world mediator, Wilson refused to consider the petition. Zitkala-Ša expected no more, but she had made a tactical blunder in setting yet another goal that the organization could not achieve.

Still other issues split the SAI membership. In her search for allies within the Society, Zitkala-Ša appealed to Montezuma by using the 1918 conference to pass a resolution calling for the immediate abolition of the Indian Bureau. This stance alienated the bureau and Indian people who were bureau employees. Moreover, the plank alarmed many other SAI members who feared what the sudden absence of bureau protection might mean to many, especially older, Indian peoples. In their eyes the SAI had taken a radical stance.

In the end, tribalism had come to the forefront of the SAI. With their vision of a pan-Indian movement, the founders of the Society had hoped to submerge individual and tribal interests into a wider Indian identity, one that encompassed a commitment the welfare of all Indian peoples. By 1919, however, it was clear that a Sioux coup had taken place, engineered in large part by Zitkala-Ša. In addition to a Sioux president, Eastman, and a Sioux secretary-treasurer and editor, Zitkala-Ša, the editorial board of the magazine had a large Sioux representation. Board member Elaine Eastman also provided a controversial element for not only was she the wife of the Society president, but an Anglo—the first non-Indian to be given an office in the organization.

At the annual conference in 1919, peyote supporters returned in force and secured the election of Thomas Sloan as SAI president. Stunned by Sloan's victory and refusing to bend on the issue of peyote, Zitkala-Ša resigned all of her offices within the organization.

Her association with the SAI at an end, Zitkala-Ša began to look for other platforms to voice her views on Indian affairs. In 1920 she began assembling the stories she had published decades earlier in journals. In the following year, these collected stories, many of which were autobiographical accounts of her childhood, were published in her second book, *American Indian Stories*. This second book is different from her first one, *Old Indian Legends*, published twenty years before when a young and idealistic Zitkala-Ša still believed that her stories could bridge the misunderstandings between the Anglo and Indian worlds and point "a steady finger toward the great brotherhood of mankind."[12] Her adult experiences had taught a hard lesson—that the separation between Anglo and Indian resulted from greed, not just from misunderstanding. By 1921 Zitkala-Ša knew that brotherhood, while still a noble objective and possible perhaps in the next generation, took second place to Anglo hunger for Indian land and water.

For Zitkala-Ša the questions of land and cultural survival were inseparable. Without a guaranteed land-base, Indian cultures could not continue as ongoing societies. Yet the land-base was being rapidly diminished. During the era of the Indian Allotment (or Dawes) Act (1887 to 1934), over two-thirds of Indian landholdings in the United States were lost. The appointment of Albert B. Fall in 1921 as secretary of the interior for the Harding administration raised the stakes even higher. Fall's hostile attitude and flagrant intention to divest Indian peoples of their remaining lands was well known.

Zitkala-Ša had lost the public voice she had used through the Society of American Indians to fight for the protection of Indian lands. She needed new allies to continue, and she found them in the General Federation of Women's Clubs (GFWC).

One of the largest and perhaps most prestigious women's organizations in the country, the GFWC established the Indian Welfare Committee in 1921 and invited Zitkala-Ša to serve as its opening speaker. Probably the most articulate Indian woman of her generation, and certainly at home behind the podium speaking to large groups, Zitkala-Ša would work often with the GFWC in the following years.

She also sought an ally in a young reformer, John Collier, who organized a new group called the American Indian Defense Association (AIDA). Collier, for his part, welcomed Zitkala-Ša's support. Her position as a speaker and investigator for the GFWC's Indian Welfare Committee, combined with the notoriety she had gained while serving as a leader of the SAI, made her a useful tool for Collier's ambitions to form an effective Indian defense.

Nowhere was Anglo greed for Indian land more blatant than in Oklahoma, where Indian probate decisions and guardianship responsibilities had been moved from the Indian Bureau to Oklahoma county courts. After the discovery of oil, a small group of attorneys and businessmen scrambled to find ways of declaring Indian property owners incompetent and to have themselves appointed to guardianships. In late 1923, under the auspices of the Indian Rights Association, Zitkala-Ša traveled to Oklahoma along with Matthew K. Sniffen of the IRA and Charles H. Fabens, an attorney, to investigate cases of land theft. What they found were truly horrifying instances of murder, kidnapping, rape, and wholesale abuse. They printed their findings the following year in a thirty-nine page pamphlet entitled *Oklahoma's Poor Rich Indians: An Orgy of Graft and Exploitation of the Five Civilized Tribes, Legalized Robbery*, published by the IRA.

The authors concentrated on six counties containing large Indian populations, and demonstrated through abundant evidence that guardians, courts, and lawyers had taken up to 70 percent of Indian estates as "administrative costs" for their so-called guardianships. Indian children died of malnutrition while their court-appointed guardians grew rich by squandering their estates. While Sniffen reviewed the growth of the professional guardian scheme in Oklahoma, Fabens outlined its basis in federal and state jurisprudence, exposing the corrupt state political system by which county court judges were elected for two-year terms on the basis of political patronage that they repaid with lucrative guardian appointments. Zitkala-Ša drove the point home by providing heartrending accounts of children who had been brutalized and stripped of their land and mineral rights.

One example was the case of Ledcie Sechi, a seven-year-old Choctaw girl, who had inherited twenty acres of oil-rich land from her mother. In the fall of 1922, the courts appointed an Anglo guardian, a Mr. Whiteman, to manage her property, which was valued at close to twenty thousand dollars. From this rich estate, the guardian paid little Ledcie and her grandmother a living allowance of fifteen dollars a month, reducing them to a state of near starvation. "The little Choctaw girl, with her feeble grandmother came to town carrying their clothes, a bundle of faded rags, in a flour sack. Ledcie was dirty, filthy, and covered with vermin. She was emaciated and weighed about 47 pounds." Employees of the Indian Health Service quickly took charge of the little girl, providing her with medical attention and proper nourishment. By July 1923 she had improved to the point where she could be placed in an Indian school, the Wheelock Academy. But the Indian Bureau could not act in defiance of the county courts to protect this little girl from her "guardian."

> Mr. Whiteman, evidently fearing to lose his grasp on his ward, demanded the child, and Ledcie Stechi, child of much abuse, was returned to the custody of her legal guardian 24 hours after she was taken to the school where she would have had good care. The last time the aged grandmother had seen Ledcie, and only for a few minutes was on the 12th of July.
>
> A month later, on the 14th of August, word was brought to the hills that Ledcie was dead. . . . The following day, at dawn, before the corpse had arrived, parties of grafters arrived . . . and harassed the bereaved old grandmother about the future disposal of Ledcie's valuable properties. . . . The Court has already appointed a guardian for the grandmother. . . . She, too, will go the way of her grandchild, as sheep for slaughter by ravenous wolves.[13]

The publication of *Poor Rich Indians* prompted a congressional investigation into the Oklahoma probate courts in 1924. But powerful interests in Oklahoma blocked any congressional action. A warrant was even issued for Zitkala-Ša's arrest, which effectively prevented her from being present in the state while the committee hearings were under way. In the end, it was a whitewash; the Senate subcommittee exonerated the county courts, ironically declaring them "lily-white."

Disgusted by her perceived failure in Oklahoma, Zitkala-Ša turned again to John Collier and accepted a position on the American Indian Defense Association's National Advisory Board. In these early years of the 1920s, there existed a strong kinship of ideals between Zitkala-Ša and Collier. Both rejected assimilation and viewed Indian cultures as superior to those of Anglo America. Collier's defense of the ongoing viability of Indian societies could not help but win the glowing admiration of Zitkala-Ša, as did his active efforts to protect Indian lands. For his part, Collier recognized Zitkala-Ša's importance as a spokesperson for reform. Without Collier, Zitkala-Ša might have been omitted entirely from the reform movement of the 1920s. She had made too many enemies, both in the bureau and among the Indian leaders of her day. She was not invited, for example, to join the Department of Interior's Committee of One Hundred, formed in 1923 and composed of many of her old friends from the SAI, to advise on Indian policy reform. Collier, on the other hand, offered her a role to play through AIDA. Their friendship was strong. Collier often made

Zitkala-Ša his hostess for visiting delegations of musicians and artists, particularly Indian people, who came to Washington. Zitkala-Ša delighted in this role, organizing Indian music and dance concerts.

Still, Zitkala-Ša continued to believe in the idea of a political pan-Indian movement whose leadership and active membership would be composed of Indian peoples. With the rapid demise of the SAI, Zitkala-Ša founded a new organization, the National Council of American Indians (NCAI), in 1924. In large part Zitkala-Ša's formation of the NCAI came about as a direct response to the political corruption she had viewed in Oklahoma and to the passage of the Indian Citizenship Act in June 1924. One of the organization's principal purposes was to develop an Indian political bloc and organize the Indian vote, particularly at the state and county levels, to bring pressure on politicians. In this endeavor, Zitkala-Ša made perhaps her most significant contribution to the pan-Indian movement as it evolved in the twentieth century. Indian peoples, she argued, must seek more than merely influence in national policy decisions, which was the goal of the SAI. Rather, they must actively involve themselves in Anglo government to protect their rights to their land and cultural inheritance.

Ensuring her right to lead, Zitkala-Ša appointed herself president of the new organization, while her husband assumed the supportive role of secretary-treasurer. Zitkala-Ša immediately set about to legitimize the National Council of American Indians as the national pan-Indian movement in the eyes of both Indian and Anglo America. She rented offices in the Bliss Building in Washington, the site of the Indian Bureau and the American Indian Defense Association, and formerly the headquarters of the SAI. She and her husband traveled endlessly throughout the country visiting reservations, organizing the vote, and bringing back evidence of federal and state corruption and policy failures. These firsthand accounts of bureau mismanagement, impoverished lands, and inadequate health care provided Zitkala-Ša with the ammunition she needed to testify frequently before the Senate Subcommittee on Indian Affairs. The Bonnins were often at Yankton, trying to help protect sacred sites from mining interests and, most crucially, lending their support to the traditional tribal council. While in Washington, Zitkala-Ša was often in Congress, lobbying on behalf of Indian peoples and publishing her written pieces in the NCAI's *Indian News Letter*. She never relented in her goal of organizing Indian voting blocs. Political power, she argued, was the only protection for Indian self-determination. "Remember This and Organize" became her slogan.

The Indian right to self-determination was always uppermost in Zitkala-Ša's heart and mind. So dedicated was she to the concept that Indian

peoples and Indian peoples alone must decide what is in their best interest, that she finally found herself in a position in which she had to oppose
her old friend John Collier.

In 1934, after Franklin D. Roosevelt was elected president, Collier finally achieved the position he needed to make significant policy reforms:
he was appointed commissioner of Indian Affairs. The onset of Collier's
tenure as commissioner brought to an end the fifty-year period of allotment begun under the Dawes Act. Collier wanted to protect the Indian
cultures and land-base, promote economic development, and restore
tribal self-government primarily through passage of the Wheeler-Howard
Act (otherwise known as the Indian Reorganization Act) in 1934. To that
end, Collier offered Indian peoples the opportunity to accept written constitutions outlining tribal governments. Collier called the day of the act's
passage "Indian Independence Day." Not all Indian peoples agreed; in all,
seventy-seven tribes voted not to accept the act despite the enormous financial benefits attached to their doing so.

The failure of the act can be attributed directly to Collier's determination to push through his programs without regard to opinions of the Indian peoples involved. Looking always to Taos, where he had first so admired the culture and society of Pueblo peoples, Collier seemed unable to
understand that other tribes had vastly different cultures and alternative
traditions of political leadership. While Collier undeniably brought
change for the better to the Indian Bureau, he was handicapped by an in-
tolerance of criticism and a refusal to compromise or even recognize any
view other than his own. His often abrasive personality alienated many
Indians like the Bonnins, who sought real self-determination in the 1930s
and refused to accept yet another new U.S. policy dictated by the bureau.

In the end the Bonnins were principally responsible for the decision of
the Yankton people to reject the act. By November 1935 Indian Office representatives seeking to impose the act at Yankton reported to Collier that
everywhere they went the Bonnins had "beat us to it," and the situation
appeared hopeless.[14]

The failure of the bureau to consult with the Yanktons on drawing up
their new constitution and its implicit assault on self-determination lay
at the heart of Zitkala-Ša's opposition. But there were other issues as well.
Zitkala-Ša wanted a recognition of tribal membership extended to all
Yankton Sioux, both those living on the reservation and those, like herself,
who lived apart. She also wanted tribal membership extended to all Yankton children born off the reservation. Such questions would be central to
twentieth-century American Indian identity, but Collier refused all com-

promise. His only concession was to urge the Bonnins to persuade Yankton to accept the tribal constitution as it was, with the promise that they could make whatever changes they wanted later. This offer smacked of old white paternalism—sign the treaty and trust us. Such a proposal was anathema to all that both Zitkala-Ša and Raymond Bonnin represented.

In the midst of this final battle over the rights of Indian people to self-determination, Zitkala-Ša died suddenly on 21 January 1938 shortly after returning to Washington from Yankton. She died a sad and profoundly disillusioned woman, frustrated at what she perceived to be her failure to achieve any measurable change in American Indian policy. At her death, the Indian was still, in her view, "a veritable prisoner of war" at the mercy of the Indian Bureau.[15]

Yet Zitkala-Ša's life was of profoundly more value than she recognized. She was the first to insist on an equal role for Indian women in national Indian organizations. She played an active leadership role in the Society of American Indians, the twentieth century's first political pan-Indian movement. Following its demise, she kept the ideal of a pan-Indian political organization alive during those crucial decades of the 1920s and 1930s, leading directly to the formation of subsequent groups later in the century that still exist today: the National Congress of American Indians and the American Indian Movement. She led the way in identifying the issues that would be of primary importance to the survival of Indian communities: the protection of land-bases and natural resources. Perhaps most important, she insisted upon the recognition of an Indian identity for all Native American peoples, not just those who live on reservations. Today, over 50 percent of American Indian peoples live off reservations. It was Zitkala-Ša who, in those vital early decades of the twentieth century, led the fight to protect their rights and their identity.

NOTES

1. Zitkala-Ša, *American Indian Stories* (Glorieta NM: Rio Grande Press, 1976).

2. Zitkala-Ša, *American Indian Stories*, p. 67.

3. Zitkala-Ša, *American Indian Stories*, p. 69.

4. "Cheers for the Indian Maiden," *Indianapolis News*, printed in *The Earlhamite*, 2 (16 March 1896): 187. Issues of "The Earlhamite" (the student newspaper) are housed in the archives of Earlham College, Richmond IN.

5. See Peter Iverson, *Carlos Montezuma and the Changing World of American Indians* (Albuquerque: University of New Mexico Press, 1982).

6. Mrs. Gertrude Bonnin to Francis Leupp, 17 January 1905, National Archives and Record Service, RG 75, no. 4487 (Washington DC). See also the correspondence of Captain W. A. Mercer, 7th Calvary, acting agent of the Uintah Reservation, 1904–1906, National Archives, RG 75.

7. "A Christmas Letter from Zitkala-Ša," *Quarterly Journal of the Society of American Indians* 3 (October–December 1915).

8. Zitkala-Ša to Carlos Montezuma, 13 May 1913, *The Papers of Carlos Montezuma* (Madison: Wisconsin State Historical Society).

9. *Quarterly Journal* 3 (April–June 1915): 106.

10. *American Indian Magazine* 6 (spring 1918): 196–97.

11. *American Indian Magazine* 6 (spring 1918): 179; (summer 1918): 168.

12. Zitkala-Ša, *Old Indian Legends* (Boston: Ginn & Co., 1901), preface.

13. Gertrude Bonnin, Charles H. Fabens, and Matthew K. Sniffen, "Oklahoma's Poor Rich Indians" (Philadelphia: Indian Rights Association, 1924), pp. 24–28.

14. Paul L. Hallam to Joe Jennings, Field Administrator Indian Organization, 13 November 1935, Yankton Box 3, University of South Dakota Archives. See also telegram from Superintendent Roberts to the Indian Office, 14 November 1935, Yankton Box 3, complaining about how the Bonnins "dominated" every meeting.

15. Zitkala-Ša to Elaine Eastman, 25 March 1935, Sophia C. Smith Collection, Smith College, Northampton MA.

Robert Yellowtail

Crow

BY FREDERICK E. HOXIE AND TIM BERNARDIS

Robert Summers Yellowtail, a tribal leader who defended the Crow community from greedy ranchers, designing senators, and indifferent presidents, came into the world at one of the most difficult moments in the tribe's history. The future councilman, tribal chairman, and agency superintendent was born at the end of the 1880s, a decade that witnessed the tribe's relocation and confinement within the boundaries of a reservation in a small corner of the vast, abundant landscape that had once made up "Crow country."[1]

Yellowtail was probably born in 1889. Over the course of his life he had at least three Crow names. He was first called Bíawakshish, or "Summer," later Shoopáaheesh, or "Four War Deeds," and finally Axíchish, or "The Wet" (the name of a nineteenth-century war chief who was a member of the same clan as Robert Yellowtail). The first of these names stayed with him to some degree throughout his life. Yellowtail was born to a family that, like its neighbors and kinsmen, would be forced to dwell within the reach of government agents and to transform their way of life so they would resemble—at least outwardly—the Anglo-American ranchers and farmers who were beginning to take up homesteads in eastern Montana's Yellowstone Valley. Like others of his generation, Yellowtail would be tracked by the record keepers at Crow Agency, the reservation headquarters. When those records indicated that he was of school age, he would be taken forcibly from his parents and deposited in dreary government classrooms. As he grew to maturity, he and his family would be inspected and harassed by agents and government "matrons" who would count them, scrutinize their dwelling, test their facility with English, record their style of dress, and inventory their belongings. The Office of Indian Affairs would even insist that Robert and his siblings abandon the tribe's tradition of giving every member a unique name and take instead their father's name—Yellowtail—as their own.[2]

Robert Yellowtail and his family would suffer these indignities as part of the government's effort to "raise up" American Indians to "civilization." In the late nineteenth century, agents and missionaries believed their efforts would save the last remnants of a dying race; their solutions make modern readers wince, but their fears were grounded in fact. As a child, Yellowtail and his family witnessed illness and death on a daily basis. In 1887 the Office of Indian Affairs reported that there were nearly 2,500 Crows living within the boundaries of the tribal reservation; by the time Yellowtail was a teenager that figure had dropped to less than 2,000—a 20 percent decline. Because the Crows maintained a high birth rate, this decline can only be attributed to pervasive illness and widespread infant mortality. During the 1890s between a third and a half of the community reported serious illnesses to agency physicians each year. The tribe's agent summarized these conditions in 1888 when he wrote that "hereditary diseases and the abrupt change from a nomadic life and an all-meat diet to living in houses and an almost vegetable diet is causing the enormous death rate."[3]

But despite these hardships, Robert Yellowtail grew up knowing much more than regimentation and suffering. He was born beside the Little Bighorn River in the Crow way. His mother was surrounded by relatives who welcomed the new baby to her clan—the Whistling Water people. His father's clan relatives in the Big Lodge clan joined in the celebration. Government officials might view a child born in the country in a traditional camp as backward, but the child belonged first to a vast family that extended outward across the length and breadth of the Big Horns and their surrounding prairies, and reached back through time to the chiefs and elders who had guided the Crow people for generations.

Throughout his life, Yellowtail celebrated his ties to clan and kin despite the fact that non-Indians, obsessed with racial boundaries and what they called "blood," would regularly deride him as a "mixed-blood," a concept that had no meaning in his tribe at the time of his birth. The boy's mother was Elizabeth ("Lizzie") Frazee Chienne, the granddaughter of a French-Canadian trader who had settled with the Crows in mid-century, and his father was Yellowtail, who had been too young to win war honors against the Sioux, but who is still remembered as a resourceful young man who was a good farmer, a good singer, an expert rifleman, and a prominent member of the tribe's tobacco society. With three sisters and two brothers, and dozens of members of an extended family, Yellowtail easily fit the Crow definition of a wealthy child. Blessed with many relatives, and lucky enough to see his siblings survive into adulthood, he grew up with ready-made allies and supporters.

Robert Yellowtail's relatives were always important to him, not only for the emotional comfort they could provide in times of stress but also because they formed a cadre of devoted volunteers who would stump for him in elections, argue his case before his enemies, and open their homes and pockets to him during political campaigns. Because he was married four times and had seven children and dozens of grandchildren, Yellowtail's family connections extended even farther. In 1911 he married the daughter of Spotted Horse, one of the most outspoken leaders of the early reservation years. Following her death in the 1920s he married Lillian Bull Shows (Hogan), a union that ended in divorce. In 1932 he married Margaret Pickett (whom he outlived) and in 1960 he married Dorothy Payne, a Choctaw woman from Oklahoma.[4]

Much of Robert Yellowtail's success can be attributed to his extensive bicultural skills. Reared in the Crow way, he nonetheless learned many of the ways of the whites as one of the first generation of Crows educated in schools. He deftly combined both to achieve high status. Though he lacked the aura of mystical power held by many nineteenth-century Crow leaders, he adhered to kinship reciprocities and respect for Crow values and traditions as demonstrated in giveaways to clan fathers and others. This made him respected among his own people and played a key role in his political career. His ambitions for political influence and status paralleled the goals of traditional careers. His oratorical powers in both the Crow and English languages were renowned, recalling the skill of orator chiefs of the buffalo days. He was high-strung and impatient, flamboyant and bombastic. He had an excellent command of the English language, both oral and written, and had studied the law extensively. He had the support of the people as a result of helping ward off the pressures to open the reservation to white homesteading from 1913 to 1920, much like the old chiefs who had remained in power as long as they were successful in war and fending off tribal enemies.

Yellowtail also possessed certain personal characteristics that served him well; he was remarkably intelligent, shrewd, dynamic, and humorous. He could also be very precise and businesslike. He had diverse interests, performing as a boy soprano in his youth, picking up the clarinet at boarding school, singing Indian tunes (especially Crow Round Dance tunes) in adulthood and belonging to the Ree dance society. Yellowtail was a lifelong sports fan, often traveling to (and betting on) college football games across the West. Yellowtail's critics charged him with being ill-tempered, a bully, and of working primarily for his own interests, but his lifelong, consistently self-stated goals were for human rights, self-determination, tribal autonomy, and economic rehabilitation for his people.

Robert's boyhood was centered in the ranching country at the head of the Little Big Horn valley. His parents and other relatives farmed and raised horses and cattle along the eastern slopes of the mountain range, thereby providing a living in an area far enough away from Crow Agency that their life was only occasionally interrupted by outsiders.

One of the first of these disruptions came within days of Yellowtail's birth: Father Pierpaolo Prando, an Italian Jesuit who had come to live among the Crows soon after their relocation to the reservation in 1884, appeared to baptize the infant. Fittingly for a community that found Christian ideals attractive but cared little for doctrinal disputes among Christian sects, Yellowtail was later re-baptized by James Burgess, a Protestant missionary, and as an adult would attend all six Christian churches in the nearby village of Lodge Grass. Yellowtail and most of his family eventually identified with the Baptist congregation in Lodge Grass, but he maintained his ties to traditional Crow religious societies, consulted traditional healers, and supported the revival of the Sun Dance among the members of his tribe. During his career in government and politics, Yellowtail worked closely with dozens of powerful non-Indian officials but he never shared their distaste for Indian "heathenism."[5]

Even though he would always remember the day White Arm, a member of the Indian Office's local police force, took him away from his parents and enrolled him in Crow Agency's boarding school, Yellowtail never resisted schooling. He was articulate and curious and he learned very quickly. He was only four years old when White Arm took him to school. Naturally he hated being away from home, but he was fascinated by the world of learning—so fascinated in fact that he later recalled that he sought a place at one of the government's off-reservation boarding schools. He was a curious young man and, he told relatives later, he left the school "in disgust" after seeing the way Crow children were treated at the local school. Despite the prospect of a lengthy separation from his family, he may have wanted to transfer for he always spoke warmly of his years at Sherman Institute in Riverside, California. Modeled on the famous off-reservation boarding school in Carlisle, Pennsylvania, Sherman was created to extend the Victorian philosophy of "Kill the Indian, Save the Man," to the Southwest. But despite its stiff uniforms and authoritarian culture, Sherman opened broad realms of learning to the young Montanan. Yellowtail graduated from the institute's high school division in 1907. Fascinated by American history and law, he managed to land a position in the office of the local justice of the peace and decided to remain in California. His dream was to become a lawyer. Still a teenager, Yellowtail sensed that an understanding of legal procedures would help him deal with the government and its agents. He came back to Montana in about 1910, still hoping to attend law school, but events at home would soon draw him into the political arena; he would stay in that arena for the rest of his life.[6]

Following the example of his hardworking siblings and kinsmen, Yellowtail used whatever cash he could gather to buy horses and cattle, which he could raise in the upper reaches of the Little Big Horn valley and sell at the rail yards in nearby Hardin and Billings. Like others in his family, Robert sought enough economic independence to free him from government support and the controls that went with it. His younger brother Tom recalled years later that the farming routine of their youth also deepened their affection for their homeland. "I enjoyed working and being outside," Tom wrote in 1991. "We would plow and plant in the spring, do our haying in the summer, and then harvest crops in the fall. . . . Our outside lives kept us close to the beauty of nature and made us physically and spiritually strong."[7]

Yellowtail married in 1911 and began to settle into this new life, but he didn't concentrate on business for very long. He soon became aware of a burgeoning confrontation that set the impoverished and isolated Crows against the assembled might of the Indian Office and Montana's political establishment. Young, energetic, and self-confident, Robert must have approached this struggle with some of the same excitement his father, his clan uncle "The Wet," and their old comrades had described when they told their stories of plains warfare. In the nineteenth century the Crows were frequently outnumbered and outgunned on the battlefield, but they dodged, shifted ground, and found some way to survive. Robert would teach the members of his tribe to apply those warriors' tactics to this new, bloodless fight.

Not surprisingly, the new fight was over land. Between 1851 and 1868, the officially recognized boundaries of "Crow country" shrank to such an extent that the tribal lands were reduced from thirty-eight million to eight million acres. In the years just prior to Robert's birth, tribal leaders who felt hemmed in by federal officials and who were under attack by the Sioux and Blackfeet decided to abandon their ancient hunting grounds in Wyoming's Big Horn Basin along the upper Missouri and in far eastern

Montana (the two areas consisting of more than one and a half million acres) in exchange for what they believed would be secure reservation boundaries in the Yellowstone Valley. When the government relocated its agency headquarters to the new town of Crow Agency in 1884, it told the tribe the sixty-mile swath of prairie running along the northern slopes of the Bighorn Mountains would be the tribe's final homeland. "The greatest and most important question facing the Crows today," their agent wrote in 1882, "is to locate them permanently on the best part of their country. . . ." The relocation of 1884 seemed to accomplish that goal.[8]

Although the Indian Office established its agency headquarters at Crow Agency, along the banks of the Little Bighorn River, Crow families like Yellowtail's, who had complied with the order to relocate, avoided making their homes too close to the government's offices. During the 1880s four major communities emerged on the new reservation, each some distance from Crow Agency. These four "districts" were Pryor (along Pryor Creek, sixty miles west of the Little Big Horn), Big Horn (in the Big Horn valley some twenty miles west of the agency), Black Lodge (ten miles north of the agency, near the site of modern Hardin, Montana), and the Yellowtails' community of Lodge Grass, twenty miles south of the reservation headquarters. These districts were actually clusters of family residences and farms rather than organized towns; their centers were usually a collection of government supply sheds and missions. For the most part the Crow families who gathered in these four communities lived like Robert Yellowtail's parents. They set up camps and cabins near kinsmen, grew hay for their horses and cattle, kept a truck garden for subsistence, and steered clear of the agent.

As peaceful and cooperative as this gradual process of adaptation and resettlement into agricultural districts may appear today, it did not fit the expectations of the white bureaucrats and politicians who had advocated it. They wanted to "dissolve the bonds of tribalism"; they expected the tribe to evolve into a collection of independent farmers who would care more for their individual crops than for their common tribal heritage. During the 1880s Crow families who gave up the idea of crossing reservation boundaries to hunt and gather and who began turning to new forms of subsistence believed they were embarking on a new future. It did not occur to them that this future would not include continuing to think of themselves as Crows. Outsiders who witnessed the shift from hunting to farming insisted that the transition also include a decline in tribal allegiance. They therefore readied plans for what they believed would be the next stage in the tribe's march towards "civilization."

During the years Robert was attending high school, Indian Office personnel, spurred on by local non-Indian ranchers and settlers, began calling for the sale of "unused" Crow pastureland to homesteaders. They also urged tribal members to relocate themselves once again—this time to one-hundred-sixty-acre farms that they would own individually and operate alone. This campaign was part of a national effort that had begun decades earlier but that had gathered steam in the 1880s and culminated in 1887 with congressional approval of the General Allotment Act (or Dawes Act). That law empowered the Indian Office to act unilaterally to divide or "allot" reservations into homesteads and sell off the "surplus" to white settlers. It also established individual landholding as a national policy goal. Implementation of the new law began slowly, but in 1892 the Indian Office applied it to the Southern Cheyennes, an Oklahoma tribe with no interest in agriculture and little power to resist the active lobbying of the region's boosters and "sooners." Calls for the allotment of other homelands were somewhat muted amid the agricultural depression of the 1890s, but when prosperity returned and agricultural interests organized, the pressure resumed. Crow leaders resisted these demands, but government threats and the prospect of individual cash payments succeeded in winning approval for a kind of appeasement policy in which tribal leaders agreed to modest land cessions involving two thinly populated areas of the reservation. As the new century began these leaders hoped that the whites were now satisfied.

When Robert Yellowtail returned home from Sherman Institute, the Crows' recent policy of resistance and appeasement was about to be tested once more. The reservation had been surveyed and allotted during the years he was in California and now the government sought to dispose of millions of acres of "surplus" lands that had not been assigned to individuals as part of their individual allotments. Tribal leaders insisted these lands were needed for future allotments and for communal grazing pastures. The Indian Office's demand became public in 1908 when James McLaughlin, a tough-talking former agent (he had ordered the fatal "arrest" of Sitting Bull in 1890), was dispatched to Crow Agency to place an ultimatum before a gathering of Crow district headmen. The united opposition of Plenty Coups and other reservation leaders of Robert's father's generation blunted McLaughlin's assault, but the grizzled bureaucrat and his superiors made it clear that they would be back. The tribe continued to hold fast, but in 1909 and 1910 the Montana congressional delegation began to campaign actively for the issue and to vie with one another to see who would be the first to succeed in getting congress to mandate the sale.

Prior to this final confrontation over the sale of "surplus" lands, the Crows had dealt with the United States through a general council of "chiefs and headmen," which was dominated by senior men. In the preservation days these leaders had been band leaders and veteran warriors who carried great personal prestige and could count on the support of their clans and warrior societies. During the 1890s these older men began to pass from the scene and were gradually replaced by reservation politicians. The most successful of these was Plenty Coups, who had been a successful war leader in the 1870s, but who did not come forward as a tribal spokesperson until after the relocation of the agency to Little Big Horn.

Plenty Coups became a remarkably able leader of the general council, but the tribe's confrontation with the Indian Office and Montana's political leaders over the unallotted lands pushed the old war leader's skills to the limit. The conflict was persistent—congressmen filed their bills year after year—and the battle had to be waged on several fronts—in the local county, in the statehouse, in Congress, and before the general American public. Plenty Coups was determined to resist, but younger, better-educated Crows who were comfortable with English and aware of potential allies in Washington and elsewhere began to propose new tactics. Sensing the rise of progressive reform in national politics, these younger leaders presented the Crows as victims of corporate avarice and government insensitivity and looked for support from reformers who had access to national press outlets.

This new language of resistance drew Yellowtail into Crow political leadership. His first official position was as a district representative on a tribal business committee set up to negotiate grazing leases with large cattle interests and to give the tribe an ongoing and credible voice in the continuing land dispute. Robert Yellowtail joined the business committee in 1912. He was initially absorbed in the struggle to defend Crow land, but his energy and quick wits soon won the attention of older men like Plenty Coups and drew him into a wide range of issues. In February 1913, less than a year after being named to the committee, Yellowtail made his first trip to Washington DC. Ostensibly serving as an interpreter for Medicine Crow, Plenty Coups, and other older men at the dedication of the National Indian Memorial in New York City, Yellowtail also accompanied the leaders when they called on the commissioner of Indian Affairs to protest the lease that Frank Heinrich, a cattle owner, had recently signed despite the tribe's objections. (Interestingly, Yellowtail later claimed that it was this visit that made him a lifelong "Teddy Roosevelt Republican.")[9]

Yellowtail soon became an indispensable member of the Crow business

committee. A charismatic speaker and fluid writer, he could draft petitions, fire off blistering letters, and charm potential allies. The first report
of his oratory appeared in the *Hardin Herald* on 3 September 1915. Not surprisingly the weekly newspaper in that white town bordering the reservation was sympathetic to the campaign to "open" the reservation, but its
reporter could not resist Yellowtail's appeal. The news story noted that at
a recent summit meeting of tribal leaders and local ranchers called by
Senator Henry Myers of Montana and Governor John Benjamin Kendrick
of Wyoming, a young man named Robert Yellowtail had captured most of
the attention by delivering "an extended speech" that mustered legal and
moral arguments to urge his adversaries to withdraw. The paper pronounced the young man "quite an orator."[10]

At the end of his life Yellowtail would recall his days as a young councilman with considerable pride. Sitting at Plenty Coups's elbow, he felt he
had accomplished a kind of twentieth-century "war deed," and he often
told stories about his adventures in the same way he must have heard
"The Wet" and Spotted Horse talk of their own youthful victories. In later
years Yellowtail would fondly recall a meeting in a hotel room the evening
before one of the hearings. The elder leaders wanted to hold a traditional
war medicine-making session but they lacked the dried buffalo dung necessary for the ceremonial fire. Someone was dispatched to the national
zoo, the essential ingredient appeared, and the next day the Crows were
triumphant once again.[11]

Each time a Montana congressman or senator brought up a bill to seize
Crow land, the tribe would send a delegation to Washington to speak out
against it. Yellowtail never failed to be part of the group. He traveled east
in 1915, 1916, and 1917. Returning to the Crows' nineteenth-century
strategy of using outside allies to defeat powerful enemies, Crow politicians such as Robert Yellowtail were able to slow the alienation of Crow
lands. As the battle wore on, Yellowtail and the others developed close ties
to sympathetic progressive politicians such as Robert La Follette, lobbyists from the Indian Rights Association, and a small group of Washington
attorneys who were beginning to represent tribal interests. Each trip required orchestrating the support of these allies and presenting the Crow
case in the most politically appealing language.

In 1917 an exasperated Senate leadership invited the Crow leaders to
draft their own bill. The politicians expressed sympathy for the tribe's position but said the pressure from local white ranchers and farmers was so
intense—and the wartime need for grain and beef so great—that some
compromise was necessary. The invitation divided the Crows, with the

seventy-year-old Plenty Coups insisting on further resistance and younger delegates declaring that this would be their last chance to cut a deal. Yellowtail and his allies proposed to divide the entire reservation among its members. No land would be opened immediately to whites and strict limits would be placed on the amount of land outsiders could lease or rent, but tribal members who gained fee-simple title to their portion would be allowed to sell. Debate over the proposal raged across the reservation for two years. Yellowtail supported the plan, but Plenty Coups and other elders—calling themselves "long hairs" in contrast to the well-shorn boarding school graduates—resisted. Finally, in the summer of 1919, Plenty Coups declared his support for a division of tribal land and the tribe unanimously endorsed a bill that became law the following year.[12]

Making it more difficult for non-Indians to gain access to reservation resources, Yellowtail and his colleagues accomplished something of a victory. In addition the entire process allowed a younger generation and new type of Crow leadership to emerge. But while the faces of the leaders changed, the goal remained the same: to defend Crow lands from attack by outsiders. In later years, Joseph Medicine Crow summed up the significance of Yellowtail's actions when he stated that Yellowtail "saved our reservation . . . he has been a warrior. . . . That's why we are still Crow Indians to this very day."[13]

While Plenty Coups would live until 1932, Yellowtail's role in the passage of the Crow Act propelled him into both tribal and national prominence. Significantly, the elder warrior was not part of the 1919 tribal delegation that testified before the Senate Subcommittee on Indian Affairs on behalf of the new bill. When the moment to address the senators arrived, the delegation's principal spokesperson was Robert Yellowtail. He used the occasion to serve notice that despite their willingness to compromise after more than a decade of resistance, the Crows had no intention of fading from view. Observing that President Woodrow Wilson was at that very moment deeply engaged in bringing the ideal of self-determination to the colonized peoples of the globe, the young orator observed that "within the boundaries of his own nation are the American Indians, who have no rights whatsoever." Brilliantly linking the idealism of the recent war to the interests of his tribe, Yellowtail informed the committee that "the Crow Indian reservation is a separate, semi-sovereign nation . . . not belonging to any State, nor confined within the boundary lines of any state. . . . No Senator or anyone else," he warned, "has any right . . . to tear us asunder." Crow country, he declared, is "ours . . . not given to us by anybody."[14]

Yellowtail remained at the center of reservation political life throughout the 1920s. He served on the business committee, the "competency commission" created by the Indian Office to determine which tribal members should receive fee patent titles to their lands, and was active in the negotiations related to grazing and mineral exploration leases. Comfortable with businesspeople and confident in his abilities as a rancher, he was sympathetic to various proposals to "develop" the economic resources of the reservation. He was also an outspoken defender of tribal prerogatives, calling for the ouster of incompetent agency superintendents at several points during the 1920s and, in 1926, supporting the filing of a land claim suit against the government in claims court. He was also visible in national and state politics. In 1923 he served as a member of the Committee of One Hundred, a group assembled by Secretary of the Interior Hubert Work to evaluate the government's policies for Indians, and in 1926 he ran unsuccessfully for a seat in Congress as an independent. He also attended the Republican National Convention in 1928. While a lifelong Republican, he was less motivated by party loyalty than by whoever might best support the Crows.

Throughout the 1920s Yellowtail tried to earn a living from his ranch, called "Little Horn Ranch," located in the hills south of Lodge Grass. Running cattle near the Wyola Railway Station and along Percheron Creek, he battled brutal winters and falling prices. Devastating weather in 1919 and 1920 nearly wiped him out; he carried a debt that may have been as high as fifty thousand dollars for most of the following decade, setting off rumors that he was using political payoffs to keep himself solvent.[15]

Despite his Republican loyalties, Yellowtail was hopeful that the election of Franklin Roosevelt in 1932 would encourage change in the stultifying bureaucracy of the Indian Office and bring about support for the self-determination ideals he had pronounced before the senate in 1919. Offended by the patronizing attitudes of agency employees and worried that the deepening depression would finally bring the extinction of the Crows so many had predicted for so long, Yellowtail was eager to lobby the new president on behalf of change. He drafted a letter to be signed by representatives of each Montana reservation and requested funds from the agency superintendent so that a Crow delegation could attend Roosevelt's inauguration. When the agency superintendent turned him down, Yellowtail persuaded his brother-in-law Donald Deer Nose and fellow council member James Carpenter to ride along with him to the capitol in his own car. In Washington, Yellowtail, Deer Nose, and Carpenter talked with anyone who would listen about the need for change in the Indian Office. Their candidate for commissioner of Indian Affairs was John Collier, the former New York City social worker who had been an outspoken advocate of greater Indian self-determination since the Harding administration. To their delight, Collier was named commissioner soon after the new president took office.

For a year after his return from the Roosevelt inauguration Yellowtail led a campaign to remove James Hyde as superintendent of the Crow Reservation. By the end of 1933 the stream of letters and petitions orchestrated by Yellowtail and his allies was successful: Hyde was transferred to Crow Creek Agency in South Dakota. The next order from Washington was even more welcome. Not content with simply agreeing to Yellowtail's request that Hyde be removed, Collier appointed Yellowtail to succeed Hyde.

It is not clear what led Collier to make this unprecedented decision. Never before had a member of an Indian tribe been appointed to supervise the agency at his home reservation. Collier and Yellowtail probably met in 1923 when both served on the Committee of One Hundred, but there is no evidence that they worked together beyond that point. One possible connection was the University of California anthropologist Robert Lowie, who knew Collier and who had been conducting fieldwork on the Crow Reservation since 1907, and whose principal informant was Yellowtail's traveling companion, James Carpenter. Whatever the reasoning, Collier's decision was generally welcomed by the Crows and condemned by local whites. His predecessor as agency superintendent told a reporter from nearby Hardin, "This is something I never dreamed of."[16]

Yellowtail's political rivals—a distinct minority within the tribe—complained that the Lodge Grass rancher was being forced on the tribe without consultation. Max Big Man, Russell White Bear, Frank Yarlott, and Harry Whiteman were all council members who frequently clashed with Yellowtail and who now feared his new power. In response, Collier took yet another unprecedented action. He ordered a referendum on the appointment. The vote took place on 4 May 1934 and produced a ringing endorsement. More than 80 percent of the eligible voters on the reservation turned out and more than 70 percent of them cast their ballots for Yellowtail.

Displaying his flair for the dramatic and his wonderful ability to capitalize on his opponents' ill-humor, Yellowtail proposed that he take office in a colorful inauguration ceremony at the end of the summer. With three months to prepare, the new superintendent's supporters created an event that celebrated his achievements and burnished his image as the proper successor to the recently deceased Plenty Coups. The centerpiece of the inauguration was a stirring address that Yellowtail delivered in the park in front of the agency headquarters and that was reprinted in full the next day

on the front page of the local newspaper. From its confident opening—
"Friends, this is our home, this is our domain, and this is our country"—to
its self-congratulatory climax—"a new era . . . has dawned for the American Indian"—Yellowtail's speech reflected his determination to define the
Crow community as a distinct political entity within the United States.[17]

Specifically, Yellowtail used his inaugural address to lay out five goals
for his administration and, by extension, the administration of John Collier. He called for the adoption of Indian preference in all Indian Office
hiring, total Indian control of leasing decisions involving cattle ranchers
and mineral resource developers, distribution of lease proceeds to individuals, the rapid development of reservation resources, and tribal control of tribal funds. While modern readers might view this list with some
skepticism (many of these policies were implemented with limited success in later years), it is remarkable that a tribal member who had been
dismissed by a government official only a few months earlier as "totally
without principle" was now the government spokesperson on the reservation. It is also significant that many of his ideas concerning tribal self-determination became general government policy decades later.

Almost immediately after his inauguration, Yellowtail faced a losing
battle with his political enemies. Commissioner John Collier insisted that
the Crows adopt the recently signed Indian Reorganization Act and form
a federally approved tribal government. With a half century of antagonis-
tic relations with local agents behind them, Crow leaders were deeply dis-
trustful of the new program. While grateful for Collier's sensitivity to
their concerns, many Crow leaders feared that the new body would be
manipulated by the government, the superintendent, or a small group of
insiders. They also feared the proposed council's power to control tribal
land and to possibly acquire individual allotments. As for the new superintendent, he gave lip service to the plan but did not stump for it with his
characteristic enthusiasm. As the appointed day of the tribal vote on the
plan neared, the commissioner insisted that Yellowtail speak out. "I feel
that it is your job to put yourself forcibly into this campaign," the commissioner wrote a week before the vote. "It is an administration policy
and program and must have the earnest support of the superintendents."[18]

With only a few days to go, Yellowtail began to speak out. Interestingly,
however, his defense of the new law did not focus on its support for the
creation of tribal governments. The new superintendent felt comfortable
with the councils the Crows had created over the previous half century and
did not believe the tribe was without a voice. What interested him were
the powers these councils might wield, particularly the power to manage

and protect reservation lands. He urged his listeners not to worry about the Indian Office. "The sale of our lands is what is ruining us," he told one gathering. He added that if land sales continued, "we will be landless in ten years and beggars on the highway." Skeptics—including James Carpenter—replied that the new law would take away all the gains the tribe had won in recent years and reduce their council to a puppet regime.[19]

Yellowtail assured Collier that with more time he could have stemmed the tide running against him, but suspicion of the Indian Office ran so deep—and had been so frequently justified—that it could not be overcome. Yellowtail told an election-eve gathering that the law promised to "fix" the system and that he promised the commissioner he would "rout" the opposition, but it was not to be. The main problem with Crow acceptance of the act was perception. Past federal policies had been disastrous; now they were being asked to consider another major change initiated in Washington. They simply said "no." Eighty percent of the eligible Crow voters turned out to cast their ballots on 17 May; the motion to adopt the Indian Reorganization Act was defeated by a margin of nearly seven to one. Interestingly, Crow oral traditions indicate that Yellowtail opposed the law. Tribal historian Joseph Medicine Crow recalls that Yellowtail's protégé and ally Hartford Bear Claw was asked to work against passage of the law.

The defeat of the Indian Reorganization Act reminded Crows that Yellowtail was now a government employee. The referendum on the law cooled some of the ardor of the previous summer's inauguration, but it did not discourage Yellowtail from embarking on an ambitious series of economic development projects. He introduced new breeds of horses and cattle to improve the quality of Crow livestock. Another Yellowtail idea had great symbolic significance. The superintendent reached agreement with the National Park Service and other federal agencies to transfer "excess" bison and elk from Yellowstone and surrounding national forests to Crow lands in the Bighorn Mountains. The tribe maintains a bison herd to this day.

Yellowtail had long advocated reducing the power of local ranchers and others who leased Crow lands, but he recognized that many of them were so large and well-entrenched that he would be unwise to attempt to evict them. He recalled near the end of his life that he called together the major lessees and told them he thought they had not been paying adequate rents. He offered them an olive branch: "I'll stay with you and protect you against any unreasonable moves. You help me and I'll help you—we are a great family." Critics later claimed that this kind of moderation allowed lease-holders to establish ties to Crow landholders—and through them, control over Crow lands—that proved impossible to break. Yellowtail called his policy "cooperation."[20]

In the end, the superintendent worked closely with some lessors and opposed others. Matt Tschirgi and other large operators made their peace with Yellowtail and entered a relationship that resembled that between Plenty Coups and an earlier generation of ranchers. "Cooperation" meant fair prices, but it also meant informal promises to hire individual Crows or to provide support for community gatherings or other special events.

Yellowtail's political opponents repeatedly charged that he compromised the interests of his people and profited personally from his office. His acquisition of a fine ranch on Rotten Grass Creek only increased suspicion and jealousy. But Yellowtail did not seem always to side with or support the large reservation lessees. He declared in 1934 that he wanted to break up the large cattle leases with smaller ones, and in 1940 he attempted to increase the competition among potential lessees by inviting Texas ranchers to bid on tribal land. In 1939 he was even sued by some of the larger lessees over his handling of certain leases. Nevertheless, in 1957 he spoke out in favor of repealing section 2 of the 1920 Crow Act, which limited the number of acres non-Crows could own on the reservation. He argued that he was too busy to enforce it while he was superintendent. Though eventually cleared of the charges, the superintendent was accused of playing favorites with lessees, accepting gifts from a mining company, and using government materials and funds for personal projects. At one point in 1939 he even submitted his resignation but withdrew it after a vote of confidence from the tribal council.[21]

Supporters regularly outnumbered Yellowtail's critics, however, particularly among those who benefited from the New Deal federal recovery programs he brought to the reservation. Beginning in 1935 the Crows were the beneficiaries of programs funded by the Works Progress Administration and the Indian Emergency Conservation Works. These programs provided employment while improving reservation resources. Activities included building reservoirs, improving roads, establishing mountain trails, and both repairing and creating new corrals and homes. Civilian Conservation Corps (Indian division) members also worked as logging crews, fire fighting units, and pest control teams. Federal efforts to reduce unemployment even supported reservation sewing cooperatives and informal Indian dancing clubs.

These recovery programs brought a sudden infusion of cash to the impoverished reservation, but they also brought about a subtle reorganization of Crow society. The shifting of individuals to paid government-funded jobs drew people away from school and provided them with an alternative to subsistence farming and ranching. Individuals found it was more convenient to live near their jobs at Crow Agency or some other settlement, so they were more likely to lease their land to a non-Indian rancher or to give up their kitchen garden. This movement from the farm to a cash-paying job "in town" (a trend hardly limited to the Crow Reservation), undermined Crow agriculture because it increased tribal members' dependency on marginal and seasonal employment. Non-Indian farmers, cultivating ever-larger tracts of land, remained behind to raise crops on Crow allotments.

By 1940 Yellowtail became aware that welfare laws and recovery programs were undermining the reservation's "traditional" subsistence activities. He set out to increase local production by creating a cattle purchase program and encouraging tribal members to participate. As a rancher, the superintendent had few qualms about recommending cattle raising over farming; his advice was also reinforced by the rapid rise in the cost of equipment necessary for large-scale agriculture in the Big Horn and Little Big Horn valleys. In 1916 the Crows had farmed only twenty thousand acres. By the outbreak of World War II Yellowtail could boast that the tribe's cattle ranchers were using nearly six times that amount. Half of all Crow household income still came from leasing, however, and the vast majority of land was still leased to outsiders.

Yellowtail introduced a number of other innovations. An outspoken advocate of education, the superintendent worked to improve funding for schools and urged children to go to college. He oversaw the establishment of the first Crow hospital in 1937 and supported community health programs. Yellowtail also took delight in reversing the Indian Office's long-standing opposition to traditional tribal dancing and ceremonial life. He welcomed the introduction of the Shoshoni Sun Dance in 1941 and presided over a revival of Crow Fair. The latter, which had been imposed on the tribe as a "harvest festival" in the first decade of the twentieth century, had frequently been a scene of struggle between superintendents who wanted to re-create a Midwestern county fair and tribal leaders who favored dancing and horse racing. Under Yellowtail, the fair was moved to August and the focus shifted to a celebration of Crow culture and family life. Families camped for several days along the Little Big Horn south of Crow Agency, gathering with dispersed relatives and visitors from Indian communities across the West and Canada. For the past sixty years, this festival of Crow life has remained largely in the form it assumed during the 1930s.

Both the benefits and the drawbacks of a cash economy on the reservation became vividly evident during World War II. Soldiers and war industry workers brought their paychecks home, crop prices rose, and federal spending continued to rise. But unfortunately these trends continued to undermine family farming and to promote migration to reservation towns or nearby cities. Yellowtail himself was an exception to this trend. He expanded his herd during his years in Crow Agency, running cattle in Rotten Grass Creek, west of his family holdings, and racing his horses at rodeos across the West as well as in Mexico.

The prosperity of the New Deal and the war years was deeply dependent on federal spending. Dollars from Washington helped revive the reservation economy and provide employment for many people but, as tribal historian Eloise Pease has noted, after the war "the bubble burst and the Crows went into their depression." In the spring of 1945, as the "bubble" of wartime prosperity reached its bursting point, Yellowtail decided the time had come to step down as superintendent. He was motivated in part by his long tenure, in part by his patron, John Collier (Collier too left office in early 1945), and in part by a desire to run for Congress. His bid failed. His defeat was mitigated by another massive confrontation that was about to take place between the Crows and their off-reservation enemies—a confrontation that made Yellowtail realize he didn't want to be saddled by an official government position.[22]

Eastern Montana had always been a difficult place for homesteaders to make a living. Even when farmers had control of more than the mythical 160 acres that had constituted a homestead in the well-watered east, it was difficult to wring a living from the arid conditions and short growing season of the vast Montana prairies. Almost from their first farming season in the Yellowstone Valley, weary planters looked to some sort of irrigation project to save them. Ditch and diversion systems began in the Little Big Horn valley in the 1880s, but by World War I attention focused on the Big Horn Canyon, particularly its solid granite mouth through which spewed billions of gallons of water, cascading downhill from the central Wyoming plains. It seemed a perfect site for a dam, but it was on Crow land.

Local farmers had been calling for a Big Horn dam for decades, but there was no serious federal interest until 1937 when the Army Corps of Engineers announced its support for the project. Superintendent Yellowtail had opposed the idea, noting that this was not a Crow project and arguing that tribal resources were needed to serve tribal ends. (He also noted that the recently introduced Crow bison herd made its home in the canyon bottom.) As had been the case thirty years earlier, however, local farmers and their congressional supporters would not accept this position. Like their predecessors in the Crow land disputes, they lobbied their congressional delegation to seek a federal mandate for the project. The farmers were finally successful in 1944 when Congress authorized construction of the proposed dam as part of the massive Missouri River hydroelectric and irrigation system then being planned. Crows were horrified, and under Yellowtail's leadership were able to prevent the project from going forward.

At the same time, Yellowtail and his fellow tribal politicians turned to an internal problem that had been ignored ever since the Indian Reorganization Act was rejected in 1935. The Crow tribe's informal system of general councils and business committees continued to function in an age when most tribes operated under written constitutions. Major disputes frequently revealed how confusing, unpredictable, and unstable the Crow political structure could be. Many reservation leaders thought the time had come to agree on a written tribal constitution.

In 1947 a committee appointed by the Crow general council drafted an initial proposal calling for a business committee. This draft was rejected by the council and, after considerable debate, three alternatives were produced. Yellowtail became the champion of one, and it carried the day two weeks after his election as tribal chairman in 1948. A tribal referendum approved the draft constitution in June 1948 by a vote of 295 to 130. The constitution called for the establishment of the office of tribal chairman, a person who would be elected by the entire membership. The constitution also specified that all legislation be approved by the general council, which would comprise all enrolled adult tribal members.[23]

Late in his life Robert Yellowtail claimed that he wrote the Crow constitution of 1948. But some critics charged that the document was originally drafted by the attorneys representing the large ranchers who leased Crow lands and that it was advocated by Yellowtail in exchange for cattle and land. They believed the former superintendent favored this "pure democracy" because he knew he could dominate its proceedings. Regardless of the role Yellowtail may have played in drafting the 1948 charter, the constitution conformed to a tradition that had been in place for most of the twentieth century. Crows were generally suspicious of legislative bodies where elected representatives acted on behalf of constituents. They feared these elected officials could be bribed by wealthy ranchers, intimidated by powerful government officials, or controlled by a few well-connected tribal members. They held to this position throughout the 1930s—there appeared to have been no second thoughts regarding the tribe's rejection of the IRA.

In 1951 federal authorities increased the pressure on the tribe to approve the use of its land for the Big Horn dam. The Bureau of Reclamation had already announced the dam would be called "Yellowtail Dam" in honor of the former Crow superintendent. Now the agency offered to purchase the dam site for one and a half million dollars. The tribe's response was adamant: No sale. After considerable discussion Yellowtail proposed (and the council endorsed) a contingency plan based on the experience of the Flatheads in western Montana. The Crows would lease the dam site for fifty years.

Matters remained locked between the two intransigent parties until the local ranchers and farmers managed—as they had in 1917—to persuade Congress to act unilaterally. In 1954 an opinion from the U.S. Department of the Interior's solicitor reinterpreted a federal law that had prohibited further work on Crow irrigation systems without the consent of the tribe. The opinion argued that the statute's restrictions applied only to existing irrigation projects, not to new ones. Senator James Murray of Montana promised to press ahead by moving to condemn the dam site. The tribe was warned that once condemnation proceedings began the Crows would likely get only the assessed value of the land, which Interior Department officials estimated could be as little as fifty thousand dollars. As with the Crow land dispute of 1917–19, the tribe had to choose between compromise or continued resistance. This time Yellowtail played the role that Plenty Coups had played in 1919; he refused to make a deal with the relentless Montana congressmen.[24]

The Crows were deeply divided over the proposed dam. Few people would be displaced by the project, and it seemed reasonable to expect a considerable financial settlement despite the tough talk emanating from Washington. On the other hand, the canyon was a unique cultural and economic resource that should either be preserved or shared only after the tribe had extracted the greatest possible payment for it. Yellowtail, who had become tribal chairman in 1952, led the forces of opposition. He was supported by a group that called itself the Mountain Crows. His opponents, calling themselves the River Crows (the name of another preservation group within the tribe), was led by William Wall and Edward Posey Whiteman. Wall became chairman in 1954; Whiteman succeeded Wall two years later. Yellowtail, always interested in Republican Party politics and events on the Crow Reservation, ran unsuccessfully in the Republican primary for the U.S. Senate in 1954.

As the dam debate reached its climax, divisions within the tribe deepened. It caused wounds that have not entirely healed and have affected Crow people down to the present. Neighbors refused to speak. Families divided. At one point the Crow Fair itself divided into two competing celebrations. Each side struggled to extract an honorable agreement from the federal government. In 1955 Yellowtail and his allies proposed a deal: one million dollars per year for fifty years. Title to the dam site would revert to the tribe for renegotiation following expiration of the term. They knew this would be unacceptable to the Bureau of Reclamation and hoped it would thus have the effect of preserving the land. Yellowtail's opponents proposed an outright sale for five million dollars with the tribe retaining all mineral rights to the land. Each side accused the other of accepting bribes and making backroom deals. Yellowtail claimed a white rancher offered him twenty-one thousand dollars to drop his opposition.

In 1956 the tribe's general council rejected Yellowtail's lease proposal and accepted the idea of selling the dam site. These decisions required several meetings, the last of which lasted thirteen hours. The final offer included the sale of land, retention of mineral rights and a provision for Crows to obtain access to irrigation without fees. Backed by the Montana congressional delegation, the Crow proposal won congressional approval in 1956 but was vetoed by President Eisenhower as an extravagant expenditure. Angered and still divided, the Crow council then rescinded its offer and approved the Yellowtail lease plan. Warned that the lease idea would not be approved, the council then reversed itself and repeated its endorsement of the five-million-dollar sale. Worried about another veto, Montana's congressional delegation reduced the price to two and a half million; Eisenhower signed the bill into law on 15 July 1958. The politicians tried to mollify the disappointed Crows by amending the bill just before passage to allow the Crows to sue the United States for the balance of the price. (The tribe won a judgement for two million dollars in 1962 but half of the award was used to pay attorneys' fees.)[25]

After years of intense struggle, the Yellowtail Dam and reservoir were opened in 1964. Benefiting largely the local white community, the project seemed finally to vindicate the namesake who had opposed it. Yellowtail's former opponents admitted that he had been right to hold out for a lease on the land, but once the concrete barriers went up to shut off the river's flow, their change of heart had no meaning.

Yellowtail himself developed some pride in the project, allowing himself to be photographed before it wearing his warbonnet and reveling in the publicity it generated for him. But the aging leader never wavered in his conviction that selling the dam site had been a mistake and that the project would have little—if any—positive impact on the tribe.

The dam fight was Yellowtail's "last hurrah" as a tribal politician. He had retreated to his Red Rim ranch house on Rotten Grass creek and devoted himself to his cattle herd. When a fire swept through the house in 1961 he moved back to the hills south of Lodge Grass, the country he had known as a child. Widowed in 1956, he married for the last time in 1960. Dorothy Payne was a Choctaw from Oklahoma, but she had grown up among the Crows and took on the role of Robert's companion with great skill. He continued to be active in tribal affairs, but now he was more effective behind the scenes, promoting the careers of his protégés such as John Cummins and blocking the paths of his enemies such as Edward Whiteman and Edison Real Bird. He was persuaded to run for chairman once more but his supporters preferred younger men.

During the 1970s Yellowtail came forward for a final time when the council debated how best to manage and exploit its coal resources. Consistent with this lifetime commitment to reservation development, Yellowtail advocated tribal ownership of the coal and canceling leases that did not pay a significant dividend. While he brought tremendous experience to the issue, he was rapidly losing his power to communicate. His speeches grew longer and his audiences smaller. Of course, by the 1970s, Yellowtail was well into his eighties. His wife Dorothy declared that although she wished that when he had grown older he would quit politics, she knew he never would. "He just has to be in there," she observed, "that's his life . . . politics is it."[26]

In the early 1980s Robert worked with a group of film makers from Missoula, Montana, to produce the 1986 documentary, *Contrary Warriors: A Film of the Crow Tribe,* much of which chronicled his life. It includes many interviews with him and Dorothy. Robert Yellowtail died on 18 June 1988 at his home on the Little Horn Ranch south of Lodge Grass. An independent "Teddy Roosevelt" fighter to the end, he had refused offers to move to a nursing home. He died only a few yards from where he had been born on the banks of the Little Bighorn River.

Robert Yellowtail was one of the first generation of school-educated Crows who used the ways and means of the whites to achieve traditional Crow goals—the preservation and perpetuation of Crow lands and ways of life. Similar to earlier Crow leaders, he accomplished his ends by compromising and by varying his tactics according to the situation before him. In his early years he was an insurgent, an outsider who opposed the actions of the U.S. government. By the 1930s he had become an insider, a government official who could use the power and resources of a federal agency to promote Crow nationhood. At the end of his life he returned to the outsider role, leading the opposition to the Big Horn Canyon dam project.

Yellowtail was not always successful, but he consistently used both his Crow cultural ties and the skills he learned in boarding school to establish a different type of leadership in the new era of reservation life. He was the first Crow leader whose influence was not rooted in battlefield achievements but in a new type of warfare: confrontations in tribal council halls, government courtrooms, and congressional hearings. In his struggle he helped the Crows endure the white invasion and become "a separate, semi-sovereign nation" within the United States.

Notes

1. For a history of the Crow people during the time of Yellowtail's birth and early adulthood, see Frederick E. Hoxie, *Parading through History: The Making of the Crow Nation in America, 1805–1935* (New York: Cambridge University Press, 1995), especially chapters 7–11.

2. Joe Medicine Crow, interview with Tim Bernardis, 26 July 1995.

3. Hoxie, *Parading*, 135.

4. Joe Medicine Crow, interview with Tim Bernardis, 26 July 1995; Carson Walks Over Ice to Tim Bernardis, personal communication, 15 August 1995; Lorena Mae Yellowtail Walks Over Ice to Tim Bernardis, personal communication, 15 July 1995; Addison Bragg, "Tribe's Elder Statesman—a 'Crooked Heel Cowpuncher,'" *Billings Gazette*, 1 December 1974, p.77.

5. For a description of Crow religious life in the early reservation era, see Hoxie, *Parading*, chapter 7.

6. Robert Yellowtail Sr., "The Crow Reservation: A Brief Review of the History of Big Horn County: The Crow Reservation and the Crows 1884–1973," in *Lookin' Back, Big Horn Country* (Hardin MT: Big Horn County Historical Society, 1976), 316; Joseph Medicine Crow, "Robert Yellowtail—1889." Little Big Horn College Archives, Crow Agency, Montana, n.d.

7. Quoted in Michael Fitzgerald, *Yellowtail: Crow Medicine Man and Sun Dance Chief: An Autobiography* (Norman: University of Oklahoma Press, 1991), 29–30.

8. See Hoxie, *Parading*, 258.

9. For details of the 1913 trip, see Hoxie, *Parading*, 289–91. Robert Yellowtail Sr. to Tim Bernardis, personal communication, May 1984.

10. See Hoxie, *Parading*, 258.

11. Robert Yellowtail, *Robert Summers Yellowtail, Sr., at Crow Fair, 1972* (Albuquerque NM: Wowapi, 1973), 2–6.

12. See Hoxie, *Parading*, 261–65.

13. Transcripts of meeting filmed for documentary, *Contrary Warriors: A Film of the Crow Tribe*, Little Big Horn College Archives, Crow Agency, Montana, GX-4.

14. Quoted in Hoxie, *Parading*, 264.

15. Charles Crane Bradley Jr. and Susanna Remple Bradley, "From Individualism to Bureaucracy: Documents on the Crow Indians, 1920–1945," Little Big Horn College Archives, Crow Agency, Montana, 1974, 34.

16. Quoted in Hoxie, *Parading*, 326. The entire New Deal era at the Crow Reservation is discussed in Hoxie, chapter 11.

17. The full text of Yellowtail's speech was carried on the front page of the *Hardin Tribune Herald* on 3 August 1934.

18. Quoted in Hoxie, *Parading*, 340.

19. See Hoxie, *Parading*, 341.

20. Transcripts of interviews compiled for documentary film, *Contrary Warriors: a Film of the Crow Tribe*, Little Big Horn College Archives, Crow Agency, Montana, G-22.

21. Bradley and Bradley, "From Individualism to Bureaucracy," 139, 144, 168–69, 233–35; Hoxie, *Parading*, 335; Eloise Whitebear Pease, interview with Tim Bernardis, 26 July 1995; Lorena Mae Yellowtail Walks Over Ice, personal communication to Tim Bernardis, 15 July 1995.

22. Eloise Whitebear Pease, interview with Tim Bernardis, 26 July 1995.

23. Joseph Medicine Crow, "Crow Tribal Government Development," in *Crow Tribal Report Presented to the Indian Policy Review Commission, Washington DC* (Crow Agency MT: The Crow Tribe, 1976), 86–87; Charles Bradley, *The Handsome People: A History of the Crow Indians and the Whites* (Billings MT: Council for Indian Education, 1991), 269; Audrey Black Eagle, "The Crow Constitution: A Breeding Ground for Division," *Voices: Writings from the Students of Little Big Horn College* (spring 1994), 2–3; and "Constitution and By-Laws of the Crow Tribe, Montana," in *Charters, Constitutions, and By-Laws of the Indian Tribes of North America, Part IIA; The Northern Plains*, by George E. Fay, comp. (Greeley: Museum of Anthropology, Colorado State University, 1967), 50–60.

24. William M. Brooke, "Yellowtail Dam: A Study in Indian Land" (honors thesis, Department of History, Carroll College, 1981), 29, 32, 35.

25. Brooke, "Yellowtail Dam," 36–44.

26. Transcripts of interviews compiled for documentary film, *Contrary Warriors*, Little Big Horn College Archives, G-86.

Vine V. Deloria Sr., *right*

Vine V. Deloria Sr.

Dakota

PHILIP J. DELORIA

What man or woman, looking back over the course of a life, cannot find cause for both pride and regret? My grandfather, the Reverend Vine V. Deloria Sr., was no different. He could take satisfaction in having served as a leader for his community, his people, and his church. Many valued that service. In 1954 he was given the Indian Council Fire's Indian Achievement Award, appointed to a high-ranking position in the national office of the Episcopal Church, and awarded an honorary doctorate from his alma mater, Bard College. In 1977 he was inducted into the South Dakota Hall of Fame during his first year of eligibility. South Dakotans—both Indian and non-Indian—continue to remember him with great affection. Yet he also had regrets. Federal Indian policy, his church's social outreach programs, Indian Christianity in general—it wasn't that all these important things had gone so terribly wrong; it was that they hadn't gone quite right. And there was the fact that, despite his best efforts, he had been helpless on so many critical occasions.[1]

Whatever late-life disquiet he may have felt stemmed, I suspect, from the particular kinds of cross-cultural leadership burdens he took on. Those burdens, shared by many Native American leaders, grew increasingly heavy during the middle years of the twentieth century. Deloria had to negotiate complicated historical changes—the Great Depression, the Indian New Deal, World War II, and the postwar termination and relocation programs. He did so through an equally complex set of cultural frames—Dakota culture, a Dakota-inflected Christianity, an Indian political culture turning to American governing institutions, and an Episcopal Church vexed by issues of power, race, and politics. His success stories—and there were many—need to be seen in the context of these complicated, overlapping arenas that, by their very nature, compromised his efforts and sent him staggering back in retreat more than once.

Deloria was born at Wakpala, on South Dakota's Standing Rock Reservation. His family history was characterized by marriage and mediation across the sometimes-blurred cultural lines that marked Indians and non-Indians. His great-great-grandfather, a late-eighteenth-century French traveler on the Missouri named Francois Des Lauriers, married a Yankton Dakota woman and settled along the river. Francois's son Francis, born around 1784, followed a similar path. The Missouri River took him to the north, where he met and married a woman of the Blackfeet band of Lakota. Their son Frank, also known as Saswe, was born in 1816 and he too settled near the Missouri.

If one were counting blood-quantum shares, Saswe would have been three-fourths Dakota. But few people—at least few Indian people—were counting, and by his generation (the third), the family was thoroughly Yankton. Saswe took three wives, made a name for himself as a powerful—and perhaps dangerous—spiritual leader, and served as headman for Yankton's "half-breed band." As "E-ha-we-cha-sha," or "the Owl Man," he signed the Yankton treaty of 1858. In 1866 he received government recognition as "Chief of Yankton half-breed band at their request," and the following year traveled to Washington DC as part of the tribe's negotiating team.

Saswe was as engaged with missionaries as he was with agents and government negotiators. He seems to have perceived missionaries (correctly, one might add) through lenses that were at once spiritual and political in nature; to him missions looked like places where one might negotiate questions of power. By the 1860s Saswe was attending services, and was baptized into the Episcopalian Church on Christmas Day 1871. During this time he encouraged one of his younger sons, Philip J. Deloria (Tipi Sapa), to think seriously about how the church was coming to be a powerful organization on the reservation and how it might best be used to help the Yanktons.

Philip attended the mission day school with some of Saswe's other children, eventually being taken by the missionaries to off-reservation Episcopal boarding schools. Like his siblings, he had been baptized at an early age. Well-educated and biculturally adept, Philip seemed destined to follow his father into politics. He had apparently been serving as a headman since his return from school in 1874. In 1878 he was presented with the medal that the government used to signify its appointed chiefs and was formally registered by the agent John Gassman as the leader of Yankton Band 8. Three years later he represented the Yanktons at a railroad negotiation in Carlisle, Pennsylvania. Sometime shortly afterward, however, he resigned this commission, having decided to devote his life to the Episcopal Church.

After returning home in 1874 Philip began serving as a lay reader and catechist. In 1883 the dynamic missionary Bishop William Hobart Hare made him a deacon. Deloria's entry into the church came at almost the precise moment when Hare assumed control of the Dakota mission district, dedicating himself to the training of Indian ministers, catechists, and deacons. By the time he retired in 1905, Hare had helped develop six ordained Indian priests and sixty lay ministers. One hundred chapels serving perhaps ten thousand Native Americans dotted the landscapes of the ten Sioux reservations. Philip Deloria was ordained in 1892 and, as a fully empowered minister, he rapidly became an influential leader within the community of Christian Indians.[2]

That community was enormous, for many Native Americans saw in the church what Saswe did: a place of social power and opportunity. Following military repression and confinement to reservations, Dakota and Lakota people confronted unimaginably deep cultural anxieties most visible, perhaps, in the meanings and practices surrounding masculinity. While traditional female activities—gathering, cooking, childrearing—tended to remain more or less the same, traditional male activities—hunting and war—had been all but eliminated. Likewise the power of the reservation agent, who made decisions on behalf of the tribe, rendered men's social leadership roles superfluous; a few momentous decisions were made in consultation with Indian leaders, but only a few. For men in particular, Dakota culture had been wrenched inside out. Many responded by turning to Christianity, which espoused a social structure that both men and women found they could utilize in their lives.

Men's religious societies had distinct connections to prereservation warrior societies. Likewise, powerful women's church groups reproduced prereservation women's societies. The yearly Convocation meetings—which drew numerous Indian people from every Dakota reservation—bore a familial resemblance to the social gatherings that had once marked the Sun Dance ceremony. Ministers and lay readers exercised a style of leadership that looked something like the consensual authority once vested in chiefs and headmen. When Philip Deloria strode across the mile-wide camp circle at the annual Convocation gatherings of the early twentieth century, he was participating in a cultural system that was at once very new and very old.

The religious belief systems of such Christian Indians pointed to broader cultural complexities. Philip Deloria was a true believer, and he could deliver a fire-and-brimstone sermon that made his listeners quake. And yet he was far more respectful of traditional beliefs than were his non-Indian missionary counterparts. He was almost certainly aware of the precarious opportunities of his own position, rooted simultaneously in two cultures and serving as a mediator between them. His Dakota parishioners also tended to reject the rigid Christian/pagan boundaries laid down by conventional missionaries, letting Christian and traditional beliefs and practices overlap and come together to create something new.

At the same time Dakota and Lakota clergy of all stripes were often more interested in their common Indianness than in the contests that went on among the four main missionary denominations—Catholic, Episcopal, Congregational, and Presbyterian. In 1872, for example, a group of Sioux deacons and clergy began meeting as the Brotherhood of Christian Unity (BCU), a leadership organization dedicated to singing, socializing, and fellowship across denominational lines. The home of a distinctive Sioux Christianity—particularly for Episcopalians and Presbyterians—the BCU continues to function today. By the early twentieth century, then, Indian Christianity was a powerful social force on the Dakota reservations, and its clergy and lay ministers had become important leaders in almost every sphere of Native American life.

This was the family—and the world—into which Vine Deloria Sr. was born in 1901. He was the last child of Philip Deloria's third marriage, which also produced two watchful sisters—Ella, a gifted linguist and ethnographer who worked with Columbia University anthropologist Franz Boas, and Susan, a socially dysfunctional artist who traveled constantly with her sister. When Vine was born, his father, according to family tradition, opened the Bible at random; eyes closed, he pointed to a verse. His finger landed at John 15:1: "I am the true vine; my father is the vinedresser." And so the child had one of his names. His Dakota name meant "Winner." The name proved apt, for Vine Deloria built much of his early life around his formidable athletic skills. He became accustomed to open competition and a certain clarity of result, with him usually coming out on top.

He attended school at St. Elizabeth's mission at Standing Rock until his mother's death in 1916. He then was sent to the Kearney Military Academy, a non-Indian Episcopal boarding school in Kearney, Nebraska. Although alone, impoverished, and barely able to speak English, Deloria made the best of his situation. He came to enjoy the school's military structure, and by the time he graduated had risen to Kearney's highest rank, cadet major. With an affable and charismatic personality, he developed many close friends. He rarely confronted racial prejudice at Kearney and, indeed, taught his friends bits and pieces of the Dakota language while they in turn renamed him "Pete," a transformation he seems to have thoroughly appreciated. It is probably no accident, however, that he was the dominant figure on the school's football, baseball, and track teams. He was quick, strong, and tough, and if personable and friendly, also capable of a powerful anger.

In 1922 his athletic prowess won him a scholarship to St. Stephen's College, an Episcopalian school of barely a hundred students attempting to gain a name and an alumni base through a newly created football team. The experiment lasted only a few years before an enrollment scandal shut down the sports program. A series of events eventually turned the school into Bard College. Deloria thought his scholarship support stemmed from Indian philanthropy and the church's support of its mission clergy, but in retrospect it seems clear that he was part of the college's efforts to build a strong team. And indeed, while at St. Stephen's, Deloria lettered in his three major sports, briefly held a national college record for longest forward pass, and served as the captain of the football team. Today he is remembered at Bard College as the greatest athletic hero to attend St. Stephen's.[3]

If he had been able to make a career choice that had the clarity of a football score, it seems likely that Vine Deloria would have chosen a life as an athletic coach. After graduating in 1926 with a B.A. in liberal arts, he began working as "boys athletic advisor" at the Fort Sill Oklahoma Indian boarding school. But just as Saswe had pushed Philip Deloria to think seriously about Indian Christianity, so too did Philip push Vine in the same direction. Philip, who retired in 1927 and was perhaps contemplating his familial, theological, and Native American legacies, strongly encouraged his son to follow in his footsteps. In 1928 a reluctant Vine entered the Episcopal Church's General Theological Seminary in New York City.

In New York, Deloria wrestled with the tension between his own inclinations and the burden of his family legacy. He began to refine his involvement in coaching and education, working at the nearby St. Luke's settlement house after his studies were finished for the day. Moving away from his father's and grandfather's brand of Indian leadership and toward a ministry more focused on youth development and education, he nonetheless felt the continual pull of the family linkage between spirituality and politics. A tangible reminder of that legacy haunted him: although in poor health, his father was determined to stay alive until Deloria's graduation, almost willing his son through the seminary program. In the spring of 1931, his coursework completed, Deloria returned to South Dakota to be ordained a deacon. Only a few days later, after seeing Vine commit to the ministry, Philip Deloria died. Already something of a church icon, his statue would later be enshrined in the Episcopal National Cathedral.

Vine Deloria was first assigned to the Pine Ridge mission, where he lived in an unheated garage and performed rites for marriages, burials, and baptisms at the many small chapels scattered throughout the central part of the reservation. After six weeks, however, he resigned in anger, fully intending to return to New York City. South Dakota's Episcopal bishop, Blair Roberts, had promised a salary of a hundred dollars per month to the graduates he recruited from the General Seminary earlier that year. Deloria found that despite his seminary degree, he was being paid "Indian wages"—fifty dollars per month—while his classmate Frank Thorburn, also at Pine Ridge, was receiving the full amount. The resignation of Philip Deloria's son promised to be a church scandal, and Roberts relented. Thinking in categories that were racial rather than religious, Roberts rationalized his decision to pay Deloria the promised amount by pointing to Deloria's impending marriage to a white woman, who needed the extra comfort the meager salary would provide. Regardless of the outcome, the stage had been set for decades of conflict between Deloria and his church—and his bishop in particular.

In May 1932, newly married and ordained, and accompanied by his wife, Barbara Eastburn of Sloatsburg, New York, Deloria returned to Pine Ridge. For a married couple, the garage left much to be desired, and it was no doubt with a sense of relief that the Delorias learned in October that they were to be reassigned to All Saints Church in Martin, South Dakota. Martin was a curious town, almost equidistant between the Pine Ridge and the Rosebud reservations on a large squared-off parcel of land that had been carved out of Pine Ridge barely twenty years before. One main street led through a small business district, and neatly laid blocks on either side housed residences and the town's five churches (Episcopal, Catholic, Lutheran, Presbyterian, and Christian Reform). It was a white town, but one with a mixed-blood history. Martin had "founding fathers" who were Lakota—Edgar Fire Thunder, Howard Bad Wound, Robert White Eagle, and Clarence Three Stars—and many Indian people still made the town their home. All Saints was not itself an "Indian" church, though Deloria also was responsible for two Indian chapels in the nearby communities of LaCreek and Gamble.[4]

His first career challenge, then, involved exactly the kinds of cross-cultural mediation for which he had been so well prepared. One might argue that this challenge prefigured his subsequent career. On the one hand, he was required to lead the way in maintaining and strengthening local Indian communities. On the other hand, he had to begin working his way into non-Indian social and political settings—the parish, the state and national church hierarchy, and the town of Martin itself. Each context—Indian and non-Indian—required a slightly different strategy.

In the small Indian chapels, Deloria was perhaps at his best. Raised in the Indian Christianity of his father's mission, he knew intuitively the songs and sermon themes that worked well with his congregations. A fine singer with a powerful voice, his oratory was riveting and inspirational. His genial personality, athletic skills, and interest in youth made him something of an uncle to young Lakota men. In addition to filling this important kinship role, he was fluent in Lakota (in later years, he would become well known among anthropologists for his vocabulary that comprised many archaic words) and extraordinarily well versed in the genealogical histories of many South Dakota Indian families. In short, within the Indian community he had both the cultural knowledge and the rare kind of charisma that in previous days had won followers and made leaders. During the annual Indian Convocations of the 1930s, it might take him two or three hours to walk from one side of the camp circle to the other, so large was the crowd of people wanting to speak with him.

All Saints Church was a different matter. Yet here too his personality and talent allowed him—an Indian man—to lead a white and mixed-blood congregation. Not surprisingly, he began by playing baseball with Martin's young men, organizing them into a large boy's club and teaching them a range of sports. Eventually Deloria invited the boys into the church to serve as his choir. Between the Boy's Club and choir practice, he made his church into one of the key locales for Martin's young men and, in doing so, won the affection and respect of his church members.

Deloria made similar overtures to the town's adults. He helped power Martin's town baseball team and volunteered to coach the Bennett County High School football team. He joined the new Freemason's lodge, and served as its chaplain. A visible presence, he combined his winning personality with clerical dignity and a sometimes intimidating physicality. At one point his parishioners asked him to tone down his enthusiasm for baseball, since they found it inappropriate that a man of the cloth should slide into second base with his aggressive intensity.[5]

A family story may illustrate the kind of effect Deloria could have when his angry streak got the better of him. Deeply concerned about Indian drinking, Deloria was disgusted by Martin's bars, which refused to allow Indian people inside, but would nonetheless sell alcohol to them from the back door. As a result, Indian people ended up drinking on the streets, where he often had to take care of them. One night he snapped. Grabbing a baseball bat, he strode into the Buckhorn, Martin's largest saloon, and pounded on the bar. "If anyone here sells anymore alcohol to Indians from the back door, they'll have to answer to me!" He stared down the silent proprietor and crowd. If he'd have been any less tough or carried any less moral authority, he might have been asking for a terrible retribution. But the combination of those traits allowed him to threaten his captive audience and to insist upon moral reform at the same time. And indeed, the Buckhorn shut down its back-door business.

His dealings with Bishop Roberts and the Episcopal Church proved more worrisome, for here his personal skills and sense of moral certainty did not fit especially well. The church was about hierarchy and obedience more than it was about creating new kinds of ministries, winning people over, or enforcing moral approaches to such questions as race and drinking. It certainly was *not* about the preservation of a distinct Indian Christianity. Perhaps twice each year, Deloria found himself fighting his church. On one occasion, for example, he physically restrained a white missionary who was attempting to prevent Indian women from placing food on a burial site. He often had to fend off the church's threats to the autonomy of the Brotherhood of Christian Unity. And he frequently questioned the disparities in salary for Indian clergy and the lack of reimbursement for the often substantial automobile expenses that they all incurred on the dirt roads of the reservations.

A key ally in his dealings with the church proved to be his wife Barbara. Barbara Sloat Eastburn grew up in an Episcopalian household in the Hudson River valley town of Sloatsburg, New York. Her family, which included military heroes and inventors, had lived in the area since the early seventeenth century. She rode the commuter line into New York City every day to work at the American Telephone and Telegraph Company. She met Deloria at his 1931 graduation. They enjoyed a whirlwind courtship and then suffered through a year's separation while Vine worked as a deacon at Pine Ridge. Her status as a white woman helped bring his salary to parity with the white clergy, and she proved willing and able to use the dynamics of race and gender to gain the ear, and occasionally the sympathy, of the bishop.

In July 1939 a tornado devastated All Saints Church and its rectory. When Deloria petitioned the bishop for help, he was told to deal with the problem himself. An old seminary friend, Cliff Cowan, now a church business manager in Ohio, agreed to help. Cowan set up a schedule in which Deloria would barnstorm Ohio churches for six weeks, lecturing and raising funds. When the tour concluded, he had raised sixteen thousand dollars for a new church and had, in the process, drawn the attention of both the national media and the upper echelons of the Episcopal Church. Deloria had undertaken speaking tours for the church before, but the Ohio campaign was different in two respects. First, it enabled him to emerge at last from the shadow of his father, whose revered status within the church had hung over him like a brilliant cloud, always defining him as "PJ's son." Second, the widespread and favorable exposure gave him much-needed leverage in his relationship with Bishop Roberts.

Throughout the 1930s, Deloria successfully consolidated his ministry and his leadership role within local communities and regional institutions that were both Indian and white. In addition, his tour of Ohio gave him a brief moment of national prominence, both inside and outside the church. Although he had focused on youth and local social issues more than politics, he worked within the intercultural paradigms that had housed his father and grandfather so well. Harder times lay on the horizon, however, and they were directly connected to the rapid social and economic transformations that characterized America's move from the Great Depression and the New Deal to World War II; and on to a postwar culture of consensus. Looking back, it would become apparent that 1939 and 1940 (when Deloria was able to build his new church, St. Katharine's) marked the end of a successful era for his ministry and for the Dakota church itself.

In 1943 Roberts reassigned Deloria to the Sisseton-Wahpeton mission in eastern South Dakota, where he was to serve as the superintending presbyter, with sole responsibility for a large set of reservation chapels, deacons, and parishioners. In many ways his three years at Sisseton passed pleasantly. Unlike the mingled and mixed-blood communities of Martin and the eastern part of Pine Ridge, Sisseton had distinct groupings of whites and full-bloods. The Delorias moved easily between the two communities, bridging them together on occasion. Yet for Vine Deloria the defining event of his years at Sisseton was a losing battle to secure the church's sponsorship of an Episcopal boarding school for Indian boys.

The Indian boarding school experience has been seen as both a site of forced acculturation and as a place where Native American children reinforced tribal identities and developed senses of themselves as "Indians" in ways that transcended tribal lines. Deloria saw the boarding school through a somewhat different lens. Through the late 1930s and early 1940s he watched as many of the small communities on South Dakota reservations began to break apart. He believed firmly in the social and cultural power of the Indian church to hold such localities together. Religious boarding schools, he argued, were critical in developing the Native American clergy so vital to such communities. Taking his own experience as a model, he sought to develop an educational program that would not only train Indian youth to negotiate white American society and prepare for careers in the church, but also allow them to retain the "Indian" in Indian Christianity.[6]

He worked out an agreement through which the church, if it promised to establish a school, could acquire title to old Fort Sisseton for one dollar. The idea was popular among many South Dakota Indians, who had watched several smaller schools close down. The bishop, however, absolutely refused to consider the idea, arguing that there was no real need for an educated Indian clergy. Educated white missionaries could do the job just as well. For Deloria, this course spelled disaster for the Episcopal Church—and hardship for the many Indian communities who had been well served by the Indian clergy. Since the bishop blocked the plan, however, there was nothing to be done.

It was a discouraged man, then, who was transferred back to Martin in 1946, this time as the presbyter of the Corn Creek district of the Pine Ridge Reservation. Moving back to familiar ground made it clear how quickly things had changed since the glory days of the decade before. By 1946 most of the boys who had sung in his choir had served in World War II or had left the area to work in defense plants. Some had gotten married and were now church members. When Deloria tried to rebuild the group with a new generation of boys, however, he encountered the significant social distinctions that existed between the tough times of the Great Depression and a new economy spurred on by wartime production.

In the 1930s, when times were tight and amusements few, young men flocked to social outlets like the Boy's Club baseball team and the choir. In the 1940s, however, wheat prices skyrocketed with wartime scarcity, and young men often leased fields and, with the help of their parents, planted crops. With cash in their pockets, or perhaps a new car in the garage, The Boy's Club no longer seemed very compelling.

Likewise, as the church cut resources and staff, Deloria's work in the Indian community was completely transformed. Now, instead of a pair of rural chapels, he found himself the only priest covering fourteen churches spread across the broad geography of the eastern half of Pine Ridge. On Sundays he faced an exhausting schedule: drive to a chapel and conduct an early service, drive to another chapel and conduct a late morning service, drive to another chapel and conduct still another service, stop to visit one of the fifteen hundred parishioners in the district, and wearily make his way home. The boys who didn't join The Boy's Club were not the only ones who had changed. Military service, war work, and out-migration had shrunk the congregations of most of the chapels. A decade earlier one might have found sixty parishioners waiting for a communion service; now a long dusty drive brought him to ten elderly holdouts. Support from the church was rare, and Deloria was constantly in debt, worrying about automobile expenses and the duties he felt obliged to fulfill.

And then there were the changes in Indian politics created by Franklin D. Roosevelt's Indian New Deal. Anchored by the Indian Reorganization Act of 1934 (IRA), the reforms of the Indian New Deal transformed many reservation communities, and these transformations were particularly visible in the structures of Indian leadership. The IRA gave tribes the opportunity to establish tribal councils modeled after American constitutional governments, with elected representatives from reservation districts. Federal and state governments, as well as private industry, insisted that IRA governments serve as the primary venue for Dakota and Lakota decision making; many Sioux people learned that speaking collectively meant speaking through the councils.

As a new and important vector for the limited money and power that came through Indian Country, the councils quickly became the places where talented leaders sought to exercise their influence. Whereas people once followed leaders because they already *had* character, charisma, and power, now voting itself became the act that *conferred* power on individuals. It often did so in divisive ways, for there were now winners and losers, arguments and counterarguments, supporters and opponents. These political institutions were strikingly different from the leadership structures of the Indian church, which, ironically, came now to look more like a reflection of the older traditions of the nineteenth century.

The reforms of the Indian New Deal, then, drained power away from the churches and created more rigid boundaries between church and state. Church leaders like Deloria no longer bridged these borders so easily, particularly at local levels. By the 1940s politics and religion were drifting apart and Indian leaders found themselves forced into unaccustomed—and increasingly marginal—categories. At the same time, the church continued to cut back on the resources available to its Indian missions. Schools and chapels closed or consolidated. Greater numbers of Indian children began attending public, private, and, later, tribal schools. Already in decline, the number of Indian clergy plummeted as a whole generation of young Indians turned to a different kind of leadership opportunity.

The Brotherhood of Christian Unity had been the heart of Dakota Christianity, but in the mid-1940s some of its most influential clergy began to slip away to death, illness, age, and exhaustion. Deloria worked hard to hold the organization together and, with BCU assistance, even opened a small boarding school—the Bishop Hare School for Boys, located in Mission, on the nearby Rosebud Reservation. In 1949 however, the demands of the school, the BCU, his chapel assignments, and the disheartening changes in Indian Christianity and Indian politics proved too much. He suffered a severe breakdown, losing his voice for almost two weeks. Desperate, he began applying for positions in other parishes, only to find his requests blocked by Bishop Roberts. Eventually, he had to resign yet again.

In 1951 he found respite in Denison, Iowa, where, with the help of Iowa bishop Gordon Smith, he escaped Roberts, South Dakota, and the Indian ministry for a smaller assignment serving three rural parishes. From 1951 to 1954 he tried to regain his perspective and his energy. While he rested, however, critical changes were occurring in federal Indian policy. During these years, the federal government sought to repudiate the underlying tenets of the Indian New Deal—Native American self-government and collective landholding—through a program called "termination." When Deloria returned to the church's Indian mission field in 1954, this time in a national capacity, he would find that the politics swirling around Indian America had changed yet again.

World War II had looked like an assimilationist dream to many white Americans. Indian people participated in proportionally large numbers in both the military and the industrial production that had characterized the homefront. In addition, the reform programs of Indian commissioner John Collier had come under fire in Congress and had by the 1940s been largely neutralized. As early as 1937 the co-sponsor of the IRA, Montana senator Burton Wheeler, sought to overturn his own legislation. By 1945, when Collier resigned, many in Congress believed that the time was ripe for putting an end to the federal Indian bureaucracy altogether.

Termination attempted to bring Indian people inside the American fold by disassembling collective institutions—tribal councils and any other type of consensual governing structures—and by pulling Indian people into the wage-work opportunities the cities offered. With the help of the Indian Claims Commission, terminationists sought to eliminate any lingering legal, political, institutional, and cultural differences between Indians and non-Indians. Since there were, in fact, many such differences, termination represented a colossal threat that, if carried out, would sweep away the very idea of Indianness.

Among the many different varieties of termination efforts, two pieces of legislation and one program have become significant signposts. House Concurrent Resolution 108, passed in June 1954, set forth the policy goal: Indians were to assume all the rights and responsibilities of American citizenship, while any governmental obligations to Indian people were to be eliminated. Public Law 280, passed in August 1953, sought to move those federal responsibilities to state governments, which proved to be ill equipped and hostile. Finally, the relocation program, inaugurated in the early 1950s, set up training and employment bureaus in many large cities. There reservation Indians were to learn quickly the ways of the time clock and the bus schedule so that they could become like white urban Americans.[7]

At almost the very instant of the formal codification of the termination program, Vine Deloria Sr. was appointed the Episcopal Church's assistant secretary for Indian Work. In early 1954 the Church began to reorganize its central office, with Indian missions and other social outreach efforts assigned a high priority. The organizers took the novel step of putting an African American clergyman in charge of outreach to black communities, and an Indian in charge of Indian missions. Deloria left Iowa in March 1954 and promptly began his tenure by touring reservations across the country. Shocked by what he found, he developed a detailed proposal for revitalized church activity on reservations, which he presented to the church's executive council in the fall of 1955. The program was sophisticated and comprehensive: boarding and day schools, scholarships at Episcopal colleges, a national training center for Indian clergy, and strategic placement and support for Indian priests and catechists. The proposal was patterned after his own life and missions, of course, but hadn't those efforts been successful? And hadn't they started to fail not because of any structural flaws but because of the lack of will and resources?

More intriguing—and more problematic—the proposal offered a complex understanding of what it meant to be Indian—an understanding that, to many, looked like a direct attack on the government's termination programs. Indeed, when he presented the proposal to the council, it was opposed by the assembled bishops, who said they resented being offered a radical program that would keep Indians distinct and separate from other Americans at a time when the nation was trying hard to eliminate such differences. Deloria's own life—which could easily serve as a case study in assimilation, if one chose to view it that way—suggested a more complicated scenario, one that emphasized continuing service to Indian people rather than the rapid and wholesale abdication of Indianness proposed by the government. Nonetheless he was branded as a separatist, a voice speaking against "progress," and was increasingly marginalized at church headquarters.

In autumn 1955 Deloria attended the conference of the National Congress of American Indians (NCAI), an Indian lobbying group that was, in some ways, the product of the Indian politics created by the IRA. A collection of tribal council members, military veterans, and members of the Indian intelligentsia, the NCAI used congressional lobbying and public relations campaigns to present a vehement case against termination. In 1956 and 1957 Deloria spent considerable time in Washington DC, attending congressional hearings and personally lobbying against termination to those in church circles willing to listen.

For centuries, "becoming civilized" and "becoming Christian" had been inseparably twinned. And if termination had a new urban industrial wrinkle, the program was nonetheless part of the old tradition of "civilizing the Indian." For many in the church, then, to argue against termination was to reject much of the mission effort. The opposition to the program of the church's secretary for Indian Work constituted an intolerable contradiction in the Episcopal position. The more he spoke out, the greater the political pressure swirling around him grew.

Ironically, like Indian politics, those of the church had changed since his father's time, becoming increasingly bureaucratized. As secretary for Indian Work, Deloria reported to the secretary for Domestic Missions, the Reverend William G. Wright, who doubled as director of the Home Department, which, along with Domestic Missions, also took responsibility for colleges, the military, and rural America. Wright in turn reported to the National Council and to the inner cabinet of the presiding bishop, Most Reverend Henry Knox Sherrill. In addition, the church had a semi-separate mission entity: the Domestic and Foreign Missionary Society.

The church offices could be intensely political, with all manner of jockeying for position and resources. Although the position of presiding bishop originally had been occupied by the most senior bishop available, in 1919 the church began to elect presiding bishops and council members. Therefore, in addition to a contradictory position on termination, Deloria confronted a multifold bureaucracy that dulled his power and his options, and a political culture that required cautious navigation.[8]

That kind of navigation had never worked particularly well for him. As the heir to a particularly Indian type of Christianity, he'd been attuned to consensual politics, and this upbringing proved difficult to reconcile with his place in the hierarchy. As an athlete, he had come to appreciate a certain kind of moral clarity that did not serve him well in the ambiguous realms of politics. He found himself hamstrung by a refusal to see anything but intellectual and moral ground. If he presented a logical argument and it was obviously the right thing to do, then why not do it? This kind of character served him well at the congregational level, but it spelled disaster at church headquarters. By the end of 1957 he was almost completely isolated and deeply depressed. His superiors let it be known that he could finish out the academic year, but that by spring 1958, he would need to find a parish.

As in 1951, he sought peace, quiet, and the reassurance of a congregation at a small church in Iowa. After a few years there, however, he once again reentered the church establishment, accepting an appointment as the archdeacon of South Dakota. Returning to Pierre, South Dakota, in 1961, he took on the responsibilities for regional organizing of the state's Indian mission work. The years between 1961 and his retirement in 1967 were among the most productive and important in his life.

The new job took him back among Indian people and he thrived, as he had once thrived locally in Martin, on the connections he was able to make between Indian and white communities. As he had once insisted on church education as the way to promote a cadre of Indian clergy, he now continued the job of developing that clergy. He traveled widely throughout the state, giving the Episcopal Church its most significant presence in years. He sought to strengthen the annual Convocations and the cross-denominational meetings of the Brotherhood of Christian Unity. And he argued effectively for South Dakota's Indian people in a variety of state and local venues.

Indeed, Deloria may have exercised his greatest influence in this more pedestrian position, for here he was able to model—for both Indians and non-Indians—a cross-cultural kind of leadership, one that originated in his family heritage and cultural background, but that carried his own personal stamp as well. It was the kind of leadership he had tried and failed to develop at the national level. The incredible affection with which younger generations of South Dakota Indian people remember him stems from these years and the years of his retirement during which he remained active around the state. He continued to be a popular and visible presence at Convocations, at the meetings of the Brotherhood of Christian Unity, at Huron College where he taught courses. In all capacities he brought together Indians and non-Indians. It is appropriate, perhaps, that his death in 1990 came during South Dakota's "Year of Reconciliation."

Yet in his later life he also looked back at his career with questioning eyes. "Since my retirement," he said in 1982, "I have come to look differently on the church. It seems to me now that the church leaders were wrong. . . . Maybe the recent movement on the part of us Sioux to revive our old religion, the religion of our ancestors, is a sign of the failures of the Christian situation. . . . In desperation, we blow balloons and let them go in church, and hug each other and kiss each other and add more and more ceremonies, as if that will give vitality to the church. But services like these are just programs and pageantry. I've been in faded Indian chapels where they sang simple hymns and said simple prayers and they read the Bible beautifully."[9]

In the end, these two settings—the institutional church and the small Indian and non-Indian communities he served—distinguished Deloria's career. He remained loyal to both. By doing so and by seeking to bring them together, he helped lead Indian people through some of the most troubled years of the twentieth century.

NOTES

1. Much of the information in this essay comes from a set of oral histories collected from Vine Deloria Sr., Vine Deloria Jr., Barbara Deloria, Margaret Rednour, Catherine Boswell, and Phil Lane Sr. Much of this information has, over the years, made its way into my own memory, but material from Deloria Sr. is contained in a set of twelve audiotapes my father and I made between 1970 and 1990. Material from Deloria Jr. is contained in a set of twenty-four videotapes made during December 1996. Barbara Deloria left behind two written accounts of her courtship, marriage, and first year in South Dakota, both of which are in my possession, as are three audiotapes made in 1987 and 1988. I recorded interviews with Rednour in January 1997, Boswell in September 1999, and Lane in March 1997 and October 1999. In addition, see Sarah Emilia Olden, *The People of Tipi Sapa* (Milwaukee WI: Morehouse Publishing, 1916); Vine Deloria Jr., *Singing for a Spirit* (Santa Fe: Clearlight, 1999); Vine Deloria Sr., "The Standing Rock Reservation: A Personal Reminiscence," *South Dakota Review* 9 (1971): 167–95; Raymond J. DeMallie and Douglas R. Parks, eds., "The Establishment of Christianity among the Sioux," *Sioux Indian Religion: Tradition and Innovation* (Norman: University of Oklahoma Press, 1987), 91–112; and Philip J. Deloria, "I Am of the Body: Thoughts on My Grandfather, Culture, and Sports," *South Atlantic Quarterly* 95 (spring 1996): 321–38.

2. On Hare, see M. A. DeWolfe Howe, *The Life and Labors of Bishop Hare: Apostle to the Sioux* (New York: Sturgis and Walton, 1914). On Philip Deloria, see Olden, *People of Tipi Sapa*, 1–23. On numbers, see Vine Deloria Sr., "Establishment of Christianity," 108–9. On Episcopal missions, see Virginia Driving Hawk Sneve, *That They May Have Life: The Episcopal Church in South Dakota 1859–1976* (New York: Seabury Press, 1977). On BCU (Brotherhood of Christian Unity), see Joseph H. Cash and Herbert T. Hoover, eds., interview with Father Vine Deloria, *To Be An Indian: An Oral History* (St. Paul: Minnesota Historical Society Press, 1995), 27–28. On the Deloria family, see Robert Craig, "Christianity and Empire: A Case Study of American Protestant Colonialism and Native Americans," *American Indian Culture and Research Journal* 21 (spring 1997): 26–29.

3. On St. Stephen's and on Deloria's athletic career, see Deloria, "I Am of the Body," and Reamer Kline, *Education for the Common Good: A History of Bard College: The First 100 Years, 1860–1960* (Annandale-on-Hudson NY: Bard College, 1982), 78–79.

4. On Martin, see *70 Years of Pioneer Life in Bennett County, South Dakota, 1911–1981* (Martin SD: Bennett County Historical Society, 1981).

5. On Deloria as a freemason, see William R. Denslow, *Freemasonry and the American Indian* (William R. Denslow, 1956), 152–57. Philip Deloria was also a freemason.

6. There are numerous recent studies of the boarding school experience. See, for example, David W. Adams, *Education for Extinction: American Indians and the Boarding School Experience, 1875–1928* (Lawrence: University Press of Kansas, 1995); K. Tsianina Lomawaima, *They Called It Prairie Light: The Story of Chilocco Indian School* (Lincoln: University of Nebraska Press, 1994); Clyde Ellis, *To Change Them Forever: Indian Education at the Rainy Mountain Boarding School, 1893–1920* (Norman: University of Oklahoma Press, 1996).

7. On Collier, see Kenneth Philip, *John Collier's Crusade for Indian Reform, 1920–1954* (Tucson: University of Arizona Press, 1977), 187–213; Vine Deloria Jr. and Clifford Lytle, *The Nations Within: The Past and Future of American Indian Sovereignty* (New York: Pantheon, 1984), 171–99. On termination, see Donald Fixico, *Termination and Relocation: Federal Indian Policy, 1945–1960* (Albuquerque: University of New Mexico Press, 1986).

8. See, for example, Raymond Albright, *A History of the Protestant Episcopal Church* (New York: Macmillan, 1964), 341–66; *The Episcopal Church Annual, 1956* (New York: Morehouse-Gorham, 1956), 36–37.

9. Vine Deloria Sr., "Establishment of Christianity," 110–11.

D'Arcy McNickle

Métis-Flathead

BY DOROTHY R. PARKER

If people today recognize D'Arcy McNickle's name, it is probably because they are familiar with his novel *The Surrounded*, considered by many to be the precursor of modern Native American literature. But writing was only one of McNickle's many talents. He was recognized by his peers as an anthropologist, a teacher, an administrator, and a tireless fund-raiser—a person who could make things happen. Awakening to his Indian identity in his late twenties, he spent the rest of his life working to assure the survival of Indian people and Indian tribes in the United States, and he became one of the most influential Native American leaders of the twentieth century.

D'Arcy McNickle's enrollment as a member of the Flathead Tribe in Montana was based only in part on his heritage.[1] His tribal membership also reflected federal Indian policy as decreed by the Dawes Act of 1887. The Dawes Act decreed that tribal lands be divided up and allotted to individual tribal members according to a roll that listed all members by name. According to the act, tribal elders could admit as members people of other Indian tribes and, if they had lived among the Flathead people for a prolonged period of time and were of good repute, even those with no Indian blood at all could be admitted. D'Arcy's mother and his two sisters, and perhaps even his father, William, might qualify. William, however, had no reason to consider tribal membership. The McNickle family had emigrated from Ireland to the United States in the late 1840s, and William had settled in Montana after helping build the transcontinental railroad that crossed the territory in the 1870s.

D'Arcy's mother's ancestry was different, however. Her family, the Parenteaus, were Métis people from Canada. Of mixed-blood French and Indian descent, they traced their European ancestry back to the voyageurs who had worked in the early fur trade, many of whom had taken Indian wives and raised families "after the manner of the country." Generations later, Isidore Parenteau, McNickle's grandfather, participated in the Riel Rebellion of 1885; after the rebellion failed and Louis Riel was executed, Isidore fled with his family (McNickle's mother, Philomene, was three years old) across the border to the Flathead Reservation in northwestern Montana, where they settled among the Flathead people. As Métis (mixed-bloods with an obscure ancestry), they apparently made no effort to establish an Indian identity.

William McNickle and Philomene Parenteau were married in 1899 and had two daughters when D'Arcy was born in 1904. By that time William was farming on tribal land and had established a reputation for honesty and hard work among both the Indian and non-Indian population. In addition to maintaining a farm, he worked as a "maintenance engineer" at the local mission school. William was ambitious and realized that the allocation of tribal land, if implemented according to the Dawes Act and the Flathead tribal census, might provide a way to legitimize and expand his farm. But first Philomene and the children would have to be enrolled as tribal members. Encouraged by William, Philomene and the children applied and in due time were adopted, with the children listed as one-fourth Cree. Although there was no hard evidence to prove that their Indian ancestors were indeed Cree, there was no question about their having Indian blood. When the reservation land was allotted, each of the children was given forty acres of land (Philomene received eighty acres) where William was already farming. He was able later to acquire still more land after the allotment process had been completed and nonallotted reservation acreage was made available to homesteaders.

While D'Arcy and his two older sisters were thus considered Indians, they were not raised as traditional members of the Flathead Tribe, and their parents discouraged them from playing with their Indian classmates. The McNickle farm was five miles from the mission and school at St. Ignatius, so the children boarded at the school (which enrolled both white and Indian children), and attended the Catholic church, where D'Arcy served as an acolyte.

Unfortunately Philomene and William's marriage was far from amicable, and when it finally ended in divorce, William wanted to remove the children from what he considered an unhealthy environment. With the help of the local reservation agent, the children were enrolled in the off-reservation Indian boarding school at Chemawa, near Salem, Oregon. Here for the first time the children met students from different tribes, many of whom spoke no English. The McNickle children spoke little else:

English was their native tongue, with an occasional French phrase added for emphasis. The children stayed at Chemawa for three years while their parents struggled over their custody.

Few details are known about McNickle's childhood, aside from the fact that while at Chemawa, he learned to play the violin. When he returned to Montana, he lived with his mother, who at that time was married to a man named Gus Dahlberg. Gus did not legally adopt D'Arcy, but Philomene wanted her son to assume Gus's name, so for almost fifteen years D'Arcy carried Dahlberg as his surname. The family moved to the Tacoma area in 1916, since jobs were plentiful in the shipyards during World War I. While in Tacoma, D'Arcy attended public high school, where he continued to play the violin, became interested in drama, and read voraciously.

After the war, the Dahlbergs returned to Montana, this time to Missoula, where D'Arcy enrolled at the University of Montana. Although he was poorly prepared for the rigors of the academic program there, he had begun to realize that without an education he had few options for the future. He knew that he did not want to farm with his father on the reservation. What he really wanted was to be a writer, a profession that he knew required more education. He was fortunate in finding a mentor—his English professor, Dr. Harold G. Merriam. Merriam was impressed with D'Arcy's ability and encouraged him to continue his studies, even suggesting that D'Arcy consider going overseas for graduate work.

McNickle's education, however, was interrupted in his senior year by the death of his grandfather Isidore. D'Arcy had loved his grandfather and was so distracted by the old man's death that he began cutting classes and eventually was suspended from the university. Nevertheless, Professor Merriam continued to support him, and with his mentor's encouragement, D'Arcy sold his forty acres of reservation land and went to Oxford University in England. Regretfully, however, he failed to graduate. Many of his college credits were not transferable, and he did not have enough money to continue his studies.

In 1926, after less than a year abroad, D'Arcy Dahlberg (he still used that name) returned to New York City. He was admittedly confused about the future and certain of only two things: he still wanted to be a writer, and he did not want to return to Montana. So he struggled to survive in the city, taking odd jobs in the publishing industry as they came along, and even selling automobiles, which he heartily detested. For the first time he began to develop a critique of American capitalism that grew stronger as the Great Depression ravaged the country in the 1930s. Those years were also difficult because D'Arcy, with almost no resources, had married Joran

Birkeland, his college sweetheart from Montana. She too aspired to a career in writing and also had difficulty finding regular employment.

But some good things did come out of those hard years. For one thing, D'Arcy enrolled in classes at Columbia University, hoping to accumulate enough credits to graduate. His research in American literature and history led to his discovery of journals written by some of the early explorers of North America. He was especially interested in stories of the French voyageurs, who were, after all, his mother's ancestors. Excited by these accounts, he looked further and found volumes of folk tales and stories that had been collected by anthropologists. Many of these stories he had heard from his grandfather Isidore, whose death had so troubled him a few years earlier. He even began to write a short story that reflected his sense of loss when Isidore died.[2] This emerging sense of his family's place in history also led him to begin an inquiry into his own immediate heritage. He had not contacted his mother since before he went to England, so he wrote to the tribal agency in Montana for her address. He also asked about his own tribal status and about the annuity checks he had been receiving from the tribe for years. He was only vaguely aware that they represented his share, as an enrolled tribal member, of income from timber royalties and tribal leases.

D'Arcy never finished that short story; instead, he put it aside and began to work on his first full-length manuscript, a novel that he first titled "Dead Grass," then changed to "The Hungry Generations," and finally called "The Surrounded." As is true of many first novels, this one was to a large extent autobiographical. Harold Merriam had encouraged his students to keep a daily journal, and a large portion of the early drafts was drawn from D'Arcy's account of his six months in Paris.[3] The novel's hero, Archilde, is a mixed-blood youth from Montana, educated at an off-reservation boarding school, who has been earning his living in Portland playing the violin. The boy sees no future on the reservation, so he returns home to say a final goodbye to his Indian mother, intending never to return. But before he can leave for good, he becomes implicated in a murder he did not commit. Frightened, he takes his violin and flees to Paris, hoping to study music. Finally realizing that he does not have any exceptional musical talent, he returns to Montana, where he successfully farms the acreage left him by his father. As the story ends, Archilde awaits the arrival of a woman he had fallen in love with in Paris, and presumably they live happily ever after. It was a classic Horatio Alger success story.

For over five years, D'Arcy wrote and rewrote this novel, changing the story line and the title, adding new characters, and submitting it over and

over again to various publishers. Responding to their editorial suggestions, he eventually dropped the entire Paris section and instead developed the story of Archilde's growing appreciation of his mother's culture
and his own involvement in it. Inevitably, the ending changed as Archilde
became further enmeshed in the question of the murder. Gone was the
"happily ever after" conclusion of the earlier draft. Reflecting his deepening awareness of the tragic story of the Native Americans with whom he
increasingly identified, D'Arcy's novel became instead an indictment of
America's attitude toward its indigenous peoples. That theme was reflected in the novel's published title *The Surrounded*.

The name of the novel was not the only thing D'Arcy changed. In 1933,
while registering to vote, and on a seeming impulse, he recorded his name
as D'Arcy McNickle, not D'Arcy Dahlberg. As he later explained to John
Collier, he and Joran were expecting their first child, and he wanted the
child to have its proper name. Antoinette Parenteau McNickle was born
on 2 January 1934.

Critics occasionally have questioned McNickle's motive in changing his
name at that particular time. They suggest that since he was trying to get
the novel published, his claim to an Indian heritage might have been to
his advantage. It is certainly possible that this thought did occur to him.
But it seems more likely that D'Arcy's growing awareness of his mixed
ethnic heritage was giving him a new sense of his own identity. D'Arcy
Dahlberg had been a fiction, while D'Arcy McNickle had legal reality.
While obviously not an Indian name, it was the name by which he was enrolled in the Confederated Salish and Kootenai Tribes, and, as he was discovering, it was a name that gave him a usable past. When *The Surrounded*
was accepted for publication in 1935, it was described as the work of an Indian author.

Not long after publication of *The Surrounded*, McNickle finally obtained
a full-time position on the editorial staff of the Works Progress Administration's recently established Federal Writers Program and, with Joran
and daughter Toni, moved to Washington DC. He soon found common interests with those in the program who were writing about Indian matters
for the state guide series, but he really wanted to work for John Collier,
who recently had been appointed commissioner of the Bureau of Indian
Affairs (BIA). Twice McNickle submitted his application to the Indian Office, and Collier, who had become aware of McNickle's work for the state
guide series, hired him.

Thus began D'Arcy McNickle's education as an anthropologist. His
first assignment as Collier's administrative assistant was to help explain

to various tribes the complexities of Collier's Indian Reorganization Act (IRA). Under this act, tribes were to be given one year to vote on adopting a formal constitution, which would provide the first step in establishing them as recognized political entities within the legal structure of the whites. The IRA was complex however, and such things as constitutions were quite outside the experience of most tribal people. They were understandably suspicious and reluctant to agree to any program the BIA proposed. It was McNickle's task to inform and persuade them.

McNickle soon became part of Collier's inner circle. Collier was a humanist and a man of some vision, although his experience with tribal affairs was limited to Native American groups in the Southwest. McNickle became an increasingly effective writer and speaker, and Collier relied on him to assist in all aspects of Indian reorganization. McNickle also contributed frequently to *Indians at Work,* the BIA's house publication, and he wrote articles and book reviews for outside publications. The more he learned about the administration of Indian affairs, however, the more he was disturbed by one major problem: the Indian Office's historic reluctance to accept the possibility that Native American people could and should govern themselves. Most older tribal members, the traditional leaders of their communities, spoke no English, and they had been deliberately and systematically excluded from positions of leadership. Meanwhile, young people, who had learned English at BIA schools, were not trained as interpreters (the capacity in which they could be immensely useful) or in any other leadership capacity. Someday, McNickle thought, perhaps he would have the opportunity to effectively alter that policy. For the time being he assumed ever-greater responsibility as he worked his way up within the bureaucracy.

One of McNickle's more interesting assignments during World War II resulted from the Indian Office's relatively brief but important role as manager of the largest war relocation center for Japanese-American evacuees, at Poston on the Colorado River in Arizona. Collier saw this project as a rare opportunity to develop a theory of personality development that might, after the war, be useful in administering the Indian reservations. For eighteen months a select group of young anthropologists including Laura Thompson, Dorothea and Alexander Leighton, Clyde Kluckhohn, Edward and Rosamond Spicer, and Ruth Underhill investigated various aspects of communal life as it evolved among the displaced Japanese-Americans at Poston. While most of the BIA's Washington office had moved to Chicago during the war, a skeleton staff, including McNickle, remained in the nation's capital, and he acted as liaison between those conducting the study and the Chicago office.

Also during the war years McNickle became one of a number of people, both in and out of the Indian Office, who began to discuss the possibility of gathering together leaders from various tribes to establish a national organization of some kind. The last such attempt, the Society of American Indians, had disbanded in the 1920s, but the renewed interest in Indian affairs occasioned by Collier's reforms in the 1930s suggested that another attempt might be more successful. Because he traveled a great deal, McNickle was in a position to meet with tribal leaders across the country, and finally, with Collier's encouragement, a group met in Denver in 1944. The group founded the National Congress of American Indians (NCAI), which has continued to be a respected and powerful forum for Native Americans.

Not surprisingly, McNickle's education in anthropology began during his years with the BIA. While he never enrolled in classes, he became an avid reader in the field, and his contact with Indian leaders and young scholars exposed him to the cutting-edge theory and provided him with rigorous training. After the war he began systematic research for his first monograph, a narrative history of Native Americans, which was published in 1949 as *They Came Here First*. This book was soon followed by a long article called "The Indians of North America" for the *Encyclopaedia Britannica*, 16th edition, published in 1952. Drawing on the research he conducted for these two publications, he wrote a fictionalized account of Native Americans in the Southwest for a Young Adult series published by Lippincott. *Runner in the Sun*, with illustrations by Alan Houser, was published in 1954. McNickle's growing expertise was recognized with his appointment in 1949 and 1950 as a fellow of both the American Anthropological Association and the recently formed Society for Applied Anthropology.

By that time, McNickle had become chief of the Branch of Tribal Relations, a major position in the Indian Office. But John Collier had resigned, and most of the people McNickle had worked with earlier had either retired or transferred elsewhere. Congress was taking a more conservative position regarding Indian affairs, even reversing some of what the Indian New Deal had accomplished under Collier, and the few Collier people who remained in the Indian Office were increasingly demoralized. Collier had succeeded in stopping, at least temporarily, the alienation of reservation lands, and had sought to strengthen tribal organizations and tribal autonomy through the Indian Reorganization Act. Successive commissioners, however, centralized the BIA's bureaucratic structure in Washington, which in effect placed the Indians themselves even further than they had been from the decision making process. In addition, Congress initiated a move toward terminating those tribes that were thought to possess sufficient resources for self-government. While McNickle was not opposed in theory to the eventual termination of government support, he knew from experience that no tribes were ready at that time to govern themselves without federal assistance. He feared, and rightly so, the outside interests that were eager to take advantage of so-called self-determination. If termination were to happen, it must not take place until tribal members were sufficiently trained to hold their own against those who would exploit tribal resources for their own gain. He considered the development of an indigenous leadership absolutely necessary in implementing any policy of termination.

Therefore, while still under the aegis of the BIA in 1951 and 1952, McNickle conducted a series of summer workshops as an addendum to the Indian Office's summer teacher training program at the Intermountain Indian School in Brigham City, Utah. He invited a number of tribal leaders and educators to attend several two-week sessions at which they "brainstormed" about contemporary Indian issues. Participants discussed local problems on their own reservations, and in doing so they discovered that other tribes faced the same kinds of problems. McNickle hoped to make them aware, by sharing their problems and exploring other tribes' solutions, that they had the resources and the ability to make significant changes in their own communities. He knew only too well that the tribes shared common concerns in areas of health, education, housing, and jobs, and also realized that the Indians themselves were unaware of how universal those concerns were. Unfortunately, while those who attended the workshops were excited about sharing their experiences, their excitement failed to translate into effective action at home. McNickle had hoped that some tribal leaders, at least, would gain greater self-confidence in identifying and solving local problems, but a two-week workshop with sporadic attendance did not begin to address the real problems. The lack of leadership required to solve problems was endemic, and only a dedicated long-term effort could nurture the kind of leadership that would ensure tribal survival. He would obviously have to explore other avenues of assistance.

The obstacles he faced if he hoped to continue working on this crucial problem within the BIA were extensive. First there was the explicit rejection by Congress of many of Collier's initiatives that might have moved reservations toward independence. The centralization of authority in Washington, while undeniably leading to greater bureaucratic efficiency, in effect reduced the number of opportunities the tribes had to participate in their own governance. If congressional wishes prevailed, terminated tribes would be at the mercy of outside forces waiting to exploit tribal resources. (The experience of the Klamath and Menominee tribes, which were being terminated at that time, showed only too clearly how great was the danger.) Although Congress conceded that some tribes might not survive termination, the Indian Office seemed unable or unwilling to implement a practical plan for developing Native American leadership that might eventually challenge the Indian Office's control. Another problem McNickle faced stemmed from the nature of the Indian Office's funding. Operating as it did on an annual budget passed by Congress, any long-term planning such as McNickle was considering became highly unlikely.

At this point, McNickle began to look outside the federal government for a solution. There was always the possibility that the National Congress of American Indians would support an alternative program. In 1950, the NCAI had established an adjunct organization called American Indian Development (AID), with McNickle as its director. AID's stated purpose was to promote community action; it already had provided a modicum of financial support for the summer workshops. Encouraged by NCAI's willingness to assist, McNickle sought additional funding from private organizations, and by 1952 he had raised thirty thousand dollars—enough, he thought, for a two-year project. Ten thousand dollars of that amount was designated for health education, while the remainder was to be used as needed. He decided to take a one-year leave of absence (or possibly two) from the Indian Office and devote himself to full-time community development.

The concept of community development was relatively new at that time and was quite unknown within the BIA's policy of managing Indian reservations. With termination apparently only a matter of time, however, the need for developing local leadership was obvious. For McNickle, the question was where to begin, because all reservations faced the same problem. He had to find the most desirable location for his project. With the help of AID's board of directors, he developed a list of desirable components for an ideal site. First, he hoped to find a place where a core of potential leaders, who perhaps had some experience with the non-Indian world through military service or attendance at an off-reservation boarding school, would be open to new ideas. Then he looked for a place with some basic medical facilities. Last but not least, he wanted some reasonable access to outside transportation, as he was also involved at that time with two other AID projects.

After an intensive search, McNickle finally decided that Crownpoint, New Mexico, was the place for his project. Crownpoint was just east of the Navajo Reservation, in what was known as the "checkerboard area" because of its ethnically diverse land ownership—part Navajo, part Hispanic, part Anglo, and part federal government. Until the 1930s, Crownpoint had been headquarters for the Eastern Navajo Agency, which had a run-down Indian hospital consisting of sixty beds, and a boarding school with four hundred students. The tribal authorities had more or less neglected the people in the surrounding area since 1935, when the Navajo capital was established at Window Rock, seventy-five miles to the west. Since they didn't live on the reservation, they also felt ignored by the Bureau of Indian Affairs.

There was another reason why McNickle chose Crownpoint. In the 1940s, at Collier's request, he had assisted in the publication of *The Navajo Door*, a seminal book by Alexander and Dorothea Leighton. The authors of this pioneering anthropological study had written about those aspects of the Navajos' culture and their worldview that affected their physical well-being. For instance, even though the Navajos had a well-developed traditional explanation of why disease occurred, their language lacked the vocabulary that might have enabled them to understand modern scientific theories of disease. In their book, the Leightons discussed some of the problems inherent in conveying scientific information to people who had no vocabulary for understanding such material and no interest in acquiring such information.

As an anthropologist, McNickle saw at Crownpoint the possibility of initiating procedures to overcome some of the cultural and linguistic obstacles described in the Leightons' study. With the hospital and school in the area, the potential for effective communication and growth was great; he found several people with the kind of experience in the outside world that he considered essential. One man, John Perry, had attended the Albuquerque Indian School as a boy, had served several terms as a representative of the area on the Navajo Tribal Council, and had worked as chief of the tribal police. Perry was sixty years old when McNickle began working at Crownpoint, and he became the project's translator.

Meanwhile, American Indian Development launched a broad search for someone to direct the health education portion of McNickle's program. After several months and repeated interviews with Viola Pfrommer, McNickle selected her as the new health educator. Pfrommer brought to

Crownpoint extensive experience in the field of health education and hygiene among indigenous peoples. She held a master's degree in public health and a doctorate in education, and since WWII she had worked as a health educator for the American Friends Service Committee in Egypt, Germany, Mexico, and El Salvador. She was willing to accept a considerable reduction in salary to come to Crownpoint because her family did not want her to leave the United States again. She knew very little about the Navajos, however, and McNickle was concerned that the stark landscape and Spartan living conditions at Crownpoint would discourage her. To his relief, she adapted efficiently and with good humor to her new situation. She lived and worked at first in a large house trailer loaned to McNickle by the BIA, until rooms at the local teacherage became available.

McNickle reluctantly accepted the BIA's assistance. He was no longer part of that bureaucracy, and he wanted to separate himself from it in the minds of the local people. He also chose to maintain some physical distance from the local project. The emphasis of community development was to empower the people to make their own decisions, not to "do things" for them. He intended to be available as a kind of catalyst, providing information about resources and options when asked, but he wanted the Navajos to identify their own needs and realize their own capacity in meeting those needs. Boulder, Colorado, was close—but not too close—to Crownpoint. It was also convenient to the Denver airport, which allowed him to maintain contacts with NCAI people and various funding organizations. In 1953, therefore, he moved his family to Boulder.

Viola Pfrommer's role at Crownpoint was more content-oriented than McNickle's and required that she live on-site, yet it also focused on empowering people to help themselves. Pfrommer, who was soon known as "Vi," quickly found that she had an ally in the extraordinary person of Annie Dodge Wauneka, the first woman to be elected to the Navajo Tribal Council (1951), who had recently been appointed chair of the Navajo Tribal Health Committee. Pfrommer and Wauneka made a formidable pair as they confronted the problem of tuberculosis, which was a major cause of death among Navajos on the reservation. As McNickle had anticipated, the problem was as much cultural as medical. The scientific cause of the disease was unknown, its transmission was not understood, and the cure, which included a prolonged stay in a hospital for whites, was often rejected in favor of more traditional healing practices.

McNickle and Pfrommer were not the only ones concerned with combating disease among the Navajos in the 1950s. The Crownpoint project, which began in the summer of 1953, was concerned primarily with public health and hygiene, while a second project, coordinated by a team of medical personnel from Cornell University, focused more on the direct application of medical resources—especially the newly developed antibiotic isoniazid. The Cornell project began in 1955 and was based at Many Farms, Arizona. Because both projects were temporary—McNickle had funding for health education for only two years and the Cornell project for five—they emphasized training Navajo people to apply resources and knowledge without assistance.

Much of what both groups emphasized in this training focused on the cultural differences between traditional healing as practiced by Navajo singers, or medicine men, and the modern scientific world of doctors and hospitals. McNickle and Pfrommer invited Dr. Kurt Deuschle, who was stationed at the Navajo hospital at Fort Defiance, to come to Crownpoint and meet with influential medicine men from the eastern part of the reservation and the checkerboard area. The exchange of information that followed was hailed as the first time that practitioners of traditional Navajo healing methods and modern medical personnel had met as equals and listened constructively to each other. Medicine men who looked through the doctor's microscope at tuberculosis bacilli saw what actually caused the disease, and several of them later asked to get an X-ray.

After Dr. Deuschle's visit, Vi Pfrommer and Annie Wauneka worked with traditional medicine men as their allies rather than their antagonists. Together they organized two major working conferences on tuberculosis, in Gallup in 1954 and in Albuquerque in 1955, that drew sponsors and participants from all over the country. In addition they cooperated with other state and federal health agencies in planning an exhibit that reached more than eleven thousand people at the Gallup Ceremonial and the Navajo Tribal Fair in 1954. Dr. Deuschle and Annie Wauneka both began working with the Cornell group at Many Farms when McNickle's funding for health education ran out. By 1960, when both the Crownpoint project and the Cornell project came to an end, the reservation had experienced a significant drop in tuberculosis-related deaths.

It must be remembered, however, that the health education part of the Crownpoint project was funded for only two years. When that money ran out in 1955, McNickle obtained additional financial support for another five years of community development, primarily from the Schwartzhaupt Foundation of Chicago. He was able to incorporate much of Pfrommer's work into the community development program, and Pfrommer remained very much a part of the project. As always, the emphasis was on empowering the people in the Crownpoint area to deal effectively with their own needs and problems.

As the project began, the most active and influential Crownpoint people had organized themselves into what they called the Navajo Development Committee and, with McNickle as a resource person, met frequently to deal with a number of concerns. Alienation from the tribal government was seen as a major problem, and several times the committee invited tribal officials from Window Rock to visit and to keep them informed. Another area of concern among the people of Crownpoint involved the local school. In addition to the BIA boarding school, which drew students from the entire eastern area, Crownpoint had a public school that was part of the Gallup school system. School officials from Gallup, invited to attend one of the committee's regular meetings, were initially shocked when the Navajos presented them with a list of demands for better service. But the demands were reasonable and the school officials responsive. Such a conference had never before even been considered a possibility.

The most visible accomplishment of the Navajo Development Committee was the building of one structure and the remodeling of another to provide a meeting place and overnight facilities for families who came to visit patients in the hospital and/or children at the boarding school. The committee raised money for supplies, hauled rock for the walls, and furnished the necessary labor. These buildings eventually provided showers, beds, laundry and kitchen facilities, and even movies (for a small fee). Local people managed the entire operation. Crownpoint had had no overnight facilities of any kind for visitors, and the buildings provided a solution to a major community problem. They were also, understandably, a source of considerable pride among the people of Crownpoint.

McNickle had never intended for his project to be permanent; indeed, the whole purpose of it was to work himself out of a job. In late 1960, as he and Pfrommer prepared to withdraw, they tried to assess the results of their efforts, but they were perplexed. For the last eighteen months or so, the project that had begun with such enthusiasm had lost its momentum. This was due partly to dissension within the tribal council at Window Rock, over which the Crownpoint people had little or no control. Young people with modern ideas had been elected to the council, and McNickle believed that they posed a threat to the Navajos' traditional social structure. They were too young to be accorded the respect reserved for tribal elders, and they did not know or value the old traditions. They could not even speak the language properly.

There were local problems, too. John Perry, who served as interpreter for the entire project, became involved in a dispute with relatives over the use of peyote, an issue that divided the tribal council itself. The dispute caused a serious rift within the Navajo Development Committee. Still another pressing problem concerned the selection of a permanent manager for the new community buildings. The issues here revolved around kinship ties and a general distrust of whoever controlled the money. McNickle wrote to Pfrommer on New Year's Eve of his discouragement, and he began to reexamine his basic concept of building local leadership.

The Crownpoint project's original premise was that tribal people who had been deprived of decision making opportunities by the federal government's paternalism could regain the ability to solve their own problems if given time and sufficient information about options and resources. McNickle had hoped that the traditional leadership of elders could become the avenue for effective change. He based the project on the assumption that the way to assure the survival of Native American tribes was to encourage traditional elders to exercise the kind of leadership they once did among their people. But he began to realize that these elders, especially the ones who spoke no English, had lost much of their influence. Younger people were bringing unanticipated changes and were leaving their elders behind.

In the early 1960s the BIA finally began discussing the possibility of training young Native American people for clerical and technical positions, but McNickle was not optimistic about this approach. While Congress had officially abandoned the idea of termination, many congressmen continued to press for opening the reservations to outside development of tribal resources. It seemed to McNickle that training Indians for clerical and technical positions would in effect still keep them away from the actual decision making positions. He insisted that economic development of tribal resources, if it came at all, must come at the direction and under the control of the Indians themselves. In a 1963 letter to John Collier, he wrote that the training the BIA proposed "will come to nothing if the men who sit in the tribal councils and on business committees are required to play the passive role of signing checks and adopting resolutions and are not helped to come to an understanding of the culture in which they are asked to lose themselves."[4] In other words, Indian people must learn enough about business operations to participate as equals in decisions concerning tribal resources.

Fortunately McNickle soon became involved in another approach to the problem that offered greater potential for preparing Indian tribes for self-rule. In 1956, while he was preoccupied with affairs at Crownpoint, a small group of people in Washington, sponsored by the independent (that is, nongovernmental), Council on Indian Affairs, had launched still another summer workshop program. They designed this program for Native American college students, some of whom were like the young people challenging the traditional leadership of tribal elders. The council was disturbed by the alarmingly high dropout rate of Native American college students. Most of them seemed at first glance to be well prepared for college. But a large percentage of the students came from rural areas or reservations; they were not only homesick, but they felt isolated in the larger college communities, where they often faced the additional burden of racial discrimination. One of the early workshop directors diagnosed the students' problem: "Many young Indians, whether of tribal or detribalized background, suffer from anxieties and confusions that the sociologist has attributed to 'marginality': They are unable to see themselves as either Indians or as white people."[5] What could be done to keep these young people in school?

McNickle first became involved with these summer workshops as a consultant and a guest speaker, and after the 1960 workshop, American Indian Development assumed responsibility for the entire operation. McNickle and the workshop staff were continually amazed at how little these students knew about their own tribal histories. Like the young people who were challenging traditional leadership in Window Rock, they no longer spoke the language of their people and knew little of their own culture. At the same time, they were trying to adapt to another culture about which they also knew almost nothing. Their confusion was quite understandable. It seemed to McNickle, tragically, that the very survival of tribal identities was endangered by this lack of self-knowledge, and his concern was reflected in the title of a small book he wrote called *The Indian Tribes of the United States: Ethnic and Cultural Survival,* which was published in 1962.

McNickle and the workshop staff, in an effort to provide the participants with essential information about themselves and the non-Indian world, developed a unique curriculum that was based on an objective comparison of Indian and European cultures. First they provided an overall view of Indian history and culture as it evolved before the European invasion, from both the Indian point of view and from the point of view of the whites. Then they provided a more detailed examination of some of the tribes represented by the various students in the workshop. They discussed mythical stories of tribal origins and compared those stories with the understanding of modern science, not to debunk the myths but to explain how myth and science provided alternative views of creation. They discussed the roots of tribal languages and kinship systems. They compared traditional cultures with contemporary tribal organizations and brought in Native American speakers who were active in tribal politics. They discussed varied concepts of land ownership as held by Indian peoples and by Europeans. Finally, by using McNickle's role-playing scripts, they analyzed the cultural dichotomies that had made the young people feel alienated among their fellow students. In other words, the staff attempted to encourage the students' self-awareness and pride in being Indian, while at the same time familiarize them with the culture in which they found themselves at college.

Reaction to this curriculum was mixed, but most students found these comparisons very enlightening. Some students examined the stereotypes that whites held about Indians and decided that if they were perceived as drunks, then they would drink. Others, however, realized that they were learning about their own history and people for the first time. As McNickle explained when discussing the workshops in his 1963 letter to Collier, "The young students who go through this short course emerge with what must be for most of them a wholly new concept of themselves and the society around them." Then he added, "Some of them get so excited they want to go right out and start a war against all the teachers and administrators they have ever known who all along were telling them that as Indians they were dead."[6] For most participants, the workshops provided information about their world that they sorely needed, and many of them became active leaders in the "Red Power" movement of the late 1960s.

Unfortunately, no attempt was made to follow up on the more than three hundred young men and women who attended the workshops from 1956 through 1967 (McNickle was unable to raise funds for such a study), but their significance might be observed in the participants' later careers. At the tribal, state, and federal level, many of them became educators, administrators, scientists, businesspeople, and artists, often working directly with and for Indian people. They were effective leaders because they were able comfortably to identify themselves as Indian and at the same time to relate constructively to the non-Indian people around them. McNickle had made that very concept the goal of the workshops, and, as he wrote in 1975, "Of the young Indian leaders who have come to national attention in recent years, and who have contributed markedly to the development of their own communities, many came through the workshop.

The thing that made the difference in their lives, I am confident, was the exposure to the social sciences, which provided insights into their own and the general society as well as the analytical tools for analyzing the forces around them."[7]

McNickle was involved with the workshops through the summer of 1967, and by that time other educational opportunities had appeared on the horizon for Native American students. One was the Opportunity Fellowship Program sponsored by the John Hay Whitney Foundation. McNickle served on the Awards Committee for that program from 1957 to 1971, and he recommended a number of promising students for those fellowships. The United Scholarship Services, which evolved from the independent Council on Indian Affairs, was also focusing on Native American students, and the National Indian Scholarship Training Program was in the planning stage. Other programs would soon follow.

While the early 1960s had been frustrating and McNickle was ready to move on to other things, those years had actually been productive. First, as he and Pfrommer withdrew from Crownpoint in December 1960, they began to prepare a lengthy report on the project for the Schwartzhaupt Foundation, which had been so generous in its funding since 1955.[8] Compiling that report took almost three years. McNickle also became involved almost immediately in planning for what became known as the American Indian Chicago Conference (AICC). This conference, which took place in June 1961, has become a watershed event in modern Indian history. It originated as the brainchild of anthropologists at the University of Chicago, who subsequently enlisted the support of the National Congress of American Indians. The stated purpose of the conference was to provide a voice for Indian people in determining a new direction for federal Indian policy. John F. Kennedy had been inaugurated as president the preceding January, and a new commissioner had not yet been appointed. The policy of termination in the 1950s had proven disastrous, and the future for Indian tribes was still unclear. Here was a unique opportunity to express tribal needs and hopes for the future.

The NCAI responded enthusiastically to the idea of gathering tribal representatives and leaders together at this crucial time, and McNickle, as chairman of the planning committee, was assigned the task of drafting a statement to be used as the working basis for the conference. He and his committee developed a number of specific topics, along with a set of questions relating to them, and mailed the material to tribal councils and interested individuals for discussion. The NCAI then followed through by organizing regional meetings to clarify the responses. On the basis of the information thus gathered, McNickle wrote a position paper and submitted it to the conference. With relatively minor changes, this document, "A Declaration of Indian Purpose," became the official report of the conference, and it has had considerable impact on administrative policies since that time.

Students who were enrolled in the 1961 summer workshop attended the Chicago conference as aides to the delegates, and they spent the first week of their six-week program running errands and delivering messages before returning to Boulder for the remainder of the session. For many of them the conference was truly an eye-opener. It reflected a unity and a common purpose among Indian tribes that surprised even those who had organized it. The students were excited and energized by their experience, and they decided to create their own organization to reflect their newfound purpose. Sixteen of them met in Gallup after the workshop, and, building on a small regional youth group already in existence, they founded what became known as the National Indian Youth Council (NIYC), an activist organization that continues to this day. Several years later McNickle served on NIYC's advisory council.

After the Chicago conference, however, McNickle was at a crossroads. Although he received a government pension and a small salary as director of American Indian Development for running the summer workshops and two other small projects in community development, it was his wife's salary that supported his family. His ailing mother had become part of the family in Boulder and he relished the time he could spend with her, but after her death in 1964 he was increasingly frustrated with the lack of focus in his life. He began to work again on a novel that he had begun in the 1930s and he was frequently invited to write articles and book reviews on Indian affairs, but he was looking for employment. He was now over sixty, and jobs did not come easily.

What finally ended this period of uncertainty was something he could not possibly have anticipated. In December 1965 he was totally surprised by the offer of a tenured faculty position, along with an offer to become chairman of the Department of Anthropology, at a new branch campus of the University of Saskatchewan in Canada. He had never before taught a regular college course; he did not have a college degree and had never even considered teaching. But he was assured by his many friends and by the university administration that he was the right person for the department. While he was still considering this offer, he received another surprise, a deeply gratifying one, when he learned that he had been nominated for an honorary doctorate of science from the University of Colorado for his thirty years of commitment to the American Indian, to be awarded at spring commencement. Suddenly he once again had a future.

But it was with some trepidation that he finally agreed to go to Canada for the fall term in 1966. He had signed a contract in the spring of 1965 to write a biography of the Pulitzer Prize–winning author Oliver La Farge, whom he had known for years, and he spent the summer before heading north doing the preliminary research and agonizing in spare moments over how he would teach an introductory course in anthropology. At this time he also terminated his marriage, which had been deteriorating for years.

With the exception of one year, 1968–69, during which he took a leave of absence to complete the La Farge biography, McNickle remained in Canada as promised until 1971, when he reached the mandatory retirement age of sixty-seven. The late 1960s were tumultuous years for colleges and universities on both sides of the border. Many young American men moved to Canada to avoid military service in Vietnam, and campuses in both countries had become alarmingly politicized. McNickle was not about to be drawn into any political battles, however. Instead, he labored to establish a traditional anthropology department with fieldwork among indigenous peoples of North America, and eventually his vision was fully realized, although he did not live to see it happen. The tensions he encountered within the university were extremely stressful and he suffered a heart attack while he was there, so he was more than willing to leave Canada, and academia, in 1971.

Retirement provided some respite. Vi Pfrommer, whom he married in 1969, had earlier bought an old schoolhouse in Albuquerque's North Valley. She had remodeled it into a comfortable home and had lived there for several years before she and D'Arcy married. They later built another house adjacent to hers, but she was never really comfortable in the new place. Her difficulty in making the adjustment may have been due to the onset of Alzheimer's disease, about which little was known at that time. She had gone to Canada with D'Arcy after their wedding, but she was disoriented and mostly confined to their apartment. When McNickle could no longer care for her at home in Albuquerque and when she no longer recognized him, he moved her into a nursing home, where she lived until the summer of 1977.

Fortunately, McNickle was able to continue consulting by phone and writing during that time. The La Farge biography was published in 1971, and by 1975 he had revised and brought up-to-date his other historical works, all of which were once again in print. He had also been asked by the Smithsonian Institution to serve on the editorial board of its proposed multivolume revision of the *Handbook of North American Indians*. His one unfinished project was the novel that he had begun in the 1930s and worked on for years. Now he practically rewrote it, and *Wind from an Enemy Sky* was accepted for publication early in 1977.

By this time, McNickle was recognized as one of a small number of elder statespeople on Indian affairs. Few of the people who had worked in the Collier administration were still living; indeed, he was the only one of NCAI's founders to attend the Chicago conference in 1961. It was not surprising, therefore, that he became the first director of the Center for the History of the American Indian at the Newberry Library in Chicago in 1971. He had helped to write the center's original proposal and to present its prospectus to both the Indian community and to the academic world. Recognition by both constituencies was essential, as the center was to be linked academically to a consortium of the Big Ten universities and the University of Chicago. As Lawrence Towner, director of the Newberry Library, wrote to him in 1973, "Without your help, we would never have gotten funded by the white community, and without your help, we would never have been accepted by either the scholarly or the Indian community."[9]

The primary concern of McNickle and others who established the center was to make the Ayer and Graff collections of Native American materials at the Newberry Library more available for scholars and at the same time to create a new conceptual basis for Indian history, which had until that time been recorded only from the point of view of whites. It was as though Native Americans had had no life prior to the coming of the Europeans—no culture, no history of their own. The staff at the center hoped to reorient the study of Indian history, shifting the focus of the narrative from the perspective of the whites to a description of tribal cultures, traditions, and events that had occurred and developed from within, independent of European/American influence. Using techniques of both anthropology and history (a disciplinary approach now called 'ethnohistory'), the center "hoped to reconstruct the story of Indian people from the Indians' point of view." As McNickle observed at the time, "no people should have to depend on another and possibly hostile party to give its account to the world."[10]

This new approach was obviously a very broad mandate for researchers and teachers, and it would require the full participation of Native American scholars and traditionalists. Access to the Newberry Library, which was essentially a research institution, had previously been limited to predoctoral and postdoctoral scholars, and McNickle knew only too well that very few Native Americans could qualify on that basis. Therefore, as the center's first director, he established fellowships for tribal historians and others, bringing the library's resources within their reach.

He had accepted the position as director, however, only on the condition that it be temporary; a permanent director was to be selected as soon as possible. Robert Bieder and Martin Zanger worked as full-time assistants under McNickle's direction until 1976, when Francis Jennings, the well-known Indian scholar, accepted the appointment to replace him. McNickle kept in close touch with the center by telephone, however, and his contribution to its development was crucial.

In September 1977, McNickle learned that he had been nominated for the Newberry Library's most esteemed position: that of distinguished research fellow. In addition to a small stipend, this fellowship would provide him the opportunity to work on his own research at the center, as well as gratuitous housing in Chicago while doing so. He was eager to accept, if only he could find someone to stay in his house in Albuquerque for extended periods of time. He planned to respond at the center's October board meeting.

However, McNickle never got to that meeting. On Tuesday, October 15, he had a massive heart attack at his home in Albuquerque and apparently died almost instantly. When he failed to arrive at the board meeting in Chicago as scheduled, the Albuquerque police were asked to investigate, and they reported the sad news to the board members. Although McNickle had a history of heart trouble, his death came as a terrible shock to those who always looked forward to his arrival at the meetings. He was buried in Albuquerque, and a large group of friends and admirers gathered later in a light rain for a memorial celebration of his life. The Center for the History of the American Indian continues as an important part of D'Arcy McNickle's legacy, and under the leadership of Francis Jennings and later of Frederick Hoxie it has carried forward D'Arcy McNickle's vision of Native Americans recording their own history. In 1983, when McNickle's daughter donated her father's papers to the Newberry Library, the center was renamed in his honor.

McNickle's legacy, of course, reaches back for more than four decades. The National Congress of American Indians has evolved into a powerful voice concerning all Native American policy matters, and the National Indian Youth Council, whose members have been more activist than McNickle himself, provides a platform for young people who are not content to follow the traditional search for consensus in dealing with contemporary issues and who, instead, are willing to provoke a more direct confrontation with the bureaucracy to arrive at solutions for their problems. Many of those who participated in the leadership training workshops have emerged as leaders in these and other areas as well.

But it may well be that, for most people who are not knowledgeable about Indian affairs, D'Arcy McNickle will remain best known for his writings, especially for his three novels. *The Surrounded* is today probably the most familiar. Although it's a rather somber story and sales were poor, reviews of the book were favorable. Some who read it predicted, with considerable foresight, that it might be the first of a new Indian literature. Oliver La Farge, whose own novel *Laughing Boy* had received the Pulitzer Prize in 1929, wrote in a 1936 review that *The Surrounded* should be added "to the small list of creditable modern novels using the first Americans as theme." But when *The Surrounded* first appeared, the country was still suffering from the Great Depression, and new authors were having a difficult time even getting published. McNickle was very pleased just to see the manuscript in print. The book all but disappeared until the early 1970s, when friends urged him to seek a publisher that might be interesting in reprinting it. Although the University of New Mexico Press decided to take up the option and republish the book, McNickle did not live to see it since the reprint was not released until 1978.

McNickle's second novel, *Runner in the Sun: A Story of Indian Maize*, which was published in 1954, never did attract the attention of adult readers, perhaps because it was published as one of a series marketed for "young adults." This novel was unique in that it was the first one written by a Native American author to depict imaginatively what Indian life was like before the arrival of the European explorers. The setting is the prehistoric Southwest, where a young boy named Salt is approaching manhood. In a classic vision quest, Salt embarks on a long journey to the south, surviving various life-threatening challenges, to bring a new ceremony and a new strain of corn to his people. Allan Houser, the Apache artist who has since achieved worldwide recognition as a painter and sculptor, was teaching at the Intermountain Indian School in the early 1950s when McNickle held his summer workshops there, and McNickle asked him to illustrate this novel.

Like his first novel, *The Surrounded*, McNickle's third one, *Wind from an Enemy Sky*, was set in the Northwest, in a place that resembled the reservation area where McNickle had lived as a child. This was the story that he started in the 1930s and revised periodically until he practically rewrote it in the early 1970s. Once again the hero is a young boy, Antoine, who has returned from an off-reservation boarding school to find his people's land threatened by a new dam that was built by a well-meaning but insensitive government bureaucracy. Antoine is more an observer in this story than an actor, but he represents the future, and the future is grim. His people's hopes and fears focus on a lost medicine bundle; they believe that recovery of the bundle will assure their survival. Although the local Indian agent and the engineer who built the dam are sympathetic and attempt to retrieve the bundle, it has been destroyed by indifference and neglect. When the engineer offers Antoine's people a gold statuette from some Central American tribe instead of the medicine bundle, the gulf between the Indians and the dominant culture becomes painfully obvious, and the final tragedy appears inevitable.

McNickle carried on an extensive correspondence with the publisher while preparing this book for the press. As was his intent with *The Surrounded*, he wanted to tell a gripping story but also hoped that discerning readers might see beyond the story to a more universal message. Despite good intentions, the Indians and the whites were unable to communicate. All were limited in their understanding by their own thoughts, language, and cultural values. Although he had worked on it for years, this book, too, was published after McNickle's death.

McNickle, of course, did not limit his writing to novels. He wrote a number of short stories that have been edited by Birgit Hans and published as *The Hawk Is Hungry* (1992). These stories, not all of which were complete, provide occasional glimpses of McNickle's humor, which is seldom seen in his other work. He also wrote dozens of articles and book reviews.

McNickle's only attempt at biography was his volume about Oliver La Farge, titled *Indian Man* and published in 1971. La Farge, who died in 1963, was a contemporary of John Collier and had headed the Association on American Indian Affairs in the 1940s and 1950s. McNickle, who was never really close to him, agreed to write the biography because it provided him with an opportunity to write about Indian affairs in those crucial decades. Although the biography was nominated for a National Book Award, reviewers for the most part were not enthusiastic about it, and it was the least successful of all McNickle's monographs.

Although he also wrote several narrative histories about Native Americans, the only one still in print at this time is *Native American Tribalism: Indian Survivals and Renewals*, which was revised and updated in 1973 from *The Indian Tribes of the United States: Ethnic and Cultural Survival*. McNickle's revisions of the earlier work are especially significant, as he wrote them and a new preface in response to the troubles at Wounded

Knee and to the American Indian Movement's occupation of Alcatraz Island in San Francisco Bay. This book is often used today as a text in Native American history classes.

Finally, D'Arcy McNickle's legacy lives on institutionally. The library on the Salish Kootenai College campus, located on the Flathead Reservation in Pablo, Montana, carries his name, as does the noted D'Arcy McNickle Center at the Newberry Library in Chicago. Historians throughout the world are examining the pre-Columbian story of Native Americans with new insight because of the work of those who have had access to the material at the D'Arcy McNickle Center. Although McNickle was self-taught, he became an expert in anthropology and was, eventually, a brilliant, wise, and compassionate elder statesperson, whose concern for tribal autonomy reached out to many people, young and old, Indian and non-Indian, across the country.

Works by D'Arcy McNickle

Fiction: Novels and Anthologies

1936. *The Surrounded* (New York: Dodd, Mead). Reprint, with an afterword by Lawrence W. Towner, Albuquerque: University of New Mexico Press, 1978.

1954. *Runner in the Sun: A Story of Indian Maize* (New York: Holt, Rinehart, and Winston). Reprint, with an afterword by Alfonso Ortiz, Albuquerque: University of New Mexico Press, 1987.

1978. *Wind from an Enemy Sky* (New York: Harper & Row). Reprint, with a foreword by Louis Owens, Albuquerque: University of New Mexico Press, 1988.

1992. *'The Hawk Is Hungry': An Annotated Anthology of D'Arcy McNickle's Short Fiction*, edited by Birgit Hans (Tucson: University of Arizona Press).

Book-length Non-fiction

1949. *They Came Here First: The Epic of the American Indian*, The Peoples of America Series (Philadelphia: J. B. Lippincott). Rev. ed. New York: Harper & Row, 1975.

1959. With Harold E. Fey, *Indians and Other Americans: Two Ways of Life Meet* (New York: Harper & Brothers). Rev. ed. New York: Harper & Row, 1970.

1962. *The Indian Tribes of the United States: Ethnic and Cultural Survival* (London: Oxford University Press). Revised and updated as *Native American Tribalism: Indian Survivals and Renewals* (London: Oxford University Press, 1973).

1971. *Indian Man: A Biography of Oliver La Farge* (Bloomington: Indiana University Press).

1973. *Native American Tribalism: Indian Survivals and Renewals* (London: Oxford University Press). Reprint, edited by Peter Iverson, Albuquerque: University of New Mexico Press, 1993.

NOTES

1. The Flathead Tribe was one of several that were united as the Salish/Kootenay Consolidated Tribe by the Stevens Treaty at Hell Gate in 1855.

2. D'Arcy McNickle, "En roulant ma boule, roulant . . . ," in *The Hawk Is Hungry and Other Stories,* edited by Birgit Hans (University of Arizona Press, 1992), 13–24.

3. McNickle's papers, including many of his diaries, now are located at the D'Arcy McNickle Center for the History of the American Indian at the Newberry Library in Chicago.

4. McNickle to John Collier. Reel 57, Collier Papers, Zimmerman Library, University of New Mexico.

5. Rosalie H. Wax, "A Brief History and Analysis of the Workshops on American Indian Affairs Conducted for American Indian College Students, 1956–1960, Together with a Study of Current Attitudes and Activities of Those Students," October 1961, 3, Workshops on American Indian Affairs, box 74, series 17, NCAI records, Smithsonian Archives, Washington DC.

6. McNickle to John Collier, 12 January 1963. Reel 57, Collier Papers.

7. McNickle to Dr. Frederick Wacker, 1 February 1975. General Correspondence, McNickle Papers, Newberry Library, Chicago.

8. "Dine Txah: A Community Experience" is a 250-page report of the Crownpoint project, now located in the McNickle Papers.

9. Lawrence Towner to McNickle, 1 August 1973, CHAI Correspondence, McNickle Papers.

10. McNickle to Matt P. Lowman II, 1 February 1971. CHAI Correspondence, McNickle Papers.

LaDonna Harris

Comanche

BY GARY C. ANDERSON

John F. Kennedy's summons to do "what you can do for your country" began a new age of activism in America that dominated the period from 1965 to 1975. This age would bring the development of many federal programs designed to uplift the poor. Federal area-redevelopment grants funded job training, while Volunteers in Service to America (VISTA) recruited young people to teach leadership and provide educational instruction. This new age of activism also revealed the startling problems faced by American Indians, the poorest of the poor in America. They had the highest unemployment rate in the land and a plethora of health care needs. While Americans had discovered poverty among the rural poor of Appalachia and among African Americans in the inner city, Indians supposedly were cared for by the Bureau of Indian Affairs. Many Americans believed that Indians had no need for the opportunities and benefits provided under the expanding War on Poverty.

A young Comanche woman from Walters, Oklahoma, LaDonna Harris stepped into this new age of activism quite unexpectedly in the fall of 1964. Her husband, Fred, recently had defeated Bud Wilkinson, the almost mythical ex-football coach of the Oklahoma Sooners, in a special election for a seat in the U.S. Senate. Little in LaDonna's background would lead anyone to believe that she would play a role in the new Great Society envisioned by Kennedy's successor, Lyndon Johnson.[1] Yet LaDonna Harris soon brushed shoulders with the elite of the new liberal cause and began a program of Indian revitalization in Oklahoma that epitomized the Great Society.

To say that LaDonna Harris lacked the experience necessary to participate in public affairs would be an understatement. She was born on 15 February 1931 near Lawton, to a white man, William Crawford, and his Comanche wife Lilly Tabbytite. The Great Depression had devastated western Oklahoma, and the family had little money. Conditions improved by the 1940s, but very little thought was given to entering college, especially by a young Comanche woman. Yet while enrolled in high school at Walters, a small community south of Lawton, LaDonna met the young Fred Harris, who had dreams of moving beyond the small two-room house in which he had been born. Fred enrolled in the University of Oklahoma in the fall of 1948, and LaDonna, his sweetheart, followed him to Norman. The following spring, on 8 April 1949, the two were married amid what must have been some uncertainty regarding their future.

The newlyweds had little money to put toward education and both of them took jobs. Fortunately, Fred landed a position as a printer at the local newspaper, a job that gave him flexible hours. At first LaDonna could only baby-sit for returning veterans who had children and some money provided by the GI Bill. The financial situation tightened even further when the Harrises had their first child, Kathryn, born in January 1950. Sometime later, LaDonna found a more permanent position at the university library, helping her husband pay his tuition and finish school. As LaDonna later pointed out, the Harris marriage was "a partnership in the fullest sense." From the very start, LaDonna "played an active role in all of her husband's endeavors."[2] She even continued to help support the family after Fred decided to go to law school. He passed the bar in 1954 and the family returned to Lawton where Fred practiced law.

The Harrises entered politics two years later, and Fred was elected to the Oklahoma state senate. Commuting the roughly ninety miles from Lawton energized the young lawyer as he promoted a liberal agenda. Fred authored the Harris Act in 1958, which created the Oklahoma Human Rights Commission. This organization prohibited discrimination in state employment and opened jobs, especially to people of color, including American Indians. LaDonna spent much of her time in Lawton, tending to two new children: Byron, born in 1958, and Laura, born three years later. Yet she did find time to volunteer at the local museum, which specialized in depicting the history of American Indians, and she also joined the Lawton Community Action Board.

After Fred was named "Outstanding Young Man of Oklahoma" by the state's Junior Chamber of Commerce, he decided to enter the U.S. Senate race left open by the death of Robert Kerr. The campaign was grueling, for no one in Oklahoma had better name recognition than Bud Wilkinson. Even so, the state was still dominated by the Democratic Party and Harris had considerable energy. LaDonna campaigned at his side, often standing on a flatbed truck, cradling her three-year-old as she listened quietly to

speech after speech. In an unusual display, she made no effort to disguise
her Indian heritage, carrying her daughter in an Indian blanket. Fred's
surprising victory landed the family in Washington DC, where they found
a house in McLean, Virginia, around the corner from another rising political star, Robert F. Kennedy.

Despite the incredible differences in background, the Kennedys and the
Harrises soon became close friends. Kennedy's friendship may have been
simple altruism, yet he too had political goals that involved building
bridges into the south and the west. Soon the Harris children were common visitors at the Kennedy swimming pool, and Ethel and Bob introduced LaDonna and Fred to other relatives and political friends. These
included Eunice Kennedy Shriver, the wife of Sargeant Shriver, then head
of the Office of Economic Opportunity (OEO), the main engine of the
national War on Poverty. The Harrises also met Stuart Udall, the secretary
of the interior, head of the agency that oversaw the Bureau of Indian Affairs. Udall's wife, Lee, became LaDonna's close friend. Other liberals in
Washington who frequented their circle included the Humphreys and the
Mondales. LaDonna would later travel with Joan Mondale, visiting Indian
reservations in Minnesota.[3]

All of these politicians and politicians' wives had common views on
many issues. They all supported civil rights, but they believed that the federal government should work beyond the passage of simple legislation
that guaranteed equal access to facilities and jobs. The main problem, as
these men and women saw it, was the need to prepare the poor and members of minority groups for jobs through training and education, and to
change the attitudes that had led to racism. This could be initiated with
the children of the poor, who needed a "head start" in education. Young
people also needed direction in order to keep them in school. This could
be accomplished by leadership training. Older men and women required
work orientation in order to train them for the job market. Finally, many
minorities simply needed instruction on what programs were available
for them. The liberal challenge included finding ways to activate the local
community so that it would organize itself to fight poverty, unemployment, and despair.

By spring 1965, LaDonna Harris had decided, with strong support from
her husband, that she would join this crusade.[4] After talking with friends
back in Oklahoma, she called for a general meeting to be held at the
University of Oklahoma campus that summer that would attempt to organize a grassroots, statewide community action group, with a special focus
on helping American Indians. This idea probably came from Sargeant

Shriver, who pioneered the Community Action Board concept. Several members of the university faculty expressed an interest in the meeting, including William Carmack, who was then director of the Southwest Center for Human Relations, an organization housed in the Continuing Education branch of the university, and Chester Pierce, a physician at ou's medical school. Other participants included administrators of the Bureau of Indian Affairs (BIA), including Leslie Towle, area director at Anadarko.

The first serious discussions of the problems to be addressed occurred at Norman on 14 June 1965. Robert Jones, the new state director of Economic Opportunity was the first speaker. He spoke vaguely about economic opportunity, stressing the need to involve many people. At this point, Towle joined the discussion. He explained that people, particularly American Indians, knew little about the programs that were available. If community action were to work, it would have to find out "what is needed, raise standards, and change attitudes." He also believed that Indians needed to develop pride in themselves. Dr. Pierce, who spoke next, argued that certainly the BIA had more experience in these matters than most of the people at the meeting, but noted that Congress, through its legislation, had emphasized the need to involve more citizens, not just government agencies. He initiated a motion to create the Oklahoma Committee for Indian Opportunity. The motion passed and LaDonna Harris, after a vote, became the first chair.[5]

After gaining encouragement from this group, Harris used her husband's office to send out a large mailing, urging friends and supporters around the state to attend a formal organizational meeting to be held on 7 August 1965.[6] The letter stressed five issues; she recruited various "experts" from the community to speak on them at the next meeting. Harris secured Virginia Harrington and Earl Pierce to speak on housing. Harrington was area director for the BIA in Muskogee, while Pierce was a local attorney. Robert Stanley, a BIA official from Anadarko, and Arthur Thomas would discuss job opportunities, and Overtone Jones, governor of the Chickasaw Nation, would address health issues. Towle would speak on education. The fifth issue, which addressed finance, credit, small business loans, and so on, fell to several area bankers.[7] While capable people, most represented "the establishment," a trend that would continue as the organization grew.

The gathering attracted over five hundred people and by all accounts was a huge success. Senator Harris had asked his colleague, Senator Joseph Montoya of New Mexico, to address the crowd. Montoya stressed that the Indian population of Oklahoma and New Mexico shared many of the same problems. These included unemployment, poverty, lack of education, and inadequate health care. Separate sessions then considered all of these issues. The discussions included a host of people, including many Indian tribal leaders. In the final hours the participants agreed to form Oklahomans for Indian Opportunity (OIO), selecting LaDonna Harris as its president. Fred Harris quickly moved to incorporate the group, filing the papers in Washington in September.[8]

While OIO promptly received much attention in the media, it lacked a headquarters, a staff, and even stationery. These pressing needs were alleviated in September 1965 when John B. O'Hara, director of the Southwest Center for Human Relations at the University of Oklahoma, extended an invitation to house the organization.[9] He offered clerical assistance and suggested that the foundation should have a large board of directors (the final number arrived at was forty one) and a streamlined executive board of directors, which would make most of the decisions. LaDonna Harris would serve as president of the executive board. O'Hara even offered to appoint her to the permanent board of the Center for Human Relations. He then suggested that OIO seek a one hundred thousand dollar grant to survey socioeconomic conditions among Indians in Oklahoma. If community action were to occur, information would be needed about the educational level of Indian people, their life expectancy, and their employment. After some thought, Harris agreed, and OIO assumed an academic or research function, while at the same time attempting to organize community action on the local level.[10]

As the organization took shape, the need for action became increasingly obvious to all involved. Letters poured into Senator Harris's office in Washington from people in Oklahoma who either wanted to help or who saw the need for change. Like many other tribal leaders across the state, William McIntosh, chairman of the Creek Nation, concluded that LaDonna was "a great Lady doing a great work," and offered his assistance.[11] Leslie Towle, of the BIA, seemed convinced that with the patronage of the Harrises, the foundation could become the "rallying point" for people who wished to change the state.[12] Other writers, including secondary school teacher Edith Waswo, saw a tremendous need for changing attitudes about race. "My heart ached when one Indian boy, age seven, came in from recess crying because someone had called him an Indian," she wrote. "I replied, 'you are an Indian and you have every right to be proud." Waswo had no idea how to bring change, but she knew it was necessary.[13]

Even so, there were skeptics, particularly since the composition of the group was decidedly Democratic in its political orientation. Seneca-Cay-uga Doris Spicer wrote in a rather terse fashion that while her tribal council had voted to become involved with OIO, it also listed three immediate improvements that it wanted: sanitation for tribal ceremonial grounds, road improvements, and tribal housing.[14] In other words, talk had occurred in the past and at least some who watched OIO take shape assumed that this organization would be no different than others. Harris graciously thanked every writer and gave whatever hope she could to the skeptics.

Difficult problems certainly did exist among Indian tribes in Oklahoma. Both the BIA and many state agencies acknowledged their severity. Leslie Towle, the area director at Anadarko, had earlier (1964) published a short piece entitled "Poverty and the Oklahoma Indian" in which he pointed out that most Indians attended school only through the fifth or sixth grade, making employment very difficult. Housing often consisted of a simple tar-papered shack. The average income for Oklahoma Indians was roughly fifteen hundred dollars a year in comparison to over three thousand dollars a year for whites. Coupled with widespread alcoholism, the picture was quite grim.[15]

In contrast, the BIA had repeatedly prided itself on the high quality of its boarding schools. A report on the school at Fort Sill written in 1965, however, found that even when Indians obtained some education, the process itself was often harmful. At Fort Sill only sixty of the three hundred students attending the school were from Oklahoma, and those who came from out-of-state became so despondent at times that the move literally threatened their mental health. When these students returned to their homes, they often had little sense of belonging and little sense of commitment to their community.[16]

Such articles and reports hardly offered the kind of definitive information necessary to launch a war on Indian poverty, yet by the fall of 1965 the OIO was eager to begin such an effort. Just a few days after Harris had visited with the staff at the Southwest Center, Director O'Hara wrote a detailed letter to Dr. Warren Cardwell, the director of the Indian Section at the Office of Economic Opportunity. O'Hara had heard that Arizona State University, the University of Nevada, and the University of Utah, among others, had recently signed contracts with the OEO to administer large sums of money earmarked for Indian tribes under Title II of the OEO's mandated program. Definitive guidelines for the expenditure of this money had not yet been developed, other than to "improve conditions" on reservations. O'Hara wanted information on how the Southwest Center might apply for these funds to assist Indians in Oklahoma.[17]

Cardwell's reply was quite unexpected. He pointed out that Congress had appropriated these funds for Indians who were "members of communities." These included the federal Indian reservation communities. The universities that O'Hara had mentioned had contracts to provide "technical assistance and related training" for these reservations. Since Oklahoma had no reservations, Director Cardwell concluded, "the above-mentioned arrangement would not be applicable to the situation in your state."[18] Such logic dumbfounded O'Hara, who realized that Oklahoma's Indians might easily fall into a bureaucratic crack, unable to access funds designated for Indians, and probably ineligible to qualify for assistance grants that had been established for the poor in the inner city. O'Hara also astutely recognized that Director Cardwell had little comprehension of whom he was dealing with. O'Hara quickly wrote Senator Harris, asking that he intercede with the head of OEO, Sargeant Shriver, for if OIO could not get money designated for Indians under OEO, how could it qualify for other funds?[19]

It took approximately a month for Director Cardwell to reinterpret OEO's guidelines. He received added information for making this decision from William Carmack, who had once been the director of the Southwest Center. Carmack had joined Harris's staff in Washington only to move quickly over to the BIA, becoming an assistant commissioner. Carmack met with OEO officials, carrying with him blank applications prepared by OIO to be filled out by tribal councils. The applications indicated that the tribal councils would sanction OIO to act in their behalf "to begin necessary studies at the earliest possible time to identify the areas of poverty, social & economic."[20] In actuality, Carmack convinced OEO officials to allow OIO to apply directly for funds under the state Equal Opportunity Agency.

The grant application that emerged from these discussions was produced by an OIO subcommittee. Donald R. Sullivan, deputy director of the Oklahoma City Urban Renewal Authority, chaired the group, which also included academics Clayton Feaver, Joe Exendine, and John O'Hara. Towle brought the expertise of the BIA to the group. Lois Gatchell and Iola Taylor were added to the committee as representatives of OIO. Gatchell directed a community action group in Tulsa, while Taylor, a young woman from Lawton who was related to LaDonna Harris, currently was serving as assistant director of OIO. Taylor would soon be named state director and play a leading role in the implementation of OIO programs.[21]

The application received what must have been one of the quickest favorable reviews of any proposal in history. News that OIO would be funded reached the group in time for its meeting on 22 April 1966. Details still remained sketchy, but OEO had designated $240,733 for Oklahomans for Indian Opportunity.[22]

The grant obviously invigorated OIO. Meanwhile, membership in the organization had grown over the winter, with over five hundred people paying the small sum of one dollar to join. Others had contributed much more, providing funds for the creation of a staff that tried to redistribute resources to needy people. Referral offices were established in Oklahoma City and Tulsa, which by this time were seeing several hundred Indian people each month. The referral centers helped Indian people apply for aid, when possible, or simply handed out clothes and food when needed. Occasionally, the referral centers helped individuals obtain employment. Yet these were small efforts, aimed at helping urban Indians. With grant money, many more options suddenly appeared. But the organization still lacked a sense of direction. As Harris told the board that summer, "What is OIO?" Community action was still being defined, especially for American Indians.[23]

Harris and her colleagues argued this question throughout the spring of 1966. Obviously, the ability to acquire future grants hinged to some extent on the success of the initial one. The proposal itself had claimed that its goal was to "provide the opportunity for attitude change and leadership training for Oklahoma Indians, who will in turn be agents for change in their own community."[24] By June a decision had been made to fund an extensive leadership program. Harris introduced the program in a speech in Tahlequah: "Training on the OU campus . . . for up to three local representatives from each Indian community across the state . . . will prepare the participants to return to their people, and with the help of an OIO field agent, a specially prepared manual, films, and slides, train other Indians."[25] The first group of participants reached campus on 9 July 1966.

The training of field representatives was heavily influenced by Earl Boyd Pierce, who was general counsel for Manpower Development in Oklahoma. Pierce earlier had launched a special project to help "hardcore" unemployed Cherokees who "by reason of their inability to speak and understand English," required considerable attention. Pierce recommended the employment of at least fifteen such field representatives to work with the Cherokees alone. He felt that these individuals should be Indian, as they would be more effective. Pierce, however, was at a loss to give suggestions on what needed to be done in western Oklahoma.[26]

While such an idea had appeal, Harris decided to discuss the next step in OIO's evolution with various tribal leaders. Eight such meetings occurred around the state in July at which the OIO staff, which now included three people, were introduced and the leadership program explained. The meetings were well attended. Meanwhile, the first leadership training sessions began with seventy-five Indians between the ages of sixteen and twenty-one participating. Flushed with the success of these early efforts, the OIO staff decided to host an awards banquet at the University of Oklahoma later that fall. The banquet, sponsored and funded by OIO, would bring young Indians to the campus to receive awards and to listen to various speakers.[27]

In addition, Harris sought more assistance for the organization in Washington. Daphine Shear of the Democratic State Central Committee previously had investigated the possibility of "getting a Kennedy for Oklahoma." Shear was looking for someone to speak to the Oklahoma Association for Retarded Children's fund-raising dinner—an event that had obvious political overtones.[28] Since Harris had become a good friend of Eunice Kennedy Shriver, who had a long-standing interest in retarded children, she asked Shriver to speak at the banquet. Eunice accepted, and on 16 and 17 September, she spent two days with LaDonna, meeting various politicians and traveling about the state. At Shriver's request and with the assistance of OIO, she visited several Head Start programs that had recently been organized for Indian children. These programs, as well as others designed to help teach English to nonspeakers, were funded by OEO, her husband's agency.[29]

While demonstrating the need for the Head Start program to Eunice Shriver may have been unnecessary, Harris persuasively argued that Indians in Oklahoma needed help as much as those on reservations. She had used the same tactics on yet another dignitary who spent several days in the state in early May. Dr. Chester M. Pierce, of the University of Oklahoma Medical Center, had informed LaDonna of the visit of Joseph English, a psychiatrist and friend, who also happened to be deputy assistant director for Health Affairs at the OEO. English received a royal tour, attending OIO meetings in Anadarko and Cordell in western Oklahoma and then traveling by private plane across the state to Tahlequah. "I can think of few groups in the country more deserving of help [than the American Indian]," he wrote in his letter of thanks upon returning to Washington.[30]

But the best opportunity to display the success of OIO and its work with Indians came in the fall, at the organization's annual banquet, slated for October 9–15. LaDonna hoped to convince Stuart Udall to speak at the gathering. Unfortunately he had another engagement. In his place, John C. Gardner, secretary of Health, Education and Welfare, accepted. In her letter of invitation, LaDonna stressed at least one lofty goal of oio: "To draw Oklahoma Indians outside their own problems so that they may become part of the solution to larger national and world problems." The conference attracted over eight hundred Indians, who attended youth opportunity forums and work orientation sessions. Scholarships were given to outstanding Indian students, and various individuals from the community also received plaques for volunteer work.[31]

Clearly Harris took considerable pride in her ability to organize such events. It confirmed in her a growing realization that women in American had a role to play in public service. By the summer of 1966 that role had reached a point where she could meet only a small portion of the requests that poured into Senator Harris's office. Church groups, cultural societies, and professional organizations, often located in states other than Oklahoma, were now inviting her to come speak to them. One such engagement that LaDonna readily accepted came from the Women's Forum Program in Lawton, where in late October she gave a speech titled "A Woman's Responsibility—from Lawton to Washington DC." While some critics suggested that oio was designed to enhance the political career of Oklahoma's junior senator, LaDonna increasingly saw the organization as one that would hopefully end the isolation associated with being Indian in Oklahoma and present new opportunity to Indian people in a world dominated by the non-Indian majority.[32]

As the oio became more successful, the organization's staff, led by Director Iola Taylor, a close friend of LaDonna, administered the agency on a daily basis. Taylor established a screening committee composed of individuals loyal to Harris or herself, to assist in the hiring of agency personnel."[33] The senior staff included a field coordinator for community development, a position that served the entire state. Other positions (some Indian, some white) included field coordinators for youth activity and for work orientation. Six regional field representatives were also hired, as were directors for the two referral centers in Tulsa and Oklahoma City. The regional coordinators were Indians, who generally came from the regions that they served. Non-Indians filled other slots, including the field coordinator for community development a position held by Donald Wilkerson, who resigned from a similar position at Arizona State University to serve with oio.[34] The dozen or so staff personnel were well paid, but much was also expected of them.

This staff collected data, provided information, and implemented programs. While Harris continued to do much to promote the agency, especially in Washington, the staff published annual reports and other literature that explained the role of the agency. A major contribution was the completion of a survey in Blaine County in eastern Oklahoma, which provided clear information on the extent of Cherokee poverty and lack of education. One case showed that of 177 Cherokee students attending public school since 1960, only 4 had graduated. Cherokee people over the age of eighteen had a median of five and one-half years of education. And all Cherokees in 1967 possessed the same level of education that they had in 1930. Many could not read or write, especially in English.[35] Such information filled OIO brochures and was often offered to newspapers for publication.

To combat the poor academic performance of Indian students, OIO field representatives organized regional gatherings. Beach parties, swimming parties, and dances were used to convince students to stay in school.[36] OIO targeted sixty schools that contained many Indian students and organized youth councils, which met regularly. Top students were selected to tutor others. Essay contests were created in which Indian students won prize money, usually twenty-five dollars. By May 1967 over sixteen hundred Indian youths were participating in the program. In some locations OIO staffed these programs with VISTA volunteers. The programs attracted so much attention that community leaders, many of them Indian, supported these activities with additional funds.[37] Other approaches to keeping Indians in school included personal letters from Harris to young Indian students, congratulating them on their success and urging them to stay in high school and graduate.[38]

While youth activities seemed to produce an immediate success, raising the economic level of Indians in the state proved more challenging. In most cases, local community action committees offered the best solutions for this problem, enlisting employers to hire Indians and give them training. OIO tried to institutionalize such piecemeal approaches by developing pilot training programs. The first began at Anadarko in the spring of 1967. The agency subsidized the wages of twenty trainees, who worked for thirteen weeks in a job. The trainee received instruction in budgeting money, employer-employee relations, and dress. After the thirteen-week period, the employer had no obligation to extend the employment of the trainee. Similar programs emerged in Shawnee, where fifteen trainees were working by the summer 1967. Additional programs later were implemented in Tulsa.[39] Usually the success or failure of the training depended upon the individual. Statistics relative to the success of the programs seem never to have been compiled.

With so many programs under way, OIO began attracting national attention, helped in part by LaDonna's efforts in Washington. By spring 1967 the Harris and the Kennedy families had become close friends, so when LaDonna asked Senator Robert Kennedy to speak at an OIO meeting, he readily agreed. For his part, Kennedy had become genuinely interested in the plight of Indian people and envisioned a trip to Oklahoma, in part, as a fact-finding mission. Iola Taylor paved the way for the Kennedy visit by sending him a detailed description of the agency and its efforts. It was, she wrote, "a statewide agency," designed to "break down the continuing isolation of Indians." But, more importantly, OIO believed in "the interaction between Indians and non-Indians" and that such interaction should be "mutually meaningful, comfortable, and worthwhile in school, churches, homes, and communities." This philosophy was clearly modeled after the growing arguments regarding African-American integration. Kennedy, who was scheduled to speak at the University of Oklahoma on 13 March, would have an audience of over eight hundred Indian students, each of whom would be allowed to bring a non-Indian friend.[40]

Kennedy's arrival in Oklahoma created quite a stir. Senator Harris's office was deluged with requests for tickets to attend the speech, especially from Democratic supporters. Most were turned down. The talk went off as planned. University president George Lynn Cross opened the evening by introducing Senator Fred Harris. With dry wit, Cross recalled the young Harris, a poorly dressed freshman in 1949. Then he mused as to how useful it would be for a university president to know ahead of time which students would go to serve in the state legislature or the U.S. Senate. "After 23 years of experience," Cross concluded, turning with a smile toward Harris, "you can't rule anyone out."[41] Harris laughed, then introduced the speaker: Robert Kennedy.

Kennedy's opening line, "I'd like to be an Indian," stirred the crowd. While conceding that such a chance had passed him by, the senator went on to address many issues important to both the national War on Poverty and the status of Indians and other minority groups. Kennedy stressed the importance of Indian pride. "Minority groups have to decide that they are not going to accept roles others have put them in." He noted of non-Indians, "you know that you can always ask: when did you arrive?" Then the senator stressed education, housing, jobs, and even life expectancy. He asked why the United States was spending "Seventy-five billion dollars for defense and two billion dollars to eliminate poverty." Finally, turning to his friend LaDonna Harris, he smiled and quipped: "When I watch the next western movie on TV, I won't know whether to root for the cowboys or the Indians."[42]

The Kennedy speech was soon followed by an article in *Look Magazine*, which gave LaDonna national exposure. The *Look* article, titled "Warpaint for the Senator's Wife," stressed the incredible poverty of American Indian populations and the failure of the BIA. It also gave LaDonna a chance to showcase the work done by OIO, which was only two years old and already garnering considerable attention. The *Look* piece pronounced OIO to be "the model for a national effort."[43] The pronouncement was not all that exaggerated. Indeed, when Bruce Rosen, director of education for the Anti-Defamation League of B'nai B'rith, toured Oklahoma and surveyed the impact of OIO, he concluded that it was one of the best run community action programs in the country. Rosen also praised Iola Taylor, its director, commenting, "Frankly, I think the woman is an administrator of the first rank."[44]

Despite Rosen's comments, not everyone in Oklahoma was pleased with either the agency or Taylor's leadership. Within weeks after the Kennedy visit a crisis evolved within the agency over its goals and its leadership. The problem initially seemed to involve Taylor's role as director. She had continually evaluated the work of the field representatives, at times removing them from their positions. A typical case involved the firing of Mary McCormick, a field representative to the Seminole Tribe. McCormick, Taylor complained, had failed to submit monthly reports on time and had meddled in tribal affairs, making several Seminole elders unhappy. It also turned out that she was an enrolled member of the Sac and Fox Tribe, rather than the Seminole Tribe. McCormick countered by charging that Taylor had been rude with her and had failed to provide her with adequate support to do her job. In this case, with the tribe supporting Taylor, the appeal failed.[45] Other firings brought charges and countercharges.

The problems ultimately reached the board of directors, which met on 8 July 1967. In the days preceding the meeting, it became clear that the entire board of forty-one would likely vote to dismiss Taylor. Fearing a general vote, Harris opted to select an all-Indian subcommittee to address Taylor's role. In the meantime Taylor offered her resignation. In the session that followed on 16 July, the subcommittee allowed evidence to be presented that both supported and criticized Taylor's efforts. The charges seemed to suggest that Taylor had been too demanding of certain field representatives and, in particular, had challenged or at least threatened established tribal representatives. It was obvious that Taylor attracted extremely loyal support from some people and did not get on well with others. Her strongest critics seemed to reside in eastern Oklahoma, several coming from the Tulsa Community Action Board.[46]

While the subcommittee decided to delay acting on Iola Taylor's tenure, several interesting questions emerged during the investigation that revealed the evolving political nature of OIO. Maynard Ungerman, the chairman of the subcommittee, concluded that the entire episode represented "the anticipated conflict between OIO and the tribal organizations." Clearly, several established tribal leaders had become jealous of the success of OIO.[47] Yet another interesting dialogue occurred between Harris and one of her staunch supporters, Lois Gatchell, from the Tulsa Community Action Committee. Gatchell had just returned from Colorado where she had several meetings with Indians. To her utter surprise, she watched as Indian college students voiced their "tenacious desire" to "retain their Indianness." These young people were "clutching for group identity, and in some instances blamed government and the missionaries for destroying their languages and other vestiges of their culture." Gatchell wondered if OIO, with its integrationist philosophy, had somehow missed something and if the criticism voiced against the agency might be coming from the very youth that it hoped to assist.[48]

Leon Ginsberg, a professor of social work at the University of Oklahoma, and another close friend to Fred and LaDonna Harris, sensed some of the same problems. While he had worked from the beginning to make OIO successful, he now wondered if he could continue with the agency. He wrote LaDonna that the entire investigation was tied to the fact that certain elements within OIO now opposed its success. These people remained unimpressed with the "progress" reported and they "seem angry about the success which pleases us." While the opposition masked their true feelings, Ginsberg felt that they definitely disliked Taylor and "they have many misgivings . . . about some of the professor-types, such as me."[49]

Harris responded to the crisis by convincing the subcommittee to correct whatever deficiencies were perceived to exist. The solution that ultimately emerged reassigned some responsibilities, taking them away from Taylor and distributing them among committees formed from the board of directors. Most important, a new committee, the Personnel Committee, was established. It was empowered to hire and fire field representatives. Other committees were formed to provide advice on youth activities and work orientation.[50] These actions satisfied many critics and the controversy slowly dissipated. Taylor remained director.

Harris's presence in Oklahoma had helped rectify the administrative problems within OIO. Yet by summer 1967 she was increasingly drawn into the web of opportunities that developed in Washington. The bond between the Harris and Kennedy families had grown, and it had important political implications. Robert Kennedy called on LaDonna to assist him in hearings regarding future funding for OEO. The war in Vietnam was now consuming considerable government money, and Congress needed to be convinced of the value of OEO. LaDonna Harris, now well known as an Indian advocate and supporter of such funding, was the perfect witness.

LaDonna testified in front of a House committee on 13 July 1967. She emphasized that OEO stood for "self-reliance." Then she mentioned many examples of how the money provided under the program was being used to help the poor in Oklahoma. In Altus, Upward Bound had made strides in convincing young people to go to college. In McCloud, the Neighborhood Youth Corp had rescued "a beautiful young Indian high school girl" from a host of problems and convinced her to enter college. Legal Services and Head Start programs had helped many people across the state. In Idabel, a small, predominantly Indian community in the southeastern corner of the state, Head Start had been initiated by a single VISTA volunteer and "one box of crayons."

After surveying these general programs, Harris turned to OIO. She pointed out to Congress that the organization had been funded by OEO money and administered by the University of Oklahoma to help Indians help themselves. It sponsored Indian leadership training, work study, and youth development programs for high school students. It also administered job training and referral centers. All of these programs were essential to "help Oklahoma Indians acquire the self-confidence, motivation, and skill to become active, productive members of the total community." And, Harris pointed out, Congress should not abolish such programs, for even with their improvements, Indian people still ranked among the very poorest of the poor when it came to health care, housing, jobs, and education. As she left the House hearing room, congressional representative Carl Albert from Oklahoma handed her a bouquet of roses. In the bouquet was a note from OEO's director, which read: "To the best witness of all— whose beauty and brains have made the House a home . . . for the poor." It was signed simply "Sarge."[51]

During the following fall LaDonna became heavily involved with a host of new activities, most of which focused on the national War on Poverty. Shriver placed her on the Women's National Advisory Committee on Poverty, and the Equal Employment Opportunity Commission sought her advice on Indian unemployment.[52] And in November, she was asked to join the Joint Commission on Mental Health of Children, a commission with a budget of over three hundred thousand dollars that had been assigned the task of examining the state of children in the country. Harris would help write the report on the state of minority children.[53] Given all of these new responsibilities, Harris resigned her position as president of OIO in February 1968, leaving the agency to Iola Taylor's care.[54]

Harris's resignation was motivated primarily by her decision to focus on national issues. Late in 1967 she and her husband had convinced President Lyndon Johnson to create the National Council for Indian Opportunity, and during the summer of 1968 Johnson's administration had established such an agency. Unfortunately, however, after Richard Nixon was elected president the council collapsed, since Vice President Spiro Agnew, the designated chairman of the organization, refused to call any meetings.[55] In response, during June 1970, LaDonna formed Americans for Indian Opportunity (AIO), a national organization whose design was based on the model of OIO, but whose goals were much broader. M. Scott Momaday, Ada Deer, Peterson Zah, and other well-known Indian advocates joined her on the board of directors. Since the Nixon administration cut funding to OEO the following year, AIO sought financial support from private foundations.[56]

As the nation struggled with Vietnam and then Watergate, community action programs fell increasingly under the direction of local organizations. A few became tied to various state bureaucracies, some fell under the control of tribal bureaucracies, and others disappeared. Oklahomans for Indian Opportunity, a legacy of the War on Poverty, continued to serve Indian people in the 1990s but it is less active today than during the 1960s. Yet the agency remains as an excellent example of successful Indian activism. Obviously much of this success was due to its leadership. There is no question that many young Indians in Oklahoma were inspired to continue with their education because of the work that the agency began. And many other Indians received assistance with legal issues and job orientation.

For Fred and LaDonna Harris, OIO served a twofold purpose. It provided an outlet for the Harris's to help people they knew needed help. Dedicated liberals in an age of liberalism, they both took advantage of the opportunity to do something good. As LaDonna later said, "No good cause is hopeless." Second, OIO served as a catalyst for political activism. Many people who assisted Fred Harris in his various campaigns worked at times for OIO. And in 1968, when Fred decided to run for the presidency, LaDonna took her organizational skills to the national level, assisting with his campaign.

By the 1970s, LaDonna was spending much of her time in fund-raising activities for AIO. Although she considered fund-raising "one of the worst things I have ever done in my life," she was effective and AIO flourished. Supported by her board of directors, LaDonna used her influence to assist in the establishment of the Council of Energy Resource Tribes (CERT), and in promoting a better relationship between the tribes and the federal government. Meanwhile, in 1976, Fred launched another bid for the Democratic presidential nomination, and LaDonna campaigned hard for him in New England. Lacking adequate financial support, the campaign floundered, and Fred decided to retire from politics. The Harris family moved to Albuquerque, where Fred accepted a teaching position at the University of New Mexico. AIO also relocated to Albuquerque, and LaDonna continued to lead the organization.[57]

Yet LaDonna's participation in personal campaigns for the presidency had not ended. Nationally well known for her leadership on social issues, and recognized for her outspoken support of environmental causes, LaDonna was nominated in 1980 by the Citizens' Party as their candidate for the vice presidency of the United States. Although neither LaDonna nor her running mate, Barry Commoner, believed they had any chance of being elected, they hoped that their candidacy would spark the formation of a political party that eventually would be able to challenge the two-party system. They raised important issues, but had difficulty getting on the ballot in many states, and in the end were soundly defeated.[58]

The unsuccessful campaign was a portent for the Harris's marriage. During the 1970s both Fred and LaDonna had become heavily involved with their careers, and after the formation of AIO LaDonna found that she was forced to spend considerable time away for her husband and family. Their "partnership in marriage," in which LaDonna had taken such pride, became strained, and in 1980 the couple divorced. They still remain amicable, but they have separate lives.[59]

Following her divorce, both LaDonna and the administrative offices of AIO moved back to Washington, where they remained for a decade. In 1990 LaDonna returned to New Mexico and relocated the offices of AIO at Santa Anna Pueblo. Meanwhile, the scope of AIO's activities expanded. During the 1980s AIO addressed a series of environmental issues and assisted the tribes in establishing a "government to government" relationship with the Environmental Protection Agency. The organization also attempted to educate government officials about the advantages of providing federal funding directly to the tribes, rather than through the Bureau of Indian Affairs. Funded by the Kellogg Foundation, the AIO in 1993 initiated the Ambassador's Program, in which talented young Native American professionals participate in an intensive one-year program "aimed at rekindling and reinforcing the use of their tribal values in a modern context." Each participant is required to design and implement a community-based project that develops their leadership and benefits their communities. The participants are chosen by a panel of regional and national Native American leaders, and the program is administered by Harris and two Native American academics.[60]

LaDonna Harris's legacy continues. Oklahomans for Indian Opportunity remains, and while some critics in the state of Oklahoma described LaDonna's efforts as self-serving, such an argument has little credibility. In retrospect, the community action exemplified by oio was good for Oklahoma, and many of oio's programs are still functioning in one form or the other across the Sooner state.

Americans for Indian Opportunity also continues. Under Harris's leadership, aio still fosters Indian leadership and devises strategies to enable tribal governments to deal more effectively with the federal bureaucracy. LaDonna Harris continues to use skills she acquired during her experiences in Oklahoma and Washington to help Indian people across the United States help themselves. In LaDonna's own words, "We Comanches believe everyone has medicine, and it everyone's responsibility to help everyone else cultivate their strengths and their medicine."[61]

NOTES

1. LaDonna's Indian heritage is well documented by the family. Her great-grandfather was taken captive as a boy in south Texas or north Mexico in the 1850s. While likely Mexican, the boy became culturally Comanche. He married a Comanche woman, and they became the parents of LaDonna's grandmother, Wick-kie Tabbytite, who helped raise her. See Interview, *Washington Post*, 22 April 1965; interview with Iola Taylor, *Lawton Constitution-Morning Press*, 15 May 1966.

2. LaDonna Harris biographical sketch, Harris Papers, box 365, Carl Albert Center, University of Oklahoma; interview, *New York World Telegram and Sun*, 8 January 1965; interview, *Wichita Eagle*, 20 May 1965.

3. There are many letters and clippings demonstrating these relationships in the Harris Papers. See, for example, boxes 363 and 364. LaDonna's ties to the Udalls developed rapidly after she helped them with the All-Indian Arts Festival in March 1965 at the Department of Interior. LaDonna's grandmother, Wick-kie Tabbytite, attended the affair. See *Tulsa Tribune*, 27 March 1965 and *Washington Post*, 22 April 1965.

4. In a telling interview, LaDonna addressed her role in Washington, comparing it to what she had tried to do in Lawton in earlier years. She said that women should consider arts and crafts, community relations, international affairs, public affairs,

home life, and the social services all to be meaningful roles. But she wished to concentrate on public affairs, concluding that a woman in Washington could accomplish much simply by being "a good listener" and by "having a meaningful conversation with the persons around her." See *Lawton Constitution and Morning Press,* 9 October 1966.

5. Noted on Meeting of 14 June 1965, Harris Papers.

6. Harris draft of letter for organization, 1 July 1965, Harris Papers; Articles of Incorporation, OIO, 10 December 1965, OIO, Harris Papers.

7. "List" of individual speakers, 28 June 1965, Harris Papers; Letter of invitation, 1 July 1965, Harris Papers.

8. Notes of the 7 August 1965 meeting and Articles of Incorporation, September–December, 1965, Harris Papers.

9. The Center was created in 1961 to provide "study, analysis, and resolution of human conflict and tension." It organized workshops, seminars, and conferences. The Executive Committee included Director O'Hara, J. Clayton Feavers (Philosophy), Arrell Gibson (History), Richard Hilbert (chairman, Sociology), Chester Pierce (Psychiatry) and Glenn Snider (Education). O'Hara would resign in 1967 to be replaced by Lonnie H. Wagstaff.

10. O'Hara to LaDonna Harris, 16 September 1965, Harris Papers. The relationship with the Southwest Center is likely a result of some lobbying by William Carmack, who had been its previous director and had been offered a job in Washington on Fred Harris's staff. Secretary Udall recruited Carmack to be an assistant director for the BIA a few months later; nevertheless, Carmack maintained an interest in OIO and for years helped it and LaDonna on many occasions. Senator Harris's initial contact with the Southwest Center apparently came in June 1965 when he addressed its faculty members. This was followed by LaDonna's appearance in November 1965 when the final arrangements were made to incorporate OIO. See John B. O'Hara to LaDonna, 16 September 1965; Glenn Snider to Senator Harris, 21 September 1965; and LaDonna itinerary, November 1965, all in Harris Papers.

11. McIntosh to LaDonna Harris, 7 July 1965, Harris Papers.

12. Leslie Towle to Senator Fred Harris, 27 August 1965, Harris Papers.

13. Edith Waswo to LaDonna Harris, 10 August 1965, Harris Papers.

14. Doris Spicer (secretary-treasurer of Seneca-Cayuga) to LaDonna Harris, 4 August 1965, Harris Papers.

15. Towle, "Poverty and the Oklahoma Indian," *Sooner Magazine,* July–August 1964.

16. Dr. Daniel M. A. Freeman, "Emotional Problems in Oklahoma Indians—Problems of Adolescents and Young Adults," unpublished report in Harris Papers.

17. O'Hara to Cardwell, 23 November 1965, Harris Papers.

18. Cardwell to O'Hara, 6 December 1965, Harris Papers.

19. O'Hara to Senator Fred Harris, 29 December 1965, Harris Papers.

20. [January 1966] notes on meeting of Carmack with OEO, Harris Papers; notes on OIO board meeting, 29 January 1966.

21. The Committee met for the first time on 19 March 1966 at the Southwest Center on the Norman campus. See Sullivan memo to Committee, 14 March 1966, Harris Papers. Harold Camaron had served as director of OIO, being replaced by Taylor in the latter part of 1966. Taylor still heads the foundation, which is headquartered in Norman, Oklahoma.

22. The grant was part of a $585,596 grant authorized for training purposes in the state. Titled "Multi-Purpose Training Center Proposal," it would be administered by the Southwest Center for Human Relations. See Minutes, OIO Board Meetings, 22 April and 15 July 1966, Harris Papers.

23. The referral centers and their development are discussed in a variety of documents in the Harris Papers, as well as in several newspaper articles, including the *Oklahoma Journal*, 28 December 1966. See also Harold Cameron to Stuart Udall, 30 August 1966, Harris Papers. OIO had also attempted to survey Indian populations in Oklahoma by sending out questionnaires. Little success had resulted by summer 1966. See Lois Gatchell to LaDonna Harris, 18 February 1966, Harris Papers.

24. 1966 Grant Proposal to OEO, Harris Papers.

25. Harris Address, *Pictorial Press* (Tahlequah), 16 June 1966.

26. Earl Pierce to Honorable Glenn M. Zech, 31 May 1966, Harris Papers.

27. Harold L. Cameron to Stuart Udall, 30 August 1966, Harris Papers; Minutes, OIO Board Meeting, 15 July 1966, Harris Papers.

28. Daphine Shear to LaDonna Harris, 10 March 1966, Harris Papers.

29. Senator Harris had a role in organizing this trip. He had begun to help Sargent Shriver distribute books printed by OEO, titled *The Mentally Retarded*, all across the state. He also had inquired regarding federal funding that was available through OEO for the study of mental health problems. Senator Harris learned that Oklahoma was one of ten states that had yet to apply for any of these funds. See Senator Harris to Sargent Shriver, 1 March 1966, Harris Memo, 25 February 1966; and Norman Brawley to Robert G. Sanders, 31 August 1966, Harris Papers. One of the schools that Eunice Shriver visited in McCloud, Oklahoma, had sixty students, 80 percent of whom were Kickapoos.

30. LaDonna Harris to Chester Pierce, 13 May 1966, and Joseph T. English to LaDonna Harris, 27 May 1966, Harris Papers.

31. OIO Annual Meeting, October 9–15, 1966; Towle to Stuart Udall, 23 August 1966; and LaDonna Harris to John W. Gardner, 28 September1966, Harris Papers.

32. Mrs. Kinley McClure to LaDonna, 17 October 1966, Harris Papers.

33. Iola Taylor to Harris, 6 December 1966, Harris Papers.

34. OIO Annual Report, 30 June 1967, Harris Papers.

35. Jim Stewart to LaDonna Harris, 24 January 1967, Harris Papers.

36. See OIO "Youth Letter," 11 August 1967, Harris Papers.

37. OIO Annual Report, 30 June 1967, Harris Papers. In Hulbert, Oklahoma, Reverend Scott Bread, a Cherokee, financed youth activities to such an extent that the VISTA volunteers who worked with him asked if it were not possible for OIO to pay some compensation. See Iola Taylor to LaDonna Harris, 8 September 1967, Harris Papers. Eleven VISTA volunteers, trained in Arizona, reached Oklahoma in March 1967. They were placed directly under the "sponsorship" of OIO. See L. Mayland Parker to Senator Harris, 28 February 1967, Harris Papers.

38. Other agencies, not directed by OIO, also helped promote education, sometimes inadvertently. Charles Cooper, editor of the *Pryor Daily Times*, wrote La Donna that all of the seniors in the Salina High graduating class had finished, for the first time that anyone could ever remember. And that they were able to do so because they had received part-time jobs through the Neighborhood Youth Corp, an OEO program. See Cooper to Harris, April 1967, Harris Papers.

39. OIO Annual Report, 30 June 1967, Harris Papers.

40. Taylor to Kennedy, 3 January 1967, Harris Papers.

41. David W. Levy, "The Wit of George Lynn Cross," Sooner Magazine 15 (winter 1995): 25–26.

42. *Oklahoma City Times*, 14 March 1967.

43. See *Look Magazine*, 4 April 1967.

44. Some critics did go public. In commenting on the surveys conducted by OIO, editor Richard Jones, in *Tulsa World*, 1 August 1967, concluded: "If we were a self-supporting Oklahoma Indian with clean kids and a good neighborhood reputation, we'd tell the interviewers to go back to the teepee and cook dog." See also Rosen to Senator Fred Harris, 12 July 1967, Harris Papers.

45. William C. Waantland to James Wahpepah, 15 December 1967, Mary McCormick to James Wahpepah, 7 November 1967 and Effie G. Kivett to LaDonna Harris, 8 November 1967, Harris Papers.

46. Maynard I. Ungerman to Senator Harris, 18 July 1967, and Lois Gatchell to LaDonna Harris, 10 July 1967, Harris Papers. Ungerman was selected to head the subcommittee primarily because of his loyalty to the Harrises. He also was chairman of the Tulsa County Democratic Committee.

47. Ungerman noted an interesting comparison in his report, given the fact that it was still 1967. He wrote Senator Harris: "I think you may recall sometime when we were joking about 'red power' that we did discuss the possibility that OIO sooner or later would through its projects threaten the status-quo relationship that the tribal chiefs have with the various tribes." Ungerman to Senator Harris, 18 July 1967, Harris Papers.

48. Gatchell to LaDonna Harris, 18 July 1967, Harris Papers.

49. Ginsberg to LaDonna Harris, 25 July 1967, Harris Papers. Some evidence sug-

gests that this crisis was causing political problems for Senator Harris. See Mrs. Othol Patton to Senator Harris, 24 July 1967, Harris Papers.

50. Neal McCaleb's Recommendations, 24 July 1967, and LaDonna Harris to H. L. McCracken, 7 August 1967, Harris Papers.

51. *Tulsa World*, 14 July 1967; *Congressional Record*, 13 July 1967, in Harris Papers.

52. See OEO Women's National Advisory Committee on Poverty, and Vincente T. Ximenses to LaDonna Harris, 17 November 1967, Harris Papers.

53. This report would become extremely controversial, since it concluded that the greatest harm for minority children was "racism," something that the majority of the commissioners rejected. See the discussion in the Harris Papers.

54. LaDonna Harris to Walter H. Richter, 6 February 1968, Harris Papers.

55. LaDonna severely criticized Agnew for his actions, and was quoted extensively in a newspaper article titled "Agnew Better Watch out for Those Comanches," *Washington Daily News,* 4 August 1970.

56. Iola Taylor would come to Washington to head up AIO in 1970, leaving OIO. The Oklahoma agency fell under the leadership of James Wahpepah, who had been responsible for organizing a Head Start program for the Kickapoo Tribe. Taylor would marry William Hayden in 1970, one of her field representatives, and she would shortly thereafter return to Oklahoma and work again for the agency. She currently serves as director of OIO.

57. LaDonna Harris, *LaDonna Harris: A Comanche Life* (Lincoln: University of Nebraska Press, 2000), 99–100, 109–10.

58. *LaDonna Harris,* 110–12.

59. *LaDonna Harris,* 109–13.

60. *LaDonna Harris,* 117–25.

61. *LaDonna Harris,* 116.

Russell Means

Lakota

BY RAYMOND WILSON

Russell Means has been a leading activist of Native American reform for over three decades. Means, reflecting on his role, recalls: "I hope to be remembered as a fighter and as a patriot who never feared controversy—and not just for Indians. When I fight for my people's rights, when I stand up for our treaties, when I protest government lies and illegal seizures and unlawful acts, I defend all Americans, even the bigoted and misguided."[1] As one of the leaders of the American Indian Movement (AIM), an Indian organization established in Minneapolis, Minnesota, in 1968 to protect urban Indians from police harassment and brutality, Means participated in many Indian demonstrations that brought attention not only to the demands and needs of Native Americans, but also to himself as a controversial Indian advocate of reform who did not hesitate to employ violence to seek change. The use of militant activities, however, sometimes hurt the overall objectives of these demonstrations, unfortunately drawing attention to the violent acts rather than to the major issues of contention.

On 10 November 1939, Russell Charles Means was born at Pine Ridge Indian Reservation in South Dakota. He was the eldest of four boys (Dace and twins named Bill and Ted) born to Walter "Hank" Means, a mixed-blood Oglala, and Theodora Louise Feather Means, a full-blood Yankton. Means was especially proud of his maternal ancestors who fought against federal Indian policies and who instructed him in the traditions of his people. Although Means fondly remembers his parents, he acknowledges that his father had a major drinking problem, a problem that Means inherited, and that his mother was a strict disciplinarian who dispensed physical punishment. Yet in spite of their difficulties, they loved their children and did not want them to endure the deplorable conditions of reservation life and the horrific Indian boarding schools, which both

Hank and Theodora had attended. They wanted their children to have op-portunities that reservation life could not give them. Consequently in 1942, the Means family moved to Vallejo, California, where Hank found work as a welder at Mare Island Navy Shipyard.[2]

Means received most of his education in public schools in California, and graduated from San Leandro High School in 1958. As an Indian stu-dent, he faced racial discrimination but managed to make decent grades and to enjoy athletics. However, during his high school years, Means be-came a problem student and a juvenile delinquent, getting into fights, drinking, and taking and selling drugs.

After graduation, Means drifted aimlessly for several years, held vari-ous jobs such as working as a ballroom dancer, a janitor, an accountant, and a rodeo hand, and married his first of four wives in 1961. He attended several colleges and business schools but never received a degree. Means continued to engage in criminal activities that included disorderly con-duct and drunkenness, street scams and petty crimes, and finally assault with a deadly weapon.[3]

Means's activities during these years were not unlike those of other downtrodden individuals coming of age in the 1960s. Such people had few opportunities, faced racial discrimination, and often fell in with the wrong crowd. Fortunately the 1960s was a decade that witnessed minority groups and others increasingly questioning American ways and demand-ing economic, political, and social justice. They no longer would passively accept the dominant society's disparaging treatment. Means finally found some direction and purpose in life and became a major activist represent-ing Indian people.

In 1964, Means participated in his first demonstration—the initial and unsuccessful attempt to claim the abandoned federal prison on Alcatraz Island. Means's father, who supported the Indian movement, invited his son to join him in the occupation. The Indian demonstrators believed they had the right to take federal surplus property under a provision of the Fort Laramie Treaty of 1868. Although the occupation was short-lived, Means expressed pride in his father's involvement and in the reawakening of his own personal feelings of Indianness.[4] Indeed, by the end of the 1960s, Means had become an avid supporter and future leader of AIM. He later declared: "No longer would I be content to 'work within the system.' Never again would I seek personal approval from white society on white terms. . . . I would get in the white man's face until he gave me and my people our just due."[5]

After the unsuccessful occupation of Alcatraz Island, Means continued to move from job to job and attend several schools. In 1967 he worked briefly for the Community Action Program of the Office of Economic Opportunity on the Rosebud Reservation in South Dakota, where he designed personnel and financial reporting systems. His superior fired him for drinking on the job, a charge he successfully fought. After being rehired, Means quit. In 1968, he, his second wife, and two children took advantage of the Indian relocation program and moved to Cleveland, Ohio. The Bureau of Indian Affairs (BIA), whose management of Indian policies Means severely criticizes, directed the relocation of reservation Indians to urban areas like Cleveland in an attempt to "improve" their living conditions. Too often, Indians were not ready for such an abrupt change of environment and were not properly assisted by the BIA in securing housing and employment.

In Cleveland, Means helped establish the Cleveland American Indian Center and became its executive director in 1970. As director, he helped relocated Indians secure credit, food, and unemployment assistance. In addition, Means organized a campaign to convince the Cleveland Indians baseball team to abandon their mascot, Chief Wahoo, a racist stereotype of a Native American. Even though the campaign failed, Means's activities on behalf of Indian people, especially those as an active demonstrator, brought him praise from both Indians and non-Indians.

In December 1969, Means attended an urban Indian conference in San Francisco. At this meeting, AIM leaders such as Dennis Banks, a Chippewa who helped found the organization, were impressed with Means's speaking abilities and wanted him to join their organization. Although Means initially had little interest in AIM, he became more familiar with its sense of duty and goals at a subsequent meeting in Detroit, and joined the organization in 1970. Within six months, Means established a local chapter of AIM in Cleveland, calling it CLAIM.[6]

Indian activism and militancy increased in the 1970s as Indians and other groups protested poor conditions both on and off the reservations, and demanded fair and just treatment. Means and AIM participated in a number of important demonstrations during the decade, all of which attracted national attention to Indian matters and drew support from many white liberals.[7] Among obstructive tactics employed were "fish-ins," which protested violations of Indian fishing rights, and temporary occupations of public offices and buildings. During the summer of 1970 and in June 1971, Means demonstrated with other AIM members at Mount Rushmore, calling attention to the illegal seizure of the sacred Black Hills from the Lakotas in the 1870s. And on Thanksgiving Day, 1970, Means and other Indians boarded the *Mayflower II* in Plymouth, Massachusetts, to protest the way white settlers had mistreated Indians. These demonstrations focused on Indian demands for redress of past grievances, increased Means's stature as an Indian spokesperson, and attracted media coverage.[8] Consequently, Means and other AIM leaders, especially Banks, continued to develop strategies to deal with government officials, police, other activists, and the media.

Means took pride in his efforts to help Indian people. In addition he continued to explore his own Indian identity by participating in a Sun Dance held at Pine Ridge Reservation in August 1971. Yet he questioned the sincerity of some of the other Indian participants, and expressed regrets about the ways in which the modern Sun Dance had been "reduced to a mere shadow of what it had once been" by the federal government. Nevertheless, Means performed his ritual duties faithfully, and ultimately recognized the important balance between females and males. In fact, tribal elders praised him for his superior performance. Means later observed, "I was learning and experiencing being an Indian. That's what was important to me."[9]

From 1972 to 1974, Means and AIM continued their efforts to help Indian people, both on and off reservations. Means and AIM almost went their separate ways, however, in January 1972 because of a misunderstanding concerning an alleged statement Means made in a *Newsweek* article about his suit against the Cleveland Indians baseball team. According to the article, Means had criticized the Chippewas, calling them "hang-around-the-fort Indians." The Chippewas, who were traditional enemies of the Sioux, were outraged. Means declared he was misquoted and blamed whites for once again causing divisions among Indian tribes. He submitted his resignation from AIM because he was sickened by the lack of support he received from some Chippewas. AIM refused to accept his resignation.[10]

One month later, Means was involved in AIM's first major intervention into a reservation incident that concerned the death of Raymond Yellow Thunder, a fifty-one-year-old Oglala Lakota from Pine Ridge Indian Reservation who was killed by white men in nearby Gordon, Nebraska. In reservation border towns like Gordon, Indians had a long history of mistreatment, so the death of an Indian did not usually receive proper investigation. Yellow Thunder's body was discovered in a truck on a used car lot on 20 February 1972; the local coroner's report indicated that he died from exposure and head injuries. Relatives of Yellow Thunder suspected foul play and demanded justice. Because they were unsuccessful in their efforts to find out more details about his death from local Gordon authorities, the BIA, and federal officials, they requested help from AIM. Means and other AIM members accepted the invitation to go to Gordon to investigate what happened to Yellow Thunder.

Testimony regarding his death later revealed that Yellow Thunder had been beaten and humiliated by four whites who had been drinking and who wanted to "bust an Indian." Part of the humiliation included stripping Yellow Thunder from the waist down and forcing him into the local American Legion Club dance. The perpetrators later boasted about the incident.

Following the assault, Yellow Thunder reported the incident to law officials, then slept for several hours at the local jail. An Indian friend saw him in the truck at the car lot on the day after the beating and talked to Yellow Thunder about the incident. The friend saw him again in the truck a few days later and thought he was just sleeping, when in fact he was dead. Apparently, Yellow Thunder died sometime after talking to his friend.

The white perpetrators were charged with manslaughter and false imprisonment, and were released on low bail. Infuriated by these decisions, several hundred Indian demonstrators, led by AIM, converged on Gordon, Nebraska, demanding that the case be reviewed. In addition, they wanted the town of Gordon to stop its blatant discrimination against Indians in such areas as education, employment, housing, and medical care. National coverage of this event helped AIM achieve some of its objectives. Gordon officials agreed to form a board to study the complaints and to exhume Yellow Thunder's body for reexamination. Means and AIM came away from the incident with an enhanced reputation among some reservation Indians.[11] Indeed, during the demonstration, Means's statement, "We've come here to Gordon today to secure justice for American Indians and to put Gordon on the map . . . and if justice is not immediately forthcoming, we'll be back to take Gordon off the map," instilled pride among the Pine Ridge residents.[12]

Following the events at Gordon, Means and other AIM members held a series of "red ribbon grand jury" hearings at Pine Ridge and other Sioux reservations in South Dakota, where Indian residents vented their frustrations regarding reservation conditions and other matters. For example, Indians complained that the white owners of the Wounded Knee Trading Post and Museum at Pine Ridge grossly exploited Indian customers. In addition, it was alleged that one of the owners had physically accosted a young Indian boy, which later resulted in Indians entering the store, threatening the owners, and causing damages. This incident is significant because Dick Wilson, the newly elected tribal chairman at Pine Ridge, denounced AIM's involvement and vowed not to allow them to hold meetings on the reservation again.[13] The stage was now set for Means's subsequent challenge to Wilson's leadership as well as AIM's occupation of Wounded Knee in 1973.

AIM's cause also was inadvertently strengthened in September 1972, when Richard Oakes, a Mohawk who had led the 1969 occupation of Alcatraz, was shot and killed by a white man in San Francisco. The assailant claimed that he had killed Oakes in self-defense, and he was charged only with involuntary manslaughter and released on bail. Outraged, Oakes's Indian friends claimed that he had been unarmed and murdered.[14]

While these events occurred in South Dakota and in California, Means and other Indian activists were planning the Trail of Broken Treaties. Spurred on by incidents such as the deaths of Yellow Thunder and Oakes, Indian activists prepared for a cross-country caravan that would start at several locations on the west coast, pick up supporters as it traveled east, and arrive in Washington in the fall, during the final days of the 1972 presidential election. Means and other activists believed that Indian demonstrations in the capital would generate considerable media coverage, cause the public to become more aware of the government's treaty failings, and attract the attention of both President Richard Nixon and his challenger, Senator George McGovern.

Means was in charge of the Seattle caravan. Other Indian activists directing the operation were Robert Burnette, former Rosebud Sioux tribal chairman, and Hank Adams, an Assiniboine-Sioux and president of the Survival of American Indians Association. The caravans arrived in the Minneapolis-St. Paul area in late October, where AIM leaders compiled a list of twenty points to improve relations between the United States and Indian people. Included among the points were demands to review treaty violations, increase Indian sovereignty, and abolish the BIA.

On 1 November 1972, Indian caravans began to arrive in the nation's capital. Unfortunately, lodging for approximately one thousand protestors had not been properly arranged. Many of the demonstrators ended up staying in the rat-infested basement of St. Stephen's Episcopal Church. The next day, Means and others marched over to the BIA building to protest. Confrontations ensued, and the demonstrators spontaneously seized and occupied the facility, renaming it the Native American Embassy.

The Nixon administration hoped to avoid excessive violence and decided to negotiate with the protestors. Means, Banks, Adams, Burnette, and the Bellecourt brothers, Vernon and Clyde, who were Chippewa AIM leaders, played key roles in conferring with federal officials. As usual, Means was a main spokesperson and met frequently with the media. In addition he helped secure the building and made plans, if it became necessary, to make sure that all the Indian occupants could exit the premises if they were attacked and the building set afire.

Such extreme action became unnecessary after federal negotiators finally agreed to study Indian grievances, respond to the Twenty Points, grant the occupiers limited amnesty, and provide monetary assistance ($66,500) to help Indians return to their homes. After seven days of occupation, the Indians left the building on 9 November. Federal officials estimated damages to the building to be 2.2 million dollars and lamented the loss of large numbers of missing documents.[15]

The Trail of Broken Treaties successfully brought together Indians from many tribes who occupied the BIA headquarters, the very nerve center of federal Indian policy. Means later wrote that he regarded the demonstration as a moral and spiritual victory and believed the general public became more aware of BIA corruption.[16]

Means returned to Pine Ridge and settled at Porcupine, a small village about eight miles from Wounded Knee. Meanwhile, tribal chairman Richard "Dick" Wilson and the Oglala Sioux Tribal Council passed legislation that prohibited AIM activities on the reservation, an action that infuriated Means, who later challenged Wilson for the office of chairman in the 1974 tribal election.

Pine Ridge Reservation was a ticking time-bomb as 1972 was coming to an end. Living conditions were deplorable, unemployment rates were high, housing was inadequate, and medical care was poor. Political factionalism, which was not uncommon among Indian tribes, pitted Wilson and his supporters against traditionalists and groups such as the Oglala Sioux Civil Rights Organization and the Oglala Sioux Landowners Association. These groups blamed Wilson for the poor conditions on the reservation, supported AIM's intervention, and agreed with Means's criticism of Wilson for not addressing reservation problems. Yet federal officials recognized Wilson as the duly elected tribal leader, and he knew he could call on them for support.

Indeed, on 20 November 1972, BIA police arrested Means when he attempted to address the Oglala Sioux Landowners Association. Arguing in vain that his civil rights had been violated, Means left Pine Ridge and moved to the Rosebud Reservation, also in South Dakota.[17]

In January and February 1973, Means and AIM participated in several protests in border towns near Sioux reservations. For example, a protest in Rapid City, South Dakota, the site of blatant racism, brought some favorable results. AIM convinced Rapid City officials to establish a committee to try to improve race relations between Indians and non-Indians.

A similar protest in Scottsbluff, Nebraska, was less successful. AIM and Chicano activists met in the city to discuss similar problems they faced as minorities. Scottsbluff police, unhappy about the meeting, kept them under constant surveillance and refused to meet with the activists. Conditions worsened when a firebomb exploded at the local junior high school. Several activists, including Means, were arrested and charged with disorderly conduct, intoxication, resisting arrest, and carrying concealed weapons. Means contended that police beat him and later placed a weapon in his cell, urging him to pick it up. All charges against the activists were later dropped.[18]

Another explosive event during these turbulent months also attracted public attention. Darold Schmitz, a white man, stabbed and killed Wesley Bad Heart Bull in a fight outside a bar in Buffalo Gap, South Dakota, on 21 January 1973. Schmitz, who claimed he acted in self-defense, was released on bail set at five thousand dollars and later was charged with second-degree manslaughter. AIM and other Indians protested that Schmitz's manslaughter charge and subsequent release was another case of a non-Indian assailant being "white-washed" after murdering a Native American. An ugly riot broke out at the courthouse in Custer, South Dakota, in which dozens of people were hurt. Means, who was inside the courthouse, was beaten by the police and arrested. Although a jury later found Schmitz not guilty of all charges, the incidents surrounding Bad Heart Bull's death and subsequent verdict caused concern among many Americans across the nation.[19]

Back on the Pine Ridge Reservation, conditions continued to deteriorate. Anti-Wilson political factions invited AIM to come to the reservation to help settle matters. Fearing AIM's intervention, Wilson used BIA funds to hire about forty people, whom he called the Guardians of the Oglala Nation, to protect BIA facilities on the reservation. His opponents called them the "goon squad" based on an acronym created from their official title. In addition, U.S. marshals, trained in special operations, arrived at Pine Ridge, supposedly to forestall any violence. In this tense atmosphere, some tribal members again attempted to impeach Wilson (this was the fourth impeachment attempt in the last eleven months). Their charges included misuse of tribal funds, failure to hold meetings, and nepotism. On

22 February, Wilson convinced the tribal council to drop the impeach-ment charges. Means, who was in attendance, left in disgust.

During the next few days, Means and about two hundred other Indians held meetings to plan a course of action. The Oglala Sioux Civil Rights Organization, AIM, and some tribal elders, headmen, and medicine men decided to occupy Wounded Knee, the tragic site of the last major con-frontation between the Sioux and the U.S. Army. Means cautioned them to keep the decision quiet so their enemies would not be alerted. On the evening of 27 February 1973, carloads of Indian demonstrators seized the hamlet of Wounded Knee, which they held for the next seventy-one days.[20]

Ultimately calling themselves the Independent Oglala Nation, the In-dian demonstrators later presented some demands, which included: the U.S. Senate Foreign Relations Committee should be convened to review Indian treaties; the U.S. Senate Subcommittee on Administrative Prac-tices and Procedures should investigate the BIA and the Department of the Interior; and the U.S. Senate Subcommittee on Indian Affairs should in-vestigate conditions on the Sioux reservations. In addition, the Indepen-dent Oglala Nation demanded the removal of Wilson as tribal chairman and the replacement of the tribal government (created under the Indian Reorganization Act of 1934) by more traditional Lakota political struc-tures. In response, Bradley Patterson and Leonard Garment, White House officials who had negotiated with Indian occupiers at Alcatraz and BIA headquarters, were dispatched by the federal government to South Da-kota. Meanwhile, a heavily armed force of over two hundred U.S. mar-shals, FBI agents, and BIA police established a perimeter around Wounded Knee.[21]

One of the first issues Means addressed was federal concern over the care and safety of residents of Wounded Knee, many of whom were el-derly whites. U.S. senators George McGovern and James Abourezk, both from South Dakota, arrived at the site and requested to talk with the resi-dents, whom the FBI claimed were hostages and prisoners of war. Means later wrote that the residents were neither hostages or prisoners of war and were free to leave whenever they desired. The two senators left satis-fied that the residents were safe. Indeed some of them even sympathized with the Indian occupiers and refused to leave. McGovern and Abourezk pledged they would get senate committees to address Indian grievances.

Rounds of talks between the Indians and federal officials during the first several days produced few results. As time passed, Means and other Indian leaders worried about the safety and health of the occupiers.

Meanwhile, Wilson threatened to evict the occupiers with his followers. When federal roadblocks were temporarily removed, many Oglalas left in spite of Means's pleas to remain. Means viewed the action as a ploy to initiate a series of arrests and to diminish the number of occupiers. However, a number of new Indian arrivals from all over the United States as well as some non-Indians replaced those who had left. The Indian occupiers received supplies of food, arms, and other items from outside sources. Among prominent supporters of the demonstration were attorneys William Kunstler and Mark Lane, comedian Dick Gregory, and actor Marlon Brando.[22]

After several more abortive attempts at negotiation, Means, Banks, and others became more alarmed. Supplies were running low and the fierce firefights continued. Applying additional pressure, federal officials cut off electrical and telephone services to Wounded Knee, and on 26 March, Means and Banks secretly made their way through the federal perimeter en route to Crow Dog's Paradise on the Rosebud Reservation, about one hundred miles away, to seek assistance. At Crow Dog's Paradise, named after Leonard Crow Dog, a Lakota holy man who helped revive the traditional Sun Dance ceremony, they found needed supplies and loyal volunteers to aid them. Means and Banks returned to Wounded Knee the following day. The occupation continued.

In late March and early April, demonstrations occurred in several cities throughout the United States in support of the occupation. A Harris Poll indicated that a majority of Americans supported the Indians. On 5 April, negotiations finally became more productive when federal negotiators agreed to conduct investigations of tribal complaints at Pine Ridge and to discuss violations of Indian treaty rights in the Fort Laramie Treaty of 1868. In return, AIM agreed that all their followers at Wounded Knee would lay down their arms; some would be arrested if warrants had been issued against them. Part of the arrangement was that Means, one of the main negotiators, would be arrested but later allowed to fly to Washington DC to meet with federal officials. After his arraignment in Rapid City, Means was released on a twenty-five-thousand-dollar bond. He and several other Indians then flew first-class to the nation's capital.

In Washington, confusion arose regarding just when the Indian occupiers were to surrender their weapons and when Means and the others were to meet with federal officials. Negotiations again broke down and progress toward the proposed settlement was stymied. Each side believed that the other should act first. Means cried foul and blamed whites for lying to Indians once again. He remained in Washington and testified on conditions at Wounded Knee before the House of Representatives' Indian subcommittee. Means refused to be provoked by the committee chairman who was highly critical of the occupation. Means left Washington and embarked on a speaking tour to garner support for the Indian occupiers. As part of his bail agreement, he was not allowed to return to Wounded Knee.[23]

The occupation finally ended on 8 May 1973. It had lasted too long and did not produce the results that Means and other Indians occupiers demanded. Wilson remained as tribal chairman, and the Independent Oglala Nation vanished. Federal officials refused to seriously consider Indian concerns regarding alleged violations of the Fort Laramie Treaty of 1868. Many Indians and non-Indians were alienated by the violent actions committed by both sides. Yet the occupation alerted white America to the problems Indian America faced. Moreover, Indians who supported the occupation felt a new sense of pride and hope. Indeed, Means later observed that "Wounded Knee was and is the catalyst for the rebirth of our self-dignity and pride in being Indians."[24]

In retrospect, AIM's occupation of Wounded Knee illustrated the strengths and weaknesses of both sides. National media coverage, which Means and other AIM leaders skillfully exploited, tended to be sympathetic toward the Indians, especially during the early stages of the occupation. Although both sides established roadblocks on several occasions, people were able to circumvent them. A number of firefights broke out; amazingly, only two occupiers were killed. Both sides suffered from dissension in their ranks, a splintering that hurt their overall effectiveness. Finally, as in previous encounters, federal negotiators again were successful in convincing Indians to abandon the occupation and in promising only to study Indian grievances.

Means was arrested in late April in Los Angeles because of complications surrounding his previous bond. He was returned to Sioux Falls and sent to jail. While in jail, federal criminal charges were brought against him and other AIM leaders for their actions at Wounded Knee. Means complained about the high bail he and the others had to pay. During the summer of 1973, Means prepared for his upcoming trial. Adding to his difficulties, he was served with an arrest warrant for his actions at the Custer County Courthouse. He later pleaded guilty and received a thirty-day jail sentence. On a more positive note, Means presented eloquent testimony at federal hearings in South Dakota regarding conditions at Pine Ridge.

In November 1973 hearings began in the Wounded Knee trials. Federal officials decided to try Means and Banks together. Felony charges against them included interstate transport and use of firearms, impeding federal officers in performance of their duties, and burglary and larceny of the Wounded Knee Trading Post. The defense argued that Means and Banks were political prisoners and were ultimately allowed to use the Fort Laramie Treaty of 1868 as evidence of Indian grievances. A change of venue moved the trial from South Dakota to St. Paul, Minnesota.[25]

On 8 January 1974 the trial of Means and Banks commenced with jury selection, which lasted over a month. Aided by several attorneys including William Kunstler, Means and Banks made the trial a political event. At times it seemed as if the federal government were on trial instead of the two Indian activists. Indeed, Means and Banks initially tried in vain to serve as co-counsels. In such roles, they could have spoken without having to take the witness stand. Nevertheless, they often interrupted court proceedings by challenging testimonies of federal officials.[26] Means later wrote: "After a while, I didn't even listen to the testimony. I just looked at the liars and thought about what I was watching. It began to register in my mind why the United States of America doesn't keep its treaties."[27]

In the final summations in September, the prosecution claimed that Means and Banks were guilty of criminal conspiracy for their actions at Wounded Knee. Speaking for the defense, Kunstler was at his best. He declared Means and Banks were not guilty of criminal conspiracy charges and passionately portrayed his clients as victims, much like Socrates and Jesus, two leaders of other social movements who were also unjustly accused of crimes.

During jury deliberations, jurors voted unanimously against conviction on the conspiracy charges. However, one of the jurors suffered a stroke during the discussion of other charges. Reduced to eleven members, the jury needed the approval of both the prosecution and the defense to continue. The prosecution refused and wanted a mistrial so they could prepare a better case than the one they had presented. The decision was up to federal judge Fred Nichol, who had become more and more frustrated with the performance of the FBI and the actions of government attorneys, including their delay in supplying materials to the defense. Instead of declaring a mistrial, Nichol dismissed all charges against Means and Banks, citing government misconduct that included lying under oath, using illegal wiretaps, and altering documents. The Justice Department was unsuccessful in appealing Nichol's decision.[28]

As a result of the Wounded Knee occupation and the subsequent trials, AIM and its leadership were considerably weakened. Federal officials concentrated on keeping AIM members busy defending themselves against numerous charges in court, which prevented them from engaging in demonstrations. The drain on their limited financial resources to pay for their legal defense nearly bankrupted the organization. Moreover, divisiveness among AIM's leadership continued to contribute to its decimation. For example, Banks and Means had disagreed over several strategies at Wounded Knee and over other matters. And in an altercation of AIM leaders at Rosebud Reservation, Carter Camp, a Ponca, shot and wounded Clyde Bellecourt.[29] Nevertheless, AIM attempted to survive these major internal crises.

After the Wounded Knee occupation ended, conditions on the Pine Ridge Reservation did not improve. In January 1974, Means challenged Wilson for the tribal chairmanship, even though Means was standing trial in St. Paul. In the primary, which several people entered, Means won. He received one hundred votes more than Wilson, who came in second. On election day, however, Wilson defeated Means by a slim margin. Means protested the results, but Wilson's victory stood. In 1984, Means tried again to run for the chairmanship but was disqualified because he was a convicted felon.[30]

For the rest of the 1970s and 1980s, and into the 1990s, Means continued his activism and sometimes dangerous lifestyle, which occasionally resulted in his sustaining knife and bullet wounds. Recalling the perilous episodes, Means reflects, "I've been shot three times, stabbed and beaten unconscious, strafed and bombed, sucked down by quicksand, and chased across the ocean in a leaky canoe."[31] For example, in March 1975, Means was present at a murder in a bar at Scenic, South Dakota. He was charged with first-degree murder, despite the fact that the victim, before dying, said Means was not the perpetrator. A jury later found him not guilty.

Three months later, on the Standing Rock Reservation in North Dakota, Means was involved in another incident at a bar at Fort Yates. Later, CBIA police stopped Means and his friends on the highway, a scuffle broke out, and an officer shot Means in the stomach. In March 1976, Means was shot again, this time in the chest by another Indian during a drinking party. Finally, in 1978, while serving time at South Dakota State Penitentiary for his actions in the courthouse riot in Sioux Falls, which occurred back in April 1974, Means was stabbed in the chest by another inmate during a prison fight.[32]

Before beginning his prison sentence, Means participated in a demonstration in Washington in July 1978. Known as The Longest Walk, the Indians protested pending anti-Indian legislation. At a rally Means engaged in an argument with Senator Edward Kennedy over a piece of legislation he was sponsoring that would weaken, according to Means, Indian treaty rights. None of the major anti-Indian bills passed.

In August 1979, Means was paroled from prison after serving one year of a four-year sentence. As the new decade dawned, he resumed his activism for Native American rights. Although attempts were made to resolve differences among AIM leaders, such efforts proved unproductive. Meanwhile Means continued to work with the International Indian Treaty Council, an organization that focused on the rights of indigenous peoples. As a representative of the organization, Means traveled to several countries, including hazardous trips to Nicaragua and Colombia in the mid-1980s, in hopes of bringing an end to the mistreatment of the Native American inhabitants by government authorities. In addition, he attempted to convince the Pine Ridge, Hopi, Lummi, and Fort Peck tribal councils to engage in economic development projects on their respective reservations. Moreover, Indian tribes should pursue, according to Means, international trade relations. Means expressed disappointment when these councils failed to embrace such opportunities; he blamed the councils and the BIA for not realizing the importance of such projects to improve reservation conditions and increase Indian self-determination.[33]

Another major concern of Means was the sacred Black Hills in South Dakota. He became an avid supporter of environmental protection and joined the Black Hills Alliance, composed of Indians and non-Indians who protested the potentially dangerous environmental practices of corporations in the Black Hills. At the Black Hills International Survival Gathering, held in the sacred hills in July 1980, Means presented what he considered his most famous speech. Titled "For America to Live, Europe Must Die," it was a passionate plea to embrace the essence of Indian spirituality and its oneness with nature and to reject the materialism and destruction practiced by non-Indians.[34]

Means also became involved in supporting Sioux claims to the Black Hills, which were illegally taken from them in 1877. In a 1980 decision, the U.S. Supreme Court offered the Sioux tribes over one hundred million dollars to settle the issue. The Indians rejected the money and demanded the Black Hills be given back to them.[35]

In April 1981, Means and others decided to reclaim the Black Hills by establishing a camp in the hills, at Victoria Creek Canyon. They named their project Yellow Thunder Camp in honor of Raymond Yellow Thunder, the Oglala killed in Gordon, Nebraska, in 1972. Justifying their right to establish the camp based on provisions in the Fort Laramie Treaty of 1868, the American Indian Religious Freedom Act of 1978, and an old federal law that allowed educational and religious activities to take place on wilderness sites, they submitted an application to the U.S. Forest Service to erect a number of permanent buildings at the campsite. When the Forest Service refused, Means and others took their case to court. In 1986 the court decided in favor of the government. Although Means and other AIM members sadly abandoned Yellow Thunder Camp, the time they spent there was rewarding. They enjoyed communal discussions and activities and laid plans to found a spiritual youth camp to help Indian children.[36]

During the 1980s, Means ran unsuccessfully for both the vice presidency and the presidency of the United States. Although he really had no chance of winning either office, he entered both races in an effort to bring attention to issues involving American Indians. In 1984, Larry Flynt, publisher of *Hustler*, asked Means to join his ticket to secure the Republican nomination for president of the United States. Means accepted, hoping to convince Republican leaders to support Indian treaty rights. Flynt was more interested, however, in attacking pornography laws, and in the end, Means quit the campaign.

Means hoped to run for the nation's highest office as the presidential candidate of the Libertarian Party in 1986. He supported some of the party's principles dealing with free-market economics and limits on governmental involvement in people's lives. Means campaigned hard, received support from a good number of Libertarian Party members, but failed to secure the party's nomination.[37]

In the century's final decade, Means remains an important and controversial Indian activist. His experiences in the 1990s include presenting a number of speeches throughout the United States and in several foreign countries, playing a key role in finally getting the name of Custer Battlefield National Monument changed to Little Bighorn Battlefield National Monument, and fighting racism in the Rapid City public schools.[38] Two other activities of particular interest concern Means's decision to become an actor and his participation in bringing to an end the Columbus Day parade in Denver, Colorado.

Because Means appeared on several U.S. television news programs such as *The Today Show*, *Good Morning America*, and other talk shows in foreign countries and felt fairly comfortable in front of a camera, he accepted an offer to read for the part of Chingachgook in the 1991 film *The Last of the Mohicans*. He won the important role and gave an excellent performance. Other movies followed, including Disney's animated and controversial 1995 film *Pocahontas*, in which Means provided the voice of Powhatan, the father of Pocahontas. Critics of the film complained that it presented romanticized and stereotyped views of Indians and questioned Means's involvement in the project.[39] Means defended the film, claiming that it depicted "a very accurate relationship between a father and a daughter." Overstating his case, Means declared that *Pocahontas* was "the best and most responsible film that has ever been made about American Indians."[40] Answering critics who charged he had abandoned the Indian movement and "sold out" to Hollywood, Means explained, "I haven't abandoned the movement for Hollywood. I've brought Hollywood to the movement."[41]

Besides acting in films, Means engaged in a vociferous protest to stop the Columbus Day parade in Denver, Colorado, in 1992. It is interesting to note that Colorado was the first state to establish a Columbus Day holiday back in 1907. Means, Colorado AIM members, and others had tried unsuccessfully in the past to persuade the Federation of Italian-American Organizations of Colorado (FIAO) to stop honoring Columbus, whom Indians viewed as the destroyer, not the "discoverer" of America. Since 1992 marked the quincentenary of the "discovery," and groups throughout the nation planned special ceremonies to celebrate the event, Means and other protesters deemed it an ideal time to take action.

Several meetings between the FIAO and those who opposed a Columbus Day parade failed to reach a solution, however. At the meetings, Means argued that the parade should honor the Italian-American culture and eliminate all references to Columbus. The issue, continued Means, was not about Italians versus Indians, but about racism. The FAIO remained unconvinced and refused to remove the name of Columbus from its parade; instead they responded by once again inviting the Indian protesters to join their parade. The Indians refused.[42]

With tensions mounting, Denver authorities prepared for the worst. Hundreds of police officers stood ready to make arrests. In a meeting with the Denver police chief, Means pledged that AIM would not encourage violence. "Now, if the police make it violent," warned Means, "then we will defend ourselves to the best of our ability."[43]

The FIAO scheduled the Columbus Day parade to start at 10 A.M. on Sunday, 11 October. At approximately 9:15 A.M., the parade organizers canceled it, fearing possible violence. The protesters learned of the cancellation at 9:45 A.M. A jubilant Means exclaimed, "We won. We abolished the holiday." Later a shouting match between the protesters and Italian Americans broke out when the latter assembled on the steps of the capitol to hear speeches, sing songs, and dance.[44] In 1992, anti–Columbus Day demonstrations swept the nation. Although observance and celebration of the day continued, Means and others who had led protests against Columbus Day activities certainly presented another view of Columbus to the American public.

During the 1990s, Means sought treatment for his anger and depression. His hard living, drinking, and personal problems extracted a heavy toll. He committed himself to Cottonwood de Tucson, a treatment center in Arizona, in late December 1991. His Indian spirituality helped him through the ordeal, and his group sessions finally provided some answers to his personal torments. According to Means, his troubled behavior resulted from low self-esteem instilled in him by his mother's biting criticism and lack of confidence in him.[45] Moreover, Means realized that the major source of his mother's behavior, and for that matter, his father's alcoholism, came from the deplorable BIA-directed reservation experiences that were imposed on them. Means observed, "to avoid being crushed, my mother got by on strength and an iron will."[46]

As the twenty-first century begins, Russell Means remains a significant and controversial voice for Indian America. He continues to work for the improvement of reservation conditions and he persists in addressing many other issues that affect Indian people. Means came to prominence as an Indian activist leader during the tumultuous 1960s, when Indians and other minorities, frustrated by injustices, neglect, and unfulfilled promises, could no longer remain passive. Indians demanded more self-determination, clamored for recognition of federal treaty obligations, and rejected forced assimilation policies that had tried for centuries "to get the Indian out of the Indian." Projecting an attractive and forceful image and possessing powerful speaking skills that attracted the media, Means was among the leading Indian demonstrators who brought attention to Indian issues. But his militant methods often alienated both Indians and non-Indians and diverted attention from genuine Indian grievances.

Many Indians disapprove of Means and AIM for their violent tactics. Critics such as Tim Giago, Lakota editor of *Indian Country Today,* a national Indian newspaper, charge that AIM and Means represent only urban Indians and have lost touch with reservation issues. Giago vehemently condemns Means and AIM for the occupation of Wounded Knee in 1973. He believes that Means could be more effective if he abandoned his radical behavior.

Additionally, AIM leaders have turned on each other. Means, who is active in AIM chapters in South Dakota and Colorado, directed efforts that banished the Bellecourt brothers from AIM in 1994 for subverting the movement. Included among the litany of charges against them were misrepresenting themselves as national leaders, undermining the efforts of other AIM members, misappropriating funds, and collaborating with governmental authorities against indigenous peoples. The Bellecourts, who belonged to the AIM chapters in Minnesota, countercharged that Means was upset with them because they questioned the Indian ancestry of Ward Churchill and Glenn Morris, two Colorado AIM leaders. In addition, the brothers questioned Means's dedication to his campaign to convince the Cleveland Indians to abandon their mascot, Chief Wahoo, charging that Means had accepted a payoff to drop the issue. They declared that Means had no authority since he had resigned from AIM on several previous occasions. Eventually, both sides exiled the other from "their" AIM organizations.[47]

In his evaluation of AIM, Means writes: "The primary goal of the American Indian Movement has always been to force the United States to live up to its own laws by meeting the obligations it took on when it signed our treaties. AIM failed to do that, but we did help restore respect to our traditional elders."[48] Indeed, AIM identified a number of Indian grievances but failed to get the federal government to solve them in the manner in which AIM demanded. Yet by bringing attention to these issues, albeit sometimes in militant ways, AIM forced the nation and its leaders to become more aware of Indian complaints. Moreover, many Indian people regained a new sense of pride in their "Indianness," and recently some tribes finally have been able to increase their ability to make decisions as sovereign nations. Unfortunately, Indians are still an oppressed people and many problems remain.[49]

Russell Means remains a charismatic and controversial figure. His autobiography, *Where White Men Fear to Tread*, published in 1995, received laudatory testimonials from such well-known people as Dee Brown, Oliver Stone, N. Scott Momaday, Gerry Spence, and Tony Hillerman. Reviews of the book were generally favorable. In addition to his success as an author, Means has recorded albums, founded an Indian film company, and established a Web site.[50]

Means continues to explore and develop his Indian spiritualism and hopes that someday he can achieve the position and respect of a tribal elder.[51] Noted Indian writer Vine Deloria Jr., a Standing Rock Sioux who does not always agree with Means, wrote: "If Russell Means has faults, and we all do, he also has talent and dedication which greatly outweigh the faults and which in my mind make him one of the great Indians of our time."[52]

The saga of Russell Means continues.

Notes

1. Russell Means with Marvin J. Wolf, *Where White Men Fear to Tread: The Autobiography of Russell Means* (New York: St. Martin's Press, 1995), 535. Means's autobiography presents his interpretation of major events involving Indian and white relations and confrontations. In this essay I have relied primarily on information provided by Means and other writers and historians who have dealt with recent Indian activism.

2. Means, *Where White Men Fear to Tread*, 4, 6–8, 12–15, 17, 21–22. Because of massive layoffs after World War II ended, Hank moved his family back to South Dakota for a brief time in 1945. They returned to California when Mare Island rehired Hank as a welder. Every summer the family returned to South Dakota to visit relatives. Means, *Where White Men Fear to Tread*, 24, 27, 31.

3. See Means, *Where White Men Fear to Tread*, 25–102, for specific details involving Means during these years; Paul Chaat Smith and Robert Allen Warrior, *Like a Hurricane: The Indian Movement from Alcatraz to Wounded Knee* (New York: The New Press, 1996), 132–33.

4. Means, *Where White Men Fear to Tread*, 102, 105–6. See *American Indian Culture and Research Journal* 18(4) (1994) (special Alcatraz edition) for valuable information on the occupation.

5. Means, *Where White Men Fear to Tread*, 153.

6. Means, *Where White Men Fear to Tread*, 136–37, 140, 145, 147–55; Smith and Warrior, *Like a Hurricane*, 133–34.

7. See Troy R. Johnson, "Roots of Contemporary Native American Activism," *American Indian Culture and Research Journal* 20(2) (1996): 127–54 for a good survey of the topic.

8. Means, *Where White Men Fear to Tread*, 167–70, 175–78, 182–86; Smith and Warrior, *Like a Hurricane*, 134–36. In September 1971, Means and other activists traveled to the BIA in Washington DC and unsuccessfully attempted to arrest two federal officials for their actions against Indians. They were arrested but soon released and sent home. See Rolland Dewing, *Wounded Knee II* (Chadron, Nebraska: Great Plains Network, 1995), 28, and Means, *Where White Men Fear to Tread*, 192.

9. See Means, *Where White Men Fear to Tread*, 186–90.

10. Smith and Warrior, *Like a Hurricane*, 136–37.

11. Dewing, *Wounded Knee II*, 29–33, contains one of the best, balanced accounts of this tragedy. Three of the four whites involved in the Yellow Thunder incident received one- to six-year sentences for manslaughter. See also Means, *Where White Men Fear to Tread*, 194–201, and Smith and Warrior, *Like a Hurricane*, 112–26.

12. Ward Churchill and Jim Vander Wall, *Agents of Repression: The FBI's Secret Wars against the Black Panther Party and the American Indian Movement* (Boston: South End Press, 1988), 122.

13. Means, *Where White Men Fear to Tread*, 202–7; Dewing, *Wounded Knee II*, 33; Smith and Warrior, *Like a Hurricane*, 118–19.

14. Dewing, *Wounded Knee II*, 35; Smith and Warrior, *Like a Hurricane*, 139–41; Means, *Where White Men Fear to Tread*, 223.

15. See Smith and Warrior, *Like a Hurricane*, 142–68; Dewing, *Wounded Knee II*, 35–36; Means, *Where White Men Fear to Tread*, 223–35. The destruction and seizure of documents became a controversial issue that split Indian activists and contributed to questioning AIM's objectives. See Smith and Warrior, *Like a Hurricane*, 171–77.

16. Means, *Where White Men Fear to Tread*, 235–36.

17. Dewing, *Wounded Knee II*, 37–38; Smith and Warrior, *Like a Hurricane*, 190–91; Means, *Where White Men Fear to Tread*, 236–37, 239.

18. Dewing, *Wounded Knee II*, 39–40; Smith and Warrior, *Like a Hurricane*, 178–82, 186–88; Means, *Where White Men Fear to Tread*, 239–43.

19. Dewing, *Wounded Knee II*, 40–45; Smith and Warrior, *Like a Hurricane*, 183–85; Means, *Where White Men Fear to Tread*, 243–46, 248.

20. Dewing, *Wounded Knee II*, 37–39, 48–51; Smith and Warrior, *Like a Hurricane*, 190–92, 194–202; Means, *Where White Men Fear to Tread*, 250–60. In a recent editorial, Wilson's daughter defends her father's administration at Pine Ridge and criticizes the tribal council for making Wounded Knee II a tribal holiday. See Mona Wilson, "Oglala Sioux tribal ordinance brings pain and anguish to Dick Wilson's family," *Indian Country Today*, February 9–16, 1998, p. A5. For another pro-Wilson piece, see Konnie LeMay, "20 years of anguish," *Indian Country Today*, 25 February 1993, pp. A1, A6. Three other books to consult on the occupation of Wounded Knee are Robert Burnette and John Koster, *The Road to Wounded Knee* (New York: Bantam, 1974); Stanley Lyman, *Wounded Knee 1973: A Personal Account* (Lincoln: University of Nebraska Press, 1991); Bill Zimmerman, *Airlift to Wounded Knee* (Chicago: Swallow Press, 1976).

21. Smith and Warrior, *Like a Hurricane*, 202–5; Dewing, *Wounded Knee II*, 63, 70, 72; Means, *Where White Men Fear to Tread*, 261, 270, 275. Included among the federal negotiators from the Department of Justice who met with the Indians during the various negotiations were Joseph Trimbach, Ralph Erickson, Harlington Wood, and Kent Frizzell. Two Indians who played important roles in the discussions were Ramon Roubideaux, a Brulé attorney, and Hank Adams.

22. Smith and Warrior, *Like a Hurricane*, 206–17; Dewing, *Wounded Knee II*, 63–67, 70, 100–101; Means, *Where White Men Fear to Tread*, 266–71.

23. Smith and Warrior, *Like a Hurricane*, 223, 233–36, 241–44; Dewing, *Wounded Knee II*, 93, 96, 104–5, 107–10; Means, *Where White Men Fear to Tread*, 282–89.

24. Avis Little Eagle, "Means reminisces," *Indian Country Today*, 25 February 1993, p. A1.

25. Dewing, *Wounded Knee II*, 121, 131, 133–34, 136, 137–38; Means, *Where White Men Fear to Tread*, 289–90, 299–300, 327–28.

26. Means, *Where White Men Fear to Tread*, 301, 311–12, 319; Dewing, *Wounded Knee II*, 138–39.

27. Means, *Where White Men Fear to Tread*, 310.

28. Dewing, *Wounded Knee II*, 139–40, 141–43; Means, *Where White Men Fear to Tread*, 312–13, 330–31. It is interesting to note that Means had a low opinion of Judge Nichol when the trial began, but as the trial progressed Means's respect for the judge increased dramatically. See Means, *Where White Men Fear to Tread*, 307, 331.

29. Smith and Warrior, *Like a Hurricane*, 270–71; Dewing, *Wounded Knee II*, 107–8, 131, 134, 135–36, 171; Means, *Where White Men Fear to Tread*, 295, 477.

30. Dewing, *Wounded Knee II*, 145–46, 170; Means, *Where White Men Fear to Tread*, 304–5, 436–41; Smith and Warrior, *Like a Hurricane*, 274.

31. Means, *Where White Men Fear to Tread*, 535.

32. Means, *Where White Men Fear to Tread*, 318–19, 338–40, 343–44, 351–52, 354–55, 359–62, 377, 387–88, 392; Dewing, *Wounded Knee II*, 147, 155, 156, 167–69; Churchill and Vander Wall, *Agents of Repression*, 176.

33. Means, *Where White Men Fear to Tread*, 365, 374–75, 377–81, 398, 459–77, 481, 492–98; Dewing, *Wounded Knee II*, 168–69, 171. Means's involvement in Nicaragua caused additional splits among AIM members, who disagreed about the Sandinistas and their policies.

34. Means, *Where White Men Fear to Tread*, 400–402, 545–54; Dewing, *Wounded Knee II*, 169. See Means's autobiography for the entire speech.

35. See Edward Lazarus, *Black Hills/White Justice: The Sioux Nation versus the United States, 1775 to the Present* (New York: HarperCollins, 1991) for thorough coverage of the subject.

36. Means, *Where White Men Fear to Tread*, 407–9, 413–14, 416–25, 428–31; Lazarus, *Black Hills/White Justice*, 411–12; Dewing, *Wounded Knee II*, 169–70.

37. Means, *Where White Men Fear to Tread*, 442–47, 482–88; Smith and Warrior, *Like a Hurricane*, 278. Besides these two controversial undertakings, Means accepted an invitation from the Sun Myung Moon's Unification Church to sponsor his speaking engagements. All these activities increased AIM's difficulties. See Means, *Where White Men Fear to Tread*, 478–82.

38. See Means's Web site, *www.russelmeans.com*, for information on his international travels from 1976 to 1995 and his "many firsts"; Kevin McCullen, "Little Bighorn battle finally ends," *Rocky Mountain News* (Denver), 12 November 1992, pp. 10, 24; Pamela Stillman, "Rallies generate promises of action against racism," *Indian Country Today*, 2 June 1993, pp. A1–A2. In 1999 Means was involved in two other events that attracted considerable public interest. After allegedly beating his Navajo father-in-law on the Navajo Reservation, Navajo officials charged him

with assault. Means claimed they had no authority over him since he was a Sioux, not a Navajo. See Brenda Norrell, "Navajos claim jurisdiction over Russell Means," *Indian Country Today*, May 31–June 7, 1999, pp. A1, A3. During the summer of 1999 Means joined with other activists in protesting racism and discrimination in Whiteclay, Nebraska. See Richard Yellow Bird, "Spiritual rally goes awry," *Indian Country Today*, July 12–19, 1999, pp. A1, A3.

39. Means, *Where White Men Fear to Tread*, 511–13, 517; for the *Pocahontas* controversy, see the following sources: Elaine Dutka, "Disney tries to apply history lesson to 'Pocahontas," *The Wichita Eagle*, 13 February 1995, p. 8A; Lois Tomas, "*Pocahontas*: One of the best or worst films about American Indians?" *Indian Country Today*, week of 1 June 1995, pp. C3, C6; Betsy Sharkey, "*Pocahontas* already making a giant splash for Disney," *The Hays (KS) Daily News*, 11 June 1995, p. D2; "Arts & Entertainment," *Indian Country Today*, week of 6 July 1995, pp. D1, D2 (contains several critical selections); James Stripes, "A Strategy of Resistance: The 'Actorvism' of Russell Means from Plymouth Rock to the Disney Studios," *Wicazo Sa Review* 14 (spring 1999): 87–101.

40. Russell Means, "Letters to the Editor," *Indian Country Today*, week of 13 July 1995, p. A5. In addition to movie roles, Means has appeared on several television dramas, including *Walker, Texas Ranger, Touched By an Angel*, and *Nash Bridges*.

41. "Media," *www.russellmeans.com*, p. 1.

42. Means, *Where White Men Fear to Tread*, 519–21; Robert Jackson, "Eyes on Denver as parade showdown nears," *Rocky Mountain News*, 4 October 1992, pp. 18–19. For Means's involvement in previous Columbus Day protests in Denver, see Marlys Duran, "Indian acquitted of halting parade," *Rocky Mountain News*, 27 June 1992, p. 8.

43. Jackson, "Eyes on Denver," p. 19; Robert Jackson, "Indians, cops brace for Columbus protest" *Rocky Mountain News*, 10 October 1992, p. 8; Means, *Where White Men Fear to Tread*, 521.

44. Mark Brown, "Protesters succeed in shutting down parade," *Rocky Mountain News*, 11 October 1992, pp. 6, 12; Means, *Where White Men Fear to Tread*, 522. In October 2000, Means once again participated in protests against Columbus Day activities in Denver.

45. Means, *Where White Men Fear to Tread*, 508–10, 524–28.

46. Means, *Where White Men Fear to Tread*, 528, 530–31.

47. Deborah Frazier, "Wounded Knee leaves legacy 20 years later," *Rocky Mountain News*, 7 March 1993, pp. 10, 13; "Activist turns to acting," *The Wichita Eagle*, 21 March 1993, pp. 3C–4C; Pamela Stillman, "AIM tribunal bans Bellecourts for life," *Indian Country Today*, 16 November 1994, pp. A1, A3; Tim Giago, "Wounded Knee was never liberated, it was decimated in 1973 by AIM," *Indian Country Today*, week of February 16–23, 1998, p. A4; Means, *Where White Men Fear to Tread*, 463–64, 466, 481; Smith and Warrior, *Like a Hurricane*, 278.

48. Means, *Where White Men Fear to Tread*, 421.

49. Smith and Warrior, *Like a Hurricane*, 277–79; Dewing, *Wounded Knee II*, 175–76.

50. See dust jacket of Means, *Where White Men Fear to Tread*; *www.russellmeans.com* contains information on his book and music. For examples of book reviews, one positive and one negative, see *American Indian Culture and Research Journal* 20(3) (1996): 234–38 and *Indian Country Today*, week of 4 April 1996, pp. C1–C2.

51. John Edgar Wideman, "Russell Means," *Modern Maturity* (September–October 1995): 68–79; Means, *Where White Men Fear to Tread*, 533–44.

52. Quoted in Smith and Warrior, *Like a Hurricane*, 274.

Howard Tommie

Seminole

BY HARRY A. KERSEY JR.

The modern concept of Indian self-determination—conceived by John Collier during the New Deal, nurtured during the Great Society, and brought to full term by Nixonian pronouncement—created a new generation of tribal leaders who maneuvered adroitly in both reservation politics and Washington hearing rooms. Following a visit from Commissioner John Collier in 1935, the Seminoles voted to accept the Indian Reorganization Act but did not form a tribal government until 1957, after narrowly averting congressional termination.[1] As chairman of the Seminole Tribe of Florida during its initial phase of dynamic economic and political emergence, Howard Tommie's leadership bridged the gap between an impoverished, fragmented people, still psychologically scarred by the brush with termination, and a unified tribe with a sophisticated government, secure in its newly confirmed sovereignty.

Howard Ernest Tommie was born on 28 May 1938 at the Brighton Seminole Reservation near Lake Okeechobee. He was the third of the Reverend Sam Tommie and Mildred Bowers Tommie's nine children. Both parents were full-blood Seminoles.[2] He is a member of the Bird clan—one of the two largest Seminole clans and arguably one of the most powerful politically, since it produced many office holders during the early years of Seminole tribal government.[3] In many respects Tommie's family reflected the social changes that engulfed Florida's Seminole people during the twentieth century. His grandfather was a venerated medicine man who had always lived in the Everglades; nevertheless, Howard's father converted to Christianity, became a Baptist lay minister, and strongly advocated Seminole resettlement on federal reservations.[4] Tommie's grandmother was a traditional clan matriarch yet urged one of her sons to attend the Carlisle Indian School.[5] As a child Howard learned both languages used by the Florida Indians—the Muskogee of his mother's people and the Miccosukee spoken by his paternal grandparents. When his family moved to the urban Hollywood Reservation, the children gained fluency in English by attending nearby public schools. Howard graduated from Chilocco Indian High School in Oklahoma where he lettered in football and basketball. He then served six months of active duty in the U.S. Army and eight years in the inactive reserves. Married with children, Tommie was working in Miami as a truck driver and welder during the 1960s when the Seminole Tribe received Community Action Program (CAP) funds from the federal government. This provided an opportunity for educated Seminoles to advance economically while also assisting their people. Tommie returned to the reservation to head the Neighborhood Youth Corps (NYC) program; there he mastered the intricacies of federal grant writing. He soon gained a reputation as an outspoken advocate of a movement that was capturing national attention: Indian self-determination.

President Richard Nixon's congressional message on Indians delivered in July 1970 was a defining moment in establishing the principle of Indian self-determination. The message outlined specific proposals for tribal action, and even though never fully implemented, Philip Deloria believes that "it stands as the strongest official policy statement for Indian self-determination."[6] The Great Society of the 1960s gradually espoused Indian control over tribal economic, social, and political affairs. The virtual monopoly the Bureau of Indian Affairs (BIA) and Indian Health Service had over providing for tribal needs would be broken. Tribes adopted a strategy of establishing eligibility for the programs that were available to state and local governments and making tribal governments the primary delivery vehicle for these programs. While termination was no longer the official policy of the federal government, many tribal leaders believed that assimilationist sentiment lurked just below the surface; therefore, another part of their strategy was an attempt to establish definitive tribal roles in the administration of government programs so that any attempt to resurrect termination would be difficult. Furthermore, with funds coming from an array of other federal agencies it would be possible to apply limited BIA monies on well-defined problems such as education and health. The vehicle for implementing this strategy was the War on Poverty, which channeled funds directly to tribes and bypassed BIA bureaucrats. Funds for the Comprehensive Employment Training Act (CETA), CAP, NYC and the like were the first discretionary funds that had ever been made available to many tribes.[7]

This windfall of federal dollars can be viewed as a mixed blessing. Government funds generally had restrictions on their use, and many Indian leaders were unprepared for such limitations; they often had to re-structure tribal governments to use the funds effectively. In addition, tribal priorities were often determined by the availability of funds for particular programs rather than by the needs of the people. While many Indians developed leadership and managerial skills running these programs there was concern about how they would apply them once the Great Society faded into history. The logical development would be for tribes to assume responsibility for programs that the BIA traditionally administered. However, that would mean calling for a radical reassessment of the guardianship relationship between the federal government and Indians.

Congressional acceptance of Indian self-determination came with passage of the Indian Self-Determination and Educational Assistance Act of 1975.[8] The act had two basic components: Title I and Title II. Title II, the Educational Assistance Act, authorized significant amendments to the Johnson-O'Malley Act, which had guided Indian education since the 1930s. In particular, it required local committees of Indian parents whose children attended schools served by a federal contract; there were also provisions for expanded funding for Indian children in public schools. However, it was Title I, the Indian Self-Determination Act, that held far-reaching implications for tribal life. It provided for direct subcontracting of federal services to tribal organizations, authorized discretionary grant and contract authority, permitted federal employees to work for tribal organizations without losing their benefits, and allowed the secretary of the interior to waive federal contracting laws if deemed appropriate for specific tribal situations. This paved the way for aggressive Indian governments to assume many functions formerly performed by the BIA or IHS alone. Tribes like the Miccosukees opted to dispense with a BIA presence altogether. As Vine Deloria Jr. summarized the situation, "Congress was thus taking the lock off the barn door and inviting Indians in to seize whatever they could pry away from the suspicious bureaucrats."[9] Seminole and Miccosukee politics of the 1970s must be assessed within the context of these rapidly evolving changes in federal-tribal relations. Unexpectedly, two small Florida tribes would find themselves on the cutting edge of a national movement.

In 1971, Howard Tommie, at age 33, was elected chairman of the tribal council, handily defeating incumbent Betty Mae Jumper—the first, and so far only, woman elected to that post. He represented himself as a new type of leader and appealed to younger members of the tribe with the promise of Indian self-determination—especially direct contracting with the federal government as the Miccosukees had done. Jumper, an experienced tribal officer, had served the Seminoles for many years. Her devout Christianity appealed to many older voters who were Southern Baptists. In contrast, Howard promised more aggressive policies than those of the older generation, which had been bound by BIA policies that dictated limited Indian self-government and fostered a high degree of dependency. Tommie recalled, "It was quite an upset when I came in with my idea of self-help. I said that we have to move forward by use of our own resources, and I captured the votes of the young."[10] On the other hand, the new chairman recognized that he had the support of the large Bird clan, while Betty Mae Jumper belonged to the very small Snake clan. With a smile he confided to a reporter, "I do belong to a large clan and that was very helpful."[11]

Delivering on his promise to shake things up, Tommie hit the ground running. He pressed forward on all fronts to assure that the tribe took maximum advantage of federal funding sources. The administration embarked on a furious cycle of grant writing, and money began to pour in. To coordinate the programs, Tommie created a human resources division with its own director and accounting department. For many years Michael Tiger, a young, well-educated Indian who later became a regional Indian Health Service administrator, ran the division. Included under the division were reservation programs, social services, manpower planning, employment assistance, the CETA program, the education department, community health coordination, the Indian Action Team, the foodstamp program, community health representatives, emergency medical assistance, mental health and alcoholism, and drug abuse. Tommie also energized established tribal programs such as Head Start and the Native American Program; meanwhile, he encouraged the council to reorganize the Seminole Housing Authority and Tribal Utility Commission. He also promoted the construction of new health clinics on all reservations as well as community centers and ball fields.

Tommie constantly sought funding for special education programs at the tribal day school on Big Cypress Reservation and for adult education. Because parents were negligent in enrolling children in school, the tribal council passed a resolution reaffirming that all Seminoles must attend school until the age of eighteen unless graduated from high school or married. "Education," the council stated, "is set as a highest priority of the Tribe and children must be motivated to seek high school education."[12]

Improving law enforcement on the reservations remained a major goal for Tommie, and after the state legislature enacted a 1974 law allowing the Florida tribes to police themselves, he secured Law Enforcement Assis-

tance Administration funds to establish a tribal law enforcement program.[13] Then he initiated a tribal legal assistance program to defend the
tribe and its members; the tribal attorney aggressively pursued Seminole
land rights and sovereignty in the state and federal courts.

On the national level Tommie gained recognition as an articulate spokesperson for Indian causes. He represented the Seminoles in the National Tribal Chairman's Association, chairing its culture and tradition
committee. This committee was instrumental in negotiating a compromise with federal authorities over the Migratory Fowl Act permitting Indians to legally possess eagle feathers for religious or cultural ceremonies.
He also served on the litigation committee of the National Congress of
American Indians and testified in support of the 1975 Indian Self-Determination Act at congressional hearings. Reflecting his interest in health
care issues, Tommie received an appointment to the National Indian
Health Board, which met quarterly in Denver to advise the government
on policy issues; eventually he would become chairman. Throughout his
administration, Howard represented the Seminoles on the board of
United Southeastern Tribes, which unified tribes of the region, serving
one term as its president; in addition, he and Miccosukee leader Buffalo
Tiger co-chaired the Florida Governor's Council on Indian Affairs. All in
all, the energetic Tommie brought a new dimension to Seminole leadership in an era of increasing tribal activism.

The Seminole Tribe's unique constitutional structure provided for an
elected tribal council to handle legislative matters, and another elected
body, the board of directors, to operate its business affairs. Although the
heads of both the council and board sat ex officio on the other body, there
was great potential for conflict if the two political leaders were in disagreement. Fortunately for the Seminoles that was not the case. The 1971
election also brought change to the tribe's board of directors. The new
president, Fred Smith, was born at the Brighton Reservation in 1939, and
therefore was in Tommie's generation. After two years with the U.S. Army
in Europe, Smith returned to the reservation and managed a beef cattle
herd while taking extension courses in agricultural and business management. He was the appointed secretary-treasurer of the Seminole Tribe
from 1968 to 1971. Fred Smith's agenda for the board of directors generally
complemented Howard Tommie's goals for tribal social and economic development—the council and board frequently held joint meetings and
were generally in accord on most issues. The new president was aware of
the implications of Indian self-determination; as secretary-treasurer in
November 1970, he had read a letter from the commissioner of Indian Af-

fairs to a joint meeting of the council and board. The letter informed tribes of Nixon's policy statement. As a result the council passed a resolution asking the government to turn over control of land operations, the cattle program, education, and employment assistance to the tribe.[14] Smith "traveled extensively throughout the United States, meeting with other tribal leaders and business consultants, touring their reservations, studying their enterprises and programs to enhance his home operations."[15] Under Smith's direction the board moved to upgrade and expand tribal business enterprises. It set regulations and restrictions for the tribe's commercial frontage along U.S. 441 and made leases available to Indian businesses. The tribe started a catfish farm on the Brighton Reservation, and built a campground and marina tourist complex there with Economic Development Act (EDA) funding. The board's EDA office also secured funds for community development programs that would build swimming pools and gymnasiums. As a cattleman, Smith had definite ideas about that enterprise. He convinced the board to assume the cattle and range management program from the BIA and increase improved-pasture acreage; the cattlemen's fees were then raised so the program would be self-sustaining. In addition, the board set up a pension program for tribal employees. Only the Indian Village and Craft Shop, set up by the previous administration with BIA approval, continued to incur significant losses despite numerous infusions of cash.

The installation of new officers signaled a new parity between the council chairman and president of the board. The budgets for the council and board in FY 1972 listed salaries for both top officials at $10,660. This ended a long period in which the position of tribal chairmanship was an unsalaried one. At the installation ceremony the outgoing chair Betty Mae Jumper remarked somewhat sardonically, "Four years ago we didn't have any money to work with and had to cash a bond in order to go on. I had to work elsewhere to get money on which to live, and still work at chairman of the council without pay."[16] Jumper was employed by the public health office; she received only a few dollars of attendance money for council meetings. Moreover, the budgeted (but unfunded) salary for the chairmanship was only $3,600, less than that of the secretary-treasurer or clerk, and substantially below the $10,660 approved for the board president.[17] This disparity offers a glimpse into the sometimes Byzantine nature of tribal politics. Evidently Jumper inherited the low, often nonexistent salary that had been imposed on the council chair. An undocumented but widely circulated story on the reservation held that the BIA superintendent and a former board president planned to transfer most of the tribe's economic assets, and thus its political power, to the board of directors at the expense of the council and its chair. In the 1960s most of the money being spent on the Seminole reservation flowed into the land development and cattle enterprises that fell under the board, as did the commercial property leases. A lack of funds to pay the chair's salary forced Betty Mae Jumper's predecessor to resign the post in 1966 to head the Community Action Program. In some circles it is still believed that the old guard on the council and board resisted Jumper and limited her effectiveness; it could not have been lost on the first female chair that the council approved a decent salary for her male successor.

In an interview, Howard Tommie noted that to be effective, an Indian leader must command support from the people; he believed he was the first Seminole chairman who fully gauged tribal sentiment. Admitting that he had no experience in tribal government other than directing NYC, he recounted:

> A lot of things made me feel like something needed to be done. I wanted to see things improve. I did not have much of an idea whether I could correct these things being chairman. We had two forms of government, the board and the council. I went ahead and ran for the council, and, luckily, because of the fairly decent job I did with the Neighborhood Youth Corps, I won a lot of people on my side. Luckily they believed me. I was born and raised here, and everybody within the reservation knows me and that recognition had a lot to do with it. That is how I got into tribal government. I am not downgrading the people who were in there, but I just felt like they did not want to progress. But, in a way, I felt it could be done and still be able to keep harmony within the tribe.[18]

The new administration undertook a policy of contracting with the federal government for services, and tribal members replaced BIA functionaries wherever possible. "Of course, we had a Bureau of Indian Affairs. I do not want to say anything bad about them, but it is a bureaucracy. For some reason or another, they seem to do whatever their guidelines are, which are very minimal. They have never lived here, like I do."[19] He believed that the tribal council could make better use of the money allocated to the tribe. "For a guy sitting over there with a GS 15, 20, 30, whatever it is, I could hire two people and a secretary with that money."[20] Initially Tommie's plans encountered strong opposition from the agency superintendent and his staff. Tommie believed that many of the government employees "did not really care whether an Indian kid got an education, or that an Indian kid got a job, or that the mother and father had a steady job. These were eight-to-five people. So we hired people that would stay on the reservation or that were qualified to go out and talk to people about what they would like to do."[21] He was convinced that during the early years of tribal government local agency officials had directed revolving credit funds to a select group of Seminoles, cattlemen, or owners of heavy construction equipment, whose interests were represented by the board of directors. When asked if federal employees tried to influence the selection of tribal officers, he responded, "I felt the biggest influence that they had was on the federal purse strings. They would satisfy a certain part of the tribal government. I do not know whether there was any particular attempt to select these individuals, but they found that most aggressive Indians would see the opportunities there, so they catered to them, I am sure. They made a substantial number of loans for the purpose of assisting the tribe. But a lot of times it would benefit the present administration's personal pocketbook . . . I am pretty sure that goes on in most places."[22] In an attempt to correct these abuses by government personnel, Tommie voided many contracts and adhered to a "buy Indian" policy wherever possible.

In 1975, Howard Tommie sought reelection to a second term. His opposition came from Betty Mae Jumper and Fred Osceola, the son of a former tribal chairman. Since Osceola belonged to the Panther clan and Tommie was a Bird, the election pitted candidates from the two largest lineages against each other. More important was which candidate could capture the vote of younger tribal members. It again became a campaign in which a young candidate (Fred Osceola was in his early 30s) sought to unseat an incumbent. Osceola adopted the slogan "motivate, rejuvenate, and educate" and was given a good chance of winning.

The older members of the electorate faced a dilemma. "The Seminoles used to be ruled by the elders," explained one tribal member. "You didn't have wisdom until you were 50 or 60. But today most of the leaders don't speak English, so the question is if they can carry on the business of the tribe. Many of the old question the young, because the young have capability, but not the wisdom, to make decisions. What you need is a young man with wisdom."[23]

The Seminole Tribe allowed only a month for campaigning between the close of nominations and election day. Most eligible Seminole voters were unlikely to be swayed by campaign literature or a media blitz. That placed a premium on intense face-to-face campaigning on all three reservations. Both Howard Tommie and Betty Mae Jumper were fluent in the Muskogee and Miccosukee languages; the latter was spoken by most tribal members and by virtually everyone at the Big Cypress Reservation. Fred

Osceola, from the Brighton Reservation, spoke only the Muskogee language of that community, leaving him at a disadvantage. All three candidates spoke English fluently, but it was important to articulate their positions in the native tongue; these Seminole politicians needed to reconcile the conflicts that separated reservation constituencies, which required an ability to employ the nuances of native languages.

Seminole politicking is low-key. "It's a guerrilla style of campaigning they use," one observer offered. "It's done more by backyard talk than big campaigning. There are subtle innuendoes by candidates attacking the other candidate's efficiency or integrity. When a candidate is talking to the Christian faction, he might say that he doesn't smoke or drink and tries to say that the others do all sorts of things."[24] The favorite campaign gathering is a cookout with an entire reservation eating together, hosted by a candidate. In his campaign, Osceola butchered and cooked two cows, one at Brighton and another at Big Cypress. Howard Tommie and Betty Mae Jumper held cookouts at the Hollywood Reservation, which they felt were crucial to their campaigns. Most of the educated Indians lived there and worked for the Seminole tribal government or the BIA; they were likely to cast ballots for the candidate who could most effectively address program and government issues. The rural Brighton and Big Cypress constituencies would probably vote based on more local concerns.

Fred Osceola campaigned against what he called the "downhill slide" of the tribe since his father left office in 1966. He promised to return the tribe to the position of prestige he claimed it had enjoyed when his father and other elders dominated tribal government. Betty Mae Jumper made her appeal to the religious older voters by stating "I believe if you don't put God before you, you're nothing."[25] She also understood the necessity of making specific campaign promises, pledging to build gymnasiums on the two outlying reservations so they would have facilities equal to those at Hollywood. Howard Tommie stressed his record, pointing to new facilities for adult education and remedial education, increased social welfare assistance, jobs, nutritional programs and social activities for the elderly, and the placing of part-time doctors on the reservations, all obtained through federal funding. He admitted that more needed to be done and promised to work for additional funding for employment and cooperative food centers on the reservations.

Following one of the largest turnouts in Seminole political history, Howard Tommie was elected to a second term as chairman of the tribal council. One south Florida newspaper credited the genial chairman with being the first Seminole leader to challenge the authority of the Bureau of

Indian Affairs, noting that he had replaced government bureaucrats in health, education, and welfare programs with tribal members. The victorious Tommie was quoted as saying "Using our own people, we're getting into a system where our interests are protected."[26]

The second term of Tommie's administration saw initiation of the most significant social, economic, and political changes in modern Seminole history. The chairman was instrumental in initiating or vigorously pursuing four issues that became crucial in defining the extent of tribal sovereignty. First, he brought closure to the Seminole land claims case by urging tribal acceptance of the Indian Claims Commission's award in 1976, and then led a struggle with Oklahoma Seminoles over equitable distribution of the funds. Congress resolved the issue in 1990, awarding the Florida Seminoles some 25 percent of the commission award, and in the process implicitly recognizing Seminole tribal sovereignty. Second, he became involved in the East Big Cypress case, which set a major precedent in eastern Indian water rights. In 1987, Congress affirmed a settlement between the state of Florida and the Seminole Tribe that included a water compact regulating tribal water rights and usage; it also assured tribal sovereignty in its own lands. Third, he participated in a controversial assertion of sovereignty by reservation "smoke shops," which sold cigarettes free of Florida sales taxes. Fourth, he introduced high-stakes, unregulated bingo. The last two ventures were undertaken at some cost in negative publicity for the tribe and were opposed by Indians adverse to smoking and gambling; they also generated legal challenges to the expansion of Seminole sovereignty.

In April of 1979 a perceptive and somewhat critical article appeared in the *Miami Herald* highlighting many ambiguities of contemporary Seminole life.[27] The *Herald* noted that the tribal government no longer depended on ventures such as the Arts and Craft Center (closed after five straight years of losing money) or the unfavorable land leases with mobile home park operators that netted less than five percent of the current fair rental value. Instead, the Seminoles had developed a dynamic economy. At that time the greatest moneymakers for the tribe were the smoke shops that opened in 1976. Taking advantage of a federal court decision exempting the Colville Tribe of Washington from paying state sales taxes, the Seminoles sold their cigarettes for $4.75 per carton—or $2.15 less than local merchants charged. In addition to tax-free cigarette sales, the tribe had become proficient in securing federal grants, and there were nearly eighty-eight contracts bringing money to the reservations. As a result, from 1969 to 1977 the tribal income soared from six hundred thousand dollars to 4.5 million dollars per year, underwriting many social and economic ventures. The tribe's first full-time attorney, Stephen J. Whilden, was also busily involved in filing lawsuits challenging state and local governments that were arbitrarily using Seminole lands. Almost immediately the Seminoles were confronted with an assault on their smoke shop operations.

In July 1977, Broward County sheriff Edward J. Stack, acting as a private citizen and taxpayer but supported by a local cigarette vendor, filed suit to require imposition of state taxes on the sale of cigarettes on the Hollywood Reservation. Stack claimed that the tribe cost Florida $275,000 per month by failing to pay taxes on its cigarette operations. Florida's Division of Alcoholic Beverages and Tobacco had not attempted to collect the taxes because of ambiguities in the law. Untaxed cigarettes had long been available on military installations and in veterans hospitals, and Florida citizens could order them by mail from North Carolina. *Vending Unlimited v. State of Florida* was transferred from Broward County, home of the Hollywood Reservation, to state capital Tallahassee, in Leon County. In March 1978 the Circuit Court of Leon County ruled that sales on Indian reservations were not taxable by the state. The plaintiff appealed. The First District Court of Appeals of Florida affirmed this ruling on 22 November 1978.[28] The appellate court cited *Confederated Tribes of Colville v. State of Washington* in its decision.[29] Nevertheless, contradictory rulings by federal courts in similar cases involving Indian cigarette sales cast some doubt on the continuation of tax-free sales to non-Indians. Therefore the tribe's attorney adroitly negotiated with state officials, which got the Seminoles directly involved in supporting political candidates. In 1979, following a lobbying effort by the Seminoles and their backers, the Florida legislature passed a bill authorizing the tribe to continue its sale of tax-free cigarettes on the reservations.[30] This act was challenged in subsequent legislative sessions, but it has been successfully defended on the grounds that smoke shops operated by the Seminole Tribe assure continuing economic independence for the Indian people of the state.

Still, many within the Indian community complained that money was not a cure-all for tribal problems and that not all Seminoles were benefiting equally from the wealth. Critics argued that federal grants only created a new form of dependency; whites and blacks, they claimed, received the best jobs on the reservation while many Seminoles remained unemployed. One estimate in the 1970s had unemployment at Hollywood hovering around 35 percent with even higher rates on the rural reservations. More than half of the residents at Hollywood received some kind of government aid, while 75 percent of the employed Indians worked either for the tribe or the Bureau of Indian Affairs. Moreover, many newly affluent tribal members often lived side by side with those on welfare, thereby exacerbating the growing economic disparities.

Discontent became more pronounced as the tribe prepared for an election in May of 1979. Tommie found himself at the center of controversy when it was discovered that he drew a large salary. During his eight years in office, his salary grew from less than ten thousand dollars to thirty-five thousand dollars, all paid from federal funds on the premise that Tommie functioned as primary administrator of the various government contracts. The tribal council had encouraged this course of action due to a financial reversal of fortune. In 1973 the Seminoles' income was projected to exceed five hundred thousand dollars with over four-fifths of that sum derived from commercial property leases at Hollywood. Consequently the council approved thirteen-thousand-dollar salaries for the chairman and president while tribal employees received 11 percent raises the following year. But funds became tight in 1975 as a result of three lease cancellations, which forced the council to suspend its annual cash dividends.[31] Tommie suggested that until the situation improved, his salary could be taken from various programs under Human Resources Division. A council resolution not only endorsed this approach but encouraged the chairman to increase his salary to twenty thousand dollars from such sources.[32] Rather than being defensive, Tommie expressed pride in having been able to secure so much of the federal largess. "You can't knock it," he said. "It was there: hot meals for the elderly, an ambulance for the Big Cypress Reservation, two pairs of shoes for a kid—that's shoes the Indian would have never had otherwise."[33]

In essence, what Tommie had done was to finesse control of federal programs away from the board and place them directly under the council where funds became available for his salary and other purposes. The move allowed the council to have control over more lucrative bingo and smoke shop operations. Some tribal members and BIA bureaucrats protested that such a transfer of power violated the intent of the Seminole constitution, which set up a separate body to run business affairs, but there was never an official challenge to Tommie's actions.

Despite improvements in tribal welfare, Tommie's detractors pointed out that non-Indians held many of the jobs in the smoke shops and in his office at tribal headquarters. The chairman defended his non-Indian secretary on the grounds that he had worked with Seminoles in that position, but they did not have the requisite skills; he also complained that many

Seminoles believed they were entitled to a job regardless of whether they were competent or not. One of his opponents conjectured that the chairman did not want an Indian secretary because in such a tight-knit community there would be no confidentiality.

The CETA programs Tommie supervised were particularly criticized for not preparing Indians for advancement in the job market, especially the nonreservation one. James Billie, a young Vietnam veteran, a tribal council member, and a candidate for the chairmanship in the coming election was quoted as saying that government training programs "sure don't help any. They seem designed to keep you on the reservation, and that's all."[34] Some Indians were also concerned that Tommie had become too autocratic, pointing to a council resolution that granted him final authority to fire tribal employees.[35]

The *Miami Herald* singled out Howard Tommie, Bill Osceola (who had replaced Fred Smith as president of the board of directors in the 1975 election), and entrepreneur Marcellus Osceola for their possession of new automobiles, airboats, swamp buggies, and other signs of affluence that set them apart from the rank and file; they were the most obvious beneficiaries of the new smoke shop prosperity. Again, Tommie remained adamantly unapologetic. He explained that the sale of cigarettes on the reservation was his idea and that he was responsible for introducing Marcellus Osceola to wealthy financial backers. The partners were to pay 4 percent of income to the tribe as sales tax, and 15 percent as rent. The tribe granted Osceola and his backers an exclusive smoke shop franchise for five years; in return Osceola and his backers would assume all costs of litigation connected with the enterprise. Tommie later informed the council that the agreement with Marcellus Osceola was not intended to be for an exclusive franchise. Osceola was supposed to sell cigarettes wholesale to other tribal members; however, when the tribal council granted franchises to other Seminoles, Osceola (unsuccessfully) challenged the decision in court. The new smoke shops on the reservations, owned 51 percent by Seminoles and 49 percent by white partners, contributed approximately $1.6 million to the Seminole Tribe's budget by 1980.

Buoyed by judicial and legislative victories vindicating the smoke shops, Seminoles now entered an even more lucrative and controversial venture: unregulated, high-stakes bingo games. In the fall of 1978 the tribal council received an economic development proposal from a group known as the Seminole Management Association. Tommie, owning 50 percent of the stock in the company, had majority ownership. The company encumbered nineteen acres along U.S. 441—the most valuable vacant land remaining on the Hollywood Reservation. The investors planned to spend $2.5 million developing the Seminole Indian Plaza, which would include a smoke shop, a strip mall, and a bingo hall that could seat over fifteen hundred patrons. The tribe was to receive its usual percentage from the smoke shop, all the rent income from the shopping center, and 20 percent of the bingo-hall profits. Tommie promised to present a complete financial proposal showing how the non-Indian investors who put up the capital would be repaid. The tribal council reportedly discussed this proposal with Tommie absent from the room, then voted 4-0 for acceptance. Thus the tribe's elected leader became its leading entrepreneur.

The ease with which the proposal passed led many tribal members to accuse the council of favoritism. Some felt the council members had been bought off with offers of jobs or even a piece of the action. Joe Dan Osceola, a former board president who had announced his candidacy for the chairmanship, conjectured that "It could have been everyone scratching everyone else's back."[36] Furthermore he questioned whether Tommie was really the majority owner or just a front man for non-Indians who put up the money.

These accusations infuriated Tommie, who countered "I really don't think I've taken the tribe for anything. Why should I be treated differently than anyone else who wants to go into business? It doesn't seem fair that I should be excluded just because I'm chairman."[37] He explained how he arranged to get the $2.5 million from backers Eugene Weisman and George Simon. However, some tribal members and public officials questioned whether Tommie's associates represented organized crime. Simon had an office at the Flagler Dog Track in Miami and identified himself as a "financial consultant" to the track, not a full-time officer. Weisman and Simon produced a long list of "investors" whose stake totaled $2.5 million; no connection to organized crime was proven.[38] Still, by the early summer of 1979 no contracts had been signed.

More fuel was added to the fire that year when Marcellus Osceola sold his smoke shop interests to Howard Tommie for a rumored four hundred thousand dollars plus another one hundred thousand for inventory. The council obligingly canceled Osceola's lease on a three-acre site and transferred it to Howard Tommie.[39] At the same time, the council passed a resolution declaring a five-year moratorium on establishing new smoke shops at Hollywood, citing the danger of saturating the market and thereby reducing tribal income from sales.[40] Still another resolution made "price wars" illegal and set a minimum sale price of $4.75 per carton.[41] Although Tommie was nominal majority owner, critics again claimed that outside money really controlled the business. Some suggested that the plan all along had been for Osceola to sell his holdings to Tommie, but the chairman vigorously denied any collusion. "I honestly could say that people could understand it that way," he admitted. "[W]e didn't want to move in that particular way. . . . Never had an agreement per se between me and Marcellus, and there were differences of opinion." These differences of opinion led to lawsuits. "In a humorous way, we asked him to sell out. Because we didn't want any competition. In a joking way. But he changed his mind and arrived at a figure."[42] As part of the deal, Osceola reportedly retained a share of the profits from the first shop and subsequently leased another smoke shop, although at a less accessible location. It was a joke on the reservation that Howard Tommie, like Marlon Brando's movie character in *The Godfather,* had made Marcellus "an offer that he couldn't refuse."

Tommie's proposal for tax-free liquor sales on the reservations became another volatile issue. A joint meeting of the council and board decided that the issue should be brought before the people at community meetings.[43] Predictably it drew a storm of protests from religious conservatives in the Seminole community—especially Southern Baptists. Following a raucous meeting held in the Hollywood Reservation gymnasium, the tribal council voted 5-0 against the proposal. Even Howard Tommie could not win a confrontation with the anti-liquor sentiment prevailing among older Seminoles. When asked about this issue, he explained, "It came about during my administration many, many times. The people, of course, were highly Baptist. They told me that they did not want it. I really got into hot water with them one time, because I did authorize the sale of beer at one of our tribal fairs one time. They worked me over pretty well in tribal council . . . so after they shot it down in the community meeting, I just said 'Okay. Now I know that you really do not want it.'"[44] Some tribal members supported liquor sales because the money earned could provide emergency services—primarily ambulances—for the rural reservations. Tommie gave it a try even though he expected the old-timers to refuse the services believing they could take care of themselves. Also, he understood that the Baptists were set against liquor because they had seen the problems it could bring.

Even though he ultimately backed away from supporting liquor sales, Tommie remained convinced that his vision of the tribe's future had as much validity as that of religious conservatives who thought things were changing too fast. He told them, "The thing that you have to understand—

I cannot impress this upon you too much—is that I am an Indian, too. I live here. I have just as much right to say something, whether I am a tribal chairman or not a tribal chairman. I see things that are happening. There is only one way that something is going to get done, and that is if we do it . . . if another Indian steps up to me and asks me why are you doing this, I am going to tell him I am just as much an Indian as he is. Just because you go to church and you have your values does not mean that I would not like to have these benefits at my disposal."[45]

The national debate over appropriate forms of Indian enterprise ratcheted up sharply during the late 1970s as more tribes sought additional sources of revenue such as tax-free cigarettes and gambling. State and local governments became intently opposed to what they perceived as unwarranted and illegal activities on Indian reservations. As a result the 1980s witnessed numerous legislative and legal challenges to Indian sovereignty. Howard Tommie, having introduced tax-free cigarette sales and bingo to the Seminoles, decided to become a full-time businessman and did not seek a third term as chairman. He withdrew as head of the bingo consortium (but remained a partner) and devoted his time to Howard E. Tommie Enterprises, which included a substantial smoke shop in a prime location on the Hollywood Reservation. It fell to the administration of his successor, James Billie, to deal with the legal assault on Seminole bingo.

In 1979 the Seminole Tribe contracted with the Seminole Management Association to run the bingo emporium in return for 45 percent of the profits.[46] By running the games daily, offering large jackpots, and bussing in bingo players, the tribe expected to realize about $1.5 million the first year, or approximately what the smoke shops generated.[47] However, a new Broward County sheriff, Robert Butterworth, threatened to intervene and close down the bingo hall before it opened. According to Butterworth, the tribe violated the Florida statute that regulated bingo operations. The statute restricted the operation of bingo games to qualified (that is, charitable or nonprofit) organizations. Operators could hold games only two days per week, with jackpots limited to one per session with a top value of $250. Operators of "qualified" games formed a strong anti-Seminole bingo lobby, claiming that the tribe operated illegally and would cut into their business. Law enforcement officials were also concerned about possible underground groups involved in Indian bingo.

In *Seminole Tribe of Florida v. Butterworth* the tribe's attorneys asked the federal district court to permanently enjoin Sheriff Butterworth from enforcing Florida's bingo statute on the reservation. The court issued a preliminary injunction in December 1979 that permitted the bingo hall to

open. Florida assumed criminal and civil jurisdiction over Indian tribes in
1961 under the provisions of Public Law 280; however, the Supreme Court
held that the act did not confer general state civil regulatory control over
Indian reservations. For the state to have enforcement power over bingo
on the reservations it must rely on the grant of criminal jurisdiction contained in Public Law 280. The case then turned on whether the state's
bingo statute was civil/regulatory or criminal/prohibitory in nature.[48] On
6 May 1980, the United States District Court for the Southern District of
Florida declared the statute to be civil/regulatory and held that Congress
never authorized Florida to impose its civil regulatory power on Indian
lands. The court granted injunctive relief: "[I]n view of the congressional
policy enunciated in Public Law 280, the court must resolve a close question in favor of Indian sovereignty."[49] On 5 October 1981, the United
States Fifth District Court of Appeals affirmed the lower court decision,
thus paving the way for expansion of Seminole bingo.[50] The Seminoles ex-
perimented with bingo at both Brighton and Big Cypress with mixed results, then opened a major bingo hall on its newly acquired small reservation in Tampa, Florida. By 1985 tribal income from all sources would
exceed $10 million per year, the bulk of it coming from bingo and ciga-
rette sales.[51]

In reviewing his administration almost a decade after leaving office,
Howard Tommie spoke of the difficulty of developing progressive policies
and programs to benefit the tribe while at the same time preserving and
honoring the traditional values of his people. It has been observed that
"progressive" and "traditional" are often convenient labels used by outsiders to describe complex dynamic social and political relationships
within Indian communities.[52] Certainly Seminoles on the three reservations did not display a uniform degree of conservatism and resistance to
change despite their religious orientation; they exhibited a wide range of
acculturation and there were multiple factors at play that led to political
factionalism. Even so, the tribal government encountered a resistance to
many of its programs. When asked how he responded to this opposition,
the former chairman replied, "I am in the age group that I am the progressive. So you have to walk a fine line for political reasons. In other words,
elections are going to come, and you do not want to offend too many
people. You had to walk a fine line."[53]

Another impediment to Seminole progress stemmed from the fact that
many Indian people retained primary loyalty to their reservation community; they did not consider themselves members of a political entity
known as the Seminole Tribe of Florida, and that perception colored the

actions of their representatives on the council and board. Such parochial-
ism was never fully overcome during Tommie's administration despite
his efforts at unification. "I think we recognized that there were some
benefits by working together. But I think that you also have to understand
that there were two different cultures, even languages. I would not say
that I was successful in it."⁵⁴ The tribal council had some success in bringing children from the reservations together for workshops, summer programs, and intertribal athletic competitions, but basically the groups remained divided. Reflecting on this division, Howard conceded, "I do not
think that they want [anyone] to bring them together. The main reason is
that we were told so often that we are our own people and cannot be told
[what to do], not by the tribe, but by the Bureau."⁵⁵

The inability to resolve these differences also accounted for what Tommie considered one of his greatest failures as a tribal leader. He strongly
favored having the tribe contract to operate the Ahfachkee Day School at
the Big Cypress Reservation, which the BIA had run since the 1940s. The
school had a record of poor attendance, marginal teachers, and below
standard academic performance; moreover, most Indian parents on the
reservation were apathetic toward education. A few adults who were interested in their children's schooling agreed that the tribal council should
take charge of the facility; certainly it could do no worse. However, the
tribal council expressed great reluctance to assume responsibility. Council
representatives from other reservations argued that should the BIA contract fail to cover all expenses, tribal funds would be siphoned away from
other projects to meet costs. There were also questions concerning who
would direct the school, hire teachers, set curriculum, and so on, as well
as an unwillingness to leave affairs in the hands of the Big Cypress community. BIA education officials in Washington also raised questions about
the tribe's ability to run a school. In the face of such resistance even the
chairman, who had a reputation for getting his way, could not force the
council to agree on contracting. His critics concur that Tommie was re-
miss in not aggressively pushing contracting as his successor did, and
point to the achievement of tribal children since the tribe began running
the school in 1982.

The most sensitive issue during Howard Tommie's administration concerned the profits that he and his associates apparently reaped from the
smoke shops and bingo. Tommie earlier alluded to the BIA rewarding a
few aggressive Seminole leaders prior to his tenure. Now media reports—
some might call them exposés—such as the *Miami Herald* piece were essentially accusing Tommie of similar actions, noting that he was one of a

small group within the tribe profiting from the business ventures. When asked directly: "How much did the entire tribe benefit economically under your administration from these new ventures?" Tommie's response evolved into a lengthy justification of the benefits that his administration produced for the tribe, and if in the process a few individuals had become wealthy, well that was the natural outcome of the entrepreneurial, capitalist system. On the whole he believed that while a few individuals were disproportionately enriched, the entire tribe had gained more. He responded further:

> That is a very broad question because anytime that you have to do something it involves economics. In other words, the whole budget would have been $150,000 or $200,000 when we first started. That kind of puts you in a dilemma. As far as monetary value, I would like to think that what I did benefited everybody. Every member of the tribe gets $300 every six months. That is money that they could stick in their pockets. We were used to having volunteer lawyers come out and take care of some of the little business that we had, like land leases or maybe a Chickee that needed to be built on the area. During that time we did not have a legal department. Now the Indians can come over here, because we have a full legal department. . . . I would say maybe there are a few of them that are in the cigarette business, but the tribe taxes, and they use that money. From what I understand, Disney World does not pay any taxes . . . but the taxes they collect benefits everybody. What I am saying to you right now is that there are people going around saying it benefits only a certain amount of people. Sure, it is like that all over the world. You can say that. It does not offend me. The paper can say that. As far as aggressiveness is concerned, we introduced something that the whole tribe can benefit from. There were some aggressive people in the tribe, and aggressive people were only looking after themselves. I can sit here and say this because I can defend myself. When money came to the tribal council [in the past], somehow it would benefit the cattle people; it benefited only the cattle people and their families. Here we are benefiting the whole tribe.[56]

Howard Tommie's candid account of his administration provides insights into the motivations, conflicts, and concerns driving many American Indian tribal leaders during the self-determination era. From it comes a greater appreciation for the broad range of social, political, and technical issues that tribal leaders are required to deal with in the modern context. Yet there exists a cultural continuity that links modern tribal leaders to their progenitors: respect and support for both rested on the exercise of wisdom coupled with cultural empathy.

The memoir also illustrates how easily leaders—Indian or non-Indian—

can blur the line that divides personal and public interests. Ironically the very enterprises that generated great wealth for the Seminole Tribe also encouraged entrepreneurial skills that produced private gain. While such activities were not illegal, in the early stages they benefited relatively few Seminoles directly and created social and political cleavages within the Seminole community.

Howard Tommie's chairmanship enjoyed considerable success. He exploited every facet of the Indian self-determination movement and delivered the Seminoles to the brink of economic and political independence while markedly increasing their sovereignty. Yet his aggressive style and personal entrepreneurship engendered some significant criticism. Like other Indian leaders in the past, Tommie may have championed changes that moved too quickly for some of his more conservative kinsmen. Yet history generally has been kind to Native American leaders who have acted forcibly for their people. Tommie's place in history may be enhanced when Seminoles in the future evaluate his career in a broader historical perspective.

NOTES

1. Harry A. Kersey Jr., "The 'New Red Atlantis': John Collier's Encounter with the Florida Seminoles in 1935," *Florida Historical Quarterly* 66 (October 1987): 131–51.

2. Seminole Tribe of Florida, Inc., *Seminole Tribe of Florida Twentieth Anniversary of Tribal Organization, Saturday August 20, 1977,* mimeographed (Hollywood FL, 1977): 16.

3. Harry A. Kersey Jr., *An Assumption of Sovereignty: Social and Political Transformation among the Florida Seminoles, 1953–1979* (Lincoln: University of Nebraska Press, 1996), 83.

4. Harry A. Kersey Jr., *The Florida Seminoles and the New Deal, 1933–1942* (Gainesville: University Presses of Florida, 1989), 176–77.

5. William C. Sturtevant, "A Seminole Personal Document," *Tequesta* 16 (1956): 58. Harry A. Kersey Jr., "The Tony Tommie Letter, 1916: A Transitional Seminole Document," *Florida Historical Quarterly* 64 (April 1986): 301–14.

6. Philip S. Deloria, "The Era of Indian Self-Determination: An Overview," in *Indian Self-Rule: First-Hand Accounts of Indian-White Relationships from Roosevelt to Reagan,* edited by Kenneth R. Philip (Salt Lake City: Howe Brothers, 1986), 202.

7. Deloria, "The Era of Indian Self-Determination," 197.

8. *U.S. Statutes at Large* 88 (1975): 2204.

9. Vine Deloria Jr. and Clifford Lytle, *The Nations Within: The Past and Future of American Indian Sovereignty* (New York: Pantheon Books, 1984), 220.

10. *Miami Herald*, 13 May 1975, 1BW.

11. *Miami Herald*, 13 May 1975, 1BW.

12. Seminole Tribe of Florida (hereafter cited as STF), Council Resolution No. C-66-75, 14 March 1975.

13. *Florida Statutes Annotated* (1991), sections 285.17 and 285.18.

14. STF, Council Resolution No. C-39-71, 13 November 1970.

15. Seminole Tribe of Florida, Inc., *Twentieth Anniversary*, 18.

16. Minutes of the Special Joint Council and Board, STF, 7 June 1971.

17. STF and Seminole Tribe of Florida, Inc., budget, FY 1971.

18. Interview with Howard E. Tommie, 14 January 1988, SEM. 60A, University of Florida Oral History Archives, 1–2.

19. Interview with Howard E. Tommie, 3.

20. Interview with Howard E. Tommie, 3.

21. Interview with Howard E. Tommie, 3–4.

22. Interview with Howard E. Tommie, 3.

23. *Miami Herald*, 13 May 1975, 1BW.

24. *Miami Herald*, 13 May 1975, 1BW.

25. *Miami Herald*, 13 May 1975, 1BW.

26. *Palm Beach Post*, 15 May 1975 C3.

27. *Miami Herald*, 8 April 1979, 11–17.

28. 364 So2d 5480.

29. 446 F.Supp. 1339.

30. *Florida Statutes Annotated* (1985), section 210.05.

31. Minutes of Special Meeting of the Tribal Council, STF, 16 October 1975.

32. STF, Council Resolution No. C-38-76, 16 October 1975.

33. *Miami Herald*, 8 April 1979, 12.

34. *Miami Herald*, 8 April 1979, 13.

35. STF, Council Resolution No. C-60-74, 11 January 1974.

36. *Miami Herald*, 8 April 1979, 12.

37. *Miami Herald*, 8 April 1979, 12.

38. *Miami Herald*, 8 April 1979, 13–14.

39. STF, Council Resolution No. C-82-79, 3 January 1979.

40. STF, Council Resolution No. C-84-79, 3 January 1979.

41. STF, Council Resolution No. C-81-79, 3 January 1979.

42. *Miami Herald*, 8 April 1979, 14.

43. STF, Council Resolution No. C-142-78 and Board Resolution BD-117-78, 6 June 1978.

44. Interview with Howard E. Tommie, 7–8.

45. Interview with Howard E. Tommie, 8–9.

46. *Palm Beach Post*, 1 March 1982, 1-2. STF, Council Resolution No. C-21-80, 24 August 1979.

47. "Bingo is the Best Revenge," *Time*, 7 July 1980, 8.

48. Dale L. McDonnell, "Federal and State Regulation of Gambling and Liquor Sales within Indian Country," *Hamline Law Review* 8 (October 1985): 606–7.

49. 492 F.Supp. 1020.

50. 658 F2d 310.

51. John Taylor, "Florida's Seminoles Have Only Just Begun to Fight," *Florida Trend* 28(9) (January 1986): 111.

52. David Rich Lewis, "Reservation Leadership and the Progressive-Traditional Dichotomy: William Wash and the Northern Utes, 1865–1928," *Ethnohistory* 38 (1991): 124–42.

53. Interview with Howard E. Tommie, 8.

54. Interview with Howard E. Tommie, 10.

55. Interview with Howard E. Tommie, 11.

56. Interview with Howard E. Tommie, 5–6.

Phillip Martin

Mississippi Choctaw

BY BENTON R. WHITE AND CHRISTINE SCHULTZ WHITE

In Mississippi the long hot summer lays across the land like a huge blanket, drenching the piney woods with humidity and pouring forth heat like an oven full of corn bread. These are sleepy days, for the sweltering temperatures and sultry, dog-day afternoons stifle activity, encouraging a languor that pervades the countryside. In October the first winds of autumn sweep in from the northwest. The sky turns a brighter shade of blue and the lethargy of the past months fades into the pastures and timberlands. For the Choctaws, who have occupied the Mississippi piney woods for centuries, autumn has always been the time of harvest. They traditionally have welcomed the crisp air of autumn as a harbinger of prosperity, a friendly spirit who promises abundance.

Following an extended period of lassitude, the winds of change have blown through the Choctaw Nation. After almost two hundred years of poverty and dependency, the Choctaws have reemerged as a people in control of their own destiny. At the heart of this transformation is Phillip Martin.[1]

The Mississippi Band of Choctaws shares a common heritage of grit and determination. Throughout history they were mostly an agricultural people raising corn, beans, pumpkins, and squash on small plots, sharing their harvest with kinsmen and trading unused surplus to neighbors. Like the Cherokees, they exhibited a talent for adjusting to the pressure of advancing white settlement, adopting many of the ways and consumer goods of the Europeans. But the Euro-American frontier came too swiftly, and by 1830 the Choctaws were forced to cede nearly all of their territory in Mississippi to the United States in exchange for lands farther west in Indian Territory. Most of the tribe removed to Oklahoma, but against all odds other Choctaws held on to remote plots of oak and pine forest in eastern Mississippi. Those few, along with kinsmen who eventually drifted back from the west, ultimately became the Mississippi Band of Choctaws.[2]

Times were hard. By the early 1900s the Mississippi Choctaws were a people struggling to survive. Most had lost their few remaining patches of land—through fraud or extortion—and had been reduced to a peasantry, existing as sharecroppers or menial laborers. In 1918 the federal government purchased twenty-four thousand acres of land from the private sector and established a new reservation near Philadelphia, Mississippi, but the Choctaws remained impoverished. Desperately clinging to their heritage, they were determined to retain their separate identity. By 1920 they counted barely one thousand members. When state authorities informed them that the only public schools available to Indian children would also be attended by African Americans, they chose to keep their children home. As a consequence, most remained illiterate. Indeed during the 1920s nearly 90 percent of the Mississippi Choctaws were full-bloods and most spoke no English.[3]

In the decades that followed there was little change and less progress. As recently as 1962, inhabitants of the Mississippi Band of Choctaw Indians Reservation easily qualified as some of the most impoverished people in the United States. Even in a state that consistently ranked near the bottom on almost every socioeconomic scale, they often were the poorest of the poor. Unemployment rates on the reservation regularly exceeded 80 percent. Per capita income was less than one-seventh the national average; those on welfare included members from almost every household. Other data bore testament to rampant alcoholism, dysfunctional families, and criminal neglect, as well as nearly epidemic levels of tuberculosis, hookworm, and several other maladies. Small wonder that infant mortality rates were far above the national average, and life expectancy well below. In short, the Mississippi Choctaws had a standard of living more in common with the populations of third world countries in Latin America or western Africa than with most of the rest of the United States.[4]

Phillip Martin has done much to improve these conditions. Born on 13 March 1926, Martin grew up in a community where family members worked hard but had little disposable income; lived in wooden shanties; and became ill, aged, and died before their time. No electricity, no plumbing, no doctors: all this was a part of his early years on the reservation. But the poverty that seemed to consume and overwhelm so many of his kinsmen inspired Martin to overcome and succeed. At a time when almost no one on the reservation received more than a rudimentary education, Martin graduated from high school. Taking advantage of the Bureau of Indian

Affairs (BIA) boarding school in Cherokee, North Carolina, he left Mississippi to earn his diploma. Following graduation, Martin pursued still another opportunity: he enlisted in the United States Air Force.[5]

In the Air Force, Martin found himself assigned to the European theater
at the close of World War II. Serving in France and Germany, he encountered conditions that would leave a lasting impression. Wholesale desola-
tion, misery, and ruin were everywhere—conditions worse than any he
had ever seen. But along with the wreckage he found something else: a
people, though hungry and desperate, who had not been broken. They refused to behave or think of themselves as defeated. Furthermore, they
possessed an unshakable faith that they would rebuild and flourish. In the
years that followed, Martin, like everyone else, witnessed what happened
next in Western Europe: the Marshall Plan and the economic miracle of
reconstruction and development. The experience had an effect on Martin.
If rebuilding could happen in France and Germany, then why not in Neshoba County, Mississippi? If seed money could jump-start an economy
in Frankfurt, then why not on an Indian reservation? If the survivors of
World War II could draw strength from adversity and from their own cultural traditions, then why not the Choctaws?[6]

For the next ten years Martin remained in the military, traveling
throughout the world, working his way up to the rank of sergeant. But he
could never forget what he had seen in Europe. Neither could he forget his
home or his people. In 1955, following his military career, he returned to
Neshoba County.

Once in Mississippi, Martin encountered the same bleak conditions he
had known as a youngster. There was no work and little prospect for
change. In no small way this was a consequence of an arcane and often
contradictory code of racial etiquette unique to Neshoba County and the
surrounding area. For over a century, a tripartite system of race relations
had evolved, placing the white man at the top, blacks at the bottom, and
Indians wherever the dominant caste felt like placing them. Choctaws
were not forced to be as deferential to the whites as were African Americans, but Indians, like blacks, had been told they would never attend the
same public schools as white people, nor eat in the same public places,
nor be buried in the same cemeteries, nor share in a thousand other common life experiences. Choctaws like Phillip Martin could join the military.
In fact, there was a proud tradition of Choctaw military service dating
back to the Civil War, when more than one unit was eagerly accepted into
the ranks of the Confederate army. But once home in Neshoba County, no
Choctaw veteran need seriously consider an active role in the life of the

larger community he was expected to defend. Unable to find work on the reservation or in the nearby county seat of Philadelphia, Mississippi, Martin moved thirty miles away to Meridian.[7]

Working days as a clerk at the Meridian Air Naval Station, Martin spent his nights attending a local community college, graduating with an associate of arts degree in 1957. He also became interested in tribal politics. He returned to the reservation and in 1959 was elected chairman of the tribal council. It was a whole new career with a "salary" of $2.50 per hour.[8]

In the past the tribal council's role had been simply to rubber-stamp BIA decisions. So disdainful was the BIA of the Choctaw tribal government that council meetings were relegated to the kitchen area of the agency. In fact, no council members went to Washington for any purpose without the permission of local BIA authorities and a BIA escort. After Martin's election, things changed. Martin studied voluminous records on relations between Indian tribes and the federal government, then led a delegation to Washington DC to press for a better response to Choctaw needs. From that time forward, Martin became a familiar figure in Washington, in particular at the Interior Department and in the halls of Congress. Here he buttonholed agency heads and representatives, pleading for money to replace obsolescent schools and decrepit homes, and to pave the reservation's red-dirt roads. The same determination that had helped him achieve an education and a military career drove him once more.[9]

Martin's first significant experience managing money for the tribe came with the War on Poverty in the 1960s. The Choctaws obtained one of the first Community Action Program grants in Mississippi—a total of fifteen thousand dollars. That money would propel many economic changes. With these funds Martin devised a fiscal system of accountability and control designed to attract other and larger federal grants. Then came another grant that enabled him to hire accountants, bookkeepers, personnel managers, and planners. In certain respects, Martin had begun to move toward an economic plan of action similar to that of nations like Singapore and Taiwan. At a time when most developing countries embraced socialism as the wave of the future, Martin shrewdly concluded that corporate investment could best serve as the driving force for economic development, and that government grants used to attract private investment were seed money, not an end in themselves. The goal was to find a source of income that would lead to prosperity and independence. Martin understood that corporations wanted cheap labor, low taxes, and an honest, consistent, and stable government policy. Moreover, he was convinced that the tribe was uniquely positioned to join the international competition for low-wage labor in the manufacturing sector.[10]

From the beginning, Martin recognized the advantage the Choctaws could wield in the competition for business and jobs. The Mississippi Choctaw Reservation, like other Indian reservations, was effectively an enterprise zone. Since tribes were considered government units, Choctaw Reservation employees, businesses, and transactions were exempt from state and local taxes as well as regulations. Though subject to federal law, enterprises owned by the tribe on the reservation were exempt from federal taxes and from many federal regulations. Thus a business could be set up on Choctaw lands without the burden of zoning permits, licenses, construction permits, and so on—all of which were a woeful part of doing business almost anywhere else in the United States. Since they controlled their own civil courts, the Choctaws could also exempt businesses on the reservation from the tort madness that was beginning to plague the rest of the country. In effect, the Choctaws could offer an entrepreneurial economic environment. "We know who our competitors are," Martin asserted: places with names such as "Tapei, Seoul, Singapore, and Ciudad Jurez."[11] With this in mind, the Choctaws obtained a hundred and fifty thousand dollars from the Federal Economic Development Administration in 1973 to establish an industrial park on a twenty-acre plot. "It will attract somebody," Martin predicted. But this time he was wrong: the site stood vacant for five years. Businesses would not risk a venture in the untested waters of Choctaw country.[12]

With characteristic tenacity, Martin began writing letters to over a hundred and fifty manufacturers throughout the United States promoting the Mississippi Choctaw Industrial Park as an ideal plant site. At last one of them, Packard Electric, a division of General Motors, offered to train Choctaws to assemble wired parts for motor vehicles. Packard offered to sell materials to Chahta Enterprises, the name of a new tribal company, then buy back the parts once assembled. On the basis of Packard's commitment, the tribe obtained another $346,000 grant from the federal government, then used a BIA loan guarantee to obtain $1 million more from a local bank to construct a 42,000-square-foot plant. For a moment, it seemed to Martin and other tribal officials as if the future of the Mississippi Choctaws had been secured. But they were wrong. Within a year Chahta Enterprises faced a debt of $1 million and was teetering on the brink of bankruptcy.[13]

Basically production lagged because of problems that had undermined tribal enterprises in so many other areas. For many Choctaws, the routine and discipline associated with regular employment were alien concepts. Employees would abruptly leave work for a family function and not return for a week. Some spoke no English. Others suffered from alcoholism. Many were single mothers with small children and no reliable transportation. To salvage Chahta Enterprises, if not the economic future of the reservation, Martin turned to Lester Dalme, a professional manager from outside the reservation.

A General Motors supervisor from rural Louisiana, Lester Dalme possessed an almost evangelical attitude toward labor and employment. Every man and woman, he believed, had an obligation to serve God through work. As soon as Dalme arrived at Chahta Enterprises, he called a general meeting to examine the demoralized work force; it was not a pretty sight. The Choctaws had no idea of how to run a business, he recalled later. Few of them had ever worked in a factory; they generally were unfamiliar with concepts such as quality control or on-time delivery. Production of materials in an efficient, profit-oriented manner was alien to them, and most Choctaws had no knowledge of profit and loss statements. To help reverse these conditions Martin promised Dalme full control over the plant, freedom from politics, no pressure to hire relatives of Choctaws or to retain any unfit employee—in other words, virtual autonomy as chief executive officer at Chahta Enterprises.[14]

Dalme moved quickly to change the workplace. Wherever possible he cut back on waste, abolished managerial perks, and put supervisors to work on the assembly line. Next, he established day care for workers with small children and purchased a pair of old diesel buses to pick up those workers without cars. He implemented a zero-tolerance policy for alcohol and hangovers in the plant. Most important, he formalized the work routine: anyone late or absent from work two times in the first ninety days received a warning; three infractions resulted in probation; four absences or late arrivals meant extended probation; and five in ninety days triggered immediate dismissal. Thirty days after Dalme implemented these reforms Chahta turned its first profit. Something else changed too. People who had been totally destitute began to show up for work in new shoes, in clothes without holes, and eventually in cars. After six or seven months the Mississippi Choctaw Reservation had a core workforce of able and increasingly self-confident workers.

From fifty-seven employees in 1979, Chahta Enterprises grew to over nine hundred by the mid-1990s. In large measure this growth can be explained by a reputation for high caliber work that has become virtually synonymous with the company. For example, the national rejection rate for all United States factories assembling harness wire systems like those of Chahta Enterprises was three per one thousand. In Japan, the rate was 2.5 per thousand. On the Choctaw Reservation the rate was .08 for every thousand.[15]

Moreover, once the tribe established a track record for productivity, profit, and timely delivery, financing for other assembly plants and enterprises followed. Another sixty-thousand-square-foot plant was erected, which produced audio speakers for Ford Motor Company, the Chrysler Corporation, and McDonnell-Douglas. Then a plant that assembled circuit boards and other electronic units for AT&T, Xerox, Westinghouse, Navistar, Harley-Davidson, and the Boeing Corporation was built. Still another plant went up, this one financed by state revenue bonds—an idea of Martin's—to assemble and hand-finish greeting cards for American Greetings Corporation. As a result, today the Choctaws own and operate the largest-volume printing plant for direct mail advertising east of the Mississippi, turning out eighty-three million hand-finished cards annually.[16]

Currently the Choctaws also own and manage a construction company; produce nearly one million pieces of plastic cutlery daily for McDonald's; and own and operate a modern shopping center and a health center that includes one of the finest hospitals in Mississippi. They also manage a multimillion dollar resort hotel and casino that includes an eighteen-hole golf course and recreation complex. Altogether, the Mississippi Choctaws operate twelve major businesses with annual gross receipts and revenues in excess of three hundred million dollars. They are by far the largest employer in Neshoba County and among the ten largest in the state. They have emerged as an economic powerhouse; a diversified industrial empire that is the chief source of jobs and income for the entire region.[17]

At first glance the assembly plants owned by Choctaw Manufacturing Enterprises (formerly Chahta Enterprises) are typical of any modern facility: buildings set amid pastures and pinewoods—all spacious and well-ventilated against the withering summer heat. Inside, workers perch at long tables weaving wires onto color-coded boards. It is tedious work; as many as three hundred wires may go into some of the harnesses that must in turn be attached to dozens of terminals. The wires are made to join and bifurcate, then recombine and intertwine over and over in runic combinations. As they work, the long rows of mostly women listen to the beat of piped-in radio and swap gossip or news. Across the floor at similar tables, others assemble telephones, put together circuit boards for computers and audio speakers, or make parts for Xerox photocopiers.

In another sense, however, the factory floor is remarkable and even revolutionary. The faces bent over the wires, phones, and speakers record a transformation that few could have envisioned in Mississippi forty years before. The employees are mostly Choctaws, but among them are also whites and African Americans, scores of them, all working side by side in what was once the poorest backwater of a state that ranked second to none in its determination to keep races and cultures apart.

It is here perhaps—on the issue of race relations and the larger community—that Phillip Martin's political instincts have paid the greatest dividends. By the 1960s Martin had the novel thought—novel in some corners at least—that high profile political agitation for equal opportunity might be pointless or even self-defeating for the Choctaws. Surrounded and hopelessly outnumbered by a non-Indian population, he felt that the Choctaws could not bring to bear enough political clout for substantive change. Because of his influence, the reservation remained largely detached and even aloof from the civil rights movement that swept Mississippi during those years. Martin took more than a little criticism for this position but he remained focused on economic development. Mississippians had a common problem, Martin noted; the lack of jobs and opportunities had kept people of all races and ethnic groups mired in ignorance, poverty, and isolation. He worked to ensure that economic success on the reservation would spill over into the surrounding communities. The reservation economy, in other words, was to be integrated into the surrounding region, creating jobs and opportunity for as many as possible. Martin understood something very basic about human nature—given the choice between hating and eating, most will choose the latter. Employment and rising incomes for Indians and non-Indians alike would be the mechanism to neutralize racist hatreds and to open the doors of acceptance.[18]

As a result of tribal economic development and integration with the outside world, not only have living standards improved throughout the area, but so too have attitudes. After decades of scorn, apathy, and open hostility from much of the surrounding non-Indian population, the Mississippi Band of Choctaw Indians have largely won the support and respect of their neighbors. It is not a perfect world in east Mississippi; there are those who still resent and even despise the Choctaws. No doubt there are some who are resentful of their success. But it is difficult if not impossible for this hostile group to influence the majority the way it did in the past. Too many owe their livelihood to the Choctaws. Mayor Harlan Majors of nearby Philadelphia said it for most: "Our best industry by far is the Choctaw Nation. Our economy depends on them. If the tribe went bankrupt, we'd go into a depression."[19]

Such farsighted policy has resulted in an unemployment rate for the area that is currently lower than it has been for decades. Among the Choctaws it is below 5 percent, a complete reversal from the 80 percent unemployment rate of the 1950s. Average family income on the reservation, in fact, has climbed from two thousand dollars per year in the 1970s to twenty-two thousand dollars for a family of four; and unlike the past, only 2.7 percent of household income derives from welfare or other social programs. Substandard housing on the Choctaw Reservation has declined from 85 percent to 15 percent, with brick ranch homes the shelter of choice. Since 1975 the average education level of tribal members has risen from the sixth grade to the twelfth grade, with achievement test scores equal to the state average. At the same time, life expectancy has soared, while infant mortality has plummeted to the national average. On the reservation, nearly everywhere it seems, there is evidence of a people on the move: well-constructed homes, schools with landscaped campuses, a modern hospital and day care center, and a new tribal meeting hall with administrative offices. In one direction there is an outdoor sports complex, in another an industrial park. It is all a part of modern life for the Mississippi Choctaws.[20]

Impressive as these gains may be, many think that even more has been accomplished in the political realm. Tribal government is similar to state political systems, with sovereignty manifested through a set of elected representatives: a chief and a sixteen-member tribal council elected by the community, and a vice chief and secretary treasurer elected by the council from its ranks. In addition, there are tribal courts that exercise authority over all misdemeanors and civil cases.

Within the context of this system, the Mississippi Choctaws have emerged as a national leader in transferring the administration of government programs from the BIA to the tribes. Moreover, the driving impulse behind the surge in Choctaw empowerment has often been the same force that was so instrumental to economic development: the chief of the Mississippi Choctaws for the past two decades, Phillip Martin. Indeed, some believe that a de-coupling from the BIA was always Martin's paramount goal: first, economic independence and the clout and self-confidence that comes with money, then political freedom. Almost every task once carried on by the BIA—law enforcement, social services, forestry, credit and finance—is performed today by Choctaw tribal members. Under a contract with the federal government the tribe operates six elementary schools, a middle school, and a high school—every facility fully accredited by the Mississippi Department of Education or the Southern Association of Colleges and Schools. Thanks to a contract with the Indian Health Service, the tribe administers its own forty-three-bed hospital and several clinics. The Choctaws also manage their own transit system as well as water, sewage, and waste disposal plants through various reservation utility commissions. All of these government functions are financed without taxing tribal members, for the tribe relies on revenue from business operations and on federal funds the government is obliged to pay by treaty.

Meanwhile, Martin has continued to utilize the larger federal political system for the Choctaws' benefit. Charges that Martin is a laissez-faire ideologue, owing to his proclivity for attracting business capital or his opposition to BIA control, are simply overstated. Martin is quick to note that seed money in the form of government grants was largely responsible for triggering the economic explosion of wealth and jobs on the reservation, and he remains as skilled and adroit as anyone in seeking economic advantage meted out by government. More than anything, Chief Martin is a pragmatist, picking and choosing from government or the private sector whatever works—whatever puts food on the table and money in the bank.

There are those who have been critical of Phillip Martin and the changes he has championed, people who argue that he has "betrayed" his culture in pursuit of economic gain. It is a familiar refrain often raised against economic development projects on reservations throughout the United States. His critics charge that by embracing modern technology, hourly work schedules, corporate investment, and all of the trinkets and consumer goods they make possible, Martin has "gutted" the very soul of Choctaw culture. All that remains, Martin's critics assert, is a pathetic caricature of Indian peoples in pursuit of the white man's dollar. Interestingly, this argument often comes from individuals who are themselves largely steeped in a Western liberal frame of reference, or more typically, from white people with very definite ideas about what an Indian should be.

Those who argue that an Indian is not an Indian unless he or she is not tied to nineteenth-century cultural patterns have missed something fundamental about culture and history. No people in the present or the past have ever lived in perfect isolation, untouched and unchanged by the rest of the world. People everywhere have interacted: trading, conversing, warring, and acculturating, one with the other, and in the process improvising, compromising, and continually reshaping themselves in order to survive. Choctaw workers in the assembly plants near Philadelphia, Mississippi, live differently from their early nineteenth century forefathers, but Choctaw farmers and cattlemen in the early national period also differed markedly from their ancestors who formed part of the pre-Columbian Mississippian complex. Tribal cultures, like other cultures, are not fixed in stone. Is the population of Japan no longer truly Japanese since embracing and building on Western technology? For that matter, are the white people of Mississippi no longer Southern because they do not live like their ancestors of the 1850s? To suggest that the Choctaws and Phillip Martin, or Native Americans anywhere, have renounced their cultural heritage by seizing opportunities that exist in recent times is to say that Indian people should live outside the flow of history. Indeed, such a perspective is demeaning, for it suggests that "real" Native American culture is somehow untouched and unaltered by events that shape the rest of human civilization; that Indian people do not share in broader patterns that shape the rest of humankind.

Chief Martin and others like him have taken advantage of a global trend toward world markets and capitalist economics, set within the context of declining or even crumbling political institutions. It is a phenomenon apt to last for generations and is uniquely suited to small-scale economic enclaves ready and able to adapt to the latest consumer-driven need or technical innovation.

As long as there are those who think of themselves as Choctaw and wish to be Choctaw, the Choctaw people will survive: whether in rural Mississippi, urban Atlanta, or anywhere in the world. It is only when no one cares or when a people turn inward against themselves with hatred or contempt, feeling only shame and seeking to hide or renounce their past, that they truly die. No one who knows Chief Phillip Martin questions his devotion to the Choctaws—those of the past, the present, or the future.

With the future generations in mind, the Choctaws have increased their financial commitments to education; schools are in fact a top priority. While modern classrooms are today the norm, plans are under way to equip them with state-of-the-art computer/learning technology. Teachers at reservation elementary schools earn salaries 25 percent higher than those at public schools in neighboring non-Indian communities. The Choctaws attempt to hire the best teachers regardless of race or ethnicity. And unlike so many public schools throughout America, on the reservation a teacher who cannot perform satisfactorily is released. There is also a tribal television station—the primary local channel for the region—broadcasting an eclectic daily menu that includes Choctaw language newscasts and public service programs on topics as diverse as personal finance and microwave cooking. Small wonder that over 90 percent of reservation members remain fluent in Choctaw.[21]

On the economic front, determination to succeed in the future is reflected in the evolving nature of the Choctaw labor force. Increasingly, the tribe has offered its members technical and managerial positions in engineering, business management, teaching, or statistical analysis. The Choctaws, in essence, are creating a twenty-first-century managerial and professional class. In 1989 for example, there were four Choctaw managers at the reservation assembly plant in Carthage, Mississippi; today there are thirteen. The next generation will manage their own businesses entirely, states Sam Schisler, current CEO of the Carthage plant. Also changing is the nature of tribal business enterprises. The children of sharecroppers, for whom a trip to the nearest town was once a major undertaking, are today assembling parts for circuit boards from Shreveport, Louisiana, to Bangkok, Thailand. Soon they will be constructing their own circuit boards. Also growing rapidly in importance are tribal service and financial industries. These days "we're more into profit centers," notes William Richardson, a former venture capitalist whom Chief Martin hired to function as a resident tribal entrepreneur. "We're aggressive as hell," says Richardson, "and we take risks," though the risks are calculated.[22]

One such risk is the new $38 million Silver Star Resort Hotel and Casino. Some Indian tribes have achieved great economic success with gaming enterprises. The Choctaws hope that their casino also will be as successful. But the Mississippi Choctaws are unique, for they have already blazed a path to economic independence with highly diversified industrial and commercial operations. For the Choctaws, the casino/hotel industry is simply a part of a much larger economic strategy. In fact, the casino is only a segment of a recreation center that includes an eighteen-hole golf course and country club, and in time will include a theme park.[23]

And so it goes. For over three decades the stories of the Mississippi Band of Choctaws and Phillip Martin have been largely synonymous. During that time Martin has served as the tribe's principal elected official for twenty-one years and as the reservation's business manager for three years. He has served five-year terms as director of the Choctaw Community Action Agency and chairman of the Tribal Housing Authority. He has been responsible for establishing an industrial park with eight industrial plants and tribal businesses, a tribe-owned construction company, and several public service enterprises including the Choctaw Transit Authority and the Choctaw Utility Commission. Altogether, these undertakings have resulted in the creation of over four thousand jobs. Most of all, perhaps, Phillip Martin has been instrumental in restoring hope.

The past two decades have witnessed mounting national recognition of Martin's accomplishments and a growing list of awards. In addition to winning the United Indian Development Association's Jay Silverheels Award, Martin has received the Minority Supplier/Distributor of the Year Award from the United States Small Business Administration and the Minority Business Development Association; the "Soar Like An Eagle" Achievement Award from the United Indian Youth Organization; and an economic achievement award from the U.S. Department of Housing and Urban Development (HUD). In 1987, Martin won the American Vocational Association's Award of Merit, owing to the success of the tribe's vocational education program. The following year he received the HUD Certificate of National Merit, in recognition of excellence and innovation at the reservation's Early Childhood Education Center. In 1996, Chief Phillip Martin was inducted into the Mississippi Business Hall of Fame. He has come a long way since the day he returned home from the military and found that no one would hire an Indian ex-serviceman.[24]

If there is a flaw in all that has been accomplished, it's probably that so much has depended on the diligence and resourcefulness of a single individual. Sooner or later, the question must be raised: What happens next? What happens after Chief Martin? Has he truly wrought an economic revolution in Choctaw country? Has he created an economic powerhouse that will sustain itself and grow only stronger far into the twenty-first century? Is this the beginning of a new chapter in the history of an ancient people who have been great and prosperous before? Within the past decade political opponents within the Choctaw Nation have challenged his leadership, suggesting they could provide political and economic leadership more equitably and efficiently. Yet no Mississippi Choctaws support a return to the old days of isolation, lack of economic opportunity, and poverty. His political opponents have embraced Martin's ideas of education and controlled participation in the greater economy; they just argue that they now can manage and administer the revitalized Choctaw Nation more effectively.

Is it conceivable that Phillip Martin is part of a world phenomenon where large nations and institutions are fragmenting in favor of resurgent local and autonomous ethnic communities that have been suppressed for three hundred years? Or will the end of Martin's career also mark the collapse of a brief and brilliant moment in the history of a people who for almost two centuries have been burdened by poverty and government dependency? Only time can say for sure: Time and perhaps the cool breezes passing through the Mississippi pines in the bright afternoon of early autumn—for in the old days the Choctaws taught their children that the spirits could foretell the future and that sometimes the spirits traveled on the wind.

NOTES

1. Although a biography of Phillip Martin has recently been published, when this essay was written no study was available, and much of the information included in this essay was garnered from interviews with Martin, members of the Mississippi Choctaw Tribe, and employees of the tribe. Also see Peter Michelmore, "Uprising in Indian Country," *Reader's Digest,* vol. 125, November 1984, 69–76; Andrew E. Serwer, "American Indians Discover Money Is Power," *Fortune,* col. 127, 19 April 1993, 136–42; Peter J. Ferrara, "Choctaw Uprising: Business Acumen of Mississippi Choctaw Indian Chief Phillip Martin," *National Review,* vol. 48, 11 March 1996, 30–32; Fergus M. Bordewich, "How to Succeed in Business: Follow the Choctaws' Lead," *Smithsonian,* vol. 26, March 1996, 70–80.

2. The best general sources for Choctaw history in Mississippi are: Samuel J. Wells and Roseanne Tubby, eds., *After Removal: The Choctaws in Mississippi* (Jackson: University of Mississippi Press, 1986); Jesse O. McKee and Jon A. Schlenker, *The Choctaws: Cultural Evolution of a Native American Tribe* (Jackson: University of Mississippi Press, 1980); Richard White, *Roots of Dependency* (Lincoln: University of Nebraska Press, 1983); Clara Sue Kidwell, *Choctaws and Missionaries in Mississippi, 1819–1918* (Norman: University of Oklahoma Press, 1985); and Patricia Galloway, *Choctaw Genesis, 1500–1700* (Lincoln: University of Nebraska Press, 1995). See also Angie Debo, *The Rise and Fall of the Choctaw Republic* (Norman: University of Oklahoma Press, 1934).

3. McKee and Schlenker, *The Choctaws,* 7–39.

4. Michelmore, "Uprising in Indian Country," 69–72; Phillip Martin, interview with the authors, 7 October 1997, Spanish Fort, Alabama.

5. Martin, interview.

6. Martin, interview.

7. Martin, interview.

8. Martin, interview.

9. Martin, interview.

10. Martin, interview.

11. Fergus M. Bordewich, *Killing the White Man's Indian: Reinventing Native Americans at the End of the Twentieth Century* (New York: Doubleday, 1996), 307.

12. Bordewich, "How to Succeed in Business," 76.

13. Bordewich, *Killing the White Man's Indian*, 308.

14. Bordewich, "How to Succeed in Business," 76–77.

15. Bordewich, *Killing the White Man's Indian*, 309–10.

16. Martin, interview.

17. "Tribal Profile." *Http://allcatalogs.com/choctaw/newhistory/html*, 1999.

18. Martin, interview.

19. Martin, interview; Bordewich, "How to Succeed in Business," 70–71.

20. Martin, interview.

21. Martin, interview; "Tribal Profile," 1999.

22. Bordewich, *Killing the White Man's Indian*, 309–10, 331.

23. Martin, interview.

24. Martin, interview.

Wilma Mankiller

Cherokee

BY BRAD AGNEW

Former Cherokee chief Wilma Mankiller's career has been chronicled in numerous articles and books, but most accounts pay little attention to her years as a tribal leader. In her autobiography of about three hundred pages, only the final, sixteen-page chapter considers her tenure as deputy chief and chief.[1] Despite the volume of literature about Mankiller, there is no critical assessment of her leadership. While it is too soon to place Mankiller's career in historical perspective, it is time to start examining her contribution to the Cherokee Nation.

Born in Tahlequah, Oklahoma, in 1945, Wilma Pearl was the sixth of eleven children born to full-blood Cherokee Charley Mankiller and his Dutch-Irish wife, Irene.[2] They lived in Adair County on land allotted to the Mankillers when the Cherokee Nation was dissolved early in the twentieth century. The family barely eked out an existence on the flinty foothills of the Ozarks where Mankiller's early years were spent in a four-room, tin-roofed house built of rough lumber with no electricity or running water. Although she felt comfortable in the familiar surroundings of Mankiller Flats, her parents hoped to provide their children with more opportunities by taking advantage of a Bureau of Indian Affairs (BIA) relocation program. In 1956, just before her eleventh birthday, she and her family boarded a train for San Francisco and a new life.

Wrenched from their rural roots, the Mankillers experienced cultural shock in their new home. Teased about her name, accent, and clothes by her classmates, Mankiller found sanctuary at the San Francisco Indian Center in the Mission District. Academically, she "remained unsettled as far as goals, with no sense of direction," but "at the end of the day, everything seemed brighter at the Indian Center." The future Cherokee leader had inherited a love of books from her father, but she admitted that she only went "through the motions of attending classes."[3] Nonetheless, she completed high school in 1963. That summer she got a job and met an Ecuadorian attending college in San Francisco. Before autumn, after a whirlwind courtship, they were married, just five days before her eighteenth birthday. Nine months later she was a mother, and less than two years later she had a second daughter. By then she was beginning to chaff under the restraints imposed by a husband who viewed her primarily as a wife and mother.

San Francisco was a hotbed of social activism in the 1960s. Dissidents not only challenged America's policy in Vietnam, but also most of the nation's fundamental values. The spirit of the times shaped the future leader of the Cherokees. Dissatisfaction with the constraints imposed by marriage spurred her to enroll in a few classes in a nearby community college. Initially she took only courses she enjoyed in the areas of literature and sociology. Soon her academic success and her growing independence widened the gulf separating the couple. Along with classes and family responsibilities she worked part time and renewed her associations with the Bay Area Native American community at the American Indian Center.

Still in the process of discovering her own identity in the turbulent 1960s, the twenty-four-year-old wife and mother observed firsthand one of the defining moments in the modern history of Native Americans—the occupation of Alcatraz. Although she was not a participant, other members of the Mankiller family moved to the island. The future Cherokee chief became "totally engulfed by the Native American movement." Thirty years later Mankiller recalled that as a result of the Alcatraz experience "I consciously took a path I still find myself on today as I continue to work for the revitalization of tribal communities."[4]

During the occupation, her father died of polycystic kidney disease, a disorder his daughter inherited. Her condition was not advanced, but doctors suggested that she might experience kidney failure before middle age.

Working for Native American causes eased the loss of her father and frustrations of a suffocating marriage. Despite her husband's objections, she traveled to west coast tribal events and volunteered at the Native American Youth Center in East Oakland. There she developed a belief that "poor people, particularly poor American Indian people, have a lot more potential and many more answers to problems than they are ever given a chance to realize." The burgeoning Indian activist also volunteered to work with the Pit River Tribe in its legal struggle against Pacific Gas and Electric Company. Her work with the Indian community ultimately led her to the realization that she "could no longer remain content as a housewife."[5] She ended her marriage, resumed the Mankiller name, and found employment as a social worker at the Urban Indian Resource Center. Her final years in the Bay Area were turbulent. Child support payments were sporadic, but worse, Mankiller's former husband refused to return his younger daughter after an outing. It was almost a year before she and the girl were reunited. Fear that he might separate her from her children again was a factor in Mankiller's decision to leave California.

When she and her two daughters moved to Oklahoma in the summer of 1977, Mankiller recalled, "I had twenty dollars to my name, no car, no job, and few, if any, prospects." Living with her mother, who had recently returned to Oklahoma, she began looking for work. Adair County, one of the poorest regions in the nation, offered limited employment opportunities, and Mankiller spent several frustrating months seeking a job. In October she was hired as an economic stimulus coordinator by the Cherokee Nation of Oklahoma. Mankiller's job was to promote college training in environmental science or health for Cherokees who would return to Indian communities and help their people.[6]

For a young divorcée, schooled in the high-pressure, direct-action environment of the San Francisco Indian movement, the bureaucracy and authoritarian nature of Cherokee government evoked frustration. From her perspective, tribal programs emphasized economic development at the expense of Cherokees living in rural communities. Even programs directed at helping the poor were exploited by "sophisticated" urban members of the tribe. Operating within the system, Mankiller stayed late, worked weekends, and "went to all the meetings." Greg Combs, a young attorney who worked with Mankiller on several projects, recalled her drive and energy. He said, "Her experiences in California, with some counterculture overtones, were probably formative in her intellectual outlook, and she came equipped with ideas that other people didn't have." Her work as a volunteer for the Pit River Tribe in California was particularly valuable in preparing grant applications on which many tribal services depended. The Cherokees' senior citizens program, home-health nursing service, language survey, Indian child welfare program, and youth shelter grew out of grant applications Mankiller helped develop. When several important proposals she drafted were funded, her work came to the attention of the principal chief and the tribal council.[7]

Encouraged by her success, she completed a degree at Flaming Rainbow University and entered a graduate program in community planning at the University of Arkansas. In early November 1979, as she was driving to the

Cherokee Nation headquarters south of Tahlequah, a head-on collision ended her graduate career and almost her life. Despite seventeen operations over the next year, Mankiller's physical rehabilitation was slowed by a gradual loss of muscle control. At first she believed her condition to be a result of the accident, but when she developed double vision she suspected something else was wrong. Medical tests revealed that she had myasthenia gravis. An operation and drug therapy reversed the symptoms; within six weeks her vision had returned to normal and she had regained control of her muscles. Even more than the occupation of Alcatraz, the car accident, neurological disorder, and prolonged recovery altered Mankiller's outlook on life. During her convalescence, she wrote, "I fell back on my Cherokee ways and adopted what our elders call 'a Cherokee approach' to life." She claimed, "From that period on, I have always thought of myself as the woman who lived before and the woman who lives afterward."[8]

In January of 1981, over a year after the crash, Mankiller returned to her position at the Cherokee Nation. The dehumanizing nature of her medical treatment gave her a different outlook. Often dismissed by medical personnel as if she were incompetent to make decisions concerning her own treatment, Mankiller was determined to help Cherokees become involved in making decisions about their self-help projects. She claimed that the "fury" with which she addressed her work was not motivated by thoughts of advancement but by a "healthy anger" and a desire to see that the Cherokee people, "especially those living in rural areas, had the chance to express their own special needs."[9]

The conditions that had driven her family from Oklahoma still prevailed throughout the Cherokee Nation. In the Bell community near the Arkansas border many of the 350 residents hauled water, lived in homes classified as substandard, and earned so little that their income was far below average even in a county that had been ranked as the poorest in the United States. Enlisting the support of Chief Ross Swimmer, a Reagan Republican who stressed the concept of self-help, Mankiller raised a million dollars in grant funds and involved the residents in completing a sixteen-mile-long water pipeline, refurbishing twenty old homes, and building twenty-five new houses. During the Bell project tribal leaders appointed Mankiller as head of the newly created Cherokee Nation Community Development Department. Years later, she recalled that the Bell project validated her belief in the Cherokees' spirit of interdependence and willingness to help each other. It also launched her career in tribal politics.[10]

Before the Bell project was completed, Chief Swimmer asked Mankiller to consider running for deputy chief on his ticket. An attorney and banker, Swimmer was more effective in Washington than in poor, rural Cherokee communities. During his second term he was diagnosed with lymphatic cancer. Although he was responding to treatment, his illness had weakened him politically. In 1983 his deputy chief announced that he would oppose Swimmer in the tribal elections in June. Mankiller, who was not Swimmer's first choice, initially dismissed the invitation to run for deputy chief as "ludicrous," but the realization that she would be in a better position to influence tribal policy as deputy chief prompted her to reconsider. Swimmer's new running mate believed he "was taking a great chance" in putting a woman on his ticket and must have forgotten that she was a liberal Democrat. Actually he was aware of her liberal bent and was lobbied by "a lot of people" to dump her from the ticket. While Mankiller's grassroots connections were a factor in her selection, she recalled that Swimmer later told her, "The single most important thing to him was that I was honest with money and dedicated to the tribe."[11]

Mankiller was surprised that her advocacy of grassroots democracy and her activist past did not become issues in the campaign. Rather, opposition focused on gender and claims that election of a woman would be an affront to God and would make the Cherokees the laughingstock of Native America. While the militant opponents of female participation in government were a small minority, their tactics were ugly and ominous—hate mail, death threats, and acts of vandalism and intimidation. Apparently most Cherokees didn't share their views, for the lone male in the three-way race for deputy chief finished last. Mankiller was forced into a runoff against Agnes Cowen, a former member of the council.[12]

Swimmer, who had been narrowly reelected on the strength of the absentee vote in the general election, publicly announced that it would be "very difficult" for him to work with Cowen as deputy chief. In the July 16 runoff election, Mankiller's opponent finished 290 votes ahead among voters who cast their ballots in person in the fourteen counties that comprised the Cherokee Nation of Oklahoma. Mankiller even lost Adair County 304 to 468 and carried only five of the fourteen counties where the voters went to the polls. She won the absentee balloting, however, by a margin of 1070 out of the 2970 votes cast, which gave her a majority overall. Similar disparities between votes cast in person and by mail in the election for chief and council positions gave rise to accusations of electoral chicanery. Eight defeated candidates including Cowen sued tribal officials, alleging fraudulent voting practices. Two years later a judge dismissed the case after the U.S. attorney found nothing to sustain the charges.[13]

Later, responding to a question about absentee ballots cast in the election, Mankiller suggested that the belief that most absentee votes were cast by Cherokees living out of state was a myth. She explained that "only 10 percent of our population is outside of the primary 14 counties (in Oklahoma)." She added, "Many of our voters are rural and it's just easier for them to do it that way [vote by mail]. Most tribal employees also vote absentee ballots." Mankiller's opponents remained disgruntled over the election, but focused their accusations upon Republican supporters of Swimmer. In response, Mankiller claimed that there were enough independent observers at the counting of the ballots that the election could not have been stolen. Greg Combs believed there may be some substance to the charge of voting irregularities but felt that neither Swimmer nor Mankiller would have participated in any fraud.[14]

Ross Swimmer began his third term with a new deputy chief. Wilma Mankiller, now the highest-ranking woman ever to serve the Cherokee people, had vowed to "make things happen." The promise was more easily made than kept. The position of deputy chief is similar to that of an understudy. As long as the chief is present, the deputy's primary function is to wait. Although constitutionally she served as president of the council, Swimmer was usually present and tended to dominate the proceedings. Even though he had selected her as his deputy, many of his supporters were hostile or indifferent to her. Mankiller characterized her two years as deputy chief as "difficult—very difficult." Moreover, while Swimmer may have overlooked their political differences when he selected her, those differences became apparent after the campaign, but Mankiller had little choice as his deputy but to follow "Swimmer's line faithfully." Finally, many councillors, including the three women, offered little support; some were almost openly hostile. Shocked by the pettiness of members of the council and stifled by a position that offered more title than authority, Mankiller recalled, "Mostly, I just coped."[15]

The previous deputy chief, a Sallisaw businessman, had spent little time at the tribal headquarters in part because "he was very limited by Ross," Agnes Cowen recalled. She also suggested that Swimmer allowed Mankiller to "do the peon-labor type of stuff" among the grassroots Indians and found it useful to have a woman deputy with officials in Washington and for public relations purposes locally. Mankiller made her position a full-time job and divided her days between her office and the field, involv-

ing herself in the day-to-day operation of the more than forty tribally operated programs. Although she had little influence in developing tribal
policy, she gradually adjusted to the realities of life as deputy chief and
reached a working accommodation with some of the members of the
council.[16]

Mankiller and the chief found mutual ground in their commitment to
the rebuilding and revitalizing of their rural communities. She continued
her efforts to stimulate small-scale economic development within the
Cherokee Nation of Oklahoma by providing financial and technical assistance that enabled members of the tribe to get off welfare and open small
businesses. Mankiller favored small-scale economic development projects
but was not opposed to large-scale undertakings. While acknowledging
the success of tribally sponsored businesses such as Cherokee Nation Industries (CNI) and Cherokee Nation Distributing, the deputy chief har-
bored reservations about going into partnership with outsiders. "I think
that the projects that we've always done best are projects we do ourselves." She contended, "The best way to build an economy for us is to
build locally controlled, locally developed businesses where the decisions
are made locally, not by somebody in Detroit who could decide to move a
plant to Taiwan or someplace."[17]

In September of 1985, just as Mankiller was adjusting to her position
and establishing a working relationship with the council, Ross Swimmer
was nominated to head the Bureau of Indian Affairs. Although his confir-
mation was delayed by procedural infighting, he assumed his duties on 5
December in Washington, and Mankiller took the oath as Cherokee chief
in a private ceremony later the same day. In statements to the press, she
expressed little concern over potential objections to her becoming the
first female leader of a major tribe. Privately she believed she was inade-
quately prepared for the "daunting" task of "taking over the entire Cherokee Nation." Swimmer, who had spent much of his time in Washington
after his nomination, had little opportunity to prepare her "for all the
complex issues" facing the tribe. In fact, the only instruction he left his
successor was a one-page single-spaced list of the major issues facing the
tribe.

Over the next year, Mankiller recalled that she talked to the former
chief only once. His staff and many other people felt that the "Cherokee
Nation would crash and burn with a woman in charge." On 14 December,
in remarks following her formal inauguration, Mankiller tried to calm
fears fanned by rumors that she planned a purge of tribal employees. She
pledged little change except for more emphasis on finding funds for social

and economic development. She did, however, follow Swimmer's lead in ruling out bingo as a source of income because of her belief that it would not provide long-term economic stability. The new chief did break one tradition when she announced that she would not sit with the council as her predecessor had. In making the change she stressed the need for maintaining the separation between the legislative and executive branches established by the constitution.[18]

Mankiller had not even taken office before she was deluged by requests for interviews. The Cherokees had always been of interest to the press, but the intensity of attention from the national and even international media was new. In late November, a flattering article in *People* magazine marked the beginning of press coverage that would spotlight the Cherokee Nation and make Mankiller an international celebrity.[19]

Media attention gave the new chief a forum she used to publicize Indian and feminist issues. On 4 July 1986, the centennial of the dedication of the Statue of Liberty, Mankiller reminded Americans that federal troops "were busy moving tribes from their homelands to reservations" while New Yorkers celebrated the symbol of freedom. "This historical perspective causes mixed feelings in American Indians," Mankiller observed. About the same time, in a *Ms.* magazine article, she stressed the decisive role of women in early Indian history and suggested that great debate in councils was avoided when "women were consulted beforehand." She blamed the imposition of the "male-dominated culture" of the whites for gradually eroding the influential voice women had exercised in Indian society. In a House committee hearing, the Cherokee chief criticized a Reagan administration proposal to eliminate Indian languages from bilingual instruction as a threat to "the culture, heritage, and language of America's Indian tribes."[20]

Although Mankiller spoke out frequently and stridently against past and contemporary injustice, her measured criticism and calm demeanor made her welcome in the offices of the nation's economic and political power brokers. The communication skills that had made her effective at the grassroots level were equally effective when she began working with state and national leaders. Despite the favorable press, Mankiller soon discovered that her efforts to improve tribal services in housing and health care were blocked by council members whose allegiance remained with the former chief or who opposed additional spending for social programs. Once again, Mankiller was compelled to cope. Although she lacked an electoral mandate from the Cherokee people, as chief she controlled the Nation's bureaucracy and its promotional capacity. In a series of columns appearing in regional newspapers, Mankiller explained tribal services and organization and apprised Cherokee voters of her administration's goals. She maintained a high profile nationally with a variety of newspapers and journals featuring biographical sketches. The Oklahoma Federation of Indian Women named her American Woman of 1986, scarcely five months after she became chief; the Governor's Advisory Committee on the Status of Women selected her for induction into the Oklahoma Women's Hall of Fame; and Harvard recognized her for "outstanding contributions to American leadership and Native American culture."[21]

Her growing celebrity status did not silence local criticism. A former council member claimed, "Wilma, I will say, is a good community worker, but that does not make her a leader." Gary Chapman, a council member who had crossed swords with the new chief on more than one occasion, also cited her lack of leadership.[22] Opponents were more outspoken in accusing her of nepotism.

About six weeks after she became chief, Mankiller announced her engagement to Charlie Soap, a Cherokee full-blood who directed the tribe's community development department. The couple met shortly after Mankiller was employed by the tribe, but did not begin working closely together until the Bell project. When Soap remained at his post after their marriage in October, the chief's opponents "drummed up a war dance" at the January 1987 council meeting. In response to criticism, Mankiller announced that her husband had resigned. Continued probing revealed that the resignation would not be effective until later in the month so that he could qualify for retirement benefits. Mankiller's conduct in this episode gave her political opponents an issue in an election year.[23]

In early 1987, Mankiller announced that she would be a candidate for chief in the June election. Despite her favorable treatment by the press and growing list of honors, she was considered vulnerable and drew three opponents. The most formidable was Perry Wheeler, the former deputy chief who had run strongly against Ross Swimmer in 1983 and who also had widespread grassroots support. The two other candidates were both well-known. Mankiller countered charges of inept leadership and lack of business and managerial experience by stressing her priorities and aspirations for her people.[24]

Perhaps what she had accomplished was not as much a factor in the election as what had not happened. The dire prediction about the tribal government's crashing and burning had proven false. Moreover, the tribe had received more favorable publicity under Mankiller than at any other time since Sequoyah devised his syllabary. Charlie Soap, Mankiller's husband, was particularly effective in taking her message to the full-blood community and defusing the gender issue. Several weeks before the election the kidney disease that had claimed the life of her father put Mankiller into the hospital for ten days. When her opponents injected her health into the campaign, her staff dismissed reports of serious illness, claiming that "her overall health is excellent."[25]

In the election Mankiller finished well ahead but was again thrown into a runoff, which she won by a wide margin despite charges concerning her health and "hippy" California background. Mankiller's personal triumph did not extend to all of her supporters running for council positions. When one of Mankiller's candidates died less than a week after being elected to the council, only five of the remaining newly elected council members were in her camp. Although absentee-voting procedures had been changed following the 1983 election, the counting of absentee ballots aroused new controversy in 1987. When the tribe's election committee voted to nullify the results of a recount of absentee ballots for council members, Mankiller appealed to the Cherokee Judicial Appeals Tribunal to intervene. Another recount was held and the results favored the incumbent administration. Consequently, one more Mankiller supporter took a seat in the tribe's legislative branch.[26]

Mankiller now had the "mandate" she had lacked since her elevation to chief, but with the council controlled by her opponents, sessions could be stormy. In one meeting the council narrowly denied her authority to convert the tribe's financially ailing motel and restaurant into a job corps center. Threatening to appeal directly to the people and vowing an "all-out political war," she was able to reverse the council's decision at its next session.[27]

The Talking Leaves Job Corps Center, operated by the Cherokees since 1978, had been slated for closure by the Department of Labor. Lobbying in Washington, Mankiller was able to persuade federal officials to maintain the operation if the tribe could find a suitable site. The motel was to be used for two or three years until a permanent facility could be built. It was not until 1995 that the job corps moved into its new home; the motel did not reopen, but the restaurant resumed operation in 1996.[28]

Political infighting did not stop the tribe's community development campaign. By 1986, eight programs modeled on the Bell project were under way. One in the Kenwood community received a Certificate of National Merit from the Department of Housing and Urban Development in 1987.[29]

Organizations across the nation continued to shower honors on the Cherokee chief and extend speaking invitations to her. She used these forums to forward the cause of the Cherokees and other Indians and frequently to urge women to assert their rights. In Washington she claimed that some tribes are better off "in spite of Reagan" and attributed their improvement to programs that carried over from the Kennedy-Johnson War on Poverty programs.[30]

Within weeks of her criticism of Ronald Reagan's administration, she had an opportunity to meet with the lame-duck president at the White House. Because of remarks objectionable to Native Americans, Reagan had agreed to discuss Indian grievances with tribal leaders. In the final weeks of his second term, the president met for twenty minutes with sixteen chiefs, including Mankiller, who had been selected as one of three spokespeople for the group. The Cherokee chief, who had never been to the White House, "was overwhelmed" and felt "an enormous responsibility to have to speak for all of the tribes of the United States." Although Reagan reaffirmed a 1983 statement endorsing self-determination for Indian tribes, Mankiller considered the meeting little more than a "photo opportunity," and expressed disappointment that the president had not been more receptive to the issues they raised. Nonetheless, the Cherokee leader's image was enhanced when a picture of her, seated immediately to the left of Reagan, appeared in newspapers across the country.[31]

Despite continuing criticism of Mankiller's leadership in stimulating economic development, the chief worked throughout her administration to improve the economic environment of the fourteen counties of the Cherokee Nation. Inadequate capitalization, intratribal rivalries, and a dearth of experienced managers placed most Indian nations at a competitive disadvantage. Many tribal enterprises failed to fulfill the expectations of their planners. Acknowledging the economic realities facing the Cherokees, Mankiller continued encouraging cottage industry and sought to cooperate with nearby institutions and governments in forming "partnerships" to improve the general business climate, not just for the Cherokees but for everyone. Her efforts attracted some business to northeastern Oklahoma, but the rural nature of the area and its limited infrastructure made progress slow.[32]

Throughout her administration, Mankiller stressed cooperation, not confrontation. After she left office, she listed some of the accomplishments she and her staff achieved during workdays that often lasted ten to sixteen hours:

1. collaborative efforts with communities in northeastern Oklahoma to provide seed money to establish a multicounty environmental organization
that is still in operation;

2. development of an intertribal environmental organization to offer technical assistance to other tribes;

3. support of a campaign in Delaware County to increase the sales tax a half
cent in order to fund a solid waste disposal system, and to obtain a grant
to defray start-up costs;

4. assistance in persuading voters in Delaware County to pass a bond to establish a vo-tech system, and aid in lobbying federal officials to help fund
the program;

5. cooperation with the city of Tahlequah to provide sewer service to residents south of town, and the contribution of almost $1 million to the ex-
pansion project;

6. completion of about $40 million worth of new construction in the Chero-
kee Nation including clinics at Stillwell, Salina, Sallisaw, and Jay; a new
Job Corps center and youth shelter; purchase of a hospital in Jay; construction of roads, water systems, and a new warehouse for Cherokee Nation Industries; construction of three bingo facilities; and renovation of
the Children's Village and facilities for Head Start and day care programs;

7. involvement in nation-building activities including assumption of a responsibility for a tribal foster care system and adoptions, and reinstate-
ment of a district court system.

During the Mankiller administration the tribal budget and number of
registered Cherokees tripled. While chief, Mankiller also served as president of the Arkansas Riverbed Authority and two terms as president of
the Inter-Tribal Council of Five Civilized Tribes.[33]

Shrinking budgets for social programs and the "no new taxes" pledge of
President George Bush forced Mankiller to consider new sources of revenue. The tribe's attempts to stimulate economic development produced
more headlines than jobs, and many tribal businesses were struggling.
Mankiller reconsidered her aversion to high-stakes gambling. Pointing
out the crisis in Indian health care, which had produced overcrowding at
Indian Health Service hospitals and tribal clinics, she acknowledged,
"We've been applying a band-aid all along. There are too many patients
and not enough room." Citing the success of the Creek Nation, she suggested, "Bingo operations could help with health care." The decision was
particularly painful for Mankiller, who made it "with a lot of mixed feelings." She recalled, "I was with the Cherokee Nation for almost eighteen
years . . . and it is the only thing I ever remember doing that I came home

and cried about." By the end of her administration, Cherokee bingo par-
lors near Fort Smith, Tulsa, and Siloam Springs had become the tribe's
major money-making enterprises.[34]

The Cherokees tapped another source of revenue in February 1990
when the tribal council authorized the collection of taxes on businesses
operating on Cherokee land. Primarily concerned with regulating "wild-
cat smoke shops" operating in Indian Country, which claimed immunity
from state taxation, the law was the most significant measure enacted
during Mankiller's tenure as chief. In addition to producing revenue for
tribal social programs and economic development, the new tax code authorized the chief to negotiate a compact with the state to collect and
retain a portion of taxes on businesses operating within the Cherokee
Nation.[35]

After two years of negotiation, Mankiller, the leaders of the Choctaws,
Chickasaws, and Seminoles, and Oklahoma governor David Walters
signed an "historic compact." The Cherokee chief emphasized that the
agreement in no way limited tribal sovereignty. "At the Cherokee Nation
we plan to continue to establish our own priorities, chart our own course
and hope that every other tribe will do the same."[36]

The new tax code exacerbated a controversy with the United Keetoowah Band (UKB), a Cherokee faction recognized by Congress in 1946.
Tribal elections of 1975 had produced a schism between the Cherokee Nation of Oklahoma and the United Keetoowah Band, both claiming to represent the Cherokee people. Despite Mankiller's hope that she could
begin working with the Keetoowahs, relations remained confrontational,
and any hope of reducing tension was dashed when the band denied
the Nation's authority to tax smoke shops and other businesses of its
members.

To police Indian Country, where state and local authorities lacked jurisdiction, the tribal council established a district court in December 1990.
At the same time the tribal security force was transformed into the Cherokee Nation Marshal Service, which had expanded duties and authority.
The council authorized Mankiller to negotiate cross-deputation agreements with law enforcement agencies in the fourteen counties of northeastern Oklahoma comprising the Cherokee Nation. These agreements
were designed to resolve jurisdictional questions among Cherokee and
other law enforcement agencies. Although cross-deputation would not be
formally authorized until April 1991, local arrangements and informal
agreements between the Cherokee Nation Marshal Service and local police had already been implemented in some areas.[37]

In the fall of 1990 deputy marshals from the Cherokee Nation accompanied county law officers in raids on smoke shops licensed by the United Keetoowah Band. The raids closed fourteen of twenty-two shops in Tulsa, Cherokee, Adair, Sequoyah, and Delaware counties. Temporary restraining orders, which would have allowed the smoke shops to reopen, were denied in U.S. district court in Tulsa.[38]

The band then appealed to the Bureau of Indian Affairs, hoping federal officials would recognize its independence and right to license smoke shops and share federal funds allocated to the Nation. Although the BIA did not support the band's claims, Mankiller viewed the agency's involvement as an encroachment on tribal sovereignty. Years later, she claimed the BIA was "always stirring things up between the United Keetoowah Band and the Cherokee Nation" to make both look like they were incapable of managing their own affairs. In discussions with the secretary of the interior in October of 1990, Mankiller made it clear that "neither I nor the deputy chief or the tribal council will allow the authority of the Cherokee Nation to be diminished." The secretary promised to weigh the Cherokee Nation's arguments carefully, but the crisis persisted. The failure of officials in Washington to resolve the dispute prompted Mankiller to advise the head of the BIA, "I hold the Bureau of Indian Affairs responsible and accountable for the possibility of outbreaks of violence and a potential civil war within the Cherokee Nation." Ultimately the federal courts denied the UKB's claim that its smoke shops were exempt from state taxation, but the Keetoowah's feud with the Nation continued to simmer.[39]

Accusations concerning Mankiller's kidney deterioration, made during the 1987 election campaign, gained credence in March of 1990 when tribal officials confirmed that "recurring kidney problems over the past few years" had made Mankiller a candidate for a transplant. On 20 June the ailing chief received a kidney from her oldest brother in an operation performed in Boston. After release from the hospital, Mankiller remained in the Boston area several months before returning to her home for further recuperation.[40]

Before she left Boston, the chief entered into an historic agreement with the BIA to allow the Cherokee Nation to participate in a self-governance demonstration project. One of five tribes selected for the program, the Cherokees assumed responsibility for federal funds currently administered by the BIA. Control by tribal officials enabled the tribe to use money for priorities set locally rather than by federal bureaucrats. Mankiller signed the act personally while convalescing "because it is a significant step toward the Cherokee Nation once again assuming control over our own resources." She envisioned the agreement not as a means of isolating the tribe, but of making it "a strong, viable unit of government that works in collaboration with other governments around us."[41]

As her first full term neared its end, Mankiller expressed satisfaction with her administration's accomplishment, pointing out that "the Cherokee Nation entered the 1990s in a stronger position than ever before." She was particularly proud of advancements in health care and progress in locating clinics close to the people. One member of the tribe claimed that "she's done everything she promised the people. . . . She's probably been the most aggressive chief we've ever had."[42]

Not everyone was as laudatory. Ross Swimmer gave his successor high marks on effectiveness in representing their people in Washington and in enhancing the tribe's image nationally, but suggested she had paid little attention to economic development and questioned her "business acumen." Perry Wheeler, Mankiller's opponent for chief in 1987, said, "My only quarrel is all she's done is work on social programs." He claimed that she had failed to take advantage of millions of economic opportunities.[43]

In March of 1991, Mankiller announced that she would be a candidate for reelection. Emphasizing her record in economic development, health care, and initiatives in self-governance, she claimed, "there is much more work to do as we prepare the Cherokee Nation and its members to enter the 21st century on their own terms." Before the campaign began, Mankiller received another invitation to the White House. Among twelve Indian leaders asked to meet with President George Bush, the Cherokee chief was one of three chosen to speak for the group. This meeting was more satisfying than the session with Reagan. Bush and his advisors asked questions, engaged in a dialogue, and listened to the agenda of the tribal leaders. Impressed by the president's promise to follow-up on their requests, Mankiller believed the meeting would send a signal to top federal officials that the president wanted to deal with tribes in a "government-to-government relationship."[44]

Continuing favorable national publicity and honors made Mankiller a formidable opponent in 1991. No one active in Cherokee government challenged her; neither of the two men who did file in the race for principal chief was well-known. In the election only 48 percent of the Nation's 24,300 voters cast ballots. Mankiller received 82.7 percent of those votes and was overwhelmingly reelected in an election free of controversy—an event unique in modern tribal history. The race was unique in another respect as well; it was the first time since statehood that members of the council were elected from districts rather than on an at-large basis. Voters had approved the change in the 1987 election.[45]

After her reelection Mankiller continued stating her views on issues she considered important. At every level of government her opinion counted. While participating in a White House conference on Indian education to consider coordination of federal Indian education programs, Mankiller announced, "I'm going to do everything within my power to see that there's not a central school board. . . . It just goes counter to everything that we at Cherokee Nation have tried to do." Plans for centralizing Indian education were abandoned. When a committee of the Oklahoma House of Representatives recommended legislation to compel Indian smoke shops to collect state tax on cigarettes sold to non-Indians, Mankiller branded the measure "ill-conceived" and said it "raised serious legal and constitutional questions." Mankiller and other Indian leaders critical of the bill marshaled their allies in the legislature, who attached amendments that gutted the measure. Changes in the senate produced a compromise measure acceptable to the Cherokees.[46]

Never reticent about expressing her political beliefs, the Cherokee chief endorsed Arkansas governor Bill Clinton for president in 1992 and was active in his campaign. After his victory, Mankiller was invited to participate in the Little Rock economic conference sponsored by the president-elect. She felt her involvement in Clinton's transition "enabled Indian people to be heard by those in Washington who can make a difference." Mankiller was not exaggerating. For the remainder of her administration, she would have the attention of the president of the United States and would be the most influential Indian leader in the country. In a 1997 interview, Mankiller stressed that she had "good access to a lot of very, very high-level cabinet people." She added, "What is interesting is that I didn't make a campaign contribution, and during my tenure none of the businesses nor the tribe gave a contribution. We just didn't do it."[47]

Despite Mankiller's influence, there was one issue of considerable importance for the Cherokee Nation that she was unable to resolve. In 1970 the U.S. Supreme Court ruled that the Cherokees and two other tribes owned the bed and banks of the Arkansas River in Oklahoma as far as the stream was navigable. After exploring its options, the tribe decided to seek compensation from the federal government for the market value of resources taken from the riverbed and to exchange their title to it for other land under federal control. Early in her administration, Mankiller reactivated the Arkansas River Bed Authority to present a united front to the U.S. government. Negotiations began with federal agencies, and lawsuits were instituted. Mankiller estimated that she devoted about one-third of her time as chief to seeking a settlement with the government. Foot-dragging and obstruction in Washington frustrated all her efforts to reach an agreement and left her doubtful that the issue would ever be resolved satisfactorily.[48]

In June 1993 abdominal discomfort put Mankiller back in the hospital in Boston for two separate surgical procedures not related to her kidney transplant. The three-hour operation kept her in the hospital for ten days but was dismissed as routine and very successful by tribal officials. By September, when she delivered her annual state of the nation address at the Cherokee National Holiday, the chief reported, "I'm in as good health as I've ever been."[49]

The high point in Mankiller's career probably occurred just following publication of her autobiography. As the result of an idea proposed in a meeting between Mankiller and the U.S. attorney general, President Clinton invited the leaders of all 545 federally recognized tribes to Washington. Newspaper reports called the meeting unprecedented. Its purpose was to resolve issues involving Indian gaming and tribal jurisdiction and provide a forum for federal officials to hear the opinions of tribal leaders on management of tribal natural resources, tribal courts, law enforcement, and religious freedom.[50]

On 29 April 1994, seated immediately to the right of President Clinton in the Rose Garden, the leader of the Cherokees moderated a "nation-to-nation" summit. The president promised the 322 assembled tribal leaders to fulfill the trust obligations the government had made, respect tribal sovereignty, and protect the religious freedom of Native Americans. After the 2 1/2 hour meeting, Mankiller expressed her belief that more had been accomplished than in her meetings with Reagan or Bush. The meeting was followed by a "listening conference" in Albuquerque with the attorney general and the secretary of interior, who "literally listened all day long while members of different tribes came in and testified about various needs and issues." As a result of the listening conference, the Justice Department created an Office of Indian Justice.[51]

Before the meetings with Clinton and his officials, Mankiller called a meeting with 650 employees of the Cherokee Nation. She surprised them and others across the country by announcing that she would not seek reelection. The chief had reached the decision while she was hospitalized in Boston but insisted that her health had not figured into her decision. "I'm actually in good health now and I want to keep it that way."[52]

When asked about her successor, Mankiller said, "It's up to you to de-cide, not me. I just hope we don't see the politics of hate in 1995 that we saw in the previous election." She warned, "It's easy to tear down a house. You can do that in a day." In one of the many tributes to the retiring chief, the executive editor of the *Muskogee Daily Phoenix* credited her "strong, unifying, visionary, and contemporary leadership" for the "impressive growth and improvements for Oklahoma's Cherokees." In concluding he wrote, "What a tragedy it would be if the growth, reforms, and vision of the Mankiller years were ripped apart in a mean-spirited, ego-driven, ulti-matum-filled election in 1995."[53] The concern expressed by the chief and the editor for the forthcoming election was prophetic.

In her final year as chief, Republicans won control of Congress and be-gan introducing budget cuts. Mankiller warned that tribal distribution of food, its housing programs, and a dozen other social services could be ad-versely affected. The chief also raised concerns about the threat to the Na-tion's bingo operations posed by proposals to bring casino gambling to Oklahoma.[54]

Threats of a more immediate nature confronted Mankiller as a result of questionable management of tribal operations, businesses, and related enterprises. In 1992 she named former chief Ross Swimmer to head Cherokee Nation Industries. Just three months after Mankiller left office, her successor and the CNI board asked for his resignation for loaning over half a million dollars of company money without authorization. A few months later, when CNI laid off almost a third of its workforce, Man-killer's successor blamed poor management in the past. In December 1994 an internal memo to Mankiller revealed "a litany of concerns" about the Cherokee National Historical Society. Later, the president of the historical society's board said, "Our financial problems boil down to poor manage-ment. . . . There needs to be more accountability. We've never had that here before." In 1993 and 1995, the Cherokee Nation Housing Authority's proposals to the Department of Housing and Urban Development were not funded. HUD officials cited deficiencies in the areas of "development of sites and timely construction." When Mankiller was informed of the situation, she sent the authority's director a letter demanding "an imme-diate written explanation of what on earth is going on over there." These and other problems were not emphasized during Mankiller's administra-tion.[55]

In March of 1995, the chief endorsed George Bearpaw, the executive di-rector for tribal operations. In the June election he finished well ahead of Joe Byrd, a two-term council representative, but short of a majority. Before the runoff, the Cherokee Judicial Appeals Tribunal disqualified Mankiller's candidate because he had pled guilty to a felony over twenty years earlier. The chief pardoned Bearpaw, but the tribunal rejected pleas to reinstate him. Consequently, Byrd ran unopposed in the runoff.[56]

After the election, Mankiller granted eleven departing executives severance pay because she believed they would be fired by the new chief. Relations between Mankiller and the incoming administration were so strained that she refused to attend Byrd's inauguration.[57] Days after assuming office, the new chief charged his predecessor with misappropriating over three hundred thousand dollars—the severance pay she'd authorized. Former chief Ross Swimmer called the payments "outrageous" and asserted, "It could be called an embezzlement by trustee." Attorneys for the Nation sued Mankiller, but their indecision concerning jurisdiction left the case in limbo.[58] Animosity surrounding the transition of administrations thrust the tribal government into chaos. Whether the turmoil was the result of "sabotage" or "inept," if not "corrupt," leadership is a hotly contested issue.

In February 1996, while hospitalized with pneumonia and a urinary tract infection, Mankiller was diagnosed with lymphoma. A six-month regimen of chemotherapy in Boston and radiation therapy at Fort Smith, Arkansas, brought the condition into remission but destroyed her transplanted kidney. Continuing health problems have restricted Mankiller's involvement in public affairs, although she has remained active in some of the causes and organizations she championed as chief. On 15 January 1998, President Bill Clinton awarded Wilma Mankiller the Presidential Medal of Freedom, the nation's highest civilian award. In ceremonies at the White House, the president praised the former chief as "not only as the guardian of the centuries-old Cherokee heritage but a revered leader who built a brighter and healthier future for her nation."[59]

Mankiller's reputation did not shield the Cherokee Nation from further strife. Although the controversy surrounding the election of 1995 subsided, in February of 1997 a new crisis erupted. Mankiller refrained from public criticism of Chief Joe Byrd for a month, but on 21 March, she charged the chief with "an outrageous defiance of tribal law" and branded his accusations of a conspiracy to destroy his administration "utter nonsense." In late July Mankiller reiterated her belief that Byrd precipitated the crisis. Threats of congressional intervention produced a shaky truce in late August. Wounds left by the intratribal feud will fester for years, but it will be even longer before this controversy and Mankiller's role in it can be evaluated objectively. What seemed a Cinderella tale as Mankiller began her last year in office now resembles a Greek tragedy. Mankiller is more optimistic. While viewing the current situation as "a sad and terrible time," she considers it "part of the learning process," and believes the long-term impact will be positive.[60]

AFTERWORD

On 2 September 1997 a draft of this chapter was sent to Wilma Mankiller for comment. She returned a nine-page letter, dated 4 September, and a two-page letter, dated 5 September, suggesting revisions and providing her views on specific passages. Based on these two letters, portions of the chapter were revised. In other passages, where Mankiller challenged the interpretation, the author, after reviewing his sources, felt the original accounts were accurate and objective. In these instances no changes were made, but the author included almost all of Mankiller's comments in the endnotes, which have been eliminated. Mankiller's views are now summarized in the following paragraphs. She objected to issues raised concerning the elections of 1983 and 1987, was disappointed that the chapter did not refer to the "tremendous progress" made by the Cherokees under former chief Ross Swimmer, challenged the veracity of some of her critics, particularly Perry Wheeler, Bob Carlile, and Gary Chapman, and countered charges of nepotism arising from her marriage to Charlie Soap. Mankiller defended herself against criticism of her negotiation of the taxation compact with the state of Oklahoma.

The former Cherokee chief claimed that she had little or no control over the Cherokee National Historical Society and branded the characterization of the problems in Cherokee Nation Industries discussed in this chapter as one-sided. She could not understand why her decision not to attend Joe Byrd's inauguration attracted public attention. She pointed out that a member of Byrd's transition team requested letters of resignation from senior people in the Cherokee Nation and insisted that they knew the new chief intended to fire them. This view is supported by Lynn Howard. Mankiller also explained her decision to grant severance pay to personnel who resigned their positions and defended it, citing the tribe's long-standing implicit policy of granting departing executives severance pay. She maintained that Byrd offered to drop the suit against her to recover money paid to departing executives in return for her promise of public support of his administration. She also categorically denied claims that she conspired to embarrass the Byrd administration.

The author regrets that space constraints prevented the inclusion of the comments of Mankiller and Howard. Their responses to the drafts of this chapter would have added further insight into Mankiller's career and outlook.

NOTES

1. Wilma Mankiller and Michael Wallis, *Mankiller: A Chief and Her People* (New York: St. Martin's Press, 1993). Mellissa Schwarz, *Wilma Mankiller: Principal Chief of the Cherokees* (New York: Chelsea House Publishers, 1994). Bruce Glassman, *Wilma Mankiller: Chief of the Cherokee Nation* (Woodbridge CT: Blackbirch Press, 1992). Michelle Wallace, "Wilma Mankiller," *Ms.* Magazine, January 1988, 68–69. Jeanne Devlin, "Hail to the Chief," *Oklahoma Today* (January–February 1990), 32–37.

2. Unless noted otherwise, all material pertaining to the years before Mankiller began working for the Cherokee Nation of Oklahoma in 1977 is found in Mankiller and Wallis, *Mankiller*.

3. Mankiller and Wallis, *Mankiller*, 111, 115.

4. Mankiller and Wallis, *Mankiller*, 192.

5. Mankiller and Wallis, *Mankiller*, 201, 203.

6. Mankiller and Wallis, *Mankiller*, 215, 217.

7. Wilma P. Mankiller, interview with Brad Agnew, 28 August 1997 (audiotape in possession of the author). Greg Combs, interview with Brad Agnew, 5 August 1997 (audiotape in the possession of the author).

8. In 1989, Mankiller appeared with Jerry Lewis during a Labor Day telethon to share her experiences with a national audience. "Chief Appears on National MDA Telethon," *Cherokee Advocate*, 7 October 1989. Also see Mankiller, interview, 28 August 1997; "Mankiller Named to Ford Foundation Board of Trustees," *Indian Country Today*, 30 March 1994, A1; Mankiller and Wallis, *Mankiller*, 219, 222–29.

9. Mankiller and Wallis, *Mankiller*, 232–33.

10. Sandy Hansen, Kathy Helmer, and Wilma Mankiller, "Bell, Oak Ridge and Kirk Mountain: Community Renewal Using Self-Help," *Cherokee Advocate*, August 10–11, 1982, 10–11; Mankiller and Wallis, *Mankiller*, 233–35.

11. Martin Hagerstrand, interview with Brad Agnew, 7 August 1997 (audiotape in the possession of the author); Bob Carlile, interview with Brad Agnew, 26 July 1997 (audiotape in the possession of the author); Mankiller and Wallis, *Mankiller*, 239–40. Also see Agnes Cowen, interview with Brad Agnew, 27 July 1997 (audiotape in the possession of the author); Mankiller interview, 28 August 1997.

12. Mankiller and Wallis, *Mankiller*, 241–42; "Cherokees to Get Female Deputy— Which One," *Tahlequah Daily Press*, 3 July 1983, 1A.

13. "Cowen and Mankiller Square Off for Deputy," *Tahlequah American*, 29 June 1983, 1, 3; "Wilma Mankiller Elected," *Cherokee County Chronicle*, 20 July 1983, 1; "Judge Dismisses Election Suit," *Cherokee Advocate*, 1 July 1985, 1.

14. Kim Atkin, "Mankiller, Ketcher Sworn in Saturday," *Tahlequah Daily Press*, 17 December 1985, 3A. Also see Cowen interview, 27 July 1997; Carlile interview, 26 July 1997; Mankiller interview, 28 August 1997; Combs interview, 5 August 1997.

15. "Cherokee Nation Looks to the Future," *Tahlequah Daily Press*, 30 March 1986, 1C; Hagerstrand interview, 7 August 1997; "Cherokee Tribe Has First Woman Chief," *Sequoyah County Times*, 8 December 1985, 1; Mankiller and Wallis, *Mankiller*, 242–243.

16. Cowen interview, 27 July 1997; Gene Thompson, interview with Brad Agnew, 14 July 1997 (audiotape in the possession of the author); Mankiller and Wallis, *Mankiller*, 243.

17. Mankiller and Wallis, *Mankiller*, 243; Hagerstrand interview, 7 August 1997; "Mankiller Years," *Tahlequah Daily Press*, 24 April 1994, 6 (Cherokee Nation section); Mankiller interview, 28 August 1997.

18. Kim Atkin, "Mankiller Confident about Leadership Ability," *Tahlequah Daily Press*, 4 October 1985, 1A; Jerry Fink, "Cherokee Leader Will Use Position to Develop Economy," *Tulsa World*, 17 November 1985, 8A; Tracy Stueve, "She's Tackled Poverty, Illness, Now Cherokee Nation Is Her Goal," *Muskogee Daily Phoenix*, 1 December 1985, 1A–2A. Also see Jack Elliott, "Mrs. Mankiller Sworn in as Cherokee Chief," *Miami (Oklahoma) Daily News*, 6 December 1985, A9; Atkin, "Mankiller, Ketcher Sworn In Saturday," 1A. Also see Mankiller and Wallis, *Mankiller*, 244–245; and Mankiller interview, 28 August 1997.

19. David Van Biema, "Activist Wilma Mankiller Is Set to Become the First Female Chief of the Cherokee Nation," *People*, 2 December 1985, 91–92; Stueve, "She's Tackled Poverty," 1A.

20. John Parker, "Clashing Visions of Liberty," *Muskogee Daily Herald*, 4 July 1986, 3A; M. K. Gregory, "Wilma Mankiller: Harnessing Traditional Cherokee Wisdom," *Ms.* magazine, August 1986, 32; Lynn Simross, "Cherokee Chief Pushes Self-Help for Development," *Tulsa World*, 19 September 1986, 1D; Rob Martindale, "Mankiller Backs Native Language," *Tulsa World*, 1 May 1987, 2A.

21. Malvina Stephenson, "Wilma Mankiller Always Thrived on Challenge," *Tulsa World*, 13 April 1986; Schwarz, "Wilma Mankiller," 85–86; "Mankiller Named Woman of the year," *Tahlequah Daily Press*, 3 June 1986, 3; "Hudlin, Mankiller in Hall of Fame," *Tahlequah Daily Press*, 10 September 1986, 7A; "Principal Chief Mankiller Receives the Harvard Foundation Citation," *Cherokee Advocate*, 10 December 1986, 10.

22. Jessie Mangaliman, "Cherokee Leader Faces Determined Election Foes," *Tulsa Tribune*, 22 April 1987, 16A.

23. "Mankiller, Soap Announce Plans to Wed," *Tahlequah Pictorial Press*, 24 January

1986, 6A; Mankiller and Wallis, *Mankiller*, 235–238; Donna Hales, "Tribe Accuses Chief, Husband of Nepotism," *Muskogee Daily Phoenix*, 11 January 1987, 1A.

24. "Cherokee Tribe Has First Woman Chief, " *Sequoyah County Times*, 8 December 1985, 1; Mangaliman, "Cherokee Leader Faces Determined Election Foes," 16A; Brett J. Blackledge, "Mankiller Cites Tradition of Woman Leaders," *Miami News-Record*, 20 July 1987, 3.

25. "Mankiller in Hospital as Election Arrives," *Tahlequah Daily Press*, 21 June 1987, 1; Schwarz, "Wilma Mankiller," 93–94.

26. Donna Hales, "Mankiller Sworn in as Cherokee Chief." *Muskogee Daily Herald*, 15 August 1987, 2A; Griff Palmer and Robby Trammell, "Cherokees Go to Court on Recount," *Saturday Oklahoman and Times*, 25 July 1987, 12; *Tulsa World*, 26 July 1987, 8A; Griff Palmer, "Cherokee Tribunal Certifies Recount," *Daily Oklahoman*, 13 August 1987, 4; "Recount Upheld by Judicial Appeals Tribunal," *Cherokee Advocate*, 10 August 1987, 10.

27. Nancy Frank, "Mankiller Vetoes Move to Buy Buffalo Ranch," *Tahlequah Daily Press*, 14 July 1988, 1; Donna Hales, "Job Corps Center a Tribal Victory, Mankiller Says," *Muskogee Daily Phoenix*, 19 April 1995, 1A and 8A.

28. Wilma P. Mankiller, "Chief Testifies to Keep Job Corps Open," *Cherokee Advocate*, June 1986, 11; "Council Votes to Move Job Corps to Bacone," *Cherokee Advocate*, June 1986, 4; "Mankiller Sets Lodge Closing Date," *Tahlequah Daily Press*, 21 August 1988, 1–2.

29. Simross, "Cherokee Chief Pushes Self-Help for Development," 1D; Dan Garber, "Tribal Department Cited for Excellence," *Tahlequah Daily Press*, 25 October 1987, 1, 3.

30. "Mankiller Calls for Strong Social Programs," *Tahlequah Daily Press*, 12 June 1988, 3; Wilma Mankiller, "Native Americans Have Given Enough," *Tulsa World*, 9 February 1989, A11; "Isuzu Ad Draws Wrath of Cherokee Chief," *Tulsa World*, 30 June 1988, A3; Elmer Saville, "Tribal Ambassadors of the 1880s Not Forgotten in 1988," *Lakota Times*, 15 November 1988, 1–2.

31. "Reagan, Indians Talk Rights," *Muskogee Daily Phoenix*, 13 December 1988, sec. A, p. 1–2; Mankiller interview, 28 August 1997.

32. Mankiller interview, 28 August 1997; Lynne Howard, unrecorded interview with Brad Agnew, 18 September 1997.

33. Mankiller to Agnew, 5 September 1997 (letter in possession of the author).

34. "Tribe Holds Ceremonies for Bingo Outpost," *Cherokee Advocate*, January/February 1990, 1B; Dana Eversole, "Mankiller Says Indian Health Care Facing Crisis Situation," *Tahlequah Daily Press*, 8 December 1989, 1, 3; "Edging In: Cherokees Move Carefully," *Tulsa World*, 30 July 1990, 7A; "Government Infrastructure," *Tahlequah Daily Press*, 24 April 1994 (Cherokee Nation section), 11; Mankiller interview, 28 August 1997.

35. "Tax Code Explained; State Compact Ahead," *Cherokee Advocate*, April 1990, 1, 21; "Cherokee Nation Tax Facts," *Cherokee Advocate*, April 1990, 21; Mankiller interview, 28 August 1997.

36. *Oklahoma Tax Commission v. Citizen Band of the Potawatomi Tribe*, United States Reports, vol. 498 (1990), 506–10; "Cherokee Nation to Develop Taxation Compact," *Grove Sun*, 28 February 1990, 2C; "Tribes, State Stand Behind Historic Compact," *Cherokee Advocate*, July/August 1992, 1 and 6; Wilma P. Mankiller, "The Tobacco Wars . . .," *Cherokee Advocate*, July/August 1992, 6.

37. "New Court System Necessary to Protect Tribal Members," *Cherokee Advocate*, April 1991, 14; "Cherokee Nation Implements District Court System," *Cherokee Advocate*, April 1991, 15; "January and February Advocate Recounts Major Headlines," *Cherokee Advocate*, January 1992, 7; "Attorney General Opinion Paves Way for Cross-Deputation," *Cherokee Advocate*, April 1991, 16. Also see Jill Wheeler, "Nation Signs Multi-County Agreement," *Green Country Neighbor*, 8 April 1991, 1–3; "Tribe, State Officials Sign Law Agreement," *Green Country Neighbor*, June 1991, 1; Mankiller interview, 28 August 1997; Combs interview, 5 August 1997.

38. "Smoke Shops Remained Closed; Continuing Legal Battles Cloud Issue," *Cherokee Advocate*, March 1991, 1 and 4.

39. "Chief Mankiller Meets with Interior Secretary Lujan," *Cherokee Advocate*, December 1990, 1; "Mankiller Blames BIA for Tribal Conflict, Violence," *Saturday Oklahoman and Times*, 22 December 1990, 7; "10th Circuit Court Denies United Keetoowah Band Appeal," *Cherokee Advocate*, June 1993, 1; Mankiller interview, 28 August 1997.

40. Donna Hales, "Mankiller Needs Kidney Transplant," *Muskogee Daily Phoenix*, 30 March 1990, 3A; "Chief Mankiller Released from Hospital Following Kidney Surgery Last Week," *Tahlequah Daily Press*, 28 June 1900, 3.

41. "Mankiller Signs Agreement for Tribe Self-Governance," Tahlequah Daily Press, 15 July 1990, 2; Janey Pearson, "Tribal Governments Embark on New Era of Sovereignty," *Tulsa World*, 19 August 1990, 1A and 7A.

42. When Mankiller became chief, two clinics served the needs of the Cherokees in addition to the Indian Health Service hospitals in Tahlequah and Claremore. By the end of her administration the Nation operated five clinics (in Jay, Nowata, Sallisaw, Salina, and Stillwell). See "Mankiller Years" (Cherokee Nation section), 6; "Cherokee Chief Seeks Second Term," *Muskogee Daily Phoenix*, 16 March 1991, 3A; Doug Ferguson, "Cherokee Chief Endures Challenges with Good Humor," *Wagoner Record-Democrat*, 13 March 1991, 4.

43. Doug Ferguson, "Cherokee Chief Endures Challenges with Good Humor," *Wagoner Record-Democrat*, 13 March 1991, 4; Doug Ferguson, "Riding High, Mankiller Ponders Re-Election Bid," *Tulsa World*, 10 March 1991, 2A.

44. "Mankiller Will Seek Re-Election to Tribe's Top Office," *Tahlequah Daily Press*, 17 March 1991, 1A; "Principal Chief Mankiller Meets with President Bush," *Cherokee Advocate*, June 1991, 1, 8; Mankiller interview, 28 August 1997.

45. "Mankiller Easily Wins Race for Cherokee Chief," *Daily Oklahoman*, 17 June 1991, 9.

46. The bill, which authorized the state to work out an agreement with Indian tribes concerning taxation of non-Indians purchasing goods in shops on Indian land, led to the negotiation of the compact discussed above. See Keith White, "Mankiller Seeks Some Good Out of Conference," *Muskogee Daily Phoenix*, 23 January 1992, 3A; Kelly Rucker, "Mankiller Urges U.S. to Fund Tribes," *Tulsa Tribune*, 14 May 1992, 7A; "Chief Mankiller Speaks Out on H.B. 1979," *Green Country Neighbor*, 11 March 1992, 26. "Mankiller Wants State to Shift Focus to Tribes' Economic Impact," *Tulsa World*, 23 February 1992, A11; Mankiller interview, 28 August 1997.

47. "Tribal Leaders Encourage Voter Participation, Endorse Clinton," *Cherokee Advocate*, November 1992, 8; "Mankiller Addresses Clinton, Gore Economic Conference," *Cherokee Advocate*, February 1993, 1; Mankiller interview, 28 August 1997.

48. Wilma P. Mankiller, "Supreme Court Will Hear Riverbed Case," *Cherokee Advocate*, October 1986, 4; "Arkansas Riverbed Authority," *Cherokee Advocate*, February 1993, (eight-page supplement); Mankiller interview, 28 August 1997; Combs interview, 5 August 1997.

49. "Mankiller Recovers from Surgery at Deaconess Hospital," *Tahlequah Daily Times Journal*, 9 June 1993, 7; "Mankiller Returns Home to Recuperate from Boston Surgery," *Tahlequah Daily Times Journal*, 30 June 1992, 8; Renee Fite, "Mankiller Says Tribe in Good Shape," *Muskogee Daily Phoenix*, 5 September 1993, 1A–2A.

50. Jim Myers, "Tribes Seek Resolutions," *Tulsa World*, 22 March 1994, 1, 3; Mankiller interview, 28 August 1997.

51. Bunty Anquoe, "President Promises Hope," *Indian Country Today*, 4 May 1994, 1A–2A; "Tribal Leaders Meet with President Clinton," *Cherokee Advocate*, June 1994, 1; Mankiller interview, 28 August 1997.

52. Rob Martindale, "Chief Mankiller to Leave Post Next Year," *Tulsa World*, 5 April 1994, 1; John Young, "Mankiller Will Step Down as Leader," *Indian Country Today*, 4 May 1994, 1A.

53. Leif M. Wright, "Mankiller: I Did What I Could," *Muskogee Daily Phoenix*, 4 September 1994, 1A and 6A; George Benge, "Mankiller a Legend in Her Own Time," *Muskogee Daily Phoenix*, 5 September 1994, 7A.

54. Bunty Anquoe, "Mankiller Receives Free Spirit Award," *Indian Country Today*, 28 September 1994, 1A–2A; "Mankiller, Jones among Hall of Fame Inductees," *Muskogee Daily Phoenix*, 6 November 1994, 2A; "Mankiller to Get Civil Rights Award," *Muskogee Daily Phoenix*, 4 July 1995, 3A; "Cherokee Chief Opposes Appointment," *Daily Oklahoman*, 19 January 1995, 11; Michael Pacewicz, "Tribal Leaders Worry about Future Support from U.S. Government," *Tahlequah Daily Press*, 11 July 1995, 1.

55. "Ross Swimmer Named President, Chief Executive of CNI," *Cherokee Advocate*, April 1992, 8; Donna Hales, "CNI Loan in Jeopardy," *Muskogee Daily Phoenix*, 3 Sep-

tember 1995, 1A and 3A; "Board Forces Swimmer to Resign from Top Post in CNI," *Cherokee Observer*, December 1995, 1 and 12; "Cherokee Nation Industries Lays Off 88 Employees," *Cherokee Observer*, April 1996, 1 and 20; "Chief's Letter Calls for Oversight on Heritage Center," *Cherokee Observer*, April 1996, 1 and 20; "Cherokee Nation Heritage Center Strives to Improve Image and Future," Cherokee Observer, April 1996, 3; "The Mankiller Letter," *Cherokee Observer*, April 1996, 3; "Mankiller: This is My Life," *Muskogee Daily Phoenix*, 14 September 1994, 3A.

56. Rob Martindale, "Next Cherokee Chief Will Face Challenges," *Tulsa World*, 15 January 1995, 15; Rob Martindale, "Mankiller Backs Bearpaw for Cherokee Chief," *Tulsa World*, 25 March 1995, 10. The *Cherokee Advocate* reported, "After the general election, controversy erupted when some tribal members [who] were not allowed to vote in the election, protested the voter registration process. Many of those complaining were unregistered voters who were turned away at the polls. Some of those who were turned away thought that they should be allowed to vote with their tribal membership card [blue card]." Also see "Cherokee Nation Tribal Election Decided July 29th," *Cherokee Advocate*, August 1995, 1; "Runoff Required to Determine Leadership of Cherokee Nation," Cherokee Advocate, July 1995 (special election section), 1, 6–7; "Cherokee Nation Run-Off Election Results," Cherokee Advocate, July 1995, 8; Constitution of the Cherokee Nation of Oklahoma, article IX, section 2.

57. "Executive Staff Resign to Pave Way for New Administration," *Cherokee Advocate*, 5 August 1995, 5; Lynn Howard to Brad and Sue Agnew, memorandum, September 9–17, 1997, in possession of the author; "Byrd Accuses Mankiller of Embezzlement," *Grove Sun*, 23 August 1995, 1A; "New Cherokee Chief Outlines Plans for New Administration," *Cherokee Advocate*, September 1995, 3; David Harper, "Mankiller Case Back in U.S. Court," *Tulsa World*, 29 August 1996, A7.

58. "Byrd Accuses Mankiller of Embezzlement," *Grove Sun*, 23 August 1995, 1A; "Mankiller Hit with Second Lawsuit," *Tahlequah Daily Press*, 14 September 1995, 1 and 3; "Mankiller Sued for Records," *Muskogee Daily Phoenix*, 14 September 1995, 1A and 5A; Harper, "Mankiller Case Back in U.S. Court," *Tulsa World*, 29 August 1996, A7; Donna Hales, "Tribe to Sue Mankiller," *Tulsa World*, 1 September 1995, A1.

59. "Suit Will Continue Despite Mankiller's Illness," *Tulsa World*, 1 March 1996, 1A; "Mankiller's Cancer Inoperable," *Tulsa World*, 5 March 1996, 1A and 10A; "Surgery Out for Mankiller," *Tulsa World*, 5 March 1996, A1 and A3; Gwen Grayson, unrecorded telephone conversation, 14 August 1997. Also see "Indian Leader Honored," *Bloomington (Indiana) Herald-Times*, 16 January 1998, 3A.

60. Darrean Browning, "Cherokee Chief Claims Charges Petty," *Northeastern*, 27 February 1997, 1–2; "Key Developments in the Cherokee Nation Crisis," *Muskogee Daily Phoenix*, 14 August 1997, 2A; Rob Martindale, "Mankiller Calls Conspiracy Assertion 'Nonsense,'" *Tulsa World*, 22 March 1997, A13; "Mankiller Addresses Tribal Conflict," *Tahlequah Daily Press*, 24 July 1997, 1; Jim Myers, "Cherokees Sign Pact," *Tulsa World*, 26 August 1997, A1 and A3; Rob Martindale and Michael Smith, "Mankiller Calls for Unity," *Tulsa World*, 29 August 1997, A1 and A4.

Ada Deer

Menominee

BY CLARA SUE KIDWELL

On 11 May 1993, Ada Deer was nominated by President William Clinton to become the first American Indian woman in history to serve as assistant secretary of Indian Affairs in the Department of the Interior. She described her vision for the Bureau of Indian Affairs (BIA) as being "a progressive Federal/tribal partnership."[1] There is a certain irony in her appointment since her tribe, the Menominee of Wisconsin, was the first with which the federal government terminated its trust relationship under House Concurrent Resolution 108, passed in 1953. Her rise to political power as assistant secretary was impelled primarily by her leadership in a 1973 fight to reverse that termination and to restore the Menominees to federally recognized status. She organized grassroots organizations and lobbied tirelessly in the halls of Congress. The daughter of a politically active white mother and a Menominee father, Ada Deer's own upbringing represents the forces of assimilation and resistance in Indian communities in the twentieth century. Her resignation from the Bureau of Indian Affairs in 1993 demonstrates the difficulties of achieving true tribal self-determination in America today.

Ada Deer was born on 7 August 1935 in a log cabin near the banks of the Wolf River, on the Menominee Reservation in Wisconsin.[2] One of nine children, she was born to Constance Stockton Wood Deer, a white mother, and to Joseph Deer, a Menominee father with "a splash of French blood." Her mother was from a wealthy east coast family and had worked for a time in Appalachia. She then accepted a position as a nurse with the Bureau of Indian Affairs (BIA), moved to the Rosebud Reservation in South Dakota, and finally was stationed on the Menominee Reservation. Always a rebel, Constance Deer was an ardent champion of Indian rights, and had a profound impact on Ada's life and future career. Her father, who had an eighth-grade education, grew up on the reservation and made Ada a part of the Menominee grassroots community.[3]

Deer spent the first six years of her life on the Menominee Reservation with her parents and the four of her nine siblings who survived infancy. Yet economic opportunities on the reservation were limited, and in 1940 the Deer family moved to Milwaukee, where Joseph Deer was soon drafted into the army to serve in World War II.[4] Although the war was not the reason for the move, the Deers became part of a new wartime phenomenon, the voluntary relocation of Indian families from reservations to cities to seek better economic opportunities. They lived in a working-class neighborhood on the south side of Milwaukee, the only Indian family on the block. There, Ada, just six years old, first experienced the discrimination of urban living. She and her siblings fought with neighborhood children who taunted them because of their "Indianess." They fought back, but Ada also learned to strengthen herself in a different way. She received a significant lesson about honesty and responsibility in elementary school when a teacher scolded her for showing a classmate her work during a spelling test. The teacher told her, "If you have pride, you don't give success away." The statement impressed her with the importance of taking responsibility for her own work.[5]

The war years marked a period of increased prosperity for the Deers and many other American Indian families, but when the war ended their prosperity declined. Meanwhile her brother became ill, and when Ada was ten years old the family moved back to the reservation. Although their log cabin had no running water or electricity, the family enjoyed the freedom and fresh air of the forest after the confinement of city life, and they raised goats whose milk improved her brother's health. Ada attended public schools in Shawano, but she felt isolated from the other children because of her clothes and background. It was clear to her that Indian students were not readily accepted as equals by other students and some teachers.[6]

The Menominee Reservation to which the Deer family had returned faced a period of transition. Established by the Treaty of Wolf River in 1854, the reservation held valuable stands of timber. The treaty had provided for the construction of a sawmill, but a gang of white entrepreneurs, the "Pine Ring," soon hovered around the edges of the reservation, often illegally cutting timber on Menominee land. In 1871 the BIA granted the tribe the right to cut and sell their own timber. During the early twentieth century the Menominees operated a profitable sawmill, but tribal leaders continually struggled with the BIA over the management of the forest, the mill, and the profits from the lumber industry.[7]

Much of the tribe's conflict with federal officials focused on the effects of a disastrous windstorm that in 1905 had downed approximately forty million board feet of timber on the reservation. The BIA had appointed an agent to oversee the recovery of this timber, but he had mismanaged his assignment; large quantities of marketable lumber had been lost. In response, the Menominees sued the federal government for damages. During 1908 Senator Robert M. LaFollette of Wisconsin sponsored legislation to set standards for the sustained yield management of Menominee timber resources. Yet the BIA still retained considerable control over the Menominee sawmill and most managerial positions were occupied by non-Indians. However, LaFollette's legislation did establish structures for tribal governance: a general council composed of adult members of the tribe, and an elected executive committee of twelve tribe members. The Menominees had continued to function under such political structures throughout the first third of the twentieth century.[8]

In 1934, after the passage of the Indian Reorganization Act (IRA), Commissioner of Indian Affairs John Collier urged the Menominees and other tribes to adopt a BIA-sponsored, tribal constitution that would alter their system of government. Since Menominee leaders initially believed that the adoption of the BIA proposal would provide them with more control over their timberlands and sawmill, they urged the Menominee people to adopt the new constitution. Yet opponents of the measure pointed out that under the IRA the jobs of the non-Indian mill managers still would be protected through the federal civil service system; federal bureaucrats would continue to control hiring and firing decisions for mill operations. In response, the Menominees rejected the IRA constitution, and the tribe continued to function under the Advisory Council, which comprised twelve elected members, and the General Council, which was made up of all enrolled Menominees.[9]

When World War II ended, the timber industry still provided employment for many Menominee people, and income from the mill and its products allowed the tribe to pay for the majority of its social services. The Menominees financed their own electrical utility and community recreational facilities, and supported a local hospital managed by an order of Catholic nuns. Although many reservation families were cash-poor, and the average wage of mill workers was $2,300 per year, in general the tribe was in significantly better financial shape than most other Indian tribes in the nation.[10]

Yet the Menominees faced some significant problems. Differing acculturation patterns enabled some Menominees to gain better access to the

reservation's abundant natural resources and viable wage economy. Anthropologists who studied the Menominees during this period found that
the reservation population ranged from highly acculturated individuals to
tribespeople who still followed the old ways. Some were Christians, some
were members of the Native American Church, and others continued to
practice traditional Menominee ceremonies.[11] Differences also existed between mixed-blood and full-blood Menominees. Like many other tribal
communities, the Menominee Reservation was divided by political factions. For example, under the tribal political structure, the Advisory
Council (composed mainly of a relatively acculturated elite) was forced to
submit decisions to the General Council, a group that often expressed a
basic suspicion of leaders in general. Friction also developed between Menominee men who had seasonal or intermittent work as jobbers for the
mills, and Menominee families whose members held the better paying
jobs in the mills and the BIA agency.[12]

The end of the war also marked a shift in federal Indian policy. Many
Americans believed that the federal government's unique series of relationships with, and obligations to, Indians should be ended, and that Indian people should be "strongly encouraged" to assimilate into non-Indian
society. In 1945, Congress largely repudiated Collier's plans to enhance the
powers of tribal governments, and Collier resigned as commissioner of Indian Affairs.[13] One year later Congress approved the Indian Claims Commission Act, which gave the tribes the right to sue the government for the
violation of treaty agreements and the subsequent loss of land and resources. Ostensibly an act to correct past injustices to the tribes, it also was
an attempt to eliminate the possibility of future Indian claims against the
government and initiate the termination of federal responsibility toward
the tribes.[14] In 1947, in response to a congressional directive, William Zimmerman, assistant commissioner of the BIA, proposed a specific plan to
terminate the tribes in a phased sequence depending upon their level of acculturation, economic resources, and acquiescence, and the willingness of
state governments to assume responsibilities for their protection, social
services, and so on. The Menominees were among the ten tribal communities that Zimmerman deemed ready to be free of federal supervision.[15]

In 1951, amidst uncertainty over their future relationship with the federal government, the Menominees learned that their half-century-old
lawsuit against the federal government over the downed timber of 1905 finally had been settled, and that the tribe would receive a payment of
$8,500,000 ($7,600,000 after legal fees). Added to the almost $2,500,000
already accumulated in the tribe's Treasury Department account, the Me-

nominees potentially were one of the wealthiest tribes in the United States. The BIA was responsible for the disbursement of the money, but the tribe had the authority to review and approve expenditures. Conflicts soon emerged between BIA officials and the Advisory Council over control of the funds, and also among tribal factions over the disbursement of the money.[16]

The distribution of these funds soon became entangled in the government's emerging termination policies. In January 1953 the General Council voted for a per capita distribution (fifteen hundred dollars to each tribal member) of most of the funds from the lawsuit payment, while the BIA wanted the tribe to use the money to fund further tribal services.[17] The Menominees' plan for a per capita payment needed congressional approval, but it was held up by Arthur V. Watkins, chairman of the Senate Subcommittee on Indian Affairs, and the strongest proponent of termination (which he referred to as the "freedom program") in Congress. Watkins demanded that the Menominees accept termination as a condition for receiving the per capita payment. He was invited by a Menominee delegation to visit the reservation and spoke to the Menominee General Council on 20 June 1953. He informed the members that termination was a foregone conclusion, and that the per capita payment was dependent upon their acceptance of the policy. In response the General Council voted to transfer responsibility for services and the management of the sawmill from the BIA to the tribe. By linking termination to the per capita payment, Watkins effectively coerced the Menominees to accept the idea. The vote however, concealed a widespread misunderstanding and fear of termination.[18]

While the Menominees voted to accept termination as a condition for receiving their cash settlement, Congress moved toward finalizing its termination policies on a national basis. In July 1953 the House of Representatives passed House Concurrent Resolution 108, endorsing a policy of termination and specifically naming the Menominees as one of the tribes eligible for the process.[19] When the House and Senate Subcommittees on Indian Affairs held joint hearings on the proposed termination legislation in the spring of 1954, the Menominees offered no protest. The tribe seemed to believe that resistance was futile. The hearing focused not on whether the tribe should be terminated or not, but on establishing procedures through which the Menominees could plan for their own termination. The final bill for Menominee termination was signed into law on 17 June 1954. The deadline for the tribe to submit its plan, and for termination to become reality, was 31 December 1958. Although the tribe requested financial assistance with the planning process, it was granted only half the costs. The BIA took a hands-off attitude: bureau officials maintained that they did not want to be perceived as attempting to control the tribe.[20] By 1958 many Menominees expressed a growing concern about their earlier decision to accept termination, but it was too late. After a series of appeals and delaying tactics that extended the final deadline for the Menominee plan, the formal termination took place on 30 April 1961.[21]

While the Menominees were moving toward termination, Ada Deer progressed through her adolescence. In 1949 she entered high school at Shawano, Wisconsin. Ada's mother set high academic standards for her, and despite her feelings that she was not fully accepted by other students in the school, she tried to live up to her mother's expectations. She made good grades but initially had difficulty adjusting to the conflicting demands of the predominantly white high school and the socioeconomic standards of her family. Ada's mother, Constance Deer, earlier had been influenced by Mormon missionaries, and at the beginning of her sophomore year Ada was sent to live with a Mormon farm family in Gunnison, Utah. Although the situation in the Shawano public schools had been far from ideal, it was tolerable; when Ada arrived in Utah she found herself resident on a rural farm, attending a school system with a predominantly conservative Mormon faculty and student body, and expected by her host family to labor in their dairy barn in exchange for her room and board. She soon returned to Wisconsin.[22]

Enrolled again at Shawano High School, Ada continued to excel at everything except algebra. She edited the senior class yearbook, won the Original Oratory contest, and during her senior year she served on the Youth Advisory Board of the Wisconsin governor's Commission on Human Rights. Moreover, during her senior year, after her mother entered her picture in a national contest to select one of the "six most beautiful Indian girls in America," she won a trip to Hollywood and a one-line speaking part in the western film *The Battle of Rogue River*. Her mother and several teachers at Shawano High School encouraged her to attend college, and when she graduated from high school the tribe awarded her a scholarship of a thousand dollars per year for four years. In the fall of 1953, while her tribe was voting on the termination issue, Ada Deer enrolled as a pre-med major at the University of Wisconsin.[23]

In Madison, Deer's interest in social and political issues important to Native American people heightened. She continued to speak out on Indian issues as a member of the governor's Commission on Human Rights, and during the summer between her freshman and sophomore years (1954) she participated in the Encampment for Citizenship in New York City. The Encampment, sponsored by the Ethnical Culture Society, brought high school and college students from many backgrounds together to study democratic processes in American society. Through the Encampment she also met Eleanor Roosevelt at Hyde Park in July 1954. Becoming less interested in medicine, Deer enrolled in coursework focused on public service and, because of her ability to influence people, was encouraged by an economics professor to consider a career as a diplomat. Deer later recalled that the professor's advice "changed my whole perspective of myself," since she began to see herself not only as a Menominee, but as a "citizen of America and the world." During her senior year at Wisconsin, Deer changed her major to social work, and graduated with a bachelor of science from the University of Wisconsin in 1957.[24]

Deer's decision to pursue a career in social work was partially motivated by events occurring back on the Menominee Reservation. As the tribe moved toward termination, and the old, established support structures broke down, socioeconomic conditions deteriorated. The hospital formerly staffed and managed by Catholic nuns closed. The tribal electricity plant was sold. The General Council voted for a per capita distribution of funds, which further depleted the tribal treasury. The tribe had no administrative structure to handle the responsibilities that it was forced to assume. The tribe's education was at the eighth-grade level, which was comparable to most of the surrounding population, but there was no professional expertise in the form of doctors, lawyers, or social workers to administer programs on the reservation. Meanwhile, the leadership of the tribe remained in the hands of men who had long been involved in tribal politics.[25]

In 1957, while the tribe struggled through the termination crisis, Deer enrolled in the Master of Science in Social Work program at Columbia University, the best such program in the nation. Her first field placement was in the Henry Street Settlement House in Manhattan. She then took a two-year leave from the program and worked with African American high school students in the Bedford-Styvesant housing project in New York City. She returned to Columbia in 1960 and completed a final placement with the State Charities Aid Association of New York, supervising homes for abandoned or orphaned infants. Deer finished her master's degree in 1961, and despite, or perhaps because of the situation on the Menominee Reservation, she did not return to Wisconsin. Rather she accepted a position as program director for a project with urban Indians at the Waite

Neighborhood House in Minneapolis. There she attended community meetings and experienced firsthand the concerns of an urban Indian community.[26]

Although Deer resided in Minneapolis, she regularly visited the Menominee Reservation and it soon became apparent to her that the tribe's termination had been a disaster. In 1963 she traveled to Washington DC where she requested and received a meeting with Phileo Nash, the commissioner of Indian Affairs. A former lieutenant-governor of Wisconsin, Nash was aware of the Menominees' ordeal and sympathized with Deer's criticism of the BIA's lack of effort in preparing the tribe to deal with the complexities of the termination process. Nash was impressed with the young Menominee woman and suggested that she work for the BIA. In 1964 she accepted an offer from the BIA area director in Minneapolis to become the area's community services coordinator. Two years later Nash asked her to travel across the United States, visit Indian communities, and report on the socioeconomic conditions she found. The experiences she gained from this trip were vital to both her understanding of conditions in Indian Country and to her growing national reputation.[27]

When Deer returned to Minnesota she found that a new area director had abolished her position and that she had been reassigned as an employment counselor. Disillusioned with a job that seemed largely without influence or any chance for advancement, she resigned after six months. She remained in Minneapolis where she worked temporarily for the University of Minnesota, then accepted a position as a school social worker for the Minneapolis Board of Education. But like many school systems, the Minneapolis public school district was a highly bureaucratic structure, and Deer believed there was no real administrative support for Indian education, or sensitivity to the special needs of Indian students. In 1969, when she was offered a position as director of the Upward Bound program at the University of Wisconsin at Stevens Point, she resigned from her position in Minneapolis and moved back to Wisconsin.[28]

By 1970, Deer's activities at the local, regional, and national levels already had attracted considerable attention. She already had served on the board of directors for the Girl Scouts of America and on the U.S. Department of Health, Education, and Welfare's Urban Indian Task Force; and had attended the White House Conference on Children and Youth. The self-confidence, articulateness, and charisma that had gained her recognition throughout her undergraduate years continued to attract the attention of individuals in positions of power and influence. In 1970, LaDonna Harris, founder of Americans for Indian Opportunity (AIO) and wife of

Senator Fred Harris of Oklahoma, invited her to serve on the AIO board of directors.[29]

But 1970 also was a critical year for the Menominee people. After almost a decade of "freedom," the previously prosperous tribe was rapidly sinking into poverty. Under the provisions of termination, the former Menominee Reservation became the seventy-second county of Wisconsin, and the tribe's assets were incorporated into Menominee Enterprises Inc. (MEI), a new corporation controlled by a voting trust composed of three white and four Menominee trustees. Each of the 3,270 tribal members received a hundred shares of stock, valued at a hundred dollars apiece, in the corporation. An additional three thousand shares of stock were to be sold to obtain capital for MEI. The trust elected the board of directors, which managed the daily affairs of the corporation. This double-tiered management structure supposedly was designed to buffer MEI against factionalism and infighting within the tribe. Some Menominees alleged, however, that it was formulated to keep the control of the trust in the hands of a governing elite and out of the hands of the majority of tribal members. Moreover, in what was to become a highly controversial move, the shares allocated to minors and incompetent persons were placed in a separate trust at the First Wisconsin Trust Company of Milwaukee. Consequently, in 1961 when the Menominees were first terminated, the First Wisconsin Trust controlled approximately 40 percent of MEI.[30]

Each tribe member also received an income bond that was to pay a 4 percent annual interest, and to have a maturity value in the year 2000. The bond supplanted the annual stumpage fees from timber sales that tribe members had received under the old reservation system. Unlike the annual stumpage payments, however, the bonds were negotiable instruments. Since the Menominees now were expected to purchase the lands on which their individual homes had been built prior to termination, many tribe members used their bonds as payment.[31]

The transition from reservation to corporation was extremely difficult for the Menominee people. Services that the tribe previously had obtained through the BIA and the Catholic Church no longer were available. Now dependent upon state and local facilities, tribe members turned to county commissioners, or the state of Wisconsin for educational or medical assistance.[32] The Menominees' problems also were accentuated by the new management of the tribe's former sawmill. Prior to termination, the mill, now MEI's major asset, had been managed as a social service rather than as a "for profit" business. Its purpose had been to provide employment for as many tribe members as possible, and it generally had done so despite continuing complaints by tribal leaders that the best jobs, that is, managerial jobs, went to non-Indians. In contrast, after 1961, when the mill became the primary asset of a private corporation (which in turn became the major tax base of a county government) the enterprise was forced to function as a profitable business venture. In turn, mill managers interested in profits automated many of the mill procedures, which made the mill more efficient but markedly increased tribal unemployment. Ironically, because the termination agreement maintained the sustained-yield management of logging operations, additional timber could not be harvested and the mill could not increase its profits through greater production. Meanwhile, since the tribe had distributed most of its tribal treasury through per capita payments during the termination period, MEI had no cash reserve for operating capital.[33]

Although the loss of social services, the now-expensive electrical power, and the disproportionately low-paying mill jobs plagued the Menominee people, a more serious threat loomed on the horizon: the erosion of the Menominee landbase through the sale of land to non-Indians for use as vacation homes and recreational facilities. Short of capital, MEI's board of directors proposed the sale of lakefront acreages on a new lake to be constructed on forest lands still held in trust for the Menominees. In conjunction with a nationally known land developer, the board of directors proposed to develop and market lakefront home sites at what would become "Legend Lake." The sale of land required the approval of two-thirds of the corporation's shareholders (a majority impossible to achieve), but in 1967 the board devised a plan to lease the proposed home sites for forty years, with options to buy, and in 1968 began construction on the first of three dams that would create the new lake for the vacation community.[34]

Dominated by non-Menominee trustees and board members, MEI had not been popular with many rank-and-file Menominees. One of its most outspoken critics was Constance Deer, Ada's mother. In 1963 she founded the Citizens' Association for the Advancement of the Menominee People (CAAMP), which had generated a petition with eight hundred Memominee signatures calling for the repeal of termination. She continued to criticize MEI in "fiery letters" to public officials and in speeches at public hearings. Controversy over the Legend Lake project solidified the opposition to MEI board members, and when MEI opened sales offices to market future lakefront lots, other Menominees picketed the offices or attempted to disrupt dinner parties held for prospective buyers.[35]

As the controversy over Legend Lake became associated with the larger issue of reversing termination, political factionalism again cut across Menominee politics. Significant numbers of Menominees resided off the reservation, and many of these tribe members, willing to accept liquidation of the tribal assets to gain their shares in cash, had supported the termination legislation. Menominees resident on the reservation often questioned the nonreservation tribe members' loyalty, and accused them of wanting to vote the tribe out of existence. Those who continued to favor the termination program countered that for decades prior to 1961 the old advisory boards and general councils had been subject to the heavy hand of the BIA; termination at least provided tribe members with an opportunity to be free of bureau authority.[36]

By the late 1960s the Deer family had become embroiled in these issues. Constance continued her fight against termination, and in 1969 Ada's younger sister Connie attended an MEI shareholders meeting at which she requested a review of the costs of the Legend Lake project, a request that was promptly denied. Angered by what she envisioned as the MEI's arrogance, Ada contacted Wisconsin Judicare, a state legal services agency, and requested assistance. Joseph Preloznik, the agency's director, promptly responded with legal action, and the MEI was forced to open its records.[37]

Encouraged by the legal victory, Deer worked with other opponents of the MEI directors to gain control of the corporation. Assisted by her sister Connie, and Joan Keshena Harte, a Menominee living in Chicago, she began to organize Menominees living in Milwaukee and northern Illinois. Jim White, a gifted Menominee orator and a resident of Chicago, attracted media attention. With the help of Lloyd Powless, Deer mounted a telephone campaign in Milwaukee to organize Menominees in that urban area, and she also enlisted the assistance of Nancy Lurie, an anthropologist at the University of Wisconsin at Milwaukee, who hosted meetings in her home and who published a number of articles in scholarly journals that called attention to the Menominee plight. Meanwhile, Joseph Preloznik, the director of the Wisconsin Judicare agency met with Menominee groups in Chicago to explain the operations of MEI and the implications of the termination legislation.[38]

During the spring of 1970 a unified organization, Determination of the Rights and Unity of Menominee Shareholders (DRUMS), emerged from these efforts. Led by Jim White, its first president and most prominent spokesperson, the group began to solicit members and organize in Menominee County, where it encountered stiff opposition from MEI officials. Although MEI agents disrupted DRUMS's organizational meetings, a backlash against MEI developed when the land developer in partnership with MEI bulldozed sites around Legend Lake before legal action initiated by Wisconsin Judicare could halt it. In response DRUMS organized confrontational picket lines at Legend Lake sales offices and mass marches to the state legislature.[39] DRUMS also organized a mass mailing to Menominee shareholders, urging them to vote the MEI trust directors out of office. In response, MEI trustee president George Kenote promised to expand the number of trustees, and in a subsequent special election, Deer and another DRUMS candidate, Georgianne Ignace, won seats on the board. But in April 1971, she and other DRUMS members lost a crucial vote that would have dissolved the trust completely. According to the terms of the Termination Bill, a dissolution of the trust agreement required the consent of 51 percent of *all* shareholders. Not all shareholders cast ballots, and the First Wisconsin Trust Company cast its votes in favor of MEI.[40]

Disappointed but not daunted by the defeat, Deer and other DRUMS leaders changed their tactics. Instead of attempting to convince MEI to vote itself out of existence, they decided to petition Congress to reverse the 1961 termination legislation that had dissolved the Menominee Reservation. Ironically, by 1970 many officials in Washington acknowledged that the termination policies had failed. The Menominees teetered on the edge of economic disaster, and the state of Wisconsin was neither able nor willing to provide them with adequate services. Moreover, in an address on 8 July 1970, President Richard Nixon officially repudiated termination in favor of self-determination for Indian people. In Congress, change was in the air. By the summer of 1970 the Senate Committee on Interior and Insular Affairs already was considering Concurrent Resolution 26, rejecting termination. In response to a congressional invitation, Deer led a delegation of DRUMS members to Washington where she testified in support of the resolution on 21 July 1971.[41]

While Deer testified in Congress, DRUMS members in Wisconsin kept up their confrontational tactics. They organized a march from Keshena to Madison in October 1971; gained national media attention in the *Washington Post* and the *New York Times*; and convinced Governor Patrick Lucey to visit Menominee County to examine the poor economic and social conditions there. In addition, during November Deer was reelected and joined by three other DRUMS members on the MEI board of trustees. At the board's next organization meeting, Deer was elected chair. She immediately announced that she would open the trustees' meetings to the public, provide detailed minutes of all meetings to the shareholders, open communication between trustees and shareholders, and attempt to establish a board composed entirely of Menominees.[42]

DRUMS now controlled MEI's board of directors, but Deer knew that the battle against termination was not over. Although Congress had repudiated the termination policy, the 1961 legislation dissolving the Menominee Reservation still remained, and the Menominees would need special legislation if Congress was to reverse itself, abolish the earlier bill, and restore the reservation. To achieve such a goal, the Menominees needed the support of both officials in Wisconsin and the state's congressional delegation. In November 1971, representatives of MEI and DRUMS met with Governor Patrick Lucey and agreed on a restoration bill that would reinstate tribal status, reopen the tribal rolls, and restore all land to trust status. Assisted by Charles Wilkinson and Yvonne Knight, attorneys for the Native American Rights Fund, Deer meet with the Wisconsin congressional delegation. Senators William Proxmire and Gaylord Nelson, and Congressman David Obey agreed to sponsor legislation to accomplish these ends. Meanwhile Deer led a small delegation of Menominees to Washington where they established an office and lobbied extensively in the tribe's behalf. Their efforts were supported by Senator Fred Harris from Oklahoma, his wife, LaDonna Harris, and Phileo Nash. LaDonna Harris and Nash served as co-directors of DRUMS's Advisory Committee.[43]

Deer spent the next two years in Washington, building support for the proposed legislation. In 1971 she entered law school at the University of Wisconsin, but her responsibilities in Washington took precedence over her studies, and she withdrew from the university to spearhead the lobbying efforts. DRUMS provided some financial support, as did small contributions from individuals and an occasional foundation, but Deer and the other lobbyists often survived through the hospitality of friends, particularly LaDonna Harris. Deer traveled regularly between Washington and Wisconsin, but because funds were scarce, communication between the Washington lobbyists and rank-and-file Menominees were difficult.[44] Yet their efforts proved successful. The restoration bill passed the House by a vote of 404 to 3, and the Senate on a voice vote. Richard Nixon signed it into law on 22 December 1973.[45]

For the Menominees, the passage of the restoration bill was the first, not the final chapter. Congress had been willing to legalize the restoration of the Menominee tribal government and reservation, but it remained up to the Menominees to decide what sort of government they wanted and to ascertain just how that government would exert authority over the newly restored tribal lands. The restoration legislation provided for the formation of a restoration committee to oversee these decisions, and Deer was elected the chair. She and other committee members were faced with a formidable task. The struggle against the old guard MEI trustees and their allies had united the DRUMS activists, but with their enemy defeated, problems emerged over the establishment of a working government. Moreover, as committee chair, Deer was forced to deal both with BIA officials who still viewed their role as managers of Menominee affairs, and with disgruntled tribespeople who saw the restoration of trust status as continued federal interference in Menominee affairs.[46]

Deer also faced opposition from another quarter. Her leadership and the subsequent victory in obtaining the restoration legislation had strengthened her reputation as an effective Indian leader, but most of her efforts had taken place in Washington. While others carried on dramatic demonstrations and confrontations in Wisconsin, Deer, who was polished, articulate, and persuasive, used her skills to persuade in the halls of Congress to further the Menominee cause. Yet because her efforts had been carried out in Congress rather than on the reservation, she and other members of the committee were accused of being aloof and operating too much on their own initiative, similar to the charges that earlier had been leveled against the governing board of the MEI. DRUMS and its leaders now came under increased criticism because they had been forced to operate outside Menominee County and had not garnered the whole-hearted support of all the local Menominee communities; they were accused of not being in touch with "grassroots" Menominees. These charges stung deeply; they were particularly harsh for a woman who had given up her own career and had spent two years of her life lobbying and negotiating with congressional leaders for the benefit of her tribe.[47]

Deer's leadership abilities soon were tested. The committee faced a new organization, the Menominee Warrior Society, which adopted some of the tactics DRUMS had used against MEI. Comprising disaffected DRUMS members, old-guard MEI officers, some American Indian Movement members, and a smattering of liberal to radical white political activists seeking Indian causes, the Warrior Society on 31 December 1974 forcibly occupied a facility near Gresham, Wisconsin, recently vacated by the Alexian Brothers, a Catholic religious order. The Warrior Society publicly announced that they intended to transform the building into a reservation hospital. Angered by the seizure, the governor of Wisconsin attempted to bypass the committee and called out the Wisconsin National Guard to intervene directly with the Warrior Society. In contrast, Deer and the committee took the reasoned position that the seizure of the property was illegal, and that the committee was not empowered to accept the facility on behalf of the tribe. Although the issues never were directly joined, the Warrior Society eventually dispersed and abandoned the buildings. In response, the committee obtained several substantial federal grants and built a new health facility for the reservation. Finally, in 1978, tribe members approved a new, constitutional government that restored full self-government to the Menominee tribe.[48]

The Warrior Society's occupation of the Alexian Brothers' facilities was indicative of Native American political activism in the 1970s. Tribal leaders during this decade faced many challenges. Those who had learned the skills of political negotiation at the national level often became the target of young, disaffected Indians who demanded immediate results. Indian discontent with the policies and procedures of the BIA led to the occupation of the agency's headquarters in Washington during 1972, and one year later the American Indian Movement seized control of the tiny hamlet of Wounded Knee, South Dakota. Meanwhile, federal officials struggled to develop an appropriate response.[49]

Federal marshals and FBI agents surrounded Wounded Knee, and the confrontation eventually dissipated, but Congress responded with two pieces of legislation that eventually changed the nature of the tribe's relationship with the federal government. Led by Senator James Abourezk from South Dakota, chairman of the Senate Subcommittee on Indian Affairs, and Congressman Lloyd Meeds of Washington State, an active supporter of the Menominee Restoration Bill and a member of the House Subcommittee on Indian Affairs, in January 1975 Congress passed the Indian Self-Determination and Educational Assistance Act—legislation that established the right of tribal governments to contract with the BIA to run their own programs. During the same month President Gerald Ford also signed a bill that established the American Indian Policy Review Commission.[50] The commission was to be composed of five Indian representatives and six members of Congress. It operated under the auspices of Congress, with all the limitations of funding and political pressure that entailed. The Indian members of the commission were chosen by the congressional members. Deer was nominated by Lloyd Meeds, who stated, "In all respects she is one of the finest, most capable individuals I have met, a tremendously fine organizer who would bring to the Commission a great deal of prestige."[51]

The commission quickly became involved in controversy. Although Deer and the other Native Americans appointed to it possessed excellent credentials, their appointments immediately were challenged by the National Tribal Chairman's Association (NTCA), since none of the appointees were tribal chairs. The association charged that they did not reflect the views of all Indian people. The NTCA lawsuit was unsuccessful, and the five congressional appointees assumed their place on the commission, but the suit cast some doubt on the commission's efforts.

Yet the commission faced more important problems than the NTCA challenge. At issue was the basic nature of the relationship between Indian people and the Bureau of Indian Affairs. Some members of the commission, and many Indian people, believed that the BIA should be abol-·ished altogether—that the bureau no longer served the best interests of the tribes. Other commissioners (and other Indians) argued that the BIA should be retained as a symbol of the federal government's obligations to Indian people, but that it should better serve Indian interests rather than function as a self-serving bureaucracy with primary control over Native Americans and their resources. Yet regardless of their differences, the five Indian members of the commission agreed "that the goal of Indian self-sufficiency is indeed a matter of overriding importance."[52]

The thirty-one task force members and the majority of their staff who conducted a series of hearings and fact-finding missions across the United States were American Indians. The commission's final report, published in 1977, contained a total of 206 recommendations. The most important one stated that the BIA should be retained but reorganized into a service agency, its authority should be decentralized, and it should become an independent department within the federal government. In addition, the commission recommended that the position of commissioner of Indian Affairs be elevated to the rank of assistant secretary. Like the Indian Self-Determination and Educational Assistance Act, the commission's report also stipulated that the BIA should contract directly with the tribes to provide necessary services. Although commission Vice Chairman LLoyd Meeds had previously supported Menominee restoration and the Indian Self-Determination and Educational Assistance Act, and had nominated Deer to the commission, he disagreed with her and the other Indian commissioners over the commission's final report. Denying the principal of tribal sovereignty that the Indian commissioners so strongly espoused, Meeds characterized the report as "the product of one-sided advocacy in favor of American Indian tribes."[53]

While serving as a commissioner, Deer also was named a fellow at the Harvard Institute of Politics, and in 1978 she was appointed senior lecturer in the School of Social Work and Native American Studies at the

University of Wisconsin at Madison. In 1979 she left the university to join the staff of the Native American Rights Fund (NARF), where she utilized her lobbying experience as legislative liaison at NARF's Washington office. NARF had served as an important legal resource for DRUMS during the struggle over restoration, and she remained with the agency until 1981, when she returned to the University of Wisconsin. From 1984 to 1990 she served on NARF's board of directors, acting as chair of the board from 1989 to 1990.[54]

Back in Wisconsin, Deer became actively involved with the Democratic Party. She was well-known to party leaders through her lobbying and other political activities, and in 1978 and 1982 she was an unsuccessful Democratic candidate for the Secretary of State's office in Wisconsin. In 1978 and 1982 she was credited with introducing an Indian plank into the National Democratic Platform, and one year later Deer was appointed to the Commission on Presidential Nomination of the Democratic National Party (the Hunt Committee), which examined the presidential nomination process and recommended changes, including a system of at-large delegates, which included a substantial number of women and minorities. Deer attended the 1984 Democratic Convention as one of these at-large delegates whose votes played a significant role in Walter Mondale's nomination. She campaigned actively for Mondale in Wisconsin.[55]

In 1992 Deer won the Democratic primary for the House of Representatives from the Second District in Wisconsin. She campaigned actively in the general election (she used a campaign slogan she always had wanted to utilize: "Me Nominee"), but she lost to her Republican opponent. Yet when William Clinton won the presidency he nominated her as the first woman to hold the office of assistant secretary for Indian Affairs. Testifying before the Senate Committee on Indian Affairs, Deer championed a policy of "strong, effective tribal sovereignty. . . . The days of federal paternalism are over." Secretary of the Interior Bruce Babbit described her as "a strong leader with a lifelong commitment to American Indian rights, to improving the lives of American Indians, and to the strengthening of tribal governments . . . She is an outstanding advocate with an impressive record of success and accomplishment." The U.S. Senate confirmed her appointment on 16 July 1993.[56]

Deer served as assistant secretary for Indian Affairs from 1993 until 1997. During her term in office, 223 Native villages in Alaska and 12 tribes achieved federal recognition. The number of tribes contracting for their own services increased to 180 through 54 annual funding agreements. Tribal-state gaming compacts were signed between 130 tribes and 24

states, and a century-old boundary dispute between the federal government and the Crow Tribe was settled. During Deer's term in office Congress passed important amendments to the American Indian Religious
Freedom Act and to the Indian Self-Determination and Educational Assistance Act. Moreover, she took an active role in mediating a dispute between contesting parties of the Oneida Nation in New York over who
should exercise legitimate authority in tribal government (a role that garnered some criticism from Native Americans). Deer also attempted to reorganize the BIA in accordance with the recommendations that she and
other commissioners had advocated while serving with the American Indian Policy Review Commission in 1977. Yet her outspoken advocacy of
tribal sovereignty in an era when Congress was engaged in significant
budget reductions, and when tribal sovereignty over taxation and gaming
was creating a backlash against Indian self-determination eventually
caused her to run afoul of the Clinton administration. On 9 January 1997,
at the request of Secretary of the Interior Bruce Babbit, she resigned from
her office as assistant secretary.[57]

Reflecting on her tenure, Ada Deer described her primary goal as one
"to oversee [the BIA's] transition from paternalistic landlord to true partner on a government to government basis with American Indian tribes."
She acknowledged that "[w]hat happens in DC is about power, and power
is based on perception. But it is important to understand that we are not
always in control of how we are perceived."[58]

Throughout most of her adult life, Ada Deer has been perceived as a
leader. In addition to her career as a political activist and a public servant,
she has served on many boards: the National Association of Social Workers, Common Cause, the Robert Wood Johnson Foundation, and the Presidential Commission on White House Fellows, to name just a few. She has
served on the president's Inter-Agency Council on Women, and testified
before the United Nations Human Rights Committee. She has received
many national honors: Woman of the Year from the Girl Scouts of America; the Wonder Woman Award from the Wonder Woman Foundation in
1984; the Indian Council Fire Achievement Award in 1984, and the 1991
National Distinguished Achievement Award from the American Indian
Resources Institute.[59]

Growing up on a reservation, guided by a strong-willed mother who
championed the rights of her Indian family, Ada Deer has become a dedicated advocate with a deep sense of purpose. After recommending that
the Bureau of Indian Affairs should become a true service agency for Indian people, and that tribal sovereignty and self-governance were of para-

mount importance for Indian tribes, she had the opportunity to serve as assistant secretary and implement some of these goals. Her outspoken defense of tribal sovereignty during a period of federal budget cuts engendered criticism and eventually led to her resignation, but her resignation was not symptomatic of failure on her part. Ada Deer's tenure as assistant secretary for Indian Affairs ended because she refused to acquiesce in a political process that traditionally has hindered the development of a true sense of self-determination for Indian tribes. She remains one of the most influential Native American leaders of the final third of the twentieth century.

NOTES

1. U.S. Senate, *Hearing before the Committee on Indian Affairs on the Nomination of Ada Deer to be Assistant Secretary for Indian Affairs*, 103d Cong., 1st sess., 15 July 1993, 10.

2. Ada Deer with R. E. Simon Jr., *Speaking Out* (Chicago: Children's Press Open Door Books, 1970), 10–11.

3. Hearing, 8–9.

4. Deer, *Speaking Out*, 10–17.

5. Deer, *Speaking Out*, 22.

6. Deer, *Speaking Out*, 22–26.

7. Patricia K. Ourada, *The Menominee Indians: A History* (Norman: University of Oklahoma Press, 1979), 93–126, 142–47, 179.

8. Ourada, *The Menominee Indians*, 179; Steven J. Hertzberg, "The Menominee Indians: From Treaty to Termination," *Wisconsin Magazine of History*, 60 (summer 1977): 267–329.

9. Rachel Reese Sady, "The Menominee: Transition from Trusteeship," *Human Organization* 6 (spring 1947): 4–6, 8–9; Hertzberg, "The Menominee Indians," 290.

10. Deborah Shames, ed., *Freedom with Reservation: The Menominee Struggle to Save Their Land and People* (Madison: National Committee to Save the Menominee People and Forests, 1972), 41; Nancy Oesterich Lurie, "Menominee Termination: Reservation to Colony," *Human Organization* 31(4) (1972): 260; Hertzberg, "The Menominee Indians," 295–98.

11. George Spindler, "Sociocultural and Psychological Processes in Menominee Acculturation," in *University of California Publications in Culture and Society*, vol. 5 (Berkeley: University of California Press, 1955); Louise S. Spindler, "Menominee Women and Cultural Change," *American Anthropological Association Memoir 91*, vol. 64, no. 1, part 2 (Menasha WI: American Anthropological Association, 1962); George Spindler and Louise Spindler, *Dreamers with Power: The Menominee Indians* (Prospect Heights IL: Waveland Press, 1971), 5. The Spindlers developed a cat-

egorization for Menominee acculturation: Native oriented, Peyote Cult members, transitional, lower-status acculturated, and elite acculturated. Also see Felix Maxwell Keesing, *The Menominee Indians of Wisconsin, Memoirs of the American Philosophical Society*, vol. 10 (New York: Johnson Reprint Corp., 1971), 76, 122–28 for a discussion of Menominee acculturation patterns earlier in the century.

12. Sady, "The Menominee," 8–13. Blood-quantum seems to have played a significant role in factionalism. By 1950 there were only eighty-two full-blood Menominees, while 97.3 percent of the population had some admixture of white blood. Yet the full-blood/mixed-blood dichotomy or characterization was also used to describe cultural patterns and biological differences, and was commonly used in debates between political opponents. See Nicholas C. Peroff, *Menominee Drums: Tribal Termination and Restoration, 1954–1974* (Norman: University of Oklahoma Press, 1982), 98–99.

13. Vine Deloria Jr. and Clifford M. Lytle, eds., *The Nations Within: The Past and Future of American Indian Sovereignty* (New York: Pantheon Books, 1984), 180–82.

14. Donald L. Fixico, *Termination and Relocation: Federal Indian Policy, 1945–1960* (Albuquerque: University of New Mexico Press, 1986), 25–29.

15. S. Lyman Tyler, *A History of Indian Policy* (Washington: United States Department of the Interior, 1973), 163–65.

16. Tyler, *A History of Indian Policy*, 163–65; Gary Orfield, *A Study of the Termination Policy* (Denver: National Congress of American Indians, 1965), chapter 4, 4.

17. Deer, *Speaking Out*, 34; Orfield, *A Study*, chapter 2, 1; Peroff, *Menominee Drums*, 53.

18. David W. Ames and Burton R. Fisher, "The Menominee Termination Crisis: Barrier in the Way of a Rapid Cultural Transition, *Human Organization* 18 (fall 1959): 103. Also see Peroff, *Menominee Drums*, 54–56; Shames, *Freedom with Reservation*, 8; and Spindler and Spindler, *Dreamers with Power*, 195.

19. Arthur V. Watkins, "Termination of Federal Supervision: The Removal of Restrictions over Indian Property and Persons," *Annals of the American Academy of Political and Social Science* 311 (May 1957): 50.

20. Peroff, *Menominee Drums*, 58–59; Orfield, *A Study*, chapter 2, 8, and chapter 4, 14–18.

21. Peroff, *Menominee Drums*, 129; Orfield, *A Study*, chapter 5, 7–13.

22. Deer, *Speaking Out*, 26–27.

23. Deer, *Speaking Out*, 28–34.

24. Deer, *Speaking Out*, 34–36, 39, 43.

25. Deer, *Speaking Out*, 42; Orfield, *A Study*, chapter 3, 10–11; Ames and Fisher, "Menominee Termination Crisis," 108.

26. Deer, *Speaking Out*, 45–46.

27. Deer, *Speaking Out*, 50; Nancy Oestereich Lurie, *Wisconsin Indians* (Madison: State Historical Society of Wisconsin, 1980), 47.

28. Deer, *Speaking Out*, 51–58.

29. Hertha Wong, "Ada Deer," in *Native American Women: A Biographical Dictionary*, edited by Gretchen M. Bataille (New York: Garland Publishing Co., 1993), 76–77.

30. Peroff, *Menominee Drums*, 121; Shames, *Freedom with Reservation*, 19.

31. Peroff, *Menominee Drums*, 121; Shames, *Freedom with Reservation*, 19.

32. Shames, *Freedom with Reservation*, 36–50.

33. Sady, "The Menominee," 11–13; Shames, *Freedom with Reservation*, 23.

34. Shames, *Freedom with Reservation*, 29.

35. Orfield, *A Study*, chapter 6, 21; Shames, *Freedom with Reservation*, 70; Peroff, *Menominee Drums*, 184–185. Ames and Fisher describe a "true Menominee" faction that in 1959 had no single recognized leader but a segment of which had as its "most articulate spokesman," a white woman married to an enrolled Menominee living on the reservation. We can infer that that person was Constance Deer. See Ames and Fisher, "Menominee Termination Crisis," 25–29.

36. Robert Edgerton, "Menominee Termination: Observations on the End of a Tribe," *Human Organization* 21 (spring 1962): 11–12; Peroff, *Menominee Drums*, 164–165.

37. Shames, *Freedom with Reservation*, 70–71.

38. Peroff, *Menominee Drums*, 175–80; Shames, *Freedom with Reservation*, 73.

39. Shames, *Freedom with Reservation*, 73–78; Spindler and Spindler, *Dreamers with Power*, 90.

40. Shames, *Freedom with Reservation*, 83.

41. Richard M. Nixon, Special Message to the Congress on Indian Affairs, 8 July 1970, in *Richard Nixon: Containing the Public Messages, Speeches, and Statements of the President, 1970* (Washington: United States Government Printing Office, 1971), 564–76; Shames, *Freedom with Reservation*, 86–87.

42. Shames, *Freedom with Reservation*, 91–92.

43. Shames, *Freedom with Reservation*, 93–94, 102.

44. Deer, *Speaking Out*, 58; Ada Deer, personal communication to Clara Sue Kidwell, 28 September 1997.

45. Peroff, *Menominee Drums*, 226; Ada Deer, "Address to North American Indian Women's Association, Northern Michigan University, Marquette, Michigan, 12 June 1975," in *I Am the Fire of Time: The Voices of Native American Women*, edited by Jane Katz (New York: Dutton, 1977), 149.

46. Lurie, *Wisconsin Indians*, 53.

47. Lurie, *Wisconsin Indians*, 53; Peroff, *Menominee Drums*, 202–3.

48. Lurie, *Wisconsin Indians*, 53–54.

49. See Vine Deloria Jr., *Behind the Trail of Broken Treaties: An Indian Declaration of Independence* (New York: Dell Publishing Company, 1974), xi–xii, 43–62; and Paul Chaat Smith and Robert Allen Warrior, *Like a Hurricane: The Indian Movement from Alcatraz to Wounded Knee* (New York: The New Press, 1996), 157–68, 171–268.

50. Mark Thompson, "Nurturing the Forked Tree: Conception and Formation of the American Indian Policy Review Commission," in *New Directions in Federal Indian Policy: A Review of the American Indian Policy Review Commission* (Los Angeles: American Indian Studies Center, University of California at Los Angeles, 1979), 5–18.

51. American Indian Policy Review Commission, *Meetings of the Commission*, vol. 1 (Washington: Government Printing Office, 1977), 11.

52. Thompson, "Nurturing the Forked Tree," 17–18. Also see excerpts from a study and recommendations by Alvin M. Josephy Jr., ed., *Red Power: The American Indians' Fight for Freedom* (New York: McGraw-Hill, 1971), 93–127; and American Indian Policy Review Commission, *Final Report*, vol. 1. Submitted to Congress 17 May 1977 (Washington: Government Printing Office, 1977), 622.

53. Thompson, "Nurturing the Forked Tree," 13; American Indian Policy Review Commission, *Final Report*, vol. 1, 23, 571.

54. Owanah Anderson, ed., *Ohoyo One Thousand: A Resource Guide of American Indian/Alaska Native Women, 1982* (Wichita Falls TX: Ohoyo Resource Center, 1982), 42; Hearings, 51; Wong, "Ada Deer," 77.

55. Peroff, *Menominee Drums*, 203; Wong, "Ada Deer," 77; Hearings, 52; Thomas E. Mann, "Elected Officials and the Politics of President Selection," in *The American Elections of 1984*, edited by Austin Ranney (Durham: Duke University Press, 1985), 103–5, 108, 120.

56. Hearings, 7; U.S. Department of the Interior, "Assistant Secretary—Indian Affairs, Ada E. Deer—Biography," *http://www.doi.gov/bureau-indian-affairs.html* and *http://www.doi.gov/doi.html*. This document adabio.html. Tuesday, 12 November 1996.

57. "Assistant Secretary Submits Resignation," *Kiowa Indian News* 25(1) (January 1997): 1–2.

58. "Assistant Secretary Submits Resignation," 1–2.

59. U.S. Department of the Interior, "Ada Deer—Biography."

Ben Nighthorse Campbell

Northern Cheyenne

BY DONALD L. FIXICO

Being a leader among Indian people implies having a sincere commitment to apply the role and the responsibilities that go with it to one's community. Leadership is not about focusing on one's own ambitions or desires, but about serving one's people. When Indian leaders are mentioned, we think of Tecumseh, Sitting Bull, Crazy Horse, Geronimo, and others of the eighteenth or nineteenth centuries. Indian leaders of the twentieth century exemplify the same attributes of traditional leaders, and Ben Nighthorse Campbell demonstrates true Native American leadership.[1]

Ben Nighthorse Campbell creates an unforgettable impression. He sports a ponytail and snakeskin cowboy boots, which he prefers for riding his Harley-Davidson in the streets of Washington DC. This mixed-blood Northern Cheyenne and U.S. senator from Colorado is a former Olympian with a black belt in judo. He is also a warrior and a leader who leads by example. Much like Crazy Horse, who was an individualist and a fearless warrior of the Oglala Dakotas, Campbell deals with issues in his own way. In a political environment of partisanship, Campbell marches to the beat of his own drum, believes in his own convictions, and votes his own way amid the political swirls in Colorado and in Washington. As a politician, Campbell is a fiscal conservative and social liberal. He has won the support of environmentalists by defending mining, timber, and ranching interests, and has earned praise from liberals for supporting aid to urban areas and programs for children. Campbell supports a balanced budget amendment and a capital gains tax cut. In his own eyes, he sees himself as a person committed to "everyday people." "I know the migrant worker who has no money to see a doctor," said Campbell. "I know what it is to load trucks. And I know the little guy in the back of the room, slipping behind his classmates. You can talk about hunger, but go hungry for a while. I know it—because it was me."[2] His political colleagues call him a fierce independent, and to some he is a political maverick. Campbell comes from a multifaceted background, and he has learned the hard way to be independent in order to survive.

In his lifetime Ben Nighthorse Campbell has also been a rodeo performer, an award-winning jewelry maker, a teacher, a member of the U.S. Air Force, and a rancher. And he is still going strong. He is highly motivated, focused, and personifies action and individuality. He has emerged as a Native American leader whose efforts have shaped the course of events in the late twentieth century.

Ben Nighthorse Campbell was born in Auburn, California, on 13 April 1933 to Albert Campbell, a mixed-blood Northern Cheyenne, and Mary Vierra, a Portuguese immigrant. Campbell's mother contracted tuberculosis when he was very young. His father became an alcoholic, supporting his family only sporadically. Because of his mother's illness, Campbell and his sister Alberta were placed in an orphanage for several months until his mother recovered. A devout Catholic, Mary Campbell could not bring herself to break her marriage vows; thus Campbell's father periodically returned and lived with the family. Mary Campbell loved her children, but the transience of her husband's presence added to the instability of her son's life.

Campbell attended New England Mills Grammar School in Wiemar, California, where he received average grades. He lacked discipline and didn't seem to fit in with the other students. In the late 1940s he attended Placer High School in Auburn, California, but again he seemed to lack focus, and in 1950, at the age of seventeen, he dropped out of high school. During these years American society adhered to a homogeneous patriotism, materialism, and "mainstream values." Being "different" was not to one's advantage. Some Indian families denied their Indian blood, and parents sometimes did not tell their children about their Indian heritage. Ben Campbell knew that he was Indian, but that was about all.

As a teenager Campbell's life careened downward. He admitted years later that he was "stealing cars, drinking, fighting. I was one step away from the reformatory."[3] Ironically however, during these same years he found the one thing that would supply the discipline that had been missing in his life: judo. In the late 1940s, while working in a fruit packing plant near Newcastle, California, Campbell got into a disagreement with a young Japanese coworker who introduced him to judo "the hard way."[4] They eventually became friends, and Campbell regularly visited the local Japanese community. While he worked at other odd jobs, Campbell learned and practiced judo. He became committed to the sport, and began to develop the self-discipline that would characterize his adult life. He refused to return to high school, but his life was no longer adrift.

While others attended high school, Campbell worked at logging jobs in northern California. Accompanied by his best friend, Lowell Heimbach (also a resident of Weimar), Campbell often "jumped" the Southern Pacific freight trains and clandestinely rode home to Weimar for the weekends. Sometimes they rode in boxcars, but often they were forced to ride on top, exposed to the elements. Campbell later recalled the long, bone-chilling journeys atop the boxcars, and commented, "By the time we got off [jumped] we'd look like raccoons, just eyeballs and soot." Yet the shared experiences strengthened the friendship between the two young men; they both considered themselves to be loners, were from the same small town, and worked together in the logging camps in northern California.[5]

Seeking adventure, in 1951 young Campbell joined the U.S. Air Force. Since he hoped to pursue a career in law enforcement, he asked to be assigned to the military police. Campbell served in Korea from 1951 until 1953, attaining the rank of airman second class. While in Korea he continued to study judo, and after his discharge from the military Campbell was determined to improve his skill at the sport.

Campbell's military experience taught him the value of education. While in the air force he completed his GED. When he returned to California, Campbell enrolled at San Jose State University, and in 1957 he received a bachelor's degree in physical education and fine arts. Yet he still was obsessed with judo and often spent six hours a day practicing the sport. Determined to further hone his skills, he decided to travel to Japan, where the sport originated and where the best judo schools were located.

In 1960 he attended Meiji University in Tokyo, Japan, as a special research student. At Meiji, Campbell entered a grueling three-year program, which tested his physical stamina, and in which he risked physical injury at every practice. To finance his residency in Japan, Campbell taught classes in English and played bit roles in Japanese films when an American face was needed. His experience in Tokyo tested his character, but his exposure to Japanese judo champions increased his determination to excel at the sport. The Japanese champions were very demanding taskmasters, but like a Cheyenne warrior, Campbell fought hard and won, thus earning the respect of his adversaries.

Although Campbell represented the United States at the Pan-American Games in 1963, where he won a gold medal in judo, he remained in Japan until 1964, when he returned to California and earned a place on the U.S.

Olympic judo team. Ironically the 1964 summer Olympic games were held in Tokyo, and Campbell accompanied the American Olympic team back to his old haunts. Five thousand Olympians, representing ninety-four nations, competed in Meiji Stadium. In track and field, another Native American, Billy Mills, caught the attention of the world. A twenty-six-year-old Marine who ran track for the University of Kansas, and who was a Lakota from the Pine Ridge Reservation in South Dakota, Mills won the ten-thousand-meter race, defeating renowned favorites from Australia, New Zealand, the Soviet Union, and Great Britain. One of thirty-eight runners in the event, Mills came from behind with a strong last kick and established a new Olympic record of 28:24.4.[6]

Campbell served at the captain of the U.S. judo team. Unfortunately an injury to one of his knees impaired his performance. Competing in spite of the injury, Campbell won his first match in seven seconds. But in his second match against Klaus Glahn of Germany, a heavier opponent, Campbell felt his knee collapse and he fell to the mat. He later remembered, "I realized there was no way that knee was going to hold up, so I had to forfeit." Bowing to Glahn, Campbell hobbled in pain off the mat, hiding his disappointment. He had trained for years to perform in the Olympics, but his spirit could not will his knee to support his body. Campbell's personal career as a judo competitor was over.[7]

Antonious Geesink of the Netherlands eventually won the heavyweight division of the judo competition, while the Japanese dominated the other three divisions.[8] Yet Campbell's Olympic teammates respected the young Cheyenne for his bravery and his attempts to compete while injured. They selected him to carry the American flag during the closing ceremonies. Although Campbell experienced considerable pain during his march through the stadium, he remembered that, "My leg hurt like hell, but I wasn't going to let someone else have the flag [to carry]."[9]

No longer able to personally compete in judo matches, Campbell began teaching judo to other athletes. During the 1960s, martial arts became more popular in the United States, and Campbell introduced his own training regimen, which encountered some opposition from judo traditionalists. His methods proved successful however, and his classes were popular. In response, Campbell wrote *Championship Judo: Drill Training*, a book that explains and delineates his training techniques, making them more available to the public.[10]

During the mid-1960s, while promoting judo as a viable part of the exercise and physical education curriculum for the California public schools, Campbell met Linda Price, a high school teacher originally from Colorado.

They were married on 23 July 1966. Meanwhile Campbell continued as a judo instructor, trained members of the U.S. judo team, worked as a deputy sheriff, and counseled American Indian inmates at San Quentin and Folsom prisons. In addition he taught art and began to design and manufacture jewelry, which he sold through a gallery in Sacramento.[11]

In the late 1970s Campbell decided to relinquish his role as a formal judo instructor and in 1979 he moved his family to a 120-acre ranch in Ignacio, Colorado, where he and his wife raised their two children, Colin and Shanan ("Sweet Medicine Woman" in Cheyenne), and where they still reside. In Colorado, Campbell focused his career on designing and manufacturing jewelry, incorporating motifs he had learned from his father (also a jeweler) and from Japanese artists and sword makers he had met while living in Tokyo. Working at his ranch studio, Campbell utilized Anasazi designs from cliff dwellings in the Southwest to develop his "painted mesa" technique. He carefully inlays a variety of metals, woods, and gemstones into eighteen-karat gold or sterling silver, "creating the impression of a sand painting." His creations were immediately successful. He eventually won more than two hundred first-place and best-of-show awards, and his work is much in demand at both regional and national markets. His designs sell for as much as twenty-five thousand dollars and are displayed in about fifty galleries throughout the nation. Yet Campbell's artistry has provided him with much more than fame and financial success. According to Campbell, "Jewelry making is my catharsis, my relaxation," and although he currently has been forced to devote most of his time to politics, Campbell still considers jewelry making to be "my escape from the pressures and demands of my work." Undoubtedly, jewelry making will continue as an important part of in his life.[12]

Campbell's political career started by coincidence in May 1980. On 22 May he had planned to fly his plane from Durango to California to deliver some jewelry to a dealer in San Francisco. A storm over La Plata County Airport forced him to wait a few hours for clear weather, and as he sat and read the local *Durango Herald,* he noticed that a Democratic political meeting was being held downtown. With some time to kill, Campbell attended the meeting. He recalled, "I was just sitting on the end of the bench listening as one nominee after another declined to run [for the Democratic nomination for House District 59 in the Colorado State Legislature]; each one with a good excuse. One person, I remember was not feeling well; another person was too busy." When asked if he would run, Campbell responded, "Well, I really wouldn't know what to do. How could I learn everything in such a short time?"

"Don't worry about that," someone else said. "We can tell you every-thing you need to know."

"Well, does it take much time?" he asked.

"No, no, it doesn't take much time," everyone assured him.

"Does it cost very much money?"

"Oh no, it doesn't cost very much money. Besides, we have funds to cover most of the cost." Six months later, after a hard campaign, Dem-ocratic candidate Campbell had spent thirteen thousand dollars out of his own pocket, had worn out a set of tires, a pair of boots, and many of his three hundred campaign volunteers who attempted to keep pace with him. Although his opponents initially envisioned him as a candidate picked only to fill the Democratic slate, Campbell surprised them with his energy and determination.[13] In November 1980 the voters of the fifty-ninth district elected him to the Colorado legislature where he served un-til 1986. While in office, the new Native American legislator served on the agriculture, natural affairs, business, and labor committees.[14]

On 4 November 1986 Colorado voters elected Ben Campbell to the U.S. House of Representatives, and he was reelected to the 101st and 102d Con-gresses. He received four appointments: one to the Committee on Agri-culture and Natural Affairs, one to the Committee on Business and Labor, one to the Committee on Interior and Insular Affairs, and one to the Com-mittee on Small Business.[15] A businessman and resident of the West, Campbell felt comfortable with his assignment to these committees. But, as the only Native American in Congress, he felt the need to also represent Indian interests as well as those of his constituents in Colorado.

In 1988, Campbell championed Indian interests when he cosponsored (with Representative Bill Richardson [D-New Mexico]) an amendment to the Omnibus Trade Act instructing the United States Customs Service to produce regulations for permanent markings on imported Indian art goods.[16] Passed as Public Law 100-418, the act resulted in the Indian Arts and Crafts Act of 1990.

But other battles were brewing. In 1989, as American Indians entered the last decade of the twentieth century, a special Senate committee re-leased a 238-page report that disclosed fraud and abuse in many Indian programs and advocated the dissolution of the Bureau of Indian Affairs. The annual budgets of the Bureau of Indian Affairs, the Indian Health Service, the Office of Indian Housing, and the Office of Indian Education totaled 3.3 billion dollars. The report recommended that these funds be stripped from these government agencies and awarded to the tribal gov-ernments as part of the "new federalism." Such a plan would have emasculated the government's infrastructure of support services for Indian people.[17] The lone Indian voice in Congress, Representative Ben Nighthorse Campbell, stood with allies such as Senator Dennis Deconcini (D-Arizona) and Senator Daniel K. Inouye (D-Hawaii) to defeat the measure. Campbell later stated that "I don't think that many people in Congress are intentionally trying to hurt Indians," but many were ill-informed.[18] Yet Campbell was aware that when legislation affecting Indians reached Congress, an "Indian voice" often went unheard. Even those representatives from states with large Indian populations often ignored their Indian constituents when their interests conflicted with the concerns of non-Indian constituents, and Native Americans often received less congressional support than their numbers or interests warranted.

In 1990, when Colorado Republican William L. Armstrong announced his retirement from the United States Senate, pressure mounted for Campbell to become a candidate for the post, but he declined, stating that he was unwilling to subject his family "to 18 months of mayhem" and campaigning.[19] Two years later, however, when Tim Wirth, a Democratic senator from Colorado, also vacated his seat, Campbell was ready to campaign for the upper house.

Wirth's and Campbell's backgrounds were as far apart as possible. Wirth was a graduate of Harvard and Stanford (both costly, elitist private institutions), held a doctorate, and dressed in expensive suits. In sharp contrast, Campbell was a cowboy and a high school dropout, had earned a GED, and was a graduate of San Jose State University, a working class school that occupied a second tier in the California State University system. While Wirth "dressed to the nines," Campbell had to obtain special permission to wear his bolo ties while serving in the House of Representatives.[20] Yet Ben Campbell was a survivor. He had earned his own way, and was very different from most of his congressional colleagues who had doors of opportunity already opened for them due to their influential backgrounds and family connections.

Ben Campbell won the Democratic nomination but faced a formidable foe in Terry Considine, a former Republican state senator. The campaign became heated when both sides alleged misconduct against the other. The Republican candidate charged that Campbell was a "Washington insider" who had received special privileges. According to Considine, Campbell had been given a free trip to Alaska by an oil company with petroleum interests in the region, had often been absent from committee assignments in Washington, and had distorted his Korean War record by claiming to have been a prisoner of war. Campbell refuted all the charges and pointed out that Considine was linked to Silverado Savings and Loan, a failed financial institution in Colorado.[21]

As the campaign progressed, Campbell's support grew, including many voters from the Denver metropolitan region, and on 3 November, the people of Colorado elected Ben Nighthorse Campbell to a six-year term in the Senate; he was the first Native American to be elected to the Senate in more than sixty years. Indeed, just three other Native Americans have served in the Senate, while only eight have served in the House. Moreover, only one other Native American, Charles Curtis, a mixed-blood Kaw and former senator from Kansas, has attained a higher office in the federal government. Curtis served as vice-president under Herbert Hoover from 1928 to 1932.[22] Yet Campbell's election seemed to be part of a broader pattern in which underrepresented minorities were elected to Congress during that year. In 1991, when Campbell arrived in Washington, he found that the newly elected Senate contained four new female senators, while in the House the number of women increased from twenty-nine to forty-eight. In addition Hispanic representation in the House increased from six to nineteen. Still, Campbell remained the only Native American in the 103d Congress.[23]

While serving in both the House and the Senate, Campbell has focused his efforts on environmental, western, and Native American issues.[24] His efforts to rename the former Custer Battlefield in Montana were widely supported by Indian people, and on 10 December 1991, when President George Bush signed the Campbell Bill, which changed the name of the Custer Battlefield to the Little Bighorn National Monument, a cheer could be heard all across Indian Country.[25] Native Americans long had questioned why the battlefield had been named after the military commander who lost the engagement, and they continued to press for a separate monument that would honor the Native Americans who perished in the battle. No one wished to remove the white monolith erected to the memory of the Seventh Cavalry personnel killed in the engagement, but many Indian people believed that a separate monument should commemorate the fallen Lakota, Cheyenne, and Arapaho warriors. Indeed, Campbell's great-grandfather, Ruben Black Horse, had fought in the battle and Campbell was proud of his forefather's patriotism.[26]

It was from this relative—Ruben Black Horse—that Ben Campbell received his name: Nighthorse. Like many mixed-blood Indians in the 1940s and 1950s, Campbell had not flaunted his Native American heritage. During these decades American society discriminated against minority groups, and while Campbell was aware of his Native American lineage and readily identified as an Indian, he had been raised apart from the reservation community and had little opportunity to interact with his father's family. Finally, in 1968, he visited the Northern Cheyenne Reservation, and since that time he has returned to the reservation in Montana on a regular basis. In 1980, Campbell was enrolled as an official tribal member, and he later was inducted into the Northern Cheyenne Tribe's historic Council of Forty-Four, which traditionally was made up of the wisest and most knowledgeable of Cheyenne leaders. Campbell considers the reservation to be a wellspring for his Indian identity, a place where he has proudly replenished his Cheyenne heritage and renewed his ties to his father's family.[27]

In 1996, five years after the passage of the Campbell Bill, a competition for a design symbolizing "peace through unity" to commemorate the role of Indians in the famed battle of the Little Bighorn was held. A seven-member jury, composed of tribal representatives, historians, and artists examined and judged over 550 entries from across the United States. Philadelphia designer John R. Collins and his wife, Alison J. Towers, a landscape architect, submitted the winning design: a memorial in an open circular plaza featuring a raised platform that supported three ghost-like warrior figures on galloping horses—figures that represented the Lakotas, Cheyennes, and Arapahos.[28]

Like most politicians, Campbell has become involved in many public events. As the United States approached the quincentennial of the European "discovery" of the Americas, Campbell, in addition to many other Native Americans, was concerned that the public often failed to realize that significant numbers of Native American people inhabited the Western Hemisphere at the time of the Europeans' arrival, and that Indians also had played a major role in the subsequent history of the United States. When Robert L. Cheney, the president of the Tournament of Roses, selected "voyages of discovery" to be the theme for the Tournament of Roses parade, he invited Cristobal Colon, who was the duke of Veragua, the marquis of Jamaica, and a twentieth-generation descendant of Christopher Columbus, to lead it. Many Native Americans protested Cheney's choice of Colon as grand marshal, so Cheney turned to Campbell, asking him to serve as a co-marshal for the event. Campbell accepted. Wearing an eagle-feather headdress with a double trailer of seventy-two golden eagle feathers, and riding Black Warbonnet, one of his prized horses, he led the 103d Tournament of Roses parade in Pasadena, California.[29]

Campbell also focused his efforts toward more serious issues. Because his father drank to excess, Campbell has been particularly interested in alcohol-related problems. He has devoted much of his congressional efforts to addressing Fetal Alcohol Syndrome (FAS).[30] Singled out by the National Council on Alcoholism and Drug Dependence as one of the leading known causes of mental retardation in the United States, FAS is particularly prevalent within the Native American communities, where one in every ninety-nine infants are born with FAS, as compared with one in six hundred to seven hundred infants in the general American population. Reports indicate that in some reservation communities, such as the Pine Ridge and Rosebud Reservations in South Dakota, one in four babies born in Indian Health Service hospitals may suffer from the syndrome.

On 7 March 1992 Campbell introduced a bill, H.R. 1322, entitled the Comprehensive Indian Fetal Alcohol Syndrome Prevention and Treatment Act. The measure included provisions for federal grants to Indian tribes to develop and provide community FAS training. It also provided funds for education and prevention programs (including a grant for ten million dollars annually for two years and fifteen million dollars annually for the following ten years) to assist in the identification of women at high risk and to provide them with treatment and FAS information.[31] When Campbell's bill was given a hearing, he was strongly supported by the late Michael Dorris, whose best-selling volume *The Broken Cord* poignantly recounts the tragic story of Dorris's adopted son, a young Indian man who suffered from FAS. The book later was made into a television movie. Several other people whose families had been affected by FAS or who had been influenced by Dorris's volume also testified in support of the legislation.[32] Although the bill initially became stalled in the House,[33] on 29 October 1992 it finally emerged as section 708 of the amended Indian Health Care Improvement Act, Public Law 102-573.[34]

In the midst of his legislative successes, Campbell experienced a growing personal political crisis. Even in Congress, where there is considerable pressure to "toe the party line," Campbell had remained an individual. A westerner, Campbell continued to sport his ponytail, ride his Harley-Davidson, and vote his conscience. A fiscal conservative, Campbell had always been concerned by overspending in Congress, and on 2 March 1995 he voted for a balanced-budget constitutional amendment that failed to pass in the Senate. For Campbell, the failure of the amendment seemed to be "the straw that broke the camel's back." He had grown disenchanted with many of President William Clinton's policies, including Clinton's decisions regarding budget cuts, term limits, and capital gains tax reductions. Campbell also was opposed to Secretary of Interior Bruce Babbitt's western land-use and grazing policies.[35]

Following his conscience, on 3 March 1995 Campbell "crossed the aisle" in the Senate, declaring that he no longer could adhere to the policies of the Democrats and had decided to join the Republican Party. He telephoned Clinton to tell him of his decision, reminding the president that although he had voted for some of his policies in the past, he no longer could support many of the administration's programs. Clinton publicly seemed complaisant about Campbell's decision, but other Democrats were more contentious.[36] On 7 March, Bob Kerrey, chairman of the Democratic Senatorial Campaign Committee (DSCC), wrote to Campbell, demanding that he return over $255,000 in Democratic Party funds that had been contributed to his election campaign. Kerrey said, "As a man of honor and integrity, I would hope that you (Campbell) will reimburse the DSCC for its expenses from the race. . . ." Campbell responded that the Democrats had benefited from his congressional work prior to his decision to leave the party, and that he would not remit the campaign funds.[37]

On 3 March Campbell defended his decision before a conference room packed with representatives, senators, and members of the media. Campbell said, "I can no longer continue to support the Democratic agenda nor the administration's goals, particularly as they deal with public lands and fiscal issues." The Indian senator continued, "I have given this a great deal of thought, particularly during the past thirty days in dealing with the balanced-budget amendment. If anything, this debate has brought into focus the fact that my personal beliefs and that of the Democratic Party are far apart." Then, Campbell humorously added, "I have always considered myself a moderate, much to the consternation of the Democratic Party. . . . My moderation will now be to the consternation of the right wing of the Republican Party."[38]

If the Democrats were unhappy over Campbell's departure, the Republicans were pleased to welcome a new colleague. Majority Leader Bob Dole informed him, "We're very glad to have you on board," while other Republicans pointed out that Campbell's defection gave the GOP a fifty-four to forty-six advantage in the Senate. Meanwhile, Campbell's move to the Republican Party brought an "enthusiastic reception" from many conservative business leaders in western Colorado. Campbell also had the support of Native Americans, many Hispanics, and a coalition of labor unions, but both his local constituents and political advisors warned him to expect a primary challenge if he decided to run for reelection in 1998.[39]

Since joining the Republican Party, Campbell has continued to champion Indian issues. Throughout the 1990s, critics have charged that the Bureau of Indian Affairs (BIA) has been inefficiently administered, and since most federal funds earmarked for Native American people have been channeled through the BIA, some pundits have argued that the tribal governments also have been tainted by waste and corruption. Meanwhile, the growth of Indian gaming created the false impression that all tribes were sharing equally in this newfound largesse. As criticism of the BIA and gaming mounted, pressure emerged in Congress for drastic reforms in the traditional relationships between the government and the tribes. Some members of Congress and some Senators even suggested that tribal sovereignty be much abridged in attempts to give the federal government renewed control over the lives of Indian people. During the past decade Campbell has used his influence to deflect such legislation.[40]

In 1996, Senator John McCain (R-Arizona) stepped down as the chairman of the Senate Committee on Indian Affairs. Native Americans throughout Indian Country feared that Senator Slade Gorton (R-Washington) would succeed him. Unlike McCain who had been a friend to Indian people, Gorton envisioned Native American sovereignty as a threat and had consistently used his influence to limit tribal control over political and economic activities. Gorton previously served as the attorney general for the state of Washington, where he had attempted to limit tribal controls over taxation, and while in the Senate he introduced "many pieces of anti-sovereignty, anti-Indian legislation."[41] In 1996, Gorton attempted to strengthen the Istook Amendment, introduced by Representative Ernest Istook (R-Oklahoma) that "would have forbidden the Secretary of Interior to accept any land into trust for an Indian nation, if the tribal government had not reached agreement to collect and remit local and state sales tax on retail activity on the land in question."[42]

To many Indians' relief, Senate Majority Leader Trent Lott of Mississippi bypassed Gorton and named Campbell the new chairman of the Senate Subcommittee on Indian Affairs. For Indians, Campbell's appointment was long overdue. As Dora Young, the chief of the Sac and Fox Nation, stated, "We are heartened to learn that circumstances have provided an Indian the opportunity to chair the Indian Affairs committee. We believe that Senator Campbell's experience as a Native American will bring a human touch to legislative deliberation on issues that mean life or death to Indian people and sovereign Indian nations."[43]

The appointment strengthened Campbell's role as the foremost proponent of Native American issues in the Senate. He has continued to advocate the judicious use of natural resources on tribal lands, and he has championed Native American water rights. Moreover, he also has labored to improve health and educational standards in the tribal communities.

The *Congressional Record Index* for 1997 disclosed that Senator Campbell has co-sponsored bills and resolutions to elevate the administrative authority of both Haskell Indian Nations University (S.R. 1095) and Southwestern Indian Polytechnic Institute (S.R. 1095). He also introduced a bill calling for the United States Mint to produce coins commemorating the history and culture of Native American people (S.R. 1112). The production would begin in the year 2000, with the Treasury Department minting a limited-edition commemorative buffalo nickel. Profits from the sale of the nickel and all other coins minted under the bill would be given to the endowment and to educational funds of the National Museum of the American Indian, which is scheduled to open in the year 2002.[44]

Campbell's approach toward Indian gaming has been more cautious. In November 1996 he delivered the keynote speech to the Western Indian Gaming Conference in which he warned about the various problems that gaming had brought to the Indian nations. Reminding his audience that Indian gaming had become a twenty-seven-billion-dollar industry, he cautioned that quarrels over the proceeds from some gaming enterprises had divided tribal communities and even some Native American families. Campbell pointed out that "Suddenly, because of the casino issue, they (everyone) want to be enrolled. We're getting a lot of new Indians." Expressing his concern that many non-Indians now believed all Indians were wealthy, he commented on the perception that Native Americans lived entirely off proceeds from gaming. "When I see kids . . . come to a small rural school with $100 bills in their pockets . . . believe me, it creates some problems in the community." Concerned that some Indian children had abandoned their plans to further their education because of casino payments, Campbell warned, "We need to make sure our kids don't lose their way with the greenbacks."[45]

Ironically, Campbell's position on the gaming issues was similar to President Clinton's. Like Campbell, Clinton also supported gaming but warned that "it is a lousy basis for an economy, past a certain point. The Indian reservations have been kept dependent too long, have suffered from the patronizing attitude of the federal government, have never been empowered to seize control of their own destiny. And I do not blame the tribes for wanting the maximum possibility on gambling. But what I'd like to see is a whole range of different initiatives so we can have long term economic prosperity, because there is a limit to how much gambling that country can absorb."[46]

Campbell's concerns regarding gaming continue. Like Clinton, he understands that the industry offers Indian communities considerable economic opportunity, but he also believes that the gaming industry needs some regulation and control. In 1997 he sponsored the Indian Gaming Enforcement and Integrity Act (S. 1130), which would improve the Gaming Commission's supervision of "monitoring and regulating 273 Indian gaming establishments operated by 184 tribes in 28 states."[47] The long-term impact of gaming remains uncertain, but Campbell and many other Native American leaders are convinced that the industry needs adequate regulations and controls.

Ben Nighthorse Campbell is a U.S. senator who has championed Native American causes, but as a senator from Colorado, he also represents a much broader constituency. He remains a westerner, a resident of Colorado's western slope, and a public servant attuned to the needs of his state and the nation. An "extremely good listener," Campbell has labored as a small businessman and was one of several sponsors of S. 540, a bankruptcy reform bill particularly favorable to "small business interests."[48] In addition, he also has sponsored legislation designed to regulate and prevent fraud within interstate telephone service companies.[49]

Campbell also has addressed environmental issues. Working with Representative Hank Brown (R-Colorado) Campbell introduced a bill, H.R. 631, designating 612,000 acres in Colorado to be protected as wilderness and another 175,000 acres to be set aside for protective management. On 13 August 1993 President Clinton flew to Denver where he signed the bill, renamed the Colorado Wilderness Act, into law at Stapleton Airport.[50] As a senator, Campbell sponsored bills that specify reclamation requirements for mining and resource extraction companies and urged the United States to sign international agreements designed to limit or reduce greenhouse gas emissions.

At the end of the twentieth century, Ben Nighthorse Campbell has emerged as the foremost Native American legislator in the United States. Like many other Native American people, he has overcome personal difficulties during his early years to achieve considerable success. As a dedicated judoka, he performed in the Pan-American Games and in 1964 he captained the American judo team in the Olympics. As a jeweler, his creations have received critical acclaim and have been much in demand. In politics, Campbell has served at both the state and national levels and has been elected by the voters in Colorado to serve in the Senate, the most prestigious legislative body in the federal government. In both the House and the Senate, Campbell has worked diligently to serve his Colorado constituents, and the larger Native American community in the United States. Leading by example, Ben Campbell is a modern-day warrior will-

BEN NIGHTHORSE CAMPBELL ✳ 277

ing to address critical political issues and stand by his convictions. He is truly an Indian leader of the late twentieth century, championing issues important to Indian people and defending Native American interests in tribal councils, in congressional committees, on the floor of the Senate, and in public.

NOTES

1. For a full study of the life of Ben Nighthorse Campbell, see Herman J. Viola, *Ben Nighthorse Campbell, An American Warrior* (New York: Orion Books, 1993). For a biography of Ben Campbell written for children, see Christopher E. Henry, *Ben Nighthorse Campbell: Cheyenne Chief and U.S. Senator* (New York: Chelsea House, 1994).

2. Wallace Terry, "Success Isn't What You Have—It's What You've Given Away," *Parade Magazine*, 2 June 1996, 16.

3. Terry, "Success Isn't What You Have," 16.

4. Viola, *Ben Nighthorse Campbell*, 33.

5. Viola, *Ben Nighthorse Campbell*, 18–21.

6. In this upset of the eighteenth Olympiad held in Tokyo in 1964, Ron Clarke represented Australia, Pyotr Bolotnikov was the star for the USSR, Murray Halberg held world records in various events and represented New Zealand, and Ron Hill was one of Great Britain's greatest marathoners. Bill Henry and Patricia Henry Yeomans, *An Approved History of the Olympic Games* (Los Angeles: The Southern California Committee, 1983), 302–6.

7. Viola, *Ben Nighthorse Campbell*, 65.

8. Endre Kahlich, Laszlo Gy Papp, and Zoltan Subert, *Olympic Games 1896–1972* (Budapest: Corvina Press, 1972), 264.

9. Terry, "Success Isn't What You Have," 16.

10. Keith A. Winsell, "Ben Nighthorse Campbell 1953–," in *Notable Native Americans*, edited by Sharon Malinowski (Detroit: Gale Research Inc., 1995), 64–65.

11. Terry, "Success Isn't What You Have," 16.

12. Michael Thompson, "The Jeweler Who Would Be Senator," *Jewelers' Circular-Keystone*, December 1992, 46–48. Also see The Talk of the Town, *New Yorker*, 23 November 1992, 1104.

13. Viola, *Ben Nighthorse Campbell*, 194–96.

14. *104th Congressional Directory*.

15. *104th Congressional Directory*.

16. Gail K. Sheffield, *The Arbitrary Indian: The Indian Arts & Crafts Act of 1990* (Norman: University of Oklahoma Press, 1997), 22.

17. Michael P. Shea, "Indians Skeptical of Report Urging Program Overhaul," *Congressional Quarterly Almanac* 46 (13 January 1990): 98.

18. Shea, "Indians Skeptical of Report," 98.

19. "Jontz, Campbell Decide to Pass on Campaigns for Senate," *Congressional Quarterly Almanac* 45 (13 May 1989): 1145.

20. Philip D. Duncan and Christine C. Lawrence, "Ben Nighthorse Campbell (R)," *Politics in America 1996, 104th Congress*, 217–18.

21. "Outsider Stay There," *Congressional Quarterly Almanac* 48 (1992): 11A.

22. Thompson, "The Jeweler," 46.

23. "New Congress Convenes," *Congressional Quarterly Almanac* 49 (1993): 4.

24. "Sac and Fox Leader Heartened by Naming U.S. Senate Indian Affairs Committee Chairman—Sen. Ben Nighthorse Campbell," *Sac & Fox News*, Stroud, Oklahoma, January 1997, 6.

25. Campbell's biographer, historian Herman Viola, explains that initially Campbell persuaded Republican Ron Marlenee of Montana, whose district included the battlefield, to introduce a bill in the 101st Congress, but as it seemed easy to pass, Montana representative Pat Williams attached a rider to change the name of the battlefield, and the bill died without public hearings in Montana. Marlenee reintroduced his bill in the 102d Congress, and Campbell introduced two bills of his own—one requesting a memorial and the other requesting a name change of the battle site. See Viola, *Ben Nighthorse Campbell*, 267–70.

26. See "Ben Nighthorse Campbell, Whose Great Grandfather Fought Custer at the Little Bighorn, Is the First Native American in the Senate since 1929," *People Weekly*, 38(22) (30 November 1922): 50; and Viola, *Ben Nighthorse Campbell*, 114–22.

27. Winsell, "Ben Nighthorse Campbell," 64. For information on the Council of Forty-Four, see E. Adamson Hoebel, *The Cheyennes* (New York: Holt, Rinehart, and Winston, 1960), 43–53.

28. Charles E. Rankin, "An Indian Memorial for the Little Bighorn," *Montana, The Magazine of Western History* 47(2) (summer 1997): 58–59.

29. Viola, *Ben Nighthorse Campbell*, 280–99.

30. Laurie Jones, "Bill aimed at preventing, treating fetal alcohol syndrome," *American Medical News*, March 23–30, 1992, 12.

31. Further discussion of Senator Campbell's FAS legislation is covered in R. A. LaDue and B. A. O'Hara, "Documentation of critical issues related to the Comprehensive Indian Fetal Alcohol Syndrome (FAS) Prevention and Treatment Act," *Focus* 6 (1992): 8–9.

32. LaDue and O'Hara, "Documentation of critical issues," and Michael Dorris, *The Broken Cord* (New York: Harper and Row, 1989), 39–63.

33. Myra Shostak and Lester B. Brown, "American Indians' Knowledge about Fetal Alcohol Syndrome: An Exploratory Study," *American Indian Culture and Research Journal* 19(1) (1995): 39–63.

34. *Indian Health Care Improvement Act,* Public Law 102-573, *U.S. Statutes at Large* 106 (29 October 1992): 4526, section 708, "Fetal Alcohol Syndrome and Fetal Alcohol Effects Grants."

35. Joe Klein, "How the West Was Lost," *Newsweek,* 20 March 1995, 31.

36. Klein, "How the West Was Lost." Also see "The President's News Conference, March 3, 1995," *Public Papers of the Presidents of the United States: William J. Clinton,* vol. 1 (Washington DC: Government Printing Office, 1996), 291.

37. "Back Rent," *The Republic,* 27 March 1995, 9.

38. Jonathan D. Salent and Jennifer Babson, "Colorado's Campbell Switches to Republican Party," *Congressional Quarterly Almanac* 51 (3 March 1995): 664; Philip D. Duncan and Christine C. Lawrence, "Ben Nighthorse Campbell (R)," *Politics in America 1996, 104th Congress,* 217–18.

39. Salant and Babson, "Colorado's Campbell Switches," 664; Juliana Gruenwald," *Congressional Quarterly Almanac* 51 (11 March 1995): 764. Also see Thompson, "The jeweler," 46.

40. "Interior Provisions," *Congressional Quarterly Almanac,* 49 (1993): 629. Also see Philip Brasher, "Feds may pay tribes $600 million for missing funds," *News From Indian Country* 11(1) (mid-January 1997), 1A, 5A.

41. "Sac and Fox Leader Heartened by Naming U.S. Senate Indian Affairs Committee Chairman—Sen. Ben Nighthorse Campbell," *Sac & Fox News,* January 1997, 6.

42. "Sac and Fox Leader," 6.

43. "Sac and Fox Leader," 6.

44. *Congressional Record Index,* 143, nos. 103–12, 105th Cong., 1st sess., 30. Also see remarks by Mr. Campbell on the *Buffalo Nickel Commemorative Coin Act of 1997, Congressional Record,* 143, no. 111, (31 July 1997): S8594–S8595.

45. Sandra Chereb, "Campbell warns about greenbacks," *News From Indian Country* 10(23) (mid-December 1996), 6A.

46. "Remarks at a Town Meeting in San Diego, May 17, 1993," *Public Papers of the Presidents of the United States: William J. Clinton,* vol. 1 (Washington DC: Government Printing Office, 1994), 689.

47. Mr. Campbell's remarks on the *Indian Gaming Enforcement and Integrity Act, Congressional Record,* 143, no. 111, (31 July 1997): S8595–S8596.

48. "CO," *Aba Banking Journal* (May 1993), 39.

49. *Congressional Record Index,* vol. 143, nos. 103–12, 105th Cong., 1st sess., 30.

50. "Remarks on Signing the Colorado Wilderness Act of 1993 in Denver, August 13, 1993," *Public Papers of the Presidents of the United States: William J. Clinton,* vol. 2 (Washington DC: Government Printing Office, 1994), 1377. Also see "Congress Clears Protection of Colorado Wilderness," *Congressional Quarterly Almanac,* 49 (1993): 278.

Janine Pease Pretty-on-Top

Crow

BY DOUGLAS NELSON AND JEREMY JOHNSTON

Those of you who are wise will become educated in the white man's school . . . make of yourselves good farmers and good men. But I would have you cling to the memories of your fathers. I would have you still go up onto the mountain and see visions so that your hearts may be clean and strong. CHIEF PLENTY COUPS

They (the Navajos) had really put together their concept of what it is they wanted to do in their curricular delivery. It was very fascinating to me. I really didn't understand it all. But at least from my logical background, I had a sense of how deep-seated culture was to people, how crucial it was for their survival; how education fit into that whole scheme. JANINE PEASE PRETTY-ON-TOP

Janine Pease Pretty-on-Top, like the famous Crow chief Plenty Coups (1848–1932), whose career straddled the nineteenth and twentieth centuries, has spent much of her life attempting to bridge the gap that sometimes exists between the Indian and non-Indian worlds. Overcoming difficulties in her personal life, she has utilized her position as a professional educator, counselor, and social worker to provide avenues for the Crow people to retain the traditions that make them Crows, yet function effectively in the non-Indian world. Through her leadership, Little Big Horn College provides opportunities for Crow students to acquire the skills needed for modern reservation life and for meeting the challenges posed by their interaction with non-Indians.

Janine Pease Pretty-on-Top was born in 1949 on the Colville Indian Reservation in eastern Washington. She is the oldest of four children born to Ben and Margery Jordan Pease, both of whose families were residents of Montana. Ben Pease was a Crow high school teacher, basketball coach, and administrator originally from Lodge Grass, Montana, on the Crow Reservation. Ben Pease's maternal grandfather was White-Man-Runs-Him, one of the Crow scouts who served with George Armstrong Custer.

His paternal great-grandfather moved to Montana from Pennsylvania in the 1850s and was employed with a fur company before serving as the first civil Indian agent assigned to the Crows by the federal government. Margery Jordan, an English and history teacher, grew up in Butte, Montana. She was the descendant of tin miners who emigrated from Cornwall, in southern England, to Montana in 1880. Ben and Margery Jordan met at Linfield College, an American Baptist institution in McMinnville, Oregon, during the 1940s. Pease enrolled at Linfield through his lifelong membership in the Lodge Grass Crow Indian Baptist Mission, founded in 1903. The Baptists also established a day school at Lodge Grass and many Crow students attended the institution, including several other members of Pease's family. Joe Medicine Crow, a highly respected Crow tribal historian, also attended both the day school and Linfield College.[1]

Pretty-on-Top grew up in Washington where her parents taught school in Ellensburg, a small city in the Yakima Valley. Since her parents supported themselves and their four children on teacher salaries, Pretty-on-Top learned at an early age that cooperation among family members was a necessary attribute of family life, and that a communal spirit of working together enabled all members of her family to share in the family's resources. Her parents encouraged their children to excel in school and to compete in athletic contests. Ben Pease continued to coach basketball and Pretty-on-Top played on one of the first women's basketball teams in central Washington. Her father urged her to do her best, but he also stressed that individuals were members of a team, and that cooperation, or team spirit, should take precedence over individual recognition.[2]

Pretty-on-Top spent many of her summer vacations on the Crow Reservation in Montana, where her Crow relatives also emphasized traditional values such as cooperation, loyalty to family members, and respect for tribal ways. Nurtured by her relatives, Pretty-on-Top felt so at home within the Crow community that she didn't realize until the age of eight or nine that not everyone was a part of a tribal community with important ties to clan brothers, sisters, aunts, and uncles. Indeed, in recalling her childhood, Pretty-on-Top remembers her summers in Montana as some of the happiest moments of her life.[3]

After graduating from high school in Moses Lake, Washington, in 1967, Pretty-on-Top entered Central Washington University, also in Ellensburg, where she majored in sociology and anthropology. While an undergraduate at Central Washington, she enrolled in a Spanish class and developed such a passion for the language that she registered for other Spanish language courses that focused on the Spanish experience in Latin America. In

1969 she spent a semester in Mexico, studying in an exchange program that emphasized language, anthropology, and meso-American archaeology. Her fluency in Spanish and her familiarity with Latino culture later proved invaluable in her involvement with minority employment, education, and youth programs.[4]

In addition to her Spanish studies, Pretty-on-Top continued to pursue her courses in social science. Her years at Central Washington found her very involved in shaping campus policies, but she also entered the broader realm of social activism within the community, and lobbied for issues affecting civil rights and local and state politics. Endeavoring to temper the ivory tower of academia with the hard reality of everyday life, she lobbied successfully for a homeless person from the streets of Chicago to be employed as a visiting scholar and to assist in classes in urban sociology. The visitor's academic pedigree left something to be desired, but he was well-versed in the "school of hard knocks."[5]

Pretty-on-Top received her bachelor of arts degree in 1970, and in January 1971 she went to work for the Governor's Commission on Youth Involvement, a division of the state government in Washington. She initially edited a newsletter that championed the accomplishments of young people in the state of Washington, but she soon expanded her efforts to address a broad spectrum of issues facing young people during these years. Her efforts to extend the voting franchise to eighteen-year-olds proved too controversial for some of her superiors, however, and she resigned from her position when she realized that any advancement within her division would require compromises on moral or political issues that her values would not allow.[6]

During the academic year 1971–72 Pretty-on-Top taught Native American Studies and counseled minority students at Big Bend Community College in Moses Lake, Washington, an institution whose student body was approximately 40 percent Hispanic. She also coached the women's basketball team. In the fall of 1972 she moved to Arizona where she accepted a position at Navajo Community College in Tsaile as a counselor for women students, and as an advisor for the women's dormitory and for student government. Initially the position appeared to be attractive. Pretty-on-Top admired the Navajo attempts to develop a curriculum that incorporated both traditional Navajo values and technical expertise needed to function in a modern society. As she later recalled, "They (the Navajos) had really put together their concept of what it is they wanted to do in their curricular delivery. It was very fascinating to me. I didn't really understand it all, but at least from my logical background, I had a sense of

how deep-seated culture was to people, how crucial it was to their survival. How education fit into their whole scheme. . . ." But the task was
complicated by events beyond her control. A major controversy erupted
over charges of racism brought by several African American members of
the college's basketball team who had been recruited to the school from
non-reservation urban areas. Since Pretty-on-Top served as a counselor
and an advisor to the student government, she attempted to mediate and
then to diffuse the situation. Yet charges and countercharges escalated
and she received repeated threats of violence. She eventually was forced
to carry a pistol, and in November 1972, after a riot occurred and one student was stabbed, the college was closed. Pretty-on-Top resigned and returned to Washington.[7]

In January 1973 she rejoined the faculty at Big Bend Community College
in Moses, Washington, where she directed the Upward Bound Program, a
part of the War on Poverty. She spent the next two and one-half years at
Big Bend, working with fifty students from Moses Lake and the Wenat-
chee Valley of eastern Washington, and also teaching Native American
Studies, counseling students, and coaching women's basketball.[8]

In 1975, Pretty-on-Top returned to Crow country in Montana to serve as
the director of the tribe's Adult and Continuing Education Program. Her
duties included the organization of an adult education coalition designed
to serve three Montana reservations. At the program's height, Pretty-on-
Top supervised fifty-one employees in eleven centers and collaborated
with board members of the Crow Central Education Commission to establish the first Crow Indian educational authority. Dedicated to "tribal
control over the design and delivery of education," the commission was
designed to provide for the education of tribal members, both on and off
the Crow Reservation. GED classes were organized and arrangements were
made for Crow tribespeople to enroll in classes at Crow Agency that were
sponsored by the commission and accredited by a neighboring community college.[9]

In July 1975, Pretty-on-Top met Sam Windy Boy, a Chippewa-Cree
teacher from the Rocky Boy's Reservation who held an adult education
position with the Day Break Star Center in Seattle, Washington. Together
they moved to Crow Agency when Pretty-on-Top accepted a position
with the Crow Central Education Commission. Theirs was a traditional
marriage, recognized by the exchanges of gifts among their families. During the next several years the couple had two children—Roses, born in
1976, and Vernon, born in 1979. Windy Boy was an educational consultant,
and for eight months during 1978 and 1979, he and Pretty-on-Top shared

the position of director of Vocational Educational. In 1979 however, Sam Windy Boy accepted a position with the sawmill and post-cutting plant on the Rocky Boy's Reservation near Havre, Montana, and the Windy Boys and their children moved to the Chippewa-Cree reservation. But by 1980 Sam Windy Boy was unemployed and often absent from his home for extended periods.[10]

Her husband's absence caused considerable hardship for Pretty-on-Top. The couple's home was near a small crossroads on the reservation, but the settlement contained only a few houses, a gas station, and a small trading post. Pretty-on-Top tried to support her family by selling her beadwork, by gathering roots and berries, and by drying and preserving the venison provided by her brothers-in-law but she eventually was forced to rely on welfare to feed her children. Meanwhile, she desperately applied for jobs on the reservation and in Havre, but could find no employment despite her extensive background in education, counseling, and administration. Her experiences during these dark days reinforced Pretty-on-Top's determination to persevere, however, and they enabled her to better appreciate the sacrifices that Crow women historically have made for their families.[11]

Finally, in March 1981, Pretty-on-Top secured a position as the Indian student advocate at Eastern Montana College (now Montana State University in Billings), where she assisted Indian students with housing, tutoring, class-scheduling, and generally provided them with advice and counseling. Yet the move to Billings presented new problems, for non-Indian landlords in the community were reluctant to rent apartments to a Native American woman who was the sole support for two children, even though the potential renter held a college degree and was employed by the university. After searching for an apartment for several weeks, she was forced to live with her aunt and uncle who also lived in Billings. Eventually, through the assistance of friends employed by the Bureau of Reclamation, Pretty-on-Top found adequate housing for herself and her family. During the next eighteen months she counseled Native American students at the university while her children were enrolled in the Billings public schools.[12]

While Pretty-on-Top was struggling to keep her family together at Rocky Boy's, events were taking place on the Crow Reservation that would profoundly impact her life. Her brief tenure at the Navajo Community College in Arizona had introduced her to a tribally controlled institution of higher education, and by 1980 such schools were proliferating. Navajo Community College (now Dine College) was chartered in 1968, and several other schools emerged in the late 1960s or early 1970s, but in 1978 Congress passed the Tribally Controlled Community College Act, which provided federal funds specifically for tribal community colleges. In response, during 1980 the Crow Central Education Commission established Little Big Horn College at Crow Agency, Montana. Designed to combine instruction in Crow values and traditions with job training for a modern world, Little Big Horn College proposed to "develop Crow Indian professionals whose life work would build the Crow Indian community; . . . to develop stronger and more informed parents, grandparents, aunts, and uncles; . . . to access Crow adults to positions which would support their families; . . . and to establish . . . a good path into the future for the Crow people." In 1982 the Crow Educational Authority asked Pretty-on-Top to return to the Crow Reservation and become executive director of the college.[13]

Pretty-on-Top returned to Crow Agency to find an institution "housed" in a dilapidated old gymnasium abandoned by the Bureau of Indian Affairs (BIA) and donated to the tribe for use as a college. The roof leaked, the windows were broken, and any pretense at central heating had long been forgotten. Pretty-on-Top recruited volunteers to repair the facility, wire the building for electrical and telephone services, and scavenge and repair enough old, used, or discarded furniture to provide a minimal amount of tables, desks, and chairs. The old basketball court served as the library, a shower room was used as a science laboratory, and a former water treatment plant housed the chemistry department. Thirty-two students were enrolled in classes. Little Big Horn College was open for business.[14]

The uphill battle continued. The college lacked accreditation and was desperately short of funds. Although Congress passed the Tribal Community College Assistance Act in 1978, and mandated that between five thousand and six thousand dollars per student be provided to these institutions, it had failed to allocate sufficient funds to meet its obligations. Indeed, between 1978 and 1996 allocations to tribal colleges never exceeded thirty-two hundred dollars, and sometimes totaled no more than nineteen hundred dollars per student. In contrast, during 1994, historically black colleges received almost seventeen thousand dollars per student, while the allocation for all community colleges approached seven thousand dollars. The Crow Tribe had little money to spend on the college, and even those funds were not always forthcoming due to bureaucratic obstructions precipitated by intratribal politics. The college charged a modest tuition of twenty dollars per credit hour, but since most Crow students came from families with limited incomes, student enrollment was low. Obviously, the college would have to rely on limited financing if it hoped to survive.[15]

Fortunately, Little Big Horn College had other resources. Although many faculty members had little experience teaching at the college level, they were dedicated to the unique purpose and mission of the institution, and they were willing to make the sacrifices necessary for the school's survival. Pretty-on-Top, like other faculty members, pitched in to share in the janitorial services and maintenance of the facility. Moreover, she envisioned the faculty as a "community of scholars," and championed an equal distribution of salaries in which all faculty members (including herself) would be paid the same. She encouraged all faculty members and staff to interact with the students and to make them feel that they were a part of the intellectual community. As Pretty-on-Top later remembered: "I really liked the idea of community of scholars, and I really liked the level hierarchy. I thought that there was some real merit in it. I thought that we (the college) came about as a result of that sort of relationship. . . . I really don't like earning twice what somebody else does. You think that you have certain values, and then you try to put that in there somewhere."[16]

Pretty-on-Top's values were tested in 1985, just three years after she assumed the presidency of the college. Reflecting the Reagan administration's desire to limit social services, the BIA announced that welfare recipients would no longer be permitted to attend college. Since about one-quarter of the students enrolled at Little Big Horn College were receiving such assistance, the BIA decision placed additional financial burdens on the institution. Not only would the school lose the student tuition, it also would be denied the federal matching funds (approximately seventy-five thousand dollars), which were critical for the college's daily operation. In response, the faculty agreed to accept a 10 percent pay cut, the secretarial staff bought their own office supplies, and Pretty-on-Top took a part-time job in a nearby community to make ends meet. Two years later the Reagan administration reneged, and welfare recipients were again allowed to enroll without forfeiting their benefits, but by that time the college had weathered the financial storm and had begun to attract enough grants from private sources to assure that its future was secure.[17]

If Little Big Horn College's financial security initially seemed fraught with uncertainty, plans for the school's curriculum proceeded smoothly. Pretty-on-Top was eager for the college to develop hard-core, traditional academic subjects, but she also believed that the nucleus of the curriculum should be based in Crow studies, which were required of all students who enrolled at the school. These offerings were augmented by courses in accounting and other business courses, and during the next few years nine separate programs emerged to contain additional course offerings in physical education/health, communications arts, Crow studies, science, mathematics, information systems, humanities, social sciences, and a freshman seminar. By the 1990s nine different associate of arts degrees were offered. Meanwhile, the college took pride in the growth of a special collection of materials housed in the Crow Indian Archives, adjacent to the college library. Through the years the archives have grown to include "records, papers, scrapbooks, family histories, and photographs of Crow individuals and tribal historians; copies of federal government records; external studies and reports; and research materials from historians, anthropologists, missionaries, attorneys, and others who have studied Crow life."[18]

The college's emphasis on the special needs and interests of its students is also reflected in its methods of instruction. Instructors encourage their students to do their best, but they emphasize cooperation rather than competition. The Crows traditionally have been a communal people, and family members often cooperate in social and economic activities. At Little Big Horn College, family members are encouraged to enroll in the same classes and to assist each other with homework and other projects. Moreover, the emphasis is not on rushing through a training program or attempting to gain a familiarity with new knowledge as rapidly as possible. For the Crows, mastering a skill or quantity of information thoroughly is more important than progressing through it as rapidly as possible.[19]

Accreditation required considerable effort. Academic accreditation teams visited the campus during 1984, but because of limited library resources, a lack of a faculty salary schedule, and inadequate finances, they refused to recommend accreditation for the college. Two years later another evaluation team arrived at Little Big Horn, but this team also remained critical of the institution's makeshift facilities and low salaries. Dismayed by the appraisal, Pretty-on-Top defended the institution's curriculum as reflecting the needs of the community and pointed out that the faculty, while undoubtedly underpaid, were dedicated teachers. Moreover, most community colleges (particularly tribal colleges) suffered from a limited physical plant and from a lack of resources, and Little Big Horn certainly was not unique in this respect. The Crow elders supported Pretty-on-Top's reply, informing her that "you are not a good warrior until you have an enemy to test your abilities." In response, the accreditation agency censured the team, but Little Big Horn still was not accredited. Subsequent evaluations were made over the next five years, and Little Big Horn College received full accreditation in 1990. In 1994, after pressure from some faculty members and another accreditation team, Pretty-on-Top reluctantly agreed to a more graduated, hierarchical salary structure. The school's accreditation was renewed in 2000, and Little Big Horn College continues as a fully accredited two-year institution.[20]

In the midst of her efforts to strengthen the college and achieve accreditation, Pretty-on-Top became involved in a voting rights contest with the state of Montana that would have profound consequences for the Crow people and for their neighbors on the adjoining Northern Cheyenne Reservation. In November 1982 a Crow candidate, Ramona Howe, was elected as the county representative to the state legislature, while a white, pro-Indian candidate also was elected to the Big Horn County Board of Commissioners. Candidates for state and local offices in Big Horn County previously had been forced to run "at large" since the county had no election districts, and Crow candidates traditionally had been unsuccessful since they usually faced a "countywide" non-Indian opposition. But in 1982 both candidates enjoyed the overwhelming support of about one thousand newly registered Crow voters on the Crow Reservation. Moreover, the Crow people, by sheer numbers, gained control of the Democratic Party in Big Horn County; most non-Indian Democrats left the party and either joined with the Republicans or voted as independents.[21]

Although Crow voters elected two candidates to office, they encountered several obstacles during the election. Some had difficulty securing voter registration materials. Others encountered difficulty obtaining absentee ballots, and many Crows believed that their absentee votes had not been counted. Sometimes Crow voters were assigned to distant voting precincts, and on numerous occasions the identity of Indian voters was challenged by officials at the polls. In addition, the two successful candidates' non-Indian opponents and their supporters suggested that the Crows were guilty of voter fraud since there were more Crows registered to vote than mailboxes at Crow Agency. However, the Crows always had shared a limited number of mailboxes; there were only six hundred for the one thousand households that used them. In fact, there was no voter fraud—just people with limited resources sharing their mailboxes with their neighbors.[22]

Convinced that the Crows and Northern Cheyennes faced a continuing pattern of discrimination, Pretty-on-Top joined with other tribal leaders to initiate legal action against Big Horn County. In August 1983, attorneys employed by these individuals filed a suit in U.S. district court charging that the at-large voting system discriminated against Indian voters in county and school elections. Janine Pretty-on-Top (then Janine Windy Boy) was the leading plaintiff in the case. In addition to the obstacles and harassment mentioned in the previous paragraph, the suit stated that although approximately 46 percent of the county's residents were Native American, almost none had been elected to school boards or to county offices. In 1983 there were ninety-nine appointees to boards and committees in Big Horn County; one was Native American. Moreover, the plaintiff's attorneys illustrated that such a pattern was not an exception. In the previous fifty years approximately 265 appointees had served Big Horn County. Only 11 had been Native Americans. There were no Native Americans on the Law and Order Commission, which dealt with Indians when they left the reservation. Indeed, only 4 of the county's 180 employees were Indian, and only 10 of the 75 Crow Indians with teaching certificates were employed in the Hardin, Montana, school district, although the school's student population was about 59 percent Native American.[23]

Testimony in *Windy Boy v. Big Horn County* began in November 1985 and lasted for several days. In June 1986, Federal District Judge Edward Rafeedie decreed that the at-large election system in the county should be replaced with voting districts before the next general election since "the evidence demonstrated a strong desire on the part of some white citizens to keep Indians out of Big Horn County government." Since Native American people comprised the majority of the population in one of the three county districts and in two of the county's five school districts, they have emerged as a powerful force in county and school board politics. As the primary plaintiff in this case, Pretty-on-Top played a major role in these proceedings. Moreover, her efforts on behalf of the Crow people illustrated the close ties between the college and the community. Unlike many academics in the non-Indian world, leaders of tribal colleges are active participants in solving the problems and issues that daily confront their constituents. They live in the "real world." They are not "ivory tower intellectuals."[24]

In the midst of laying the groundwork for accreditation and leading the struggle for Native American voting rights in southern Montana, Pretty-on-Top pursued graduate degrees in education. In 1987 she was awarded a master's degree in education from Montana State University in Bozeman, and seven years later (1994) she received a doctorate in adult and higher education from the same institution. Aware of the continuing needs on the Crow Reservation, she concentrated her graduate work on adult education. Her dissertation focused on the origin of the Tribally Controlled Community College Assistant Act of 1978; she examined how tribal leaders conceived of the idea, how they developed support in Congress, and who emerged as their advocates and opponents in both Congress and the executive branch. Much of her research was based on memos, reports, and narratives of the Study Group on Indian Education of the House Subcommittee on Education, and she traced arguments and opinions found in these narratives to their antecedents in earlier legislation regarding Indian education. Pretty-on-Top ascertained that the tribal colleges' strategy was to work through members of Congress who were favorably inclined toward Native American people and who cared about education. Many of these individuals were not specialists in Indian affairs, nor were they from states or districts with large numbers of Native American constituents, but they were legislators "of good heart" who believed that everyone should have access to higher education.[25]

Pretty-on-Top found that these champions of Indian education adapted successful provisions from earlier legislation and incorporated them into the Tribally Controlled Community College Assistant Act. In keeping with the hectic pace of her life during this period, her dissertation was sometimes written in libraries; sometimes on a laptop computer while on an airplane or in a teepee; and on one occasion at a large serving table in the mess hall of Ted Turner's ranch, near Bozeman, where Crow officials were conducting an archaeological survey of sacred sites prior to a construction project.[26]

Pretty-on-Top's interest in federal legislation affecting higher education for Native American people also was spurred by her participation in national organizations that focused on this subject. She served as Little Big Horn College's representative to the American Indian Higher Education Consortium during the 1980s, and in 1983 was elected to a two-year term as president. While president, she was instrumental in reversing President Ronald Reagan's "pocket veto" of the reauthorization of the tribal colleges act. She later served as the organization's treasurer for six years. She was a trustee of the Smithsonian's National Museum of the American Indian. In 1986, after the tribal colleges established the American Indian College Fund, she served on the AICF's board of directors from 1988 to 1995, and from 1998 to the present.[27]

By the early 1990s Pretty-on-Top's personal and family life had become more stable and she felt at home on the Crow Reservation. In 1983 her marriage to Sam Windy Boy ended in divorce, but she continued to raise her children and was surrounded by friends and relatives. In 1991 she married John Pretty-on-Top, a leader in the Crow Sun Dance and a cultural commissioner for the Crow Tribe. Moreover, by 1994 Little Big Horn College continued to struggle for operating funds, but the school was firmly established as one of the leading tribal colleges in the United States. Meanwhile, Pretty-on-Top was much in demand as a public lecturer and had emerged as a nationally respected leader within the field of Native American education. In 1990 the National Indian Education Association named her their Educator of the Year.[28]

Her leadership was recognized by the John D. and Catherine T. MacArthur Foundation. In 1994 the foundation awarded Pretty-on-Top a MacArthur fellowship, one of the most prestigious awards given to individuals throughout the Western Hemisphere. MacArthur fellows are chosen from a highly select group of nominees and are provided with an income over a five-year period "so that they may have the time and the freedom to fulfill their potential by devoting themselves to their own endeavors at their own pace." Nicknamed "MacArthur genius grants," these awards provide recipients with the time and financial resources to "focus on more than one area through interdisciplinary work, to change fields if they wish, or even to alter the direction of their careers." Pretty-on-Top spent her five years at Little Big Horn College, expanding and strengthening the curriculum and providing the leadership necessary for continued growth and stability.[29]

Like college administrators at most tribal colleges across the United States, Pretty-on-Top is determined that her institution will continue to meet the changing needs of her people. When the college first opened, Pretty-on-Top and other administrators initially designed programs to train Crow students for jobs in the immediate region. That training still continues, but the number of jobs near the Crow Reservation remains limited. As a result, Pretty-on-Top has encouraged students to "think like entrepreneurs and develop their own small businesses." More than sixty students are enrolled in computer science classes in preparation for careers in business and technology, and the college recently signed a contract with the National Park Service to provide guided bus tours of the Little Big Horn Battlefield, a national historic site that abuts the Crow Reservation. The college not only trains the guides but also manages the tour buses and associated services.[30]

During the fall semester of 1999 over three hundred students were enrolled at Little Big Horn College. Administration, faculty, and staff numbered about forty. The college catalog listed over 175 separate courses that are offered on a regular basis. Seventy-three sections of these courses were offered during that semester. Pretty-on-Top continued to serve as the president of the institution, but she was assisted by three deans and a registrar.[31]

As student enrollment continues to grow, Pretty-on-Top acknowledges that Little Big Horn College will face a series of challenges in the future. The Crow population continues to increase; current projections estimate that tribal enrollment may reach sixteen thousand by 2007. Much of this increase will come from younger Crows who loom as potential students at the college. Pretty-on-Top believes the franchise for guided tours of the Little Big Horn Battlefield is a portent of things to come. The Crows expect that tourism in the region also will increase, and the college hopes to play a major role in preparing tribal members to take advantage of tourist-related business opportunities. She also believes that the college will increase its role in providing vocational education and certification for a growing number of economic activities.[32]

Yet Pretty-on-Top envisions the school as an important social, cultural, and political force within the future Crow community. She believes that the college has a role in addressing local health and substance abuse problems, and that the institution should continue its efforts to champion and preserve the Crow language and culture, particularly in response to the onslaught of a global culture promulgated by the spread of cable television and mass marketing in the region. She also believes that Crow culture and spirituality should be protected from the aggressive proselytism of Pentecostal Christianity. Pretty-on-Top hopes that the college can take the lead in promoting the tribe's judicious management of its natural resources and that it can prepare Crow citizens for a more active role in county and state politics. And finally, lest she appear too ethnocentrically focused on just the problems of the Crow Reservation, Pretty-on-Top also believes that Little Big Horn College should serve as a bridge between the Crows and their non-Indian neighbors, an institution that will work for continued improvement in the Crows's "acquaintance, collaboration, and friendship with whites."[33]

Like other administrators of tribal colleges, Pretty-on-Top presides over an institution that serves many purposes. All of the thirty tribal colleges scattered on reservation communities across the Great Lakes states and the West provide vocational training designed to match the job market within their specific regions, yet they also offer classes that provide their students with the basic courses needed to transfer into four-year undergraduate colleges or universities. Most offer intensive coursework in the specific history or culture of their tribal communities, and all employ

Native American instructors as experts in such subjects. Indeed, all of these institutions are blessed with a nucleus of highly dedicated administrators and faculty members, many of whom serve the institutions at salary levels considerably below what they might earn at comparable nontribal colleges.[34]

Low faculty salaries are symptomatic of the financial difficulties these institutions continue to face. In 1986, Pretty-on-Top and other tribal colleges created the American Indian College Fund, a nonprofit organization located in Denver, Colorado, that is dedicated to garnering support for the tribal colleges. Since 1989 the fund has raised more than thirty-five million dollars, and in 1999 received major gifts from the David and Lucille Packard Foundation, the Coca-Cola Foundation, SONY Electronics, and the Bill and Melinda Gates Foundation, among a host of others. But the colleges receive no state support and their location within impoverished communities still makes them vulnerable to financial shortages. Classes continue to be taught in substandard classrooms desperately short of adequate equipment or library facilities, and in some tribal communities the institutions remain at the mercy of internecine tribal politics.[35]

Yet coups are being counted. In 1999 nearly thirty thousand students attended tribal colleges, at least six thousand of them beneficiaries of scholarship funds provided by the American Indian College Fund. And despite the often substandard libraries, laboratory equipment, and classrooms, students at the tribal colleges are achieving some significant success. While less than 10 percent of Native American students currently graduate from public colleges, more than 40 percent of graduates of tribal colleges are now pursuing more education. Another 50 percent of these graduates are employed at permanent jobs. According to the Carnegie Foundation for the Advancement of Teaching, "Without question, the most significant development in American Indian communities since World War II was the creation of tribally-controlled colleges. . . . Considering the enormously difficult conditions tribal colleges endure, with resources most collegiate institutions would find unacceptably restrictive, their impact is remarkable."[36]

At Little Big Horn College the battle continues. Plans have been made for a new and enlarged campus, but so far they remain on the drawing board. Yet Pretty-on-Top remains optimistic. The college continues to be a reservoir and fountain of Crow culture, and its graduates have achieved considerable success. Over two hundred Crow students have completed their course work and received their diplomas. Some have gone on to four-year colleges, and some have not, but 85 percent are employed on or near the Crow Reservation where they lead full lives, supporting their families. Amid the books, reports, memos, and other materials in Janine Pretty-on-Top's crowded office is the *Little Big Horn College Catalog, 1997–1999*, whose cover is adorned with a photograph of Plenty Coups, the great Crow chief whose leadership spanned the end of the old "buffalo days" and the tribe's occupation of the Crow Reservation. Inside the catalog, adjacent to its frontispiece is a quote from this honored leader. His words still hold true. "Education is your most powerful weapon. With education you are the white man's equal; without education you are his victim."[37]

In January 2001, while this volume was in press, Janine Pease Pretty-on-Top left her position as president of Little Big Horn College after considerable disagreement and turmoil emerged within both the college's board of trustees and the Crow tribal council over the direction and leadership of the institution, particularly over the allocation of funds for future construction projects on campus. Pretty-on-Top is currently serving as an independent educational consultant.

NOTES

1. Janine Pease Pretty-on-Top, interview with Douglas Nelson and Jeremy Johnston, 25 April 1997; Janine Pretty-on-Top, personal communication to R. David Edmunds, 21 December 1999.

2. Interview, 25 April 1997.

3. Interview, 25 April 1997.

4. Interview, 25 April 1997.

5. Interview, 25 April 1997.

6. Interview, 25 April 1997.

7. Interview, 25 April 1997.

8. Interview, 25 April 1997.

9. Interview, 25 April 1997.

10. Interview, 25 April 1997; personal communication, 21 December 1999. Also see "Rocky Boy's Reservation," in *Tiller's Guide to Indian Country: Economic Profiles of American Indian Reservations*, edited and compiled by Veronica E. Velarde Tiller (Albuquerque: BowArrow Publishing, 1996), 407–8.

11. Velarde Tiller, *Tiller's Guide*, 407–8.

12. Interview, 25 April 1997.

13. Paul Boyer, "Tribal Colleges," in *Native Americans in the Twentieth Century*, edited by Mary B. Davis (New York: Garland, 1996), 649–51; *Little Big Horn College Catalog, 1997–1999* (Crow Agency: Little Big Horn College, 1997), 6.

14. Interview, 25 April 1997; Fergus M. Bordewich, *Killing the White Man's Indian: Reinventing Native Americans at the End of the Twentieth Century* (New York: Anchor Books, 1996), 286.

15. Bordewich, *Killing the White Man's Indian*, 292.

16. Bordewich, *Killing the White Man's Indian*, 292–93; Interview, 25 April 1997.

17. Bordewich, *Killing the White Man's Indian*, 293–94.

18. Interview, 25 April 1997; *Little Big Horn College Catalog*, 1–82; Little Big Horn College, fall 1999 course schedule, 1–3.

19. Bordewich, *Killing the White Man's Indian*, 289–91.

20. Interview, 25 April 1997.

21. Interview, 25 April 1997.

22. Interview, 25 April 1997.

23. Interview, 25 April 1997. *Billings Gazette*, 1 September 1983, 1A, 6A; *Billings Gazette*, 8 November 1984, 7C; *Billings Gazette*, 15 June 1986, 1A, 12A. Also, Douglas Nelson to R. David Edmunds, personal communication, 3 February 2000.

24. Interview, 25 April 1997.

25. Interview, 25 April 1997.

26. Interview, 25 April 1997.

27. Interview, 25 April 1997; "Women of Hope," *Native Peoples* (spring 1997), 11.

28. Interview, 25 April 1997; "Women of Hope," 11.

29. MacArthur Fellows Program: Overview, *http://www.macfdn.org/programs/fel/fel_overview.htm*.

30. Rene Sanchez, "At Little Big Horn, an Outpost of Learning, Tribal Colleges Helping to Revive Tradition of Self-Reliance," *Washington Post*, 12 July 1997, A01.

31. *Little Big Horn College Catalog*, 59–87; fall 1999 course schedule, 1–3.

32. Interview, 25 April 1997.

33. Interview, 25 April 1997.

34. "The American Indian College Fund—Where Are the Colleges?": *http://www.collegefund.org/colleges.htm*.

35. "The American Indian College Fund—Who Is the College Fund?" and "Getting

the Word Out,": *http://www.collegefund.org/main.htm*. Also see Bordewich, *Killing the White Man's Indian*, 295–97.

36. "The American Indian College Fund—Who Is the College Fund?": *http://www. collegefund.org/main.htm*. Sanchez, "At Little Big Horn," A01. Also see The Carnegie Foundation for the Advancement of Teaching, "Tribal Colleges: Shaping the Future of Native America," in *First Peoples: A Documentary Survey of American Indian History*, edited by Colin G. Calloway (Boston: Bedford/St. Martins, 1999), 509–24.

37. *Little Big Horn College Catalog*, ii, 5.

Walter Echo-Hawk

Pawnee

BY JOHN R. WUNDER

In today's world, every Indian is a warrior. Some have chosen the court-room, the law library, and the legislative hall as their fields of combat in the search for liberty, cultural freedoms, and sovereignty. These people are Indian lawyers from the Native American Rights Fund (NARF), a na-tional Indian law firm founded in 1970 as a special pilot project that evolved from California Indian Legal Services (CILS), an agency initially financed by the federal government's Office of Economic Opportunity. One of NARF's senior staff attorneys is Arusa To-da-hey ("Good Horse" in Pawnee), whose professional name is Walter R. Echo-Hawk.

Over the years NARF's board of directors has articulated five areas of concentration: the preservation of tribes and traditional culture, the pro-tection of tribal resources, the promotion of human rights, the account-ability of governments to Native Americans, and the development of In-dian law. Officially an apolitical organization, NARF does not participate in partisan political debates or issues, but it does assist in formulating legis-lation and in initiating and defending challenges in court that seek to pro-tect and enhance Indian rights. NARF represents Indian clients—both indi-viduals and tribes. If clients can afford to pay for NARF's services, they are asked to do so; but if they cannot they are not necessarily denied represen-tation. Representation hinges on the issues involved. NARF will not rep-resent Native Americans who seek legal assistance against other Indians.[1]

Walter Echo-Hawk graduated from the University of New Mexico's In-dian law program and passed the Colorado bar exam. Although he joined NARF as an attorney in 1973, he previously had been associated with the firm. Echo-Hawk's cousin John, one of the initial members of NARF, en-couraged him to pursue a career as an attorney, and in the summer of 1971, while a law student at the University of New Mexico, Walter served as a clerk in the NARF offices. Today, as a senior staff attorney there, he manages a large caseload and serves on the litigation management committee. Echo-Hawk does not envision himself as exceptional, but simply as one of many Indian attorneys and as a prototype for the current generation of legal warriors.

Walter Echo-Hawk was born on 23 June 1948 in the Indian hospital on the Pawnee Reservation near Pawnee, Oklahoma. The oldest of four children, Walter has a sister, Debbie, and two brothers, Roger and Lance. His father, Walter Echo-Hawk Sr., is a decorated U.S. Air Force veteran with tours of duty in Korea and Vietnam. His mother, Jeanine Echo-Hawk, is a former public school teacher. Since Walter Echo-Hawk Sr. spent his career as an enlisted man in the air force, the Echo-Hawks moved frequently during Walter's childhood. From 1956 to 1963 the family lived in Warrensburg, Missouri, near Whiteman Air Force base. Walter Sr. was then assigned to Ramey Air Force base in Puerto Rico, where in 1966 Walter graduated from high school.[2]

The Echo-Hawks are members of the Kitkahahki, or Republican, band of the Pawnee Nation. Some of their relatives are members of the Skidi band. There are two other Pawnee bands: the Chaui, or Grand Pawnees, and the Pitahawiratas. As Kitkahahkis, the Echo-Hawks belong to the warrior class. In 1777, Spanish officials at St. Louis reported that the Kitkahahkis numbered from 350 to 400 warriors and that they were a conservative people who lived in central Kansas and south-central Nebraska. During the nineteenth century, as disease decimated Pawnee villages and large numbers of non-Indians moved onto the plains, the Pawnee Nation was forced onto a reservation in Nebraska and then removed to Oklahoma. The Kitkahahkis opposed this resettlement, but pragmatically acquiesced since they needed federal annuity payments to survive in the new land. Once in Oklahoma, they agreed to occupy the Pawnee Reservation, the land upon which Walter Echo-Hawk was born.[3]

In 1966, after graduating from high school, Echo-Hawk enrolled at Oklahoma State University, where he received a B.S. in political science in 1970. During the 1960s the Indian world in the United States underwent many changes. In 1961, Indian college students and other activists founded the National Indian Youth Council (NIYC) whose statement of policy articulated a viewpoint "based in a tribal perspective" and stated "literally that the Indian problem is the white man, and further realizes that poverty, educational drop-out, unemployment, etc., reflect only symptoms of a social contract situation that is directed at unilateral cultural extinction."[4] This conclusion epitomized the dissatisfaction of many young Indians with the status quo during this decade and was a harbinger of things to come. In 1967 the Indian law program at the University of New Mexico was founded, and in 1968 young Indians in Minneapolis-St. Paul organized the American Indian Movement (AIM). One year later Native American militants occupied Alcatraz, an event that brought national attention to Indian issues. During 1969, Native American teachers formed the National Indian Education Association, and in 1970 the federal government returned Blue Lake to the Taos Pueblos, an event that established important legal and political precedents.[5]

Walter Echo-Hawk joined NIYC during the 1960s, and during the summer of 1968 he enrolled in a program at the University of New Mexico designed to assist Native American college students interested in a legal career. In 1968 he also assisted with the camp established by Martin Luther King's Poor People's Campaign, at Ponca City, Oklahoma. One year later he spent part of the summer at an NIYC workshop in Boulder, Colorado. These experiences aroused his interest in national affairs, but he also was motivated by events in northern Oklahoma. No Indians served on local school boards, and school administrators demanded that Pawnee high school students cut their hair, a violation of some Pawnees' religious beliefs and traditions. In addition, many Pawnees believed they were subject to police brutality. The unexplained death of Echo-Hawk's uncle in a local jail also piqued his concern and activism.[6]

Yet Echo-Hawk, like many other Indians in Oklahoma, initially was wary of AIM and its tactics. AIM emerged in Minneapolis, was primarily an urban-based organization, and was popular among the youth of Indian families who had been relocated off reservations and into ghetto-like conditions in major cities. Native Americans in Oklahoma debated the merits of AIM's actions, but most of the Echo-Hawks, including Walter and John, were traditionalists, and although some Pawnees, and even some members of the Echo-Hawk family, praised these urban activists, support for AIM remained limited until the occupation of Wounded Knee, South Dakota, in 1973.[7]

After graduating from Oklahoma State University, in 1970 Echo-Hawk enrolled in the Indian law program at the University of New Mexico. While a law student, he met his future wife, Pauline Sam (Yakama), a student from Haskell Indian Institute in Kansas who was enrolled as an undergraduate at the University of New Mexico majoring in anthropology. They married and have three children: Amy, a University of Colorado graduate in journalism; Walter Jr., a graduate of the Santa Fe Institute of Indian Arts and a singer; and Anthony, a ninth-grade hockey player. Walter and Pauline Echo-Hawk continue to reside in Lyons, Colorado.[8]

While enrolled in law school, Echo-Hawk acquired many of the skills needed by a modern legal warrior. In addition he envisioned how law could serve as a tool for social change and as an effective means to protect Native American rights. At first, Echo-Hawk saw himself as a plaintiff's lawyer, an aggressive pursuer of change through the courtroom, championing an active offense rather than a cautious defense. Over the years, however, his approach changed. He now envisions his role as that of a careful advocate, a warrior still dedicated to the goals necessary for the achievement of Indian rights, but more a problem-solver, a seeker of the best alternative to achieve the appropriate end. Echo-Hawk's position changed because he, like many other Native Americans, lost faith in the federal court system after the 1980s. He questions whether federal district and appellate courts provide a level playing field for Native American issues and believes that legal actions must be carefully chosen if they are to be successful. In addition he believes that other legal arenas such as Congress, state legislatures, and the United Nations also offer opportunities for the defense and protection of Native American rights.[9]

Echo-Hawk's first case as a NARF attorney, *Indian Inmates of the Nebraska Penal and Correctional Complex v. Vitek* was typical of many issues addressed by the firm since its inception. In this initial case, NARF pressed for Native American prisoners' access to spiritual leaders at state expense, and their right to meet as a group for educational purposes. In the years that followed, Echo-Hawk and other NARF attorneys defended Native American prisoners' rights to wear their hair long, in a traditional manner, and Echo-Hawk successfully championed the rights of Native American prisoners to meet with medicine men, participate in sweat lodge ceremonies, and keep sacred objects such as sage, cedar, and sweet grass in both state and federal prisons in the Southwest and Great Plains. Echo-Hawk and NARF also have addressed related problems such as mail censorship, visitation rights, adequate medical care, and prison overcrowding.[10]

NARF's initial involvement in recognition and restoration issues has continued. Recognition is the legal means through which the United States officially acknowledges the existence of a Native American group as a tribal nation. It is somewhat analogous to the official standing foreign nations have with the United States government. Recognition is important because it means that federal programs are usually extended to members of the recognized entity. Tribes achieve recognition if they have a treaty with the United States, or if they meet certain standards as articulated by Congress, the executive branch of the federal government, or the federal courts. Restoration can occur for a tribe previously recognized, but that has been terminated. The restoration process, begun in the 1970s, was a direct response to the termination acts passed for specific tribes in the 1950s and 1960s. Between 1954 and 1966, 109 tribes and bands were terminated by laws signed by presidents Dwight D. Eisenhower and John F. Kennedy. Designation of restoration comes only from Congress, and in the 1970s, 1980s, and 1990s many recognition and restoration movements have been supported by NARF.[11]

NARF was instrumental in persuading the U.S. attorney general to file a suit on behalf of the Passamaquoddys against the state of Maine, and then assisted the Passamaquoddys and Penobscots in filing land claims in 1976. Meanwhile NARF attorneys successfully pressed Congress for a bill to allow both tribes to regain part of their former land base and a restitution for lands taken illegally. In 1980, when President Jimmy Carter signed the Maine Indian Claims Settlement Act, the largest return of lands to Indians in American history was completed. NARF also assisted in the recognition of the Coushatta Tribe of Louisiana (1973), the Pascua Yaqui Tribe of Arizona (1978), the Tunica-Biloxi Tribe of Louisiana (1981), the Narragansett Tribe of Rhode Island (1982), the Poarch Creek Tribe of Alabama (1983), and the Mashantucket Pequots of Connecticut (1983). In addition, three Texas tribes, the Alabama-Coushattas, the Texas Kickapoos, and the Ysleta Del Sur Pueblos all achieved recognition with NARF's assistance during the 1980s.[12]

Not all recognition attempts were successful. NARF's efforts to obtain federal recognition for the Gay Head Wampanoags of Massachusetts and the San Juan Southern Paiutes of Arizona have so far ended in failure, but NARF's labors on behalf of Native Americans in Alaska did serve some clients well. In *Native Village of Noatak v. Hoffman* (1991), the Ninth Circuit Court of Appeals ruled that the Village of Noatak and all other villages listed in the Alaska Native Claims Settlement Act are "tribes" holding the same status as all other Indian tribes in the lower forty-eight states. This decision meant that the village governments for 226 federally recognized tribes in Alaska containing ninety-five thousand Native Alaskans were now approved by the federal government.[13]

NARF's restoration efforts are perhaps best exemplified by their support for the Menominee Tribe of Wisconsin and the Siletz Tribe of western Oregon. The Menominee Restoration Act of 1973 assigned federal trust status to the Menominees, and the Siletz Tribe was restored in 1977, receiving a 3600-acre reservation in 1980.[14]

During the 1970s NARF also became involved in the protection of Native American hunting and fishing rights—important issues since many tribes traditionally hunted and fished in order to survive under subsistent living conditions. When Indian people, particularly in the Pacific Northwest and Great Lakes region, asserted their hunting and fishing rights that had been guaranteed to them through past treaties, they were opposed by food companies, sporting enterprises, and some state and federal agencies. As a prelude to the extensive litigation on hunting and fishing rights in the 1970s, in 1968 the Supreme Court in *Puyallup Tribe Inc. v. Department of Game* (known as *Puyallup I*) opened the door for state regulation of what previously had been considered protected off-reservation Native American treaty rights to fish and hunt at customary places. As a consequence, many Indians who fished found themselves literally in bloody battles on rivers and streams, and in life-and-death litigation in courtrooms. Eventually, in 1973 federal courts in Washington state, with NARF's prodding, established the right of Indians in Washington to 50 percent of the harvestable fish in off-reservation waters.[15]

NARF also defended Native American fishing rights in the Great Lakes region and in Oregon. During the 1970s NARF represented the Bay Mills Chippewas, the Grand Traverse Chippewas, and the Sault Sainte Marie Indian community against the state of Michigan. It also has represented several tribal communities in Wisconsin. In 1970 it obtained a major legal victory when the Supreme Court upheld the decision of a federal appellate court and declined to review a case that might have had a negative impact on Indian fishing rights in the region. NARF was less successful in Oregon. Although it won a declaration that the Klamath Tribe, while terminated, still retained treaty hunting and fishing rights within their former reservation, in 1985 the Supreme Court in *Klamath Tribe v. Oregon Department of Fish and Wildlife* found that the Klamaths could not claim treaty hunting and fishing rights on all former treaty lands. Oregon, however, did agree to restore a disputed eighty-eight-thousand-acre tract to the former reservation boundary, placing it under Klamath treaty rights jurisdiction.[16]

Significant progress was achieved in Alaska. In 1989 NARF attorneys persuaded a federal district court to enjoin the state of Alaska from preventing any Native fishermen from subsistence fishing at traditional sites, and throughout the 1990s NARF has labored to extend fishing and hunting rights won by treaty Indians in the lower forty-eight states to Alaska's Natives. Issues included establishing hunting and fishing rights on the Outer Continental Shelf, preventing oil development in the Arctic National Wildlife Refuge from disturbing the caribou herds of the region, stopping the state from enforcing regulations that lessen subsistence harvests of caribou and moose, guaranteeing traditional-site fishing rights, and halting gold leases on federal lands that would interfere with fishing and hunting. A major watershed occurred in 1995 when the Ninth Circuit Court of Appeals in *Katie John v. United States* ruled that federal law recognizes as a priority the right for rural Alaska residents, who are mostly Natives, to hunt and fish for subsistence purposes, over commercial and sport hunting and fishing on public lands. The development of Native Alaskan hunting and fishing rights continues.[17]

Closely related to Native American fishing rights are the tribes' claims on the water flowing through and adjacent to reservation communities, and NARF has been in the forefront in defending these claims. Beginning with the articulation of the *Winters* doctrine, the Supreme Court in 1908 held that the establishment of a reservation guaranteed preemptive Indian rights to water inside and adjacent to the reservation. The *Winters* doctrine was further developed in *Arizona v. California* (1963) when the Supreme Court ruled that Native American water rights stood against all others, and the quantity of water reserved was based on the amount needed to irrigate the entire reservation. These were extremely important decisions preserving the viability of reservation lands, but during the past three decades they have been continually challenged.[18]

In the 1970s NARF attorneys assisted the Pyramid Lake Paiutes of Nevada in obtaining adequate water to develop and maintain their own fish hatchery, and forced the Pima Mining Company to recognize the Tohono O'Odhams rights to water in Arizona. In addition NARF buttressed the economic security of tribes along the Colorado River by urging that the Supreme Court supplement the *Arizona v. California* decision with an order declaring that these tribes were to receive their water allocations first in times of water shortages.[19]

Unfortunately, conditions changed during the 1980s. Although NARF attorneys assisted the Klamaths in obtaining sufficient water from former reservation lands, helped the California Mission Indians establish the San Luis Rey Indian Water Authority, and provided counsel to the Southern Utes in resolving water claims in southwestern Colorado, they found that federal courts that once had safeguarded tribal water rights began to chip away at their earlier decisions. In 1983 the Court overturned a lower court's decision to provide water to the Pyramid Lake Paiutes's fishery, and then stated in *Arizona v. San Carlos Apache Tribe* that old water allocations were void and that state courts should decide future ones. The latter decision represented a fundamental blow to Native American water rights and encouraged NARF subsequently to rely more on legislation than the court in water rights issues.[20]

Echo-Hawk was personally involved in one important water rights case during this period that in retrospect he considers to be the most difficult litigation that he has ever attempted. During the early 1980s the Puget Sound Power and Light Company and the city of Auburn, Washington, in an attempt to build a hydroelectric plant, endeavored to divert the White River and some of its tributaries away from the Muckelshoot Indian Reservation. The reservation, established in 1855, is the home of Skulkamish, Skopamish, Stakamish, and some south Puyallup bands of Native Americans who were guaranteed fishing rights in the White River by treaties signed in 1854 and 1855. In 1934 all the bands incorporated as the Muckelshoots under the Indian Reorganization Act, and their reservation consists of about five sections of land located twenty-five miles southeast of Seattle.[21]

The Muckelshoots believed that the diversion of the river would siphon away their water and destroy their fishing, and Echo-Hawk represented the tribe in their legal action against the power company and the city of Auburn. Following a series of hearings, in 1986 Echo-Hawk obtained an injunction preventing the diversion of the river by successfully proving that such a change would violate the Muckleshoot's water and fishing rights. After quantifying their federally reserved water rights, a settlement from the power company enabled the Muckelshoots to rebuild a salmon hatchery and obtain a fourfold increase in water flowing through the reservation from the company's dam. Yet the hostility of the defendants remained so intense that Echo-Hawk was forced to appeal to the Ninth Circuit Court of Appeals to obtain attorney fees guaranteed under the Civil Rights Attorney Fees Act.[22]

Echo-Hawk also assisted the Klamath Tribe in its battle over water with the state of Oregon. In 1994 the Klamaths challenged the jurisdiction of Oregon over its quantification and allocation of reserved water rights and its attempts to force the tribe to pay state water fees. The case achieved mixed results. The court decreed that Oregon did exercise jurisdiction over water allocation, but that it could not charge the Klamaths fees for the water. The decision led to a pending case in which irrigation districts sued the Bureau of Reclamation over changes by the federal agency in the allocation of water, which were made to protect endangered species and Klamath fishing rights.[23]

Litigation on the Klamath case continues, but during the 1990s NARF attorneys have become more wary of the courts and have embarked on a series of legislative and administrative activities that have led to at least two water compacts between states and tribes. The Fort McDowell Indian Community Water Rights Settlement Act and subsequent agreements helped to protect Indian water rights in Arizona, while, with NARF's assistance, the state of Montana and the Northern Cheyennes reached an agreement and cloture on the amount of water reserved for the Northern Cheyenne Tribe. Other tribes in the 1990s, such as the Nez Perces, the Tule River Tribe of California, and the Chippewa-Cree Tribe of Montana, continue on the long twisted road of water rights negotiations under NARF's guidance. Given NARF's administrative and legislative successes in water law, it is not surprising to find NARF representatives appointed by Congress and the president to the Western States Water Policy Review Advisory Commission, and NARF serving as a co-sponsor of the Western States Water Council symposia on the settlement of Indians' reserved water rights claims. In the 1990s NARF's legal warriors have come to the conclusion that the defense of Indian water rights may be better served by monitoring, patience, and legislation, rather than litigation.[24]

NARF also has been active in helping the tribes develop and protect their relationship with both private corporations and the states in relation to taxes. Although states have been eager to tax products sold on reservations or trust lands, and to tax the limited income of Native Americans, in general the Supreme Court initially gave states few options to tax Indian resources. NARF has worked diligently to protect the tax-exempt status of Indian assets while assisting the tribes in developing procedures through which tribal governments can obtain revenue from private corporations, such as mining or petroleum companies, who continue to do business on Indian lands.

During the 1970s, NARF attorneys argued successfully that individual Native Americans in both Montana and Minnesota were exempt from state taxation as long as they resided upon a reservation, regardless of whether they were members of the tribe that governed the reservation, and in 1980 in *Joe v. Marcum* a federal appellate court upheld NARF's position that the state of New Mexico could not garnish Indian wages earned on the Navajo Reservation. NARF also has defended individual Indians from state taxation in Oklahoma. Since there are no federally recognized Indian reservations in the state, officials in Oklahoma attempted to levy automobile excise taxes and income taxes on tribal people who lived and

worked on Indian trust lands. Sac and Fox tribal members challenged the
state, and in *Oklahoma Tax Commission v. Sac and Fox Nation* (1993), the Supreme Court decided that Oklahoma could not levy such taxes on Native
Americans who resided on and worked on trust lands. NARF filed an amicus brief on behalf of the Cheyenne-Arapaho Tribe of Oklahoma in support of the Sac and Fox Nation.[25]

Attorneys from NARF have also assisted tribal governments in their attempts to establish their own revenue systems and to protect these systems from state taxation. During the 1980s NARF assisted several tribes in
their defense of natural resource production, income, and sales taxes on
reservation or trust lands. For example, in 1981 the state of Oklahoma was
forced to reach a settlement with the Pawnees that barred the state from
collecting sales taxes on tribally licensed businesses on the Pawnee Tribal
Reservation. Walter Echo-Hawk assisted by filing an amicus brief for the
Pawnee Tribe in *State of Oklahoma, Ex Rel Oklahoma Tax Commission v.
Mays,* in which the federal district court declared Pawnee tribal lands a
reservation within the meaning of "Indian Country." In Florida in 1981 a
state appellate court ruled that the state of Florida could not sue NARF's
client, the Seminole Tribe, to collect sales taxes from reservation-based
businesses. Echo-Hawk also was the counsel of record for the Pyramid
Lake Paiute Tribe when they settled out of court with the state of Nevada
who agreed to recognize the Paiutes's inherent sovereign power to tax
non-Indians doing business on their Nevada Indian reservations.[26]

Other important tax cases included *Montana v. Blackfeet* (1985), in which
the Supreme Court held that the state of Montana did not have the authority to tax the oil and gas royalties of the Blackfeet Nation; a decision
by the Supreme Court ruling that since the Jicarilla Apache Tribe already
levied its own severance taxes on reservation oil production, that any additional severance tax by the state of New Mexico would constitute a double tax and inhibit petroleum production; and *Mustang Fuel Corporation v.
Cheyenne-Arapaho Tribe* (1989), in which the Cheyenne and Arapahos were
accorded the right to tax oil and gas production not on a reservation, but
on tribal trust lands. The *Mustang Fuel Corporation* case was initially tried
in tribal courts however, and the corporation has appealed the case in the
federal court system. The outcome of this case is still pending, but the
case suggests that tribal courts have initial jurisdiction over tribal taxation, a decision welcomed by tribal governments, and that tribes do have
the power to impose a severance tax over natural resource development.[27]

Yet not all taxation cases have gone smoothly for NARF and its clients. In
1992 the courts ruled in *County of Yakima v. Confederated Tribes of the Yak-*

ima Reservation that Yakima County, Washington, could impose property taxes on land patented in fee simple, but not on the sale of these lands. In *Department of Taxation and Finance of the State of New York v. Milhelm Attea & Bross, Inc.*, the court concluded that a state may regulate cigarette sales by collecting taxes from Indian wholesalers and retailers on sales to non-tribal members; while in *Oklahoma Tax Commission v. Chickasaw Nation* (1995), the court decided that the state of Oklahoma could not tax sales of gasoline when the tribe was the retailer and sold the fuel on tribal land. It did allow the state to tax the income of tribal members who worked for the tribe on tribal trust land but did not reside on trust land. In each case NARF filed an amicus brief, but these decisions seemed to weaken the position of tribal people and governments in their relation to state agencies.[28]

In many ways, taxation is a function of sovereignty, and NARF has been in the forefront in defending modern tribal governments as they have forged new parameters of sovereignty or have defended their respective nations. Indeed, almost all of the cases involving NARF have dealt with sovereignty to some degree, but several cases have been particularly significant. During the 1970s, NARF assisted in the defense of the Mississippi Choctaw homeland, arguing that it constituted a reservation as generally understood within the usual definitions of federal law. NARF attorneys also assisted the Cocopah Tribe in Arizona regain lands wrongfully seized by the Department of the Interior, and in a series of other legal actions they built step-by-step case law and administrative rulings that placed a protective shield around the Indian land-base. This land-base has been used by tribal government to reclaim sovereignty and to practice self-determination.[29]

One of the greatest threats to tribal sovereignty by the federal government was the passage of Public Law 280 in 1953. The law authorized certain states to assert criminal and civil jurisdiction over Indians and Indian reservations within their borders, but the law had been applied unevenly, and states differed markedly in their attempts to exercise such jurisdiction. Some states, like Nebraska, were not eager to assume jurisdiction because the federal government provided no funds for additional services, so they simply assigned jurisdiction to county officials who generally ignored the reservation communities. Others, such as South Dakota, initially attempted to exert a broad jurisdiction but then attempted to apply such hegemony selectively. In 1984, NARF prevented South Dakota from assuming criminal jurisdiction over the Cheyenne River Sioux Reservation. Two years later, with NARF's assistance, the Winnebago Tribe of Nebraska regained jurisdiction over its reservation through court proceedings and through legislation passed within the state legislature. In 1987 the Ely Colony Shoshones also regained jurisdiction over their reservation when the state of Nevada retroceded state control.[30]

NARF has also championed the sovereignty of tribal courts. In *Duro v. Reina* the Supreme Court ruled that Indian courts did not have criminal jurisdiction over crimes committed by nontribal member Indians on reservations, a jurisdiction that tribal courts traditionally had exercised. The court reasoned that Congress had never recognized this sort of tribal sovereign authority. In response NARF led a successful legislative effort culminating in the passage of federal legislation in 1991 explicitly recognizing Indian court criminal jurisdiction over nontribal member Indians. Yet other issues emerged. Questions of whether tribal courts hold civil jurisdiction over personal injury actions involving two non-Indians, whether tribal courts have jurisdiction over a civil suit by an Indian against an non-Indian company, and whether tribal courts can hear civil disputes involving a tribal member's suit against a state agency have required substantial NARF commitments. Meanwhile many states, non-Indian companies, and non-Indian individuals repeatedly have sought to limit the jurisdiction of Indian courts. NARF has anticipated this impending legal clash and has sought to find ways for tribes to strengthen and build court, governmental, and regulatory infrastructures to meet these challenges.[31]

Among all the facets of tribal sovereignty, none has attracted as much public attention as the tribes' involvement with gaming. As funding for federal programs shrank and unemployment within the reservation communities mounted during the 1980s, many tribes looked to gaming as at least a temporary means of providing jobs and revenue. NARF assisted some tribes that initially adopted this economic alternative, and not surprisingly, these tribes encountered opposition from state governments. In 1986, NARF participated in a federal district court dispute that led to a ruling that the state of Oklahoma had no jurisdiction to regulate or tax the bingo operations of the Muscogee (Creek) Nation, and in 1988 NARF assisted the St. Croix Band of Chippewa Indians of Wisconsin in placing land in trust so that a tribal bingo hall could be erected. Perhaps the most important action of NARF in this legal arena involved filing an amicus brief in the Supreme Court case of *California v. Cabazon Band of Mission Indians* (1987), which prevented states from enforcing state gambling laws on reservations.[32]

This decision and the subsequent growth of gaming led to the passage of the Indian Gaming Regulatory Act of 1988. The act recognized the tribes' "exclusive right to regulate gaming" if such activity was not prohibited by federal or state laws. The law also established three classes of gaming: traditional tribal games; basic organized games, such as bingo and lotto; and casino games, such as blackjack, slot-machines, and lotteries. Tribes conducting the third class of games must enter a "compact governing the conduct of gaming activities" that they operate with states in which the gaming occurs. The states, in turn, are required to negotiate in good faith. The act also provided for the National Indian Gaming Commission to oversee gaming activities.[33]

Since the passage of the gaming act many tribes have established casinos, and Native American gaming has proliferated. Because most tribes with gaming operations can afford their own legal representation for gaming disputes, NARF has generally withdrawn from most direct contact with the gaming enterprises, although tribes that have prospered from gaming have provided financial support to NARF and to other Indian organizations. Yet gaming remains a powerful force within Indian Country, and in 1993 Richard Hayward, chairman of NARF's board of directors, acknowledged that although Indian gaming represents less than 3 percent of the entire gambling industry in the United States, it still generated enough revenue to help tribes build housing, health clinics, schools, and water and sewer systems. Even so, the tribes recognize that they need to use the money carefully and work toward long-term stable economic development. According to Hayward, NARF will continue to be "instrumental in assisting many tribes" to explore and develop long-term sound economic enterprises.[34]

Although controversies over gaming may grab the headlines, issues focusing on religion probably are more important to most traditional Native American people. In 1978 Congress passed the American Indian Religious Freedom Act (AIRFA), which initially was envisioned as significant legislation that would strengthen the rights of Native Americans to practice their traditional religions. The act contains two primary provisions. The first called on the federal government to "protect and preserve for American Indians their inherent freedom to believe, express, and exercise traditional religions," and referred to Indians' right to gain access to sacred sites, to use sacred objects, and to practice sacred ceremonies. The second provision required the president to order federal agencies to monitor and assess their policies in regard to adherence to the first provision, and to consult with traditional Indian religious leaders about such adherence. After consulting with the agencies, the president was required to issue a report to Congress documenting favorable policy changes.[35]

Ironically, the name of the act is misleading since it contains no pro-visions for enforcement and does not protect sacred tribal sites. AIRFA does not prevent persons or government agencies from restricting the re-ligious rights of Native Americans, nor does it provide opportunities for tribes or individual Native Americans to bring lawsuits against such inter-lopers for any damages. Echo-Hawk and other NARF attorneys cautioned potential clients that the legislation would be difficult to implement, and in 1980, when the Tennessee Valley Authority initially began to plan the erection of a dam on the Little Tennessee River that would flood tradi-tional hunting lands and areas used to gather religious objects, the Chero-kees appealed to NARF for assistance and Echo-Hawk became the attorney of record. Although he argued that the construction of the dam would vi-olate Cherokee religious rights as outlined in AIRFA, the Sixth Court of Ap-peals ruled in *Sequoyah v. Tennessee Valley Authority* (1980) that the region to be flooded was not "central" to Cherokee religious practice and the construction of the dam proceeded. Echo-Hawk also wrote an amicus brief in support of the Navajos who attempted to obtain a court order to lower the water level of the Glen Canyon Dam on the Colorado River and to restrict tourist activity at Rainbow National Monument, since both the high water and tourist traffic infringed on tribal religious practices, but in *Badoni v. Higginson* (1980) the court ruled that Navajo religious interests were less important than the need for electric power. Obviously, AIRFA's effectiveness as a defense of Native American religious rights was much diminished. Echo-Hawk did assist the federal government in its study of policy as required by section 2 of AIRFA, and he also testified on federal compliance problems before Congress.[36]

With AIRFA essentially emasculated, the assault on Native American re-ligious beliefs continued. NARF filed an amicus brief in *Lyng v. Northwest Indian Cemetery Protective Association* (1988), but it could not prevent the Supreme Court from ruling that the U.S. Forest Service could pave roads and supervise the harvesting of timber in areas containing sites sacred to the Yurok, Karok, and Tolowa peoples in California. Native Hawaiians also lost their appeal to prevent the development of a geothermal project at a sacred religious site in Hawaii, but the Federal Energy Regulatory Commission did refuse permission for the construction of a dam and hy-droelectric project at a site sacred to the Kootenai people in Montana. But in this case, in which Echo-Hawk served as the counsel of record, the commission also endeavored to protect the confidentiality of the Koote-nai religion and forbade all parties, including NARF attorneys, to disclose its opinion. It also decreed that all legal records including the opinion should remain sealed. Ironically therefore, the only case using AIRFA to protect Indian religious rights cannot be referred to nor can it serve as a precedent for other legal decisions.[37]

The greatest threat to American religious freedom, however, emerged in Oregon. The controversy arose as a result of a complex legal precedent involving a Native American, a white Oregonian, their worship in the Native American Church, and the loss of their jobs and unemployment compensation. Alfred Smith, a Klamath, and Galen Black, a white man, both worked for a private drug rehabilitation company in Portland. Smith was a member of the Native American Church and Black attended church ceremonies where they both acknowledged that they had used peyote. As a result, they were fired from their jobs, and when they applied for unemployment benefits, the state denied their claim because it determined that Smith and Black were fired for misconduct. State laws of Oregon declared peyote a drug and criminalized its use, but these laws had not been enforced for many years, and most people believed that the laws were unconstitutional with regard to the Native American Church.

Nevertheless, once the case came before the Supreme Court, a majority held that Oregon could enforce anti-peyote laws and that such statutes did not infringe on the free exercise of Native Americans to practice their religion. Such a decision struck at the very heart of Native American religious freedom. When the case first reached the Supreme Court in 1988, it was remanded to the Oregon Supreme Court to clarify whether Native American Church members could use peyote as a sacrament and not be subject to Oregon criminal law. Echo-Hawk played a role in this litigation, coauthored an amicus brief, and participated in the oral argument that led to the remand. In 1990 when the case was returned to the Supreme Court after the Oregon Supreme Court ruled for the plaintiffs, Echo-Hawk again served as a member of the legal team that represented the Native American Church of North America. Yet the Supreme Court was determined to ignore all previous tests for assessing the limits of the First Amendment's free exercise clause, and upheld the Oregon court's decision. The only solace was that the court was badly divided, and the justices penned strongly worded dissents and concurring opinions that suggested that their colleagues in the majority did not know the law or much about Indian religious practices. If the court decision remained the law, Native American religious freedom would be substantially limited.[38]

In response, four years later Congress passed and President William Clinton signed the American Indian Religious Freedom Act Amendments of 1994 that legalized once and for all the religious use of peyote by members of the Native American Church. Echo-Hawk and other NARF attorneys strongly supported the bill by presenting testimony before Congress as counsel to the Native American Church, and by working with the National Congress of American Indians and the Association on American Indian Affairs to help secure passage of the legislation.³⁹

Closely related to issues of religious freedom is the defense of Native American graves and skeletal remains. In the twentieth century alone, as many as two million Native American remains have been disturbed. Grave robbers have been encouraged and employed by museums, universities, government agencies, and private tourist businesses. Reluctant to part with their stolen goods, museums and private collectors have hoarded the remains of Native Americans and associated burial objects, sometimes even refusing to discuss the size and nature of their collections.

NARF has been in the forefront of the ranks demanding that these remains be returned to tribal people, and Walter Echo-Hawk continues to consider this issue his most meaningful legal involvement. Echo-Hawk has battled in the courts, in both state and national legislatures, and in the public arena for the return of his dead relatives and for the deceased kin of other indigenous peoples of the United States. These struggles have culminated in the passage of repatriation acts in states such as Nebraska, Kansas, Arizona, California, and Hawaii, and finally in the passage of the Native American Graves Protection and Repatriation Act of 1990 (NAGPRA) by Congress. In addition, the Smithsonian Institution has also been forced to repatriate Indian remains and burial goods to appropriate tribes. And finally, NARF has helped develop federal Indian burial policies designed to protect Indian burial sites and repatriate over three hundred thousand Native American bodies stored in federal and state institutions.⁴⁰

Nowhere was the battle more personal and difficult than in Nebraska, the traditional homeland of the Pawnee people. The first reported desecration of a Pawnee grave occurred in 1820, but the thievery continued into the twentieth century. Asa T. Hill, known as the "father" of Nebraska archaeology, a used-car salesman, amateur archaeologist, and director of the Nebraska State Historical Society (NSHS) bought farmland in 1920 that held many Pawnee graves. According to Hill, "I don't play golf . . . my only recreation is this Indian investigation. I come out Sundays and dig up Indians. . . . This hill is my golf course." With Hill's enthusiasm and direction, hundreds of Pawnee bodies were exhumed in Nebraska between 1920 and 1950. In 1988, when Lawrence Goodfox Jr., the president of the Pawnee Business Council and a respected elder, requested the return of the Pawnee dead, many Nebraskans were shocked to learn that the NSHS held over one thousand skeletons, many of which were Pawnees.[41]

James Hanson, director of the Nebraska State Historical Society, refused to return the skeletal remains and led a hostile campaign to prevent the repatriation. When the Pawnees attempted to obtain access to records to verify the skeletal remains in the society's collection, the society denied them access to public records; and thus began a series of legal actions that culminated in the passage of Nebraska state law LB340 (January 1989), which was the most stringent Indian repatriation act in the United States at that time. When NARF finally gained access to NSHS records, the reason for the society's recalcitrance became obvious. At no time did either the society or the people who had robbed the Indian graves obtain exhumation permits, as required by Nebraska state law.[42]

The NARF effort on behalf of Native American repatriation in Nebraska initially was led by Robert M. Peregoy, a Flathead attorney; he was joined by Echo-Hawk who represented the Pawnees and Winnebagos. Echo-Hawk played a key role lobbying legislators for the passage of Nebraska's state repatriation statute, and he also represented his tribe in *Nebraska State Historical Society v. Pawnee Tribe and the State of Nebraska* (1990), in which the court ruled that the NSHS was a state agency and subject to state open-record laws. He also won an arbitration award granted under the new Nebraska repatriation statute, which was used to determine the identity of four hundred human remains and accompanying burial objects that the NSHS initially had refused to return. In Kansas, Echo-Hawk testified before the state legislature, helped draft and negotiate legislation, and lobbied for the successful passage of an unmarked-grave protection statute. In California he testified before the state house and senate, championing a second repatriation bill after an initial piece of such legislation was vetoed by the governor. The subsequent bill was passed and signed.[43]

During the 1990s Echo-Hawk has continued his efforts on behalf of Native American repatriation. He represented the Pawnee Tribe, the Larson Bay Tribal Council, and a cultural rights coalition composed of NARF, the National Congress of American Indians (NCAI), and the American Association of Indian Affairs in negotiating and lobbying for the passage of the National Museum of the American Indian Act, which required that the Smithsonian Institution repatriate Native American remains and funerary objects to culturally affiliated tribes upon the request of tribal officials. He then represented the Pawnees in their successful pursuit of three separate repatriation and reburial requests from the Smithsonian. He also assisted in the drafting of the Native American Grave Protection and Repatriation Act, testified before Congress in support of this legislation, and coordinated the lobbying effort of the Indian cultural rights coalition led by Susan Harjo, director of NCAI. In all these efforts Echo-Hawk has envisioned himself as a modern warrior, using his legal training in defense of his people. As he later pointed out, "This modern-day Indian War [repatriation] was fought not on a battlefield, but around conference tables, in courtrooms, and in the halls of Congress."[44]

The fight goes on. In addition to the issues discussed above, Echo-Hawk and other NARF attorneys have addressed issues such as Native American access to schools and education, child welfare rights, health care, voting rights, and mascots. In 1995, at a meeting celebrating NARF's twenty-fifth anniversary, Evelyn Stevenson, chair of NARF's board of directors noted that the legal battlefield of the last quarter-century reflected a number of "positive milestones," but she foresaw the challenges of the future. "While we've fought long and hard for the achievements realized," she stated, "we still see ourselves addressing many of the basic issues that were in the forefront twenty-five years ago." Stevenson pointed out that "basic, inalienable rights deemed sacrosanct by Indian people are continuously in jeopardy" because both legislative and judicial systems across the United States are filled with individuals who have only a minimal knowledge of Native American people and their cultures. Yet as Stevenson indicated, these people often exercise a profound influence on establishing or changing Indian policy. Moreover, this policy "often vacillates with every new swing of the political pendulum, leaving each of our generations to pick up the pieces and repeatedly start the process all over again."[45]

Stevenson's assessment accurately portrays the brief history of NARF and its legal warriors. At first there were few Native American lawyers, but those few were determined to defend the rights of their people. As the years passed, their ranks have grown. Walter Echo-Hawk's career reflects these challenges. In seeking to use the law both as an instrument to protect Native American sovereignty and rights, and as a tool for social change, he has ventured into the courtroom and legislative halls. In each case, whether defending Native American water rights, or assisting in the formulation of legislation to protect Native American religion and culture, Echo-Hawk has based his career on those elements essential to a legal warrior: skilled training and a desire to provide legal advice and representation to Indian tribes and individuals. Like other members of NARF's legal war party, he has helped to forge new policies designed to strengthen tribal self-determination and self-governance, and to protect individual Native American rights. The struggle continues.[46]

Notes

I am very grateful to Anne Diffendal, Ph.D., archivist, and public history and museums consultant in Lincoln, Nebraska, for her willingness to share her private archival information on the Nebraska repatriation controversy with me; to Jay Buckley, University of Nebraska–Lincoln, Department of History and Center for Great Plains Studies, for his research assistance; and to Walter Echo-Hawk for his generosity in providing me with materials about NARF and his personal opinions about Indian law.

1. Walter Echo-Hawk, interview with John R. Wunder, Boulder CO, 13 November 1997.

2. Walter Echo-Hawk, interview.

3. Martha Royce Blaine, *Pawnee Passage, 1870–1875* (Norman: University of Oklahoma Press, 1990), 45, 71–72, 221, 228–29, 270; George E. Hyde, *The Pawnee Indians* (Norman: University of Oklahoma Press, 1951), 116–23; Richard White, *The Roots of Dependency: Subsistence, Environment, and Social Change among the Choctaws, Pawnees, and Navajos* (Lincoln: University of Nebraska Press, 1983), 147–56, 210.

4. John R. Wunder, *"Retained by The People": A History of American Indians and the Bill of Rights* (New York: Oxford University Press, 1994), 157.

5. Wunder, *"Retained by The People,"* 156–66.

6. Walter Echo-Hawk, interview.

7. Walter Echo-Hawk, interview. Also see M. Annette Jamies, ed., *The State of Native America: Genocide, Colonization, and Resistance* (Boston: South End Press, 1992); Orlan J. Svingen, "Jim Crow, Indian Style," *American Indian Quarterly* 11 (fall 1987): 275–86; and Troy R. Johnson, *The Occupation of Alcatraz Island: Indian Self-Determination and the Rise of Indian Activism* (Urbana: University of Illinois Press, 1996).

8. Walter Echo-Hawk, interview.

9. Walter Echo-Hawk, interview.

10. *Indian Inmates of the Nebraska Penal and Correction Complex v. Vitek,* no. 72-l-156 (D. NE, orders of 31 October 1974 and 24 May 1976); *Teterud v. Burns* 522 F2d 357 (8th Cir 1975); *Ross v. Scurr,* no. 80-214-A (D. IA, order of 13 March 1981); *Bear-Ribs v. Carlson,* no. 77-3985-RJK (D. CA, order of 1979); *Marshno v. McManus,* no. 79-3146 (D. KA, order of 14 November 1980); *Frease v. Griffin,* no. 79-693-C (D. NM, order of 3 December 1980); *Little Raven v. Crisp,* no. 77-165-C (D. OK, order of 8 November 1978); *Crowe v. Erickson,* no. 72-4101 (D. SD, various orders); *Bender v. Wolff,* no. R-77-0055 BRT (D. NV, order of 5 July 1977); *White Eagle v. Storie* 456 F.Supp 302 (D. NE, 1978); *Indian Inmates of the Nebraska Penal and Correction Complex v. Greenholtz* 567 F2d 1368 (8th Cir 1978); "The Native American Rights Fund: Brief History, 1970 Highlights," (hereinafter NARF Highlights), *http://www.narf.org/intro/history/1970.htm.* Also see NARF 1986, 1987, and 1988 Highlights.

11. John R. Wunder, "Indigenous Peoples, Identity, History, and Law: The United States and Australian Experience," *Law/Text/Culture* 4 (autumn 1998): 81–114. Also see Wunder, "*Retained by The People*," 98–105, particularly table 1: Termination of Tribes and Bands, 1954–1966, and table 2: Restoration of Terminated Indian Tribes; Charles F. Wilkinson and Eric Biggs, "Evolution of the Termination Policy," *American Indian Law Review* 5(1) (1977): 139–84; Beth Ritten Knoche, "Termination, Self-Determination and Restoration: The Northern Ponca Case" (master's thesis, University of Nebraska at Lincoln, 1990), 58, 79–82.

12. NARF 1972, 1973, 1976, 1977, 1978, 1980, 1981, 1982, 1983, and 1987 Highlights.

13. Richard A. Hayward, "Chairman's Message," *Native American Rights Fund 1991 Annual Report* 1 (hereinafter referred to as NARF Report). Beginning in 1991 an extensive annual report emerged from the annual highlights. The annual reports are divided into sections that include the five goals of NARF, an executive director's report, and sometimes a chair of the board's introductory remarks. Fifteen other tribes, including the Miami Nation of Indians of Indiana, the Pamunkey Tribe of Virginia, the Shinnecock Tribe of New York, and the Houma Tribe of Louisiana, among others, are still actively seeking recognition.

14. NARF 1973, 1977, and 1980 Highlights.

15. *Puyallup Tribe, Inc. v. Department of Game* 391 U.S. 392 (1968) (*Puyallup I*). Also see *Puyallup Tribe, Inc. v. Department of Game* 414 U.S. 44 (1973) (*Puyallup II*), and *Puyallup Tribe, Inc. v. Department of Game* 433 U.S. 165 (1977) (*Puyallup III*). Wunder, "*Retained by The People*," 180–82; Jack Landau, "Empty Victories: Indian Treaty Rights in the Pacific Northwest," *Environmental Law* 10 (winter 1980): 414–37.

16. NARF 1973, 1974, 1975, 1977, 1978, 1979, 1980, 1981, 1983, 1985, 1987, and 1989 Highlights. Also see *Kimball v. Callahan* 439 F2d 564 (1974); and Mary Pearson, "Hunting Rights: Retention of Treaty Rights after Termination—*Kimball v. Callahan*," *American Indian Law Review* 4(1) (1976): 121–33.

17. "Protection of Tribal Natural Resources," NARF 1991 Report, 3–5; "Protection of Tribal Natural Resources," NARF 1992 Report, 3–4; "Protection of Tribal Natural Resources," NARF 1993 Report, 4–5; "Protection of Tribal Natural Resources," NARF 1994 Report, 5–6; "Protection of Tribal Natural Resources," NARF 1995 Report, 4–5; "Executive Director's Report," NARF 1994 Report, 1–2.

18. *Winters v. United States* 207 U.S. 564 (1908); *Arizona v. California* 373 U.S. 546 (1963). Also see Wunder, "*Retained by The People*," 120–22; Robert S. Pelcyger, "The *Winters* Doctrine and the Greening of the Reservation," *Journal of Contemporary Law* 4 (winter 1977): 19–37; and Norris Hundley Jr., "The Dark and Bloody Ground of Indian Water Rights: Confusion Elevated to Principle," *Western Historical Quarterly* 9 (October 1978): 455–82.

19. NARF 1972, 1975, and 1979 Highlights.

20. NARF 1981–89 Highlights.

21. *Uncommon Controversy: Fishing Rights of the Muckleshoot, Puyallup, and Nisqually*

Indians, report prepared for the American Friends Service Committee (Seattle: University of Washington Press, 1970), 35, 37–40, 56–60.

22. Walter Echo-Hawk, interview; NARF 1987 Highlights.

23. *Klamath Water Users' Assoc. v. Patterson,* no. 97-3033-HO (D. Ore., filed 1997); *United States and the Klamath Tribe v. State of Oregon Water Resource Dept.,* 44F3d 758 (9th Cir 1994), cert. denied, 122 L Ed.2d 302 (1995); and "Klamath Basin General Stream Adjudication and Negotiation," NARF 1994 Report, 1–2.

24. "Executive Director's Report," NARF 1991 Report, 1; "Executive Director's Report," NARF 1992 Report, 1; "Executive Director's Report," NARF 1993 Report 1; "Protection of Tribal Natural Resources," NARF 1991 Report, 2–3; "Protection of Tribal Natural Resources," NARF 1992 Report, 2–3; "Protection of Tribal Natural Resources," NARF 1993 Report, 2–4; "Protection of Tribal Natural Resources," NARF 1994 Report, 3–5; "Protection of Tribal Natural Resources," NARF 1995 Report, 2–4; Wunder, *"Retained by The People,"* 184–85.

25. NARF 1972, 1973, 1974, and 1980 Highlights; "Preservation of Tribal Existence," NARF 1993 Report, 1; "Executive Director's Report," NARF 1993 Report, 1.

26. *State of Oklahoma, Ex Rel Oklahoma Tax Commission v. Mays,* no. C-81-12 (D.C., Pawnee County, decision of 10 July 1981); NARF 1985 Highlights.

27. NARF 1985, and 1989 Highlights; "Executive Director's Report," NARF 1993 Report, 1; "Executive Director's Report," NARF Report, 1; "Preservation of Tribal Existence," NARF 1991 Report, 1–2; "Preservation of Tribal Existence," NARF 1992 Report, 1–2; "Preservation of Tribal Existence," NARF 1993 Report, 1–2; "Preservation of Tribal Existence," 1994 Report, 1; "Preservation of Tribal Existence," NARF 1995 Report, 2.

28. "Preservation of Tribal Existence," NARF 1991 Report, 1; "Preservation of Tribal Existence," NARF 1994 Report, 3; "Preservation of Tribal Existence," NARF 1995 Report, 1.

29. NARF 1972, 1973, 1978, 1979, and 1980 Highlights.

30. NARF 1984, 1986, and 1987 Highlights; *Solem v. Bartlett* 46 U.S. 463 (1984).

31. "Brief History," NARF 1990 Report, 1; "Executive Director's Report," NARF 1991 Report, 1, NARF 1992 Report, 1; NARF 1994 Report, 1; "Preservation of Tribal Existence," NARF 1991 Report, 2; NARF 1992 Report, 1; NARF 1993 Report, 1; NARF 1994 Report, 2–3; NARF 1995 Report, 1–2.

32. NARF 1986, 1987, 1988, and 1989 Highlights. Also see *Cabazon Band of Mission Indians et al. v. California* 480 U.S. 202 (1987).

33. For further insight, see William R. Eadington, ed., *Indian Gaming and the Law* (Reno: Institute for the Study of Gambling and Gaming, 1990).

34. "Chairman's Message," NARF 1993 Report, 1–2, quotation page 2.

35. *U.S. Statutes at Large* 92 (11 August 1978), 469–70.

36. *Sequoyah v. Tennessee Valley Authority* 620 F2d 1159 (1980); *Badoni v. Higginson* 638 F2d 172 (1980); Walter Echo-Hawk, interview; Howard Stambor, "Manifest Destiny and American Indian Religious Freedom: *Sequoyah, Badoni,* and the Drowned Gods," *American Indian Law Review* 10(1) (1982): 58–59; Wunder, *"Retained by The People,"* 194–96.

37. *Lyng v. Northwest Indian Cemetery Protective Association* 485 US 439 (1988); Wunder, *"Retained by The People,"* 196–97; NARF 1988 Highlights; Walter Echo-Hawk, interview.

38. *Employment Division, Department of Human Resources of Oregon et al. v. Alfred L. Smith* 485 US 660 (1988)(*Smith I*); 494 US 872 (1990) (*Smith II*); Wunder, *"Retained by The People,"* 197–98.

39. American Indian Religious Freedom Act Amendment of 1994, 42 U.S. 1996a; Walter Echo-Hawk, interview; NARF 1989 Highlights.

40. NARF 1985 and 1989 Highlights; Walter Echo-Hawk, interview; Roger C. Echo-Hawk and Walter E. Echo-Hawk, *Battlefields and Burial Grounds: The Indian Struggle to Protect Ancestral Graves in the United States* (Minneapolis: Lerner Publications Co., 1994); *U.S. Statutes at Large* 104 (16 November 1990), 3048–58 (Native American Graves Protection and Repatriation Act); Wunder, *"Retained by The People,"* 208–10.

41. Echo-Hawk and Echo-Hawk, *Battlefields and Burial Grounds,* 51–52.

42. Echo-Hawk and Echo-Hawk, *Battlefields and Burial Grounds,* 52.

43. Echo-Hawk and Echo-Hawk, *Battlefields and Burial Grounds,* 60–65; "NARF Attorney, Robert M. Peregoy," NARF *Legal Review* (winter/spring, 1996): 19; Robert M. Peregoy, "The Legal Basis, Legislative History and Implementation of Nebraska's Landmark Reburial Legislation," Native American Rights Fund, Boulder CO, August 1991; *Nebraska Unmarked Human Burial Sites and Skeletal Remains Protection Act,* sec. 12-1211 et seq., R.S. Supp. 1990. Also see *Nebraska State Historical Society v. Pawnee Tribe and the State of Nebraska,* no. 448 (DC, Lancaster County, Nebraska, filed 1990); *In the Matter of the Pawnee Tribe of Oklahoma, et al., and the Nebraska State Historical Society,* arbitration award (12 March 1991); *Kansas Unmarked Burial Sites Protection Act,* H.B. no. 2144 (1989); Kansas Appropriations Legislation, S.D. 68 (1989); California Repatriation Bill, A.B. 2577 (1990).

44. *Native American Grave Protection and Repatriation Act,* 25 USC 3001 et seq. (1990); National Museum of the American Indian Act, 20 USC 80 et seq. (1989); Also see Echo-Hawk and Echo-Hawk, *Battlefields and Burial Grounds,* 71.

45. "Chairperson's Message," NARF 1995 Report, 1–2.

46. Walter Echo-Hawk, interview; "Executive Director's Report," 1995 NARF Report, 1. For a more specific discussion of Walter Echo-Hawk's legal philosophy and that of other Indian legal warriors, see Walter Echo-Hawk, "Preface," *American Indian Culture and Research Journal* 16 (1992): 1–7; "Loopholes in Religious Liberty," *Cultural Survival Quarterly* 17 (1994): 62–65; "Museum Rights vs. Indian

Rights: Guidelines for Assessing Competing Legal Interests in Native Cultural Resources," *New York University Review of Law and Social Change* 14 (1986): 437–53; "Tribal Efforts to Protect against the Mistreatment of Indian Dead: The Quest for Equal Protection of the Laws," NARF *Legal Review* 14 (winter 1988): 1–5; "Native American Religious Liberty: Five Hundred Years after Columbus," *American Indian Culture and Research Journal* 17 (1993): 33–52; "Indigenous v. Nonindigenous Rights, Responsibilities, and Relationships," *International Affairs,* University of Nebraska, 1997, 1–9; and coauthored with Roger C. Echo-Hawk, *Battlefields and Burial Grounds;* with Dan L. Monroe, "Deft Deliberations," *Museum News* 70 (1991): 55–58; with Robert M. Peregoy and James Botsford, "Congress Overturns Supreme Court's Peyote Ruling," NARF *Legal Review* 20 (winter/spring 1995): 1, 6–25; and with Jack F. Trope, "The Native American Graves Protection and Repatriation Act: Background and Legislative History," *Arizona State Law Journal* 24 (spring 1992): 35–77.

CONTRIBUTORS

✳

Brad Agnew is a professor of history and chair of the Department of History at Northeastern State University. He is the author of *Fort Gibson: Terminal on the Trail of Tears* and *Movin' On in the Korean Stalemate: The 279th Infantry Regiment, 1950–1954,* and has written many articles on Oklahoma and military history.

Gary C. Anderson is a professor of history at the University of Oklahoma. He has written many articles and books on Native American history, including *The Indian's Southwest 1580–1830: Ethnogenesis and Cultural Reinvention; Sitting Bull and the Paradox of Nationhood* for the Library of American Biography Series; *Kinsmen of Another Kind: Dakota-White Relations in the Upper Mississippi Valley, 1650–1862;* and *Little Crow, Spokesman for the Sioux.* He has just completed a study of intertribal and political and economic development on the southern plains in the eighteenth century.

Timothy Bernardis is the library director at Little Big Horn College, the Crow tribal college in Crow Agency, Montana. He also oversees the Little Big Horn College Archives: Crow Indian Historical and Cultural Collections. He is the author of *Baleeisbaalichiweé (History) Teacher's Guide* and the updated essay on the Crows to be published in the Plains volume of the Smithsonian's *Handbook of North American Indians* (forthcoming).

Philip J. Deloria, the grandson of Vine V. Deloria Sr., is an associate professor of history at the University of Michigan. He is the author of *Playing Indian* and the coeditor of the *Blackwell Companion to American Indian History.*

R. David Edmunds is Watson Professor of American History at the University of Texas at Dallas. His numerous books, articles, and essays on Native American history include *The Potawatomis: Keepers of the Fire, The Shawnee Prophet, Tecumseh and the Quest for Indian Leadership,* and *The Fox Wars: The Mesquakie Challenge to New France* (coauthored with Joseph L. Peyser).

Donald L. Fixico, CLAS Scholar, is a professor of history and director of the Indigenous Nations Studies Program at the University of Kansas. He is the author or editor of many articles and books on American Indians in the twentieth century, including *The Invasion of Indian Country in the Twentieth Century: American Capitalism and Tribal Natural Resources*; *The Urban Indian Experience in America*; *Termination and Relocation: Federal Indian Policy 1945–1960*; (ed.) *Rethinking American Indian History: Analysis, Methodology, and Historiography,* and (ed.) *An Anthology of Western Great Lakes Indian History.*

Frederick E. Hoxie is Swanlund Professor of History at the University of Illinois at Urbana-Champaign. He is the author or editor of numerous articles and books, including *A Final Promise: The Campaign to Assimilate the Indians, 1880–1920* and *Parading through History: The Making of the Crow Nation in America, 1805–1935.*

Jeremy Johnston is an instructor of Native American history at Northwest Community College in Powell, Wyoming.

Harry A. Kersey Jr. is a professor of history at Florida Atlantic University. He has written extensively on the Florida Seminoles and served as historian and legal consultant for the tribe. For ten years he was a member of the state Indian commission in Florida. His books include *Pelts, Plumes, and Hides: White Traders among the Seminole Indians, 1870–1939*; *The Florida Seminoles and the New Deal, 1933–1942*; and most recently *An Assumption of Sovereignty: Social and Political Transformation among the Florida Seminoles, 1953–1979.*

Clara Sue Kidwell is the director of the Native American Studies Program at the University of Oklahoma. She has written extensively on Native American women and Native American history. She is the author of *Choctaws and Missionaries in Mississippi, 1818–1918.*

Douglas Nelson is a professor of anthropology at Northwest Community College in Powell, Wyoming.

Dorothy R. Parker is Professor Emeritus of History at Eastern New Mexico University and an adjunct professor of history at the University of Mexico. She is the author of *Singing an Indian Song: A Biography of D'Arcy McNickle, The Phoenix Indian School: The Second Half-Century,* and numerous book reviews, articles, and chapters in scholarly volumes.

William E. Unrau is Distinguished Professor of History Emeritus at Wichita State University. He is the author of numerous articles and books, including *The Kansa Indians: A History of the Wind People, 1673–1873*; *Mixed-Bloods and*

Tribal Dissolution: Charles Curtis and the Quest for Indian Identity; and *White Man's Wicked Water: The Alcohol Trade and Prohibition in Indian Country, 1802–1892*. Unrau resides in Louisville, Colorado, and is conducting research on myth and reality in Indian Country.

Deborah Welch is an assistant professor of history at Longwood College. A graduate of the University of Wyoming (Ph.D. 1985), Welch has published essays and presented papers on Gertrude Bonnin's (Zitkala-Sa's) life. She currently is conducting research for a biography of Bonnin.

Benton R. White is dean of Liberal and Fine Arts at Kilgore College, Kilgore, Texas. *Christine Schulz White* is an instructor of history and anthropology at Kilgore College. Both have taught for many years and have published books and articles on American history and Native American history, including their most recent coauthored work *Now the Wolf Has Come: The Creek Nation in the Civil War*.

Raymond Wilson is a professor of history at Fort Hays State University, Hays, Kansas. He is the author of *Ohiyesa: Charles Eastman, Santee Sioux* and coauthor of *Native Americans in the Twentieth Century* and *Indian Lives: Essays on Nineteenth- and Twentieth-Century Native American Leaders*.

John R. Wunder is a professor of history at the University of Nebraska–Lincoln. Wunder, who holds both a Ph.D. in history and a J.D., has written extensively on Native American law. His latest volume is *"Retained by The People": A History of American Indians and the Bill of Rights*.

INDEX

✳